The Decline of Deference

R

The Decline of Deference

Canadian value change in cross-national perspective

Neil Nevitte

broadview press

Canadian Cataloguing in Publication Data

Nevitte, Neil
   The decline of deference: Canadian value change in cross-
national perspective

Includes bibliographical references and index.
ISBN 1-55111-031-8

1. Canada - Politics and government - 1980-1984.*
2. Canada - Politics and government - 1984-1993.*
3. Canada - Politics and government - 1993-   .*
4. Political participation - Canada. 5. Canada - Social conditions
- 1971-   .* 6. Social Values - Cross-cultural studies. 7.
Authority - Cross-cultural studies. I. Title.

FC609.N48   1996   971.064   C94-932138-9   F1034.2.N48   1996

Broadview Press
Post Office Box 1243, Peterborough, Ontario, Canada K9J 7H5

in the United States of America:
3576 California Road, Orchard Park, NY 14127

in the United Kingdom:
B.R.A.D. Book Representation & Distribution Ltd., 244a, London Road,
Hadleigh, Essex SS7 2DE

Broadview Press gratefully acknowledges the support of the Canada Council,
the Ontario Arts Council, and the Ministry of Canadian Heritage.

Typesetting and assembly: True to Type Inc., Mississauga, Canada.

PRINTED IN CANADA

To Sue

Table of Contents

PART V
CONCLUSIONS

Chapter 9   Patterns of Change   285

Figures and Tables

Tables

Preface

Remarkable changes have taken place in Canada in the last decade or so, and some of these shifts have to do with values. The following investigation of Canadian values and value change is guided by two convictions, biases if you like, and I may as well be frank about these from the very start.

First, the approach adopted is an explicitly comparative one. Giovanni Sartori, a scholar who does not mince words, claims that "he who knows only one country knows none" (1991: 245). The aphorism trumpets the advantages of comparison: much can be learned about Canadian value change by taking the broad view, by examining Canadian dynamics in the larger context of the transformations that over the last fifteen to twenty years seem to have rattled all advanced industrial states. Comparing Canadian values and value change in the context of the values held by publics in eleven other advanced industrial states, and doing so across an identical time frame, tells us two things. First, it quickly becomes apparent that advanced industrial states have experienced similar value transformations during the decade 1981—1990. Second, it becomes clearer precisely where Canadians' orientations to their political, economic, and social worlds are similar to, and where they differ from, those of other publics.

The second bias of the book is also about perspective: one can investigate economic values in isolation. The same holds for the examination of social and political orientations. But we soon find that when it comes to values, changes in political life cannot be neatly separated from those that have swept across the economy or taken place in the family and society at large.

Employing the economic and social\political perspectives jointly necessarily means painting with a broad brush. This quite deliberate strategy involves trade-offs: the risks and shortcomings have to be balanced against the advantages. The safest approach would have been to stay close to home, as it were, and to examine the available evidence in more manageable chunks. There is a certain kind of satisfaction that comes from poking around in small corners and being able to say something quite definitive about a more modest area of concern. And there is comfort in staying close to home. Those who go searching for the bigger picture risk straying into areas that are less familiar. Another risk is that readers looking for evidence about a specific set of orientations may find insufficient attention given to their special interest. Still, it strikes me that, from time to time, it is worthwhile to try to say something about the bigger picture even though there are dangers in doing so.

In presenting the evidence, I aim to strike a reasonable balance between accessibility and the need for adequate technical documentation. First, basic data are always presented for each of the value domains considered, and so readers have the opportunity to see the basic findings for themselves and to work up their own interpretations of the evidence. People with different interests can treat the volume as a sourcebook. Second, wherever possible, the evidence is presented in graphic form. Readers not comfortable with statistical data generally find this kind of presentation easier to fathom. At some points, however, more sophisticated statistical treatments are unavoidable. On these occasions I follow a couple of guidelines: much of the more technical information is consigned to appendices or footnotes, and when there is a choice of statistical strategies, I stick with the same techniques as much as possible.

What follows is just one interpretation of these value dynamics. Readers who are interested in Canadian values, or value change in advanced industrial states more generally, may not agree with the interpretation. My main hope is that the perspective is a useful one and that the findings are sufficiently arresting to warrant further considerations and more detailed investigation.

No project of this scale can be undertaken without a lot of help. This one would never have seen the light of day without the generous assistance of the Donner Canadian Foundation, which courageously provided financial support at a time when large-scale survey research in Canada must have seemed risky. I am extremely grateful to the Foundation, as well as its patient project officers, for backing the enterprise. I am also very grateful to the Social Sciences and Humanities Council of Canada, whose financial support carried this project through its later stages.

I also bear large debts to a number of individuals. The project would never have been launched in the first place without the support of Ronald Inglehart of the University of Michigan. Even as he was engaged in coordinating the largest cross-national survey research project ever undertaken, Ron generously found the time to help launch the Canadian project. This book represents but one stage of a larger project. More precisely, it is an outcrop of earlier work that probed what role citizens' values played in the emergence of North American free trade. That project brought together three collaborators—Ron Inglehart (United States), Miguel Basanez (Mexico), and me—and as anyone who has tried it knows, long-term collaborative efforts are not just bloodless exchanges of ideas. One of the most valuable things I have gained from this collaboration has been the friendship and hospitality of Ron, Miguel, and their families.

There are also mountains of other debts. The project has been running for some eight years, and I have been extremely fortunate to have a number of very able research assistants along the way. Robert Burge, Lori Davis, Linda Fung and Jutta Elbe brought their intelligence and enthusiasm to the work, as did Mebs Kanji and Shainoor Virani. Mebs Kanji had the most difficult task;

he was "the closer" and did the bulk of the heavy lifting during the most complicated latter phases of the project. All of these people were more than just research assistants; they were collaborators who made important contributions to the intellectual shape of the book. The contributions of my colleagues in the Thursday evening seminar in applied probability were vital, as was the superb editorial work of Terry Teskey and Barbara Conolly.

Other people have helped in different ways, and I also thank them. Some count as direct contributors: they provided commentary on earlier versions of this work that were floated from time to time as conference papers or as preliminary drafts of articles. Others have been unwitting helpers, offering up their ideas and valuable insights about themes that emerge in various parts of the book. Among these are Paul Abramson; Keith Archer; Michael Atkinson; Herman Bakvis; Sam Barnes; Sylvia Bashevkin; Andre Blais; Henry Brady; Roderic Camp; Harold Clarke; William Flanagan; Elisabeth Gidengil; Loek Halman; Dick Johnston; Oddbjorn Knutsen; Larry LeDuc; Maureen Mancuso; Maurice Pinard; Bob Putnam; Ron Rogowski; Richard Simeon; Paul Sniderman; Fred Turner; and Kent Weaver.

The book builds on data coming from several studies, and in a very direct way it was made possible by the combined efforts of eighty-three principal investigators who carried out the 1990 World Values Surveys in 44 societies. I am grateful to Rasa Alishauskiene, Vladimir Andreyenkov, Soo Young Auh, David Barker, Elena Bashkirova, Marek Boguszak, Marita Carballo de Cilley, Pi-chao Chen, Hei-yuan Chiu, Eric de Costa, Juan Diez Nicolas, Karel Dobbelaere, Mattei Dogan, Javier Elzo, Ustun Erguder, Yilmaz Esmer, Blanka Filipcova, Michael Fogarty, Luis de Franca, Christain Friesl, Yuji Fukuda, Iavn Gabal, Allec Gallup, George Gallup, Renzo Gubert, Peter Gundelach, Loek Halman, Elemer Hankiss, Stephen Harding, Gordon Heald, Felix Heunks, Carlos Huneeus, Kenji Iijima, J.C. Jesumo, Fridrik Jonsson, Ersin Kalaycioglu, Jan Kerkhofs, Hans-Dieter Klingemann, Renate Koecher, Marta Lagos, Max Larsen, Ola Listhaug, Jin-yun Liu, Nicolae Lotreanu, Leila Lotti, V.P. Madhok, Robert Manchin, Carlos Eduardo Meirelles Matheus, Anna Melich, Ruud de Moor, Elisabeth Noelle-Neumann, Stefan Olafsson, Francisco Andres Orizo, R.C. Pandit, Juhani Pehkonen, Thorlief Petterson, Jacques-Rene Rabier, Andrei Raichev, Vladimir Rak, Helene Riffault, Ole Riis, Andrus Saar, Renate Siemienska, Kancho Stoichev, Kareem Tejumola, Noel Timms, Mikk Titma, Niko Tos, Jorge Vala, Andrei Vardomatski, Christine Woessner, Jiang Xingrong, Vladimir Yadov, Seiko Yamazaki, Catalin Zamfir, Brigita Zepa, Xiang Zongde, and Paul Zulehner.

The 1990 World Values Surveys build on the 1981 European Values Systems Survey, directed by Jan Kerkofs, Ruud de Moor, Gordon Heald, Juan Linz, Elisabeth Noelle-Neumann, Jacques-Rene Rabier, and Helene Riffault. Then there are the contributions made by participants in the two-wave Political Action Study: Samuel Barnes, Dieter Fuchs, Jacques Hagenaars, Felix Heunks, M. Kent Jennings, Max Kaase, Hans-Dieter Klingemann, Jacques Thomassen, and Jan Van Deth.

Data from the World Values Surveys are available from the ICPSR survey data archive at the University of Michigan. The Canadian data are also available from the Institute for Survey Research, York University. I extend an invitation—for anyone and everyone to use the unique, rich, and enormously valuable data that come from the Canadian and other segments of the World Values Surveys. None of the institutions and individuals who have supported the project is, of course, responsible for the interpretation that follows.

And finally, to Sue, Lee and Alex who allowed me to creep off at various times, such as Sunday mornings, so that I could do "just a little more" on this project — thank you.

Sartori, G. 1991. "Comparing and miscomparing." *Journal of Theoretical Politics* 3(3): 243–57.

1: A Decade of Turmoil

This book is about values and value change during a remarkably volatile period in recent Canadian history, 1981–1990. During that decade, Canadians confronted a bewildering array of social, economic, and political conflicts. Together, these conflicts challenged long-standing assumptions about the nature and future of the community. No single event adequately captures the flavour of the period, but on the political front two historic conflicts clearly dominated the agenda: battles over the Constitution, and the disputes about free trade with the United States.

The decade might have begun with the celebration of the patriation of the Constitution. Instead, it began with the drama of Réné Lévesque and the Quebec delegation marching away from the constitutional table leaving other first ministers to sign the Constitution Act of 1982. Quebec's refusal to "sign off" on the new Constitution unleashed successive rounds of constitutional bickering that lasted the entire decade and beyond. The search to find a political framework that would "bring Quebec back in" preoccupied political leaders, and for much of the period and beyond, normal politics—resolving issue differences within the rules of the game—became entangled with high-stakes politics—contests about the rules of the game.

Canadians from all walks of life were drawn into the constitutional debates in one way or another. Experts raised profound questions about the adequacy of parliamentary institutions and offered up proposals to redefine the rules of representation. Provincial governments pushed a variety of old and new grievances onto the constitutional agenda, including proposals, like Senate reform, that would redefine the balance of powers between federal and provincial governments. Interest groups from all corners of society seized the opportunity to press for the entrenchment of a host of particular rights and protections. Throughout the entire process citizens were urged to be patient, and to stay the course while leaders hammered out a solution that would, as the politicians of the day put it, serve Canadians into the twenty-first century.

Towards the end of the decade it looked as though a solution to the impasse and a way to bring Quebec back in had been found. First ministers gathered at Meech Lake to iron out the final wrinkles and to seal an agreement that was supposed to end the wrangling. The collapse of Meech Lake plunged Canadians into the second constitutional crisis of the decade. Once again, the immediate cause of the failure was disagreement about Quebec's claims to "distinct society" status. But on this occasion the drama was provided by Elijah Harper, a native member of the Manitoba legislature, who resolutely refused to give consent to the Meech Lake proposals.

The failure of Meech Lake had several predictable consequences. In Quebec, its collapse further poisoned Quebec's relationships with the rest of Canada; it was interpreted as a rejection of Quebec itself, and support for Quebec's independentist option increased sharply. Predictably too, the crisis sparked more finger-pointing and recriminations; it unleashed more studies, more hearings, and more proposals. Special joint committees were launched to search for new constitutional options. A citizens' forum toured the country to listen to what the public had to say about the country's future. Canadians were jostled back onto the constitutional rollercoaster for another high-stakes ride. One clear message to come from the Meech Lake episode, though, was that Canada's constitutional gridlock was no longer a two-player game, one that could be solved by simply cutting a deal between Canada's two European founding partners. Harper's role in the defeat of Meech Lake signalled another turning point and overturned another long-standing assumption. Through Harper, Canada's aboriginal peoples staked out a powerful claim to First Nation status and served notice that no new deal would be struck without the meaningful participation of Canada's first peoples. Their message was clear: If Quebec deserved status as a distinct society on the grounds of early historical settlement, and a distinct language and culture, then aboriginal peoples had an equal if not greater claim to distinct society status and all that went with it.

As the country lurched from one constitutional crisis to another, and political leaders threw themselves into the search for a framework within which Canadians could amicably live together, citizens were presented with a strikingly divergent set of visions of the country. Was Canada a two-nation country? A country of three founding peoples? Five regions? A multicultural society? A community of communities? All of the images drew attention to differences, but the increasingly urgent question became: What values hold Canadians together?

Free trade with the United States was one of the few issues to eclipse the constitutional crisis. The outcome of that debate, the signing of the Canada–U.S. Free Trade Agreement in 1988, marked another turning point. Free trade with the United States might be seen as the formalization of a trend towards greater economic integration that had gathered momentum since the Second World War. But as a formal policy, it was a historic U-turn. Moreover, that U-turn was negotiated by the Progressive Conservatives, the party that traditionally had most vigorously led the charge against free trade with the United States. The issue divided Canadians along familiar nationalist and continentalist lines (Bashevkin, 1991). Nationalists reminded Canadians that, from the outset, Canadians and Americans stood for different things and that the Canadian political community was deliberately designed to resist the revolutionary impulses and cultural orientations of the United States. They contended that in the present, as in the past, the integrity of Canada and the Canadian way of life depended on its ability to keep the United States at arm's length and to judiciously manage the continental pull of its powerful southern neighbour.

Continentalists countered with a variety of arguments, but two stood out. The first was that securing expanded trade with Canada's largest trading partner was vital to Canadian competitiveness in an increasingly competitive global economy. The pro–free trade forces conceded at the outset that a free trade agreement with the United States would likely entail some short-term marketplace adjustments. But in the long run, they argued, the deal would produce more jobs and make Canada more competitive and prosperous. Equally important, a formal free trade deal could serve tactical ends; it would limit the United States' ability to apply protectionist strategies. Second, they argued that Canadian values were strong, that those values had successfully survived the forces of "Americanization" for generations, that other states such as those in Europe had formed similarly comprehensive trade agreements without losing their identities. There was no reason to suspect, they believed, that the Canadian case would be any different (Lipsey, 1985).

Given the economic interests at stake, it came as little surprise that corporations, manufacturers, and the business community at large enthusiastically threw their weight behind the pro–free trade position. The opposition to free trade attracted a more diverse coalition. Unions, whose membership faced the prospects of open competition with an American labour force with much lower levels of unionization, lower wages, and fewer benefits, vigorously opposed the deal. The mavens of Canada's cultural industries also opposed the deal. The gap between supporters and opponents of free trade was wide and fundamental. At issue were not just competing theories about the connection between culture, economics, and policy making, but also completely different assessments of the robustness of Canadian values. Where nationalists viewed Canadian values as fragile and susceptible to outside influences, continentalists saw them as sturdy.

With the constitutional wrangling and the disputes over free trade, Canadians were forced to grapple with giant issues that had profound implications for the future of the country. Trying to cope with both at the same time heightened the sense of crisis of the period. In important respects the Constitution and free trade were very different issues, but both encouraged Canadians to reflect about their society and its future. The Constitution encouraged citizens to think about what values held Canadians together. With free trade, they confronted another question: What values set them apart from the United States? Disputes about the Constitution and free trade, though, were not the only benchmarks of turmoil. Less spectacular upheavals on a variety of other fronts also contributed to the turbulence of the era; and they challenged other long-standing assumptions about the nature of Canadian society and provided further evidence of discontinuity.

From the middle of the 1960s to the late 1980s Canadians had what by most standards qualified as a stable party system. Federal electoral politics conformed to the "two-party-plus" model common to most parliamentary systems working with similar electoral rules. Throughout the entire period, one of the two major parties controlled parliament with clear electoral majorities, with the Liberals enjoying more success in the 1970s and the Progressive Conservatives, like parties of the right in other Anglo-American democracies, enjoying more success in the 1980s. Regardless of which party held office, winning majorities typically hinged on electoral success in Quebec. Studies examining the electoral behaviour of Canadians during that period characterize the linkage between voters and parties as evidence of "stable dealignment" with a potential for fragmentation (Clarke et al., 1991; Leduc, 1984). Voter attachments to parties were "fickle" and federal parties rarely provided voters with clear or imaginative platforms. Nonetheless, stable majorities were consistently cobbled together through a combination of deft agenda setting and issue agility (Clarke et al., 1991). By 1990 that "stable dealignment" appeared to have unravelled, as the Canadian party system veered away from the conventional two-party-plus configuration to take on the look of a five-party system. Partisan fractures opened up on two fronts. In Quebec, federal members of Parliament defected from the government benches to form the Bloc Québecois, while in western Canada the populist Reform Party emerged to capitalize on dissatisfaction with the Progressive Conservatives. To be sure, during the 1980s both Reform and the Bloc were still "untried alternatives" (Pinard, 1973). But the emergence of these partisan fractures introduced new strategic difficulties for the major parties, and raised doubts about the capacity of the traditional parties to work as integrative institutions representing the whole country. The Reform Party positioned itself to cut deeply into the Progressive Conservatives' electoral stronghold in the West and presented that party with an ideological challenge "from the right." At the same time, the Bloc Quebecois provided Quebec independentists with a federal opportunity they had not seen before. The appearance of the Bloc threatened to decouple voter support for federalist parties in Quebec, the historic cornerstone of federal majorities in the preceding twenty-five years. Both fractures emerged with dramatic force in the 1993 federal election.

Significant shifts in the patterns of interest group activity during the 1980s provide yet other signals of Canada's volatile social, economic, and political climate. New life was pumped into old issues and a staggering array of new issues were pushed onto the agenda as citizens mobilized and divided over such matters as the environment, women's rights, gay rights, the family, consumer rights, peace, multiculturalism, and race.

Canadians were relative latecomers to environmental activism, but throughout the 1980s the environmental movement grew at an impressive clip. Most estimates place the size of the environmental lobby in the late 1980s at somewhere between 1,800 and 2,500 groups representing perhaps as many as two million Canadians (Bakvis and Nevitte, 1992; Wilson, 1992). The label "environmentalism" gives the impression that environmentalists are a cohesive group, organized around a single task and united on tactics and philosophy. Certainly, all share a general concern for ecological degradation, but seen up close, the picture becomes more complex. Environmentalists' theatres of action range from peace to animal rights. Some groups tackle such international problems as ozone depletion and global warming. Others pour their energies into more specific targets—clearcut logging in British Columbia, the development of dams in Alberta and Saskatchewan, nuclear power plants in Ontario and hydro-electric megaprojects in Quebec. Across the country attention focused on industrial emissions, water and air quality, waste disposal, acid rain, oil spills, recycling, the preservation of wildlife and endangered species. Far from being narrow, the environmentalists' agenda carried far-reaching implications for cultural, health, and economic policy. In pursuing that agenda, environmentalists attracted diverse allies and powerful adversaries. In some cases they found common cause with native groups whose more specific goals, typically, were to protect local habitats and traditional ways of life. More often than not, their adversaries have been processing and manufacturing industries and corporations in the primary resource sector.

Environmentalists lost some battles and won others, but the net effect of these sustained campaigns did have a significant impact. In the 1960s, it might have been easy to dismiss environmentalism as the preoccupation of a handful of vegetarian crackpots—the marginalized few. But throughout the course of the 1980s environmental concerns were increasingly embraced by the middle class. Governments and publics alike grappled with trade-offs reflecting newly relevant dilemmas: What balance to strike between jobs and environmental degradation? Profit and quality of life? Prosperity now and the legacy for future generations?

The women's movement was not new to the 1980s but, like the environmental movement, it too gathered momentum throughout the decade. Also like environmentalism, the womens' movement spanned a remarkably wide range of social, economic, and political issues. Feminist intellectuals launched stinging attacks on the patriarchal structures of society and the systematic oppression of women (Abramson et al., 1988). Research groups exposed gender biases in health care, poverty, divorce laws, business practices, pensions, and opportunities (Fox, 1989; McDaniel, 1988). A huge variety of women's groups launched vigorous and sophisticated campaigns to redress inequalities facing women in all spheres of activity—in the home, in the workplace, and in the polity. On the constitutional front, women lobbied hard and made significant gains with the entrenchment of women's rights in the Charter of Rights and Freedoms in 1982. Building on that victory, legal advocacy groups worked to test those rights in the courts. Others demanded to know why women were so under-represented in Parliament and in the higher ranks of political parties, and the potential electoral importance of women was not lost on political elites. When leaders of the major political parties were invited to address women's issues in a publicly televised debate during the 1984 federal election campaign, the party leaders accepted.

Traditional assumptions about the place of women in the economy were challenged as women's groups pressed for equal pay for work of equal value, fairer hiring and promotion practices, flexible work hours, protection from sexual harassment in the workplace, and greater access to daycare. Traditional norms about the status of women in society were challenged by groups drawing attention to violence against women, pornography, and spousal rape. Weak enforcement of wife battering, alimony, and child support legislation came under attack. Pressure mounted for more rape crisis centres and shelters for battered women. Networks supporting single mothers, native women, and women of colour expanded.

The women's movement was united in neither ideology nor tactics. Some men supported the women's movement, and some women opposed it (Burt, 1988). The pressure to advance women's rights touched off wide-ranging controversies about the status of the family, marriage, and motherhood. The disputes about abortion and sexual preference were particularly bitter. Traditionalists, men and women alike, organized to counter the lobbying efforts of "radical feminists"; they argued that feminists were "going too far" and that the agenda of "gays and lesbians" would undermine family values with disastrous effects.

On another front, relations between Canada's cultural majorities and minorities also become more abrasive during the 1980s signalling the emergence of serious social turmoil of a very different sort. The long-standing conflicts between francophones and anglophones, and between aboriginal and non-aboriginal peoples, took centre stage during the constitutional debates. Backstage and out of the constitutional limelight, newer frictions were added to old ones as troubling racial divisions became more prominent. Those divisions reshaped the social dynamics in most of Canada's major urban centres. Discrimination against visible minorities in the workplace and in accommodation was not new (Reitz, 1988); the novel development was the emergence of open conflicts between whites and non-whites. Fights between black and white students broke out in Halifax schools. Black community leaders in Montreal denounced police action against black youths as discriminatory and racist. Racial tensions erupted into open conflict in Toronto in the wake of large-scale riots in Los Angeles. Relations deteriorated between the Asian and non-Asian communities in Vancouver and elsewhere. Such issues as the wearing of turbans by Sikhs sparked public controversy about "tradition" and what it meant to be a "Canadian." Frictions in urban and rural Canada touched off more expansive debates about the wisdom of multiculturalism as a policy. Some took issue with the "community of communities" vision underpinning that policy, arguing that such a vision was a recipe for greater fragmentation at a time when unity was called for. Others debated whether new immigrants should keep, or shed, the traditions of the societies from which they came. The debates swirling around multiculturalism and immigration, and the increasingly commonplace evidence of racial tension, called into question yet another piece of conventional wisdom—how tolerant are Canadians?

Interpreting Turmoil

There is nothing remarkable about vigorous public debate, the airing of differences of opinion, the competition of interests, or controversies about what future directions a country should take. Indeed, all this is the stuff of political, social, and economic life in any open and vibrant democracy. What is striking about the Canadian experience of the 1980s is just how passionate and widespread those debates were and that the controversies engaged issues so fundamental to communal life. Equally striking is the fact that, at the end of the decade, most of the contentious matters remained unresolved. The turbulence was not confined to politics or to the easily recognizable "big issues" of the era, the Constitution and free trade with the United States; it washed across all spheres of endeavour, dividing Canadians in the home, in the workplace, and in the polity.

What explains the turmoil of the period? This book tries to answer that question, beginning with the observation that, in one way or another, many of the conflicts were battles about fundamental values—about what values divide Canadians, what values they share, and what values make Canadians distinct. If the turbulence erupting during the decade was indeed about values, then one plausible explanation for that turbulence is that the 1980s was a decade of significant value change. This book investigates that theme, and presents a great deal of evidence to show that Canadian values did change in the 1980s, and, as we shall see, were in some respects quite remarkable. It is not enough, though, simply to show that values changed. Taking up the theme of value change raises other difficult questions: Which values changed? In what ways? And what explains the shifts?

Canada as One Stage

When interpreting change, context is everything. Seen up close, the variety, scope, and depth of conflicts Canadians faced throughout the decade appear to be unique. In their details, of course, they are. But that turmoil can also be viewed from a broader perspective, and from that more distant vantage point the Canadian setting may be seen as a particular stage on which larger forces are played out. The rising levels of support for Quebec national independence and the growing pressures for greater decentralization, for example, may reflect growing concern about autonomy and shifts in communal identities. Those themes featured prominently in other settings during the same period, often with dramatic results. In some instances, shifting communal loyalties culminated in the most tragic and radical of all outcomes, the bloody collapse of the state, as in Yugoslavia. In others it brought equally significant changes in the opposite direction, such as the reunification of Germany. Both instances serve as useful reminders of the fluidity of political life. They illustrate yet again that state boundaries are neither static nor inviolate. Political communities are dynamic; they can fragment and recombine. The collapse of Meech

Lake undoubtedly was the immediate cause of sharply increased support for the independentist option in Quebec in 1990. From a longer historical perspective, though, that surge in nationalist sentiment can be regarded as but another phase in the recurrent cycles of support for national autonomy. Then again, viewing those same dynamics from a broader cross-national perspective reveals striking similarities in the rhythms of nationalist movements throughout the advanced industrial world. As in Quebec, the nationalist identities of the Catalans, the Basques, the Occitans, and the Corsicans in Spain and France, the Welsh, Scots, and Irish in Britain, the Jurassians in Switzerland, Armenians and Ukrainians in the former Soviet Union, and national minorities elsewhere have been remarkably resilient. Despite enormous and sustained pressures to assimilate, minority nationalist sentiments have not disappeared or crumbled under the weight of either authoritarian central planning or advanced industrialism, as some expected they would. Instead, to a remarkable degree communal identities have persisted, and the communal dynamics of these groups continue to shape the politics of many if not most states (Tiryakian & Rogowski, 1985).

In its details, the Canada–U.S. free trade agreement was a unique bilateral economic pact. But the formation of that larger trading bloc has parallels elsewhere. The push to North American free trade can be seen as but one example of a more general theme; most advanced industrial states are seeking to expand their trade environments. The emergence and expansion of the European Economic Community provides the most comprehensive example of economic collaboration, but there are other examples of lowered trade barriers and increased regional economic cooperation, such as the Australia–New Zealand pact and revitalized interest in economic cooperation in Latin America. The concerns raised by partners to these arrangements, particularly by publics in smaller partner states, have a familiar ring; they echo many of the worries that Canadians aired during the debate about Canada–U.S. free trade. In important respects they reflect similar dilemmas. The largely economic logic driving states to pursue such arrangements is clear: the intention is to encourage prosperity by exploiting economies of scale and comparative advantage while securing access to large markets. Canadians and publics elsewhere worried about the effects. They asked: What about autonomy? Sovereignty? Will expanded trade limit the capacity to pursue domestic public policies that reflect the particular collective aspirations of the Canadian public?

The emergence of such novel partisan formations as the Reform Party and the Bloc Québecois undoubtedly reflect a combination of social and structural tensions that are peculiar to the Canadian setting. Shifting partisan alignments, though, is hardly a trend unique to Canada. The fragmentation of party systems, the increased volatility of electorates, and the emergence of parties challenging the status quo have been the hallmarks of political turbulence throughout nearly all advanced industrial democracies since the 1970s (Dalton, Flanagan & Beck, 1984). As the West European experience illustrates, these challenges can come not only from nationalist groups, from the left, or from the right, but also from parties and political formations that have no obvious ideological roots in any part of the traditional left–right spectrum (Dalton, 1988; Muller-Rommel, 1990). Different electoral rules and institutional arrangements shape the opportunities for the mobilization of new political parties in different ways. In some cases, as in Germany, the rules of the game are deliberately designed to stack the deck against the formation of new political parties. In others, the barriers to entry are much lower. But even when these cross-national variations are taken into account, the general pattern of partisan fragmentation is a remarkably persistent one (Kitschelt, 1990).

Challenges to the status quo have come not just from new political parties; they have also come from non-partisan formations, most notably interest groups. Vigorous and increasingly sophisticated interest groups have become a much more prominent feature of political dynamics in Canada since the 1980s (Cairns, 1990; Phillips, 1991). Those very same dynamics also feature prominently in the turbulence experienced in most other advanced industrial democracies during the same period. A mountain of evidence demonstrates that the rise of issue-driven movements, movements employing a host of direct-action strategies, has so altered the substance and dynamics of state–society relations across advanced industrial states that conventional interpretations of normal political contests no longer apply (Keuchler & Dalton, 1990). The surge in activity of groups promoting women's rights, the right to life, pro-choice, gay rights, consumers' rights, the environment, peace, and a host of other concerns relating to "quality of life," "minoritarianism," or the status of historically marginalized groups, all contributed to the turmoil facing Canadians since the early 1980s. Precisely the same concerns pushed their way onto the agendas of other advanced industrial states in the 1970s and have become increasingly prominent since then (Barnes et al., 1974). To be sure, there are cross-national variations in the success of interest group activities and in the organizational forms they take. In some instances, for example, environmental movements have coalesced into political parties, as in the cases of the Greens in West Germany or Ecolo and Agalev in Belgium. But in most cases, as in Canada and the United States, ecology movements have pursued their goals through non-partisan strategies (Kitschelt, 1984). There are also significant national differences in the successes of some groups and in the dynamics surrounding those successes. In some settings, as in Canada and the United States, the emergence of an organized pro-choice formation sparked a powerful reaction on the part of pro-life forces. At issue, in both cases, was not just the legality or morality of abortion. The abortion debate spilled over to a larger set of questions; it polarized publics around the status of women and became a battleground for competing definitions of "the family" and competing values about "family life." In other settings, the reactions have been much less robust and much less organized. There are significant variations too in the goals of movements bearing the same generic label. The goals of feminists in Britain, for example, are not precisely the same as those of feminists in the United States, and neither are identical to those preoccupying feminists in Sweden (Gelb, 1990). Far more striking than the national differences in organizational form and precise focus, though, are the common impacts of these movements; all have changed their respective domestic political agendas.

Most advanced industrial states have some historical record of tension between racial majorities and minorities. With the exception of the United States, few advanced industrial democracies have sustained experience of open racial conflict. During the course of the 1980s, racial issues and the politics of immigration became more contentious and more salient to both political discourse and social dynamics throughout most of western Europe. Once again, there are very significant variations in the salience of race and in the extent to which and how racial issues shape domestic political life. In Portugal, perhaps the most multiracial of all West European societies, the politics of race has remained all but irrelevant. But in Germany, France, Belgium, Austria, Italy, Denmark, and Norway parties of the far right exploit fears about the social and economic consequences of immigration and the "invasion of foreigners." In the process, they have made striking electoral gains during the latter half of the 1980s.

Understandably, Canadians are absorbed in the details of their own lives. But when we step back from the precise details of Canadian political, social, and economic turbulence of the last decade, when the transformations are placed in the broader context of changes taking place elsewhere, Canada's recent experiences with fracturing parties, surging interest group activism, increasing public irritation with the status quo, declining satisfaction with the political classes, rising communal tensions, and increasingly abrasive relations on other social fronts all appear less isolated, and less idiosyncratic. And if the turmoil Canadians faced has much in common with the uncertainties experienced by citizens in other advanced industrial states, it may well be that the causes of the turmoil have more to do with the structures and rhythms of late industrialism than with the particular quirks of Canadians or the peculiarities of the Canadian institutional setting.

Three Perspectives on Canadian Value Change

1: Canada as an Advanced Industrial State

It is unlikely that any single explanation can provide an entirely adequate account of all the conflicts Canadians experienced during the 1980s. Undoubtedly, some of the turmoil reflects a combination of significant structural, demographic, and institutional transformations the origins of which can be traced to the 1970s or even earlier. But as scholars since the nineteenth century have noted, significant changes in economic and social structures are linked to value changes. The social, political, and economic values that prevailed during feudalism, for example, are not the same as those associated with the rise of industrialism (Tilly, 1988). Nor, for similar reasons, is there any reason to suppose that the values prevailing during early industrialism are identical to those emerging with late industrialism. Indeed, most perspectives on contemporary values in advanced industrial states begin with the observation that there are fundamental qualitative differences between early and late industrial experiences. Late industrialism has been alternatively labelled as "postindustrialism" (Bell, 1973, 1976), "technetronic" society (Brzezinski, 1970), "postwelfarism" (Lasch, 1972), and "postbourgeois" or "post-materialist" society (Inglehart, 1971, 1990). Regardless of the terminological differences, observers generally concur on two important themes.

First, advanced industrial states have crossed a series of significant thresholds.[1] Typically, all have experienced unprecedented levels of affluence; all have economies that are increasingly driven by the tertiary sector; all have undergone massive expansions in the educational opportunities available to their populations; each has experienced the "information revolution" and a corresponding growth in communications-related technologies. The social consequences of these changes have also been dramatic: they include the expansion of social welfare networks and dramatic increases in the social, geographic, and economic mobilities of populations. Moreover, from a broad historical standpoint, these developments have taken place in a relatively short time frame—in about the last twenty-five years.

The second observation, one central to the analysis that follows, is that these structural transformations are linked to fundamental shifts in the value systems of publics. Again, observers do not all agree about the emphasis to place on the various aspects of the value changes. Some characterize the shifts as change from group solidarity to self-actualization; they see a greater importance attached to "inner goals" as central (Huntington, 1974). Others describe the changes in terms of "individualization" (Ester, Halman and deMoor, 1993). There are also differing assessments of the consequences of those changes. Harding (1986), for instance, argues that the value changes have produced a "new morality." Dalton (1988) notes that the transformations have given the concept of success new meaning. Others indicate that the value shifts have transformed attitudes towards authority, conformity, religiosity, the work ethic, and autonomy (Flanagan, 1982; Naisbitt, 1982; Toffler, 1980). On the political front, these changes are sometimes seen as part and parcel of a transition from "old politics," in which such concerns as economic growth, public order, national security, and traditional lifestyles are central, to "new politics," which places more emphasis on individual freedom, social equality, and quality of life (Hildebrandt & Dalton, 1978; Miller & Levitin, 1976). The changes also extend to the family and the workplace. Despite these differences in emphasis and variations in what is taken to be most significant, there is substantial agreement about the scope and general content of the value changes.

Descriptions of the origins and consequences of advanced industrial value change might be similar, but that does not mean there is widespread agreement on why these value changes have occurred. One line of argument is that value change is chiefly the result of the inherent weaknesses of old welfare states, states that have buckled under a combination of stresses, including rising expectations about what the state should do, a declining capacity to respond to rising demands, and institutional inertia (Offe, 1984). Another plausible line of argument is that value change in advanced industrial states is a direct consequence of the changing class structures of these states, and most particularly the rise of a new class (Lipset, 1979).

Perhaps the best-documented explanation of such value changes is provided by Inglehart, who argues that the "materialist" orientations associated with earlier phases of industrialism are being gradually replaced by "post-material" orientations among publics in advanced industrial states. Inglehart relates the rise of post-materialism to the kinds of structural shifts that are characteristic of late industrialism, and comprehensively demonstrates the host of ways in which post-materialist orientations are connected to the content and dynamics of social and political behaviours in a wide variety of settings (Inglehart, 1971, 1977, 1981, 1988, 1990). Central to Inglehart's theory are the combined effects of two hypotheses. First, the scarcity hypothesis holds that an individual's priorities reflect the socioeconomic environment. "One places the greatest subjective value," Inglehart notes, "on those things that are in relatively short supply" (1988: 881). Second, the socialization hypothesis draws attention to the importance of formative experiences in shaping durable value orientations. "The relationship between socio-economic environment and value priorities," Inglehart cautions, "is not one of immediate adjustment: a substantial time lag is involved for, to a large extent, one's basic values reflect the conditions that prevailed during one's pre-adult years" (1988: 881) Armed with these twin perspectives and employing Maslow's (1954) conceptualization of a needs hierarchy, Inglehart demonstrates that those segments of the population with direct experience of the great traumas of the twentieth century, the Second World War and the Great Depression, give relatively high priority to "materialist goals"—economic security and "safety needs" (Inglehart, 1971, 1990). Those born since 1945, without direct experience of these traumas and "drawn largely from the younger segments of the modern middle class," have had very different formative experiences. They have, he notes, "been socialized during an unprecedentedly long period of unprecedentedly high affluence. For them, economic security may be taken for granted as the supply of water or air we breathe once could" (1971: 991). In effect, those with post-materialist orientations have moved up the needs hierarchy: they are no longer preoccupied with material security and instead give priority to aesthetic and intellectual needs and to the need for belonging.

Applied to the Canadian setting, this line of reasoning suggests a very wide-ranging explanation for the turbulence Canadians experienced in the last decade or so. Not least of all, it implies that Canada's recent value changes may be less distinctive than some suppose, and for that reason may not require a Canada-specific explanation; they could be attributed to the combination of structural and scarcity/socialization dynamics that, according to Inglehart, explain why across all advanced industrial states, "what people want out of life is changing."

2: Canada as a North American State

A second plausible explanation for Canadian value change works from a narrower frame of comparison; it fixes attention on Canada's position as a North American state. The United States serves as Canada's most important reference society, and there is a long tradition of interpreting Canadian values through the optic of Canadian–American comparisons. For example, there is a wealth of accumulated historical wisdom explaining the distinctiveness of contemporary Canadian values in terms of differences in "founding circumstances." These historically informed accounts emphasize the sharp contrasts between Canada's counterrevolutionary past and the revolutionary catharsis of the United States. Unlike the United States, Canada experienced no civil war, and the trajectory of Canadian sociopolitical development was shaped decisively by the presence of dual, European, founding fragments (Clark, 1962; Lower, 1964; Morton, 1961; Underhill, 1960). For generations, the one consistent thread within Canada's policy towards the United States was resistance to judicious management of the forces of continental integration. Other theorists attribute contemporary Canadian–American value differences to cross-national variations in sociostructural make-up, levels of unionization in the workforce, patterns of social mobility, institutional arrangements, elite behaviour, the workings of political parties, crime rates, and collective decisions about health care, education, and a variety of other social supports (Hartz, 1964; Horowitz, 1966; Naegele, 1971). Yet others, most notably Seymour Martin Lipset (1950, 1963, 1979, 1990), have imaginatively woven together historical, literary, sociostructural, and other scattered sources of evidence to bring Canadian–American values into focus. Collectively, this body of high-quality research has been a platform for vigorous debate about the scope and meaning of Canadian and American values; it has also been a rich source of intriguing speculations about the scope and direction of value change (Horowitz, 1973; McRae, 1964).

Moving from qualitative, contextual, or anecdotal evidence to authoritative conclusions about whether Canadian and American values are "basically the same" or "fundamentally different" is a difficult business; it requires a leap of faith. It is equally risky to rely on this kind of information to make definitive judgements about whether Canadian–American value differences of yesteryear still apply. On top of that, similar kinds of qualitative evidence can be cobbled together to make a quite different case that Canadian–American value differences have eroded with the passage of time.

The notion that Canadian values have become increasingly "Americanized" has haunted guardians of Canadian culture for generations. Certainly, it is not difficult to cobble together pieces of anecdotal evidence to fit this view. For example, such recent changes in the Canadian political system as the adoption of the Charter of Rights and Freedoms and the changing role of the courts, the calls for an elected Senate, and the circulation of the populist idea that Canadians should consider the recall of members of Parliament can all be interpreted as reflecting contemporary instances of "American influences." By the same token, some of the social and cultural markers that used to distinguish Canadians from Americans now seem less reliable benchmarks. In the 1960s and 1970s, for example, it was common practice to point to Canada's bilingualism as a characteristic clearly differentiating Canadians and Americans. In the 1990s the United States is home to some twenty-five million Hispanics; linguistic duality has become a more prominent feature of that society. Similarly, the politics of race once served as another means of distinguishing American from Canadian communal relations. But as we have seen, race has moved from the margins of Canadian communal reality to become a part of normal discourse.

Other arguments can travel in the same direction. Irving Louis Horowitz (1973), for example, takes issue with Lipset's explanation that Canadian–American value differences are attributable to variations in founding circumstances and the residual effects of those differences. According to Horowitz, the variations in the prevailing value systems of the two countries may have more to do with their basic structural differences. Canada, he argued, was a case of "lagged development." This line of speculation implies that as Canada and the United States become structurally more similar, so too will their value systems. In that sense, the United States "shows Canada the picture of its own future."

Perhaps the most widely held explanation for Canadian–American value convergence, and one that pumped life into the Canadian debate about the wisdom of free trade with the United States, centres on the consequences of Canada's geographic proximity to the United States. In many respects, Canada and the United States are probably more interdependent than any two other countries in the world and that interdependence works at multiple levels (Keohane & Nye, 1976). In the economic realm, the volume of two-way trade between the two countries is huge; they are the largest trading dyad in the world, and each is the other's most important source of exports and imports. The massive scale of American direct and indirect investment in the Canadian economy is well documented (Redekop, 1978). Less heeded, but also significant, is Canada's emerging position as a major investor in the American economy (Fry, 1980). In addition to the commercial and financial transactions, there are very substantial population flows between the two countries. The volume of cross-border media and communications transactions provides yet another indication of de facto integration. Like publics in other parts of the world, Canadians have an appetite for a wide spectrum of American cultural products. But Canadian exposure to printed, and, particularly, electronically transmitted cultural exports from the United States is far greater. About 80% of the Canadian population has access to all of the major American television networks. At yet another level, Canadians and Americans share strategic interests in the defense of the continent.

The suggestion that the combined effects of multilevel transactions between countries can produce value change is not new. When Karl Deutsch and his colleagues (Deutsch, 1952, 1957, 1968; Haas, 1958) first began exploring the dynamics of European integration some forty years ago, they argued that the volume of cross-national transactions has a lot to do with value change and with the prospects for economic and political integration. Drawing on social learning theory and armed with evidence from multiple European case studies, Deutsch and his colleagues suggested that high levels of cross-border transactions (the movement of peoples, cross-border commerce and communication flows) encourage greater similarities in "main values."[2] Such similarities, they argued, are mutually reinforcing and increase the level of trust between peoples. Higher levels of trust in turn increase the likelihood of greater cooperation and economic integration. And economic integration calls for the coordination of decision-making, and hence is conducive to political integration. Deutsch's historically inspired account of why values play an important role in the integration process remains an influential one. The links in this chain of reasoning are empirically tested and the essential elements of the theory are reflected in more contemporary renditions of the dynamics of integration (Diebold, 1988; Lindberg & Scheingold, 1970; Nye, 1977). However, the Deutsch theory plainly has implications for the North American setting. If the 1988 Canada–United States free tade agreement signifies a commitment to greater economic integration between the two countries, then the Deutsch perspective implies that the agreement will have been preceded by significant changes in cross-border transactions. Available evidence supports that prediction. The volume of Canada–U.S. two-way border crossings (the movement of peoples) rose from 72 million visits in 1980 to 94 million visits in 1989 (Statistics Canada, 1991). Commercial and financial transactions also increased sharply over the period immediately leading up to the agreement (Schott & Smith, 1988). But did Canadian and American "main values" also converge over that period? On balance, the answer is that they did.

3: Canada as an Immigrant Society

A third possible explanation for Canadian value change is even more narrowly focussed; it draws attention to changing patterns of population replacement. The dynamics of population replacement are affected by a host of factors, including fertility rates, longevity, immigration, emigration, changing attitudes to the family, the place of women in the economy, and education. In the Canadian setting, as in others, there have been dramatic shifts in long-standing patterns of population replacement over the last twenty-five years. Census data show that in 1965 Canada's fertility rate stood at 3.1 births per woman.

By 1972 the rate had dropped below the replacement level of 2.1, and by 1985 it had fallen to just 1.7 (Beaujot, 1993: 75).[3] A variety of explanations have been offered for this decline in fertility rates,[4] which amounts to a 45% decrease between 1965 and 1990. At the same time, Canadians were also living longer. Other things being equal, the combined effect of declining fertility rates and greater longevity is population aging. In 1971, for example, the average age of the Canadian population stood at just over 26 years; by 1986 it had risen to nearly 32 years, and demographers project that it will continue to rise, to about 45 years of age by the year 2036 (Beaujot, 1991). Declining fertility rates and increased longevity, according to socialization theory, will have direct consequences for value change because the impact of "formative experiences" on basic value orientations will be more attenuated, more long-lasting, than in the past.

Declining fertlity rates and increased longevity, though, tell only a part of the demographic story, particularly in Canada. Because the natural birth rate has declined below the replacement rate, maintaining current population levels has increasingly been accomplished via immigration. Given that 40,000 to 50,000 people emigrate from the country each year, some 175,000 immigrants are needed just to stabilize the Canadian population at current levels. Canada has always been an immigrant society, and with 16% of its population being born outside of the country, it relies more heavily on immigration than any other advanced industrial society except Australia (20% of whose population is non-native-born). Simply calculating the net balance of emigration and immigration, though, misses one of the most dramatic aspects of Canada's population shift over the last twenty-five years, namely, the fundamental shifts in immigrants' country of origin. Between 1956 and 1960 Canadian immigrants coming from traditional, European, sources outnumbered those coming from non-traditional, non-European sources by a huge margin, about fifteen to one. By 1980 that trend had completely reversed; immigrants from "non-traditional" sources outnumbered those from traditional recruiting grounds two to one (Beaujot & Rappak, 1988) (see figure 1).

The significant shift in country of origin has had several obvious consequences. One is that Canada has become a less European society than ever before, and the introduction of Canada's policy of multiculturalism in the 1970s reflected that changing reality. Another is that communal relations have become more complicated. To the already difficult relations between the three primary groups with historic claims grounded in founding status—Canada's First Nations and English and French settlers—have been added "new Canadians" who come from extraordinarily diverse backgrounds and make claims for social, economic, and political inclusion.

Less obvious, but of special significance here, immigrants are also a potential source of value change. Reliable evidence about what values immigrants bring to Canada is sketchy at best. And remarkably little is known, for example, about the processes of value adaptation—about how quickly or slowly new Canadians adapt, about which values newcomers tend to keep and which

Figure 1   Birthplace of Immigrants to Canada, 1961–1989

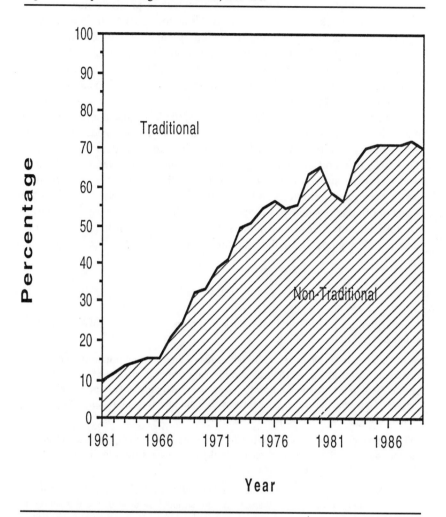

Traditional sources: Europe, Australasia, United States
Non-traditional sources: Africa, Asia, North & Central America, the Caribbean, South America, Oceania, born at sea, and not stated
Source: Immigration Statistics, 1961–1989 (Ottawa: Supply and Services).

they shed. One speculation is that the values of immigrants coming from western and northern Europe, the traditional sources of immigration, are more congenial to "mainstream Canada" than those who come from non-traditional sources. Relatedly, it might be argued that immigrants from traditional countries of origin adapt more easily than those coming from non-traditional countries. These judgements, though, remain speculations. In the absence of direct sytematic evidence, it is impossible to demonstrate precisely how, or even whether, the values of new Canadians differ significantly from those of non-immigrants. Even so, new Canadians certainly might be considered a potential source of value change, for two basic reasons: first, the basic value orientations of immigrants are not, and by definition could not have been, rooted in Canadian experience; and second, these immigrant peoples make up a sizeable percentage of the Canadian population.[5]

These three perspectives on or images of Canada—Canada as an advanced industrial state, Canada as a North American society, and Canada as an immigrant society—all point to possible explanations for Canadian value change. They are not mutually exclusive; Canadian values may have changed partly because of the structural and value shifts associated with late industrialism, partly because of proximity to the United States, and partly because of the kinds of orientations that new Canadians contribute. Nor do these perspectives exhaust the entire set of possibilities, but they are three of the more obvious ones and they guide the analysis that follows.

NOTES

[1] See Huntington (1974) "Post-Industrial Politics: How Benign Will It Be?" Comparative Politics 6: 147–77.

[2] By "main values" Deutsch and his colleagues were referring primarily to core economic and political norms. Deutsch and his team (Deutsch et al. 1957) were primarily interested in the question of how to secure peace and prosperity in post-war western Europe. They concluded that greater cross-national integration through strategic institution building was the most promising avenue.

[3] The conventional calculation is that 2.0 births are needed to replace parents and 0.1 compensates for the small number of deaths that occur before the next generation reaches reproductive age. See Beaujot 1991: 75.

[4] Political and economic factors also undoubtedly come into play. In agricultural economies, children might be seen as an "investment" because they are a source of "free" labour. They also might be seen as a form of insurance against old age. But as David notes, in the contemporary context having children may be a risky investment. And on balance, it seems, "economic rationales are relevant to explaining why people do not have more children, but they may not explain why people have children" (Beaujot 1991: 83).

[5] The point is that they are sufficiently large to potentially skew what are taken to be Canadian values.

2: Setting the Stage

Values, or deep dispositions, are important because they guide decisions about right and wrong and because they underpin a whole array of social, economic, and political preferences. They are also important because they are foundations for action, foundations that help to explain regularities, or indeed irregularities, in people's behaviour (Rokeach, 1968).[1] There is no consensus about the best way to determine the shape and substance of public values. In the absence of direct evidence, for example, some observers have attempted to get a fix on public values by delving into popular literature, sifting through laws and constitutions, and scanning the policies adopted by governments. Others have formed conclusions about public values on the basis of such indicators as crime rates or structural characteristics like levels of unionization. Each approach has its particular advantages, and investigators using these methods have generated a host of intriguing speculations about national values, about cross-national value similarities and differences, and about value change. Seymour Martin Lipset's (1990) path-breaking work comparing Canadian and American values, for example, relies primarily on an artful combination of such strategies. But these approaches also have disadvantages; part of the controversy surrounding the question of how much Canadian and American values differ hinges on the adequacy and interpretability of qualitative evidence (see Horowitz, 1973; Truman, 1971). One such problem has to do with making the logical leap from institutional or structural indicators to conclusions about the values of entire publics. To what extent, for example, do policies crafted by elites reliably reflect the preferences of the rest of the public? Or, to take another example, does the fact that people in one country save more of their disposable income than people in another provide a true indication of deep-seated differences in the way they view economic risk-taking? Might they not instead reflect different responses to variations in interest rates or tax rules? Independent researchers looking at the very same evidence can arrive at different interpretations regardless of what type of evidence is used. But the problems of inference and interpretation are particularly difficult with qualitative data, not least because qualitative evidence is typically "lumpy"; it is cumbersome and hard to synthesize. Cross-national comparisons further compound the difficulties, among other reasons because crime rates or unemployment statistics are rarely reported in precisely the same way in different countries.

This book relies on a different strategy; it draws upon a unique and enormously rich body of data that comes from survey questionnaires, the World Values Surveys. The main advantage of these kinds of data is that they minimize the need to base inferences about public values on indirect structural or behavioural indicators. Survey questionnaires provide *direct* measures of values or deep dispositions; they work from a simple principle, that the best way to find out about people's values is to ask them.[2] The World Values Surveys are a particularly powerful tool for investigating Canadian values and the broader theme of value change for a combination of reasons.

First, the only way to know if, and how, Canadian values have changed is by making cross-time comparisons. To be able to say anything about value change during the 1980s, for example, we need to know, at a minimum, what Canadian values were like at the beginning of the decade and what they were like at its end. The World Values Surveys were conducted in Canada first in 1981 and then in 1990, and with data taken from these two time points it is possible to establish the direction and scope of value change during the decade.[3]

Second, the World Values Surveys (WVS) data are useful because the surveys were conducted in some twenty-two countries in 1981 and more than forty countries (accounting for some 70 per cent of the world's population) in 1990. In fact, the WVS are the largest body of direct cross-time and cross-national data on public values ever collected. Most studies of values typically focus on one country, a good strategy for fleshing out the details and probing the nuances of values in any single setting. But it is difficult, if not impossible, to fathom what is distinctive about the values of one country by looking only at that country. How does one know which values are uniquely Canadian and which ones are not by looking only at Canada? Two-country comparisons run into a similar problem because such comparisons end up highlighting contrasts but provide no benchmark indicating which country is exceptional. A broader cross-national perspective is crucial, then, because the content and contours of what are peculiarly Canadian values can only be brought into focus by examining Canadian values against the backdrop of values held by other publics.

Third, recall the three explanations for Canadian value change outlined in the last chapter; each one works at a different level of analysis. Consequently, to be able to test all three at once requires evidence that can accommodate a broad and flexible investigatory strategy. To evaluate the "new Canadians" perspective, for example, involves two tasks. First, we have to be able to unpack the Canadian evidence so that the values of the three sub-groups— anglophones, francophones, and "new Canadians"—can be isolated. Then we have to be able to see whether, and how, the values of each group have changed during the decade. To test the "Americanization" perspective calls for aggregate national comparisons; it involves comparing Canadian values and value changes with those that have taken place in the United States. The third perspective is yet more global: Canadian value changes have to be placed in the even broader context of value changes in other advanced industrial states. The WVS are uniquely equipped to undertake these multiple comparisons; they are the only data available that allow us to undertake them all and to do so within a common time frame.

Finally, there are a variety of methodological and substantive features of the WVS that make them a particularly powerful tool for comparative analysis. The questions used in the surveys have been repeatedly tested and fine-tuned in multiple settings for more than two decades, and so we can be reasonably confident that the data coming from these surveys are reliable. Moreover, all of the surveys were deliberately coordinated with respect to both timing of the field work and content of the questionnaires. With very minor adjustments, the same survey questions were used in every setting. As a result, the data coming from these surveys are "even"; interpretations based on the WVS are less encumbered by the problems of equivalence that plague many cross-national surveys, which were either not undertaken at the same time or rely on questions that are only roughly similar.

These features of the World Values Surveys are of special significance for anyone interested in making systematic Canadian–American value comparisons. To be sure, empirical survey research that directly measures values in both countries has become increasingly popular in the last fifteen years, and this has partly been a reaction to the limitations of qualitative evidence. But the reliability of the conclusions these studies generate about the uniqueness and overlap of Canadian and American values has been undermined by a variety of methodological difficulties. Until now, for example, much of the available empirical research has been narrowly focussed; it often relies upon data drawn from limited segments of national populations. Such data may serve the researcher's particular purposes quite well, but it is not possible to generalize about the values of national publics from student samples (Frohlich & Boschman, 1986; Landes, 1977; Nevitte & Gibbins, 1990), from samples of political elites (Presthus, 1977), or from samples of single communities on each side of the border (Crawford & Curtis, 1979). Some complementary national surveys have been conducted in the two countries, but their utility in cross-national value comparisons has been undercut by other flaws. The Quality of Life Study, for example, was pioneered in the United States and replicated in Canada. In this instance, the comparability of the findings is limited by the fact that the studies were conducted six years apart (U.S. 1971; Canada 1977). Election studies, of course, have been conducted in both countries for more than a quarter of a century, and these data provide fertile ground for comparative exploration of an important, but nonetheless relatively narrow, range of political phenomenon (Beck & Pierce, 1977; Crawford & Curtis, 1979; Guppy, 1984; Wattenburg, 1979). Quite aside from variations in the content and design of these studies, however, national elections have *never* been held simultaneously in both countries. Surveys are now regularly conducted on both sides of the border by commercial agencies, and these have been particularly useful for tracking and comparing attitudes towards single issues (Lipset, 1990). But such studies are driven by the relatively narrow concerns of market research; they do not contain the rich mix of social, political, and economic indicators that allow us to analyze and interpret these single issues in the larger context.

The WVS data are the only directly comparable cross-time Canadian–American data available; no other survey has asked national samples of Canadians and Americans the very same questions at each of two different times. On the substantive front, the WVS data are unique in their scope; they were specifically designed to tap a very broad range of value domains. The WVS included detailed indicators of orientations to a host of social, economic, and political values. This means that it is possible not only to examine changes in family values, in work values, and in political values, but also to explore the intriguing questions of whether, and how, these values may be connected. The WVS would be valuable enough if they allowed us to explore the extent of value change or continuity across several broad value domains in a single country. What makes these data so useful is that, for the first time, it is now possible to undertake all of these comparisons in multiple countries and to do so systematically over precisely the same time period.

Structural Shifts in Context

The selection of other countries to include for comparison is important because context sets the benchmark, and provides the framework, for interpretation. Throughout this book, Canadian values are compared to those held by publics in eleven other countries: France, Britain, the former West Germany, Italy, the Netherlands, Denmark, Belgium, Spain, Ireland, Northern Ireland, and the United States. These countries vary significantly across a variety of fronts. In their systems of government, for example, some are parliamentary, others presidential; some, like Britain, are unitary and others, like Germany, are federal. There are also significant differences in levels of economic performance, and in the scope and depth of welfare state (Heidenheimer & Flora, 1981). Added to these are the unique religious, ethnic, and linguistic configurations of their populations. Some countries, like Spain and Ireland, are almost entirely Catholic, others are predominantly Protestant, but most have populations of mixed faiths. Despite all of these variations, the majority nonetheless share a broad commitment to the liberal version of the democratic process. To be sure, the historical routes by which these countries arrived at that commitment are different. Some became democratic early, others relatively late. In some cases the transition to democracy was relatively peaceful, in others it was plainly violent. In some the commitment to democratic processes evolved gradually and continuously, in others that process was marked by discontinuities. The significant point is that regardless of the variations in their cultural characteristics, institutional arrangements, and evolutionary trajectories, citizens in all of these states now

Table 2-1 Percentage of the Workforce Employed in Primary, Secondary and Tertiary Economic Sectors

Country	Primary Sector (1990)	Secondary Sector (1990)	Tertiary Sector (1990)
France	6.1	29.9	64.0
	(-10.2)[a]	(-9.0)	(+19.2)
Britain	2.1	29.0	68.9
	(-1.5)	(-16.6)	(+18.1)
Germany	3.4	39.8	56.8
	(-7.0)	(-7.1)	(+14.0)
Italy	9.0	32.4	58.6
	(-15.4)	(-4.9)	(+20.3)
Netherlands	4.6	26.3	69.1
	(-2.5)	(-13.2)	(+15.7)
Denmark	5.6	27.5	66.9
	(-7.9)	(-9.6)	(+17.4)
Belgium	2.7	28.3	69.0
	(-3.0)	(-15.6)	(+18.7)
Spain	11.8	33.4	54.8
	(-17.6)	(-1.0)	(+18.6)
Ireland	15.0	28.6	56.4
	(-15.4)	(+0.4)	(+15.1)
Canada	4.2	24.6	71.2
	(-4.7)	(-7.8)	(+12.5)
United States	2.8	26.2	70.9
	(-2.5)	(-9.6)	(+12.0)

Source: OECD Statistics Directorate, Paris, 1992.
[a] Parentheses enclose percentage change 1967–1990

enjoy the cluster of rights and freedoms that are essential to an open, competitive, and free democratic process. All have a free and secret vote, a free press, and guarantees of freedom of religion, expression, and association. All hold regular and competitive elections, and the barriers to citizen participation in public life are minimal.

All of the countries are similar in another equally significant respect: each one plainly qualifies as an advanced industrial state (Huntington, 1974). By 1990 at least half of those in the paid workforce in each of these countries were employed in the tertiary sectors of the economy: in government or in the service sector. Once again, and as Table 2-1 illustrates, there are leaders and laggards in this respect. The American, Belgian, British, Canadian, and Dutch economies, for example, crossed the threshold to advanced industrialism about twenty years ago, the French, Irish, Italian, and Spanish did so much later. Variations in the pace of these economic transitions aside, the general direction of economic structural change in these countries over the last twenty-five years has been remarkably similar. Without exception, the relative size of the paid workforce employed in the primary economic sectors shrank between 1967 and 1990. In all cases except one, Ireland, the workforces employed in the manufacturing sector shrank. And over the same period the size of the tertiary-sector workforce grew in every country.

That societies have economies in which most people in the paid workforce are employed in the tertiary sector has a number of implications. One is that the kind of work that most people now do is very different from the kind of work that occupied their parents. The shift from an economy driven by the exploitation of primary resources and manufacturing to one driven mainly by technology, information, and services almost certainly could not have been accomplished without a corresponding shift in the skills of the workforce. Industrially advanced economies, in other words, could hardly have emerged without a well-educated workforce. For that reason, it comes as no surprise to discover that each one of these countries has experienced progressively widening public participation in post-secondary education. As Figure 2-1 illustrates, the shifts have been quite dramatic. In the European countries, for example, slightly less than 9 per cent of those in the 20–24 age group were in post-secondary institutions in 1960. By 1989 the proportion had more than tripled, to about 32%.

The figures for both of the North American countries have been consistently higher. In 1960 for example, 32 per cent of American 20–24-year-olds were in post-secondary education. That figure jumped to just over 70 per cent by 1989. In the Canadian case, the pace of the shift has been even more dramatic. The proportion of Canadian 20–24-year-olds in post-secondary education quadrupled over the same period, rising from 16 per cent to 66 per cent between 1960 and 1989. The "education gap" between Canada and the United States has not disappeared entirely, but it has narrowed significantly over the last thirty years. What explains the sharp differences between the North American and European levels of participation in post-secondary education? There are several possibilities. One is that the differences reflect the fact that North American societies are more "open" than their European counterparts, and that North Americans attach greater importance to post-secondary education as a vehicle for social mobility. It is also possible that the actual European–North American post-secondary education gap is less dramatic than the data imply and that the apparent differences are amplified by cross-national variations in how post-secondary education is organized or by how data are reported. But even if we discount these North American-European differences and look at the cross-time changes that have taken place within each country, the evidence points to a strikingly consistent pattern: those countries, such as Italy and Spain, that were slower to become advanced industrial economies (see Table 2-1) were also slower to expand post-secondary education.

The demand for a sophisticated workforce was undoubtedly one reason for the rapid emergence of educated publics. But the explosion of educational opportunities has consequences that reach far beyond the confines of the

Figure 2-1   Percentage of Men and Women (20–24 Years of Age) in Post-Secondary Education, 1960–1989

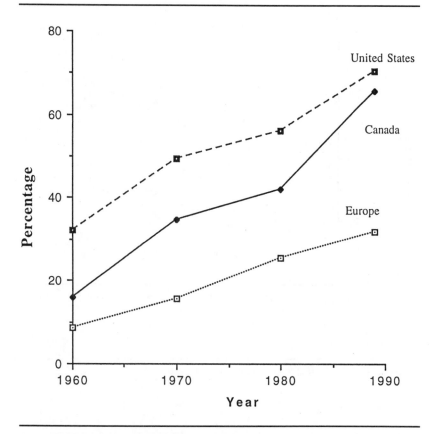

Source: UNESCO Statistical Yearbooks, 1976, 1992, Paris.

workplace. It is also clear that the sustained expansion of educational opportunities has had a greater impact on some segments of the public than others. Thirty years ago, for example, there were very striking gender imbalances in enrolments in post-secondary education institutions throughout all advanced industrial states. In 1960 the enrolments of North American men outstripped those of women by a ratio of about 2:1, and in Europe this gender gap was even wider, favouring men over women by a margin of about 3:1. As Figure 2-2 shows, between 1960 and 1989 these discrepancies all but disappeared.

Once again, there is significant variation in the rates of change. In the North American cases, for example, women achieved post-secondary enrolment parity with men by about 1980. In fact, by 1989 women actually outnumbered men in North American post-secondary institutions by a margin of about 15%.

Figure 2-2 Percentage of Men and Women (20–24 Years of Age) in Post-Secondary Education in Canada and the United States, 1960–1989

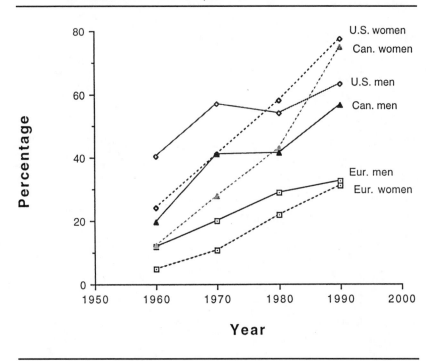

Source: UNESCO Statistical Yearbooks 1976, 1992, Paris.

In the European countries, the post-secondary gender gap in enrolments closed a little later. By 1989 the gap was insignificant in all but three countries: Ireland, the Netherlands, and West Germany.

These trends—the shifting occupational structures, the explosion of post-secondary educational opportunities, and the narrowing of the gender gap in enrollment—have been accompanied by a variety of others, such as increased geographic and occupational mobility. Not surprisingly, these changes have had an enormous impact on the character of the paid workforce, as women have entered it in unprecedented numbers. The sharp increase in the number of two-income families is one facet of that change. Another is the emerging, and corresponding, challenge to traditional conceptions of family life. People marry later, if at all. The size of the average family has fallen. Balancing career opportunities with home life has become more difficult, and the cumulative effects of these and other stresses are reflected in yet another consistent trend: higher divorce rates. As Figure 2-3 illustrates, the changes over the last thirty years are striking. In 1960, for example, Canadian divorce rates looked

Figure 2-3   Divorce Rates Per 1,000 Population: 1960–1989, Europe, U.S., Canada

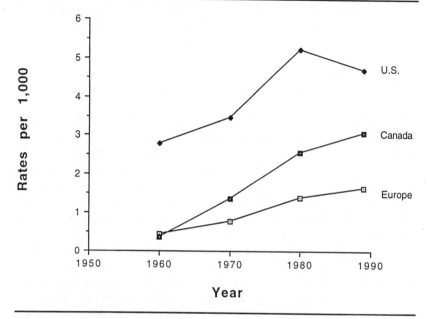

Source: UN Demographic Yearbooks, 1976, 1982, 1990, 1992, New York.

very much like those in European countries. Between 1970 and 1989, though, they became progressively less European, and moved towards American levels. With the possible exception of the United States, which appears to have peaked in 1980, divorce rates have consistently risen in every country over the thirty-year period.

The particular shifts sketched out above capture but one part of the entire array of structural changes that have swept across advanced industrial states over the course of the last two decades. But they are sufficient to illustrate two general points. First, although the rate and scope of these structural shifts vary from one setting to the next, in every country all of the changes are in the same direction. Second, it is tidier to think of each of these shifts in isolation, to regard them as analytically distinct, but the picture that emerges is far more complex. In practice, the variety of structural changes that advanced industrial states have undergone simultaneously on a number of fronts form an interrelated pattern. The structural changes that take place in one domain, such as the economy, turn out to be closely related to changes in other domains. One set of shifts cannot be neatly separated from others.

Taken together, the countries that are the focus of this analysis all share in the common social, economic, and political traditions that set the Western liberal-democratic world—Western Europe and North America—apart from most other parts of the globe. In a sense, they reflect different parts of the spectrum within that tradition. All have experienced similar structural shifts over the last twenty-five years. By examining Canadian values against this backdrop, we will be able to see how Canadian values "fit" within the context of the values of other publics that are within the same Western tradition. Where, then, do Canadian values fit? In what respects are they similar? And where are they different?

From Structural Change to Value Change

We begin by examining two very general questions. The first concerns the perspective that interprets Canadian values in terms of advanced industrialism: Is there any direct evidence that Canadians, over the 1980s, experienced the same kinds of value shifts that have been documented in the West European setting over the last two decades? The second deals with broad-gauge value priorities: To what extent are the general priorities of Canadians fundamentally different from, or similar to, those of citizens in other advanced industrial states?

That the structural transformations associated with advanced industrialism have been accompanied by changes in basic values in the last two decades is not a novel idea. And, as has already been pointed out, observers have offered a variety of interpretations of the origins, scope, and implications of the changes. Recall Inglehart's (1976, 1990) explanation: his theory unites the well-established premise that formative experiences are fundamental to the development of long-lasting basic value orientations (the socialization hypothesis) with the observation that citizens of advanced industrial states live under conditions that are historically exceptional: most do not live under conditions of physical or economic insecurity (the scarcity hypothesis). Together, these hypotheses produce quite specific predictions about both the content and the dynamics of value change. One is that periods of sustained prosperity will encourage a shift away from a preoccupation with "material goals" (money and physical security) and a shift towards "post-materialist values" and such "higher-order" priorities as the need for belonging, self-esteem, and values relating to the quality of life. Periods of economic decline will have the opposite effect. Because the dynamics of these value priorities are linked to formative experiences, the conditions that prevail during pre-adult years, the expectation is that the value changes will be gradual and will show up in generational differences. In the long run, as the generations that faced such traumatic events as the Depression and the Second World War are gradually replaced by those with no such first-hand experiences, societies will become increasingly post-materialist.

The claim that publics in advanced industrial states are becoming progressively more post-materialist was first systematically tested in 1970 (Inglehart, 1971) using surveys of national samples of publics in six European countries, all of which are also included in this study: Britain, France, West Germany, Italy, the Netherlands, and Belgium. The people interviewed were presented with a list of four items, two of which represented "materialist" goals and the other two "post-materialist" ones, and respondents were asked to rank the goals in order of importance to them. Those ranking the two materialist goals first and second were classified as the "pure materialist" value type; those ranking the post-materialist items first and second were classified as "pure post-materialists"; and the rest were classified as "mixed." The 1970 study as well as subsequent surveys of the same publics (Inglehart, 1990; Inglehart, Nevitte, & Basanez, 1996) produced striking support for the theory. All the available evidence corroborated the two key predictions: that post-materialist orientations were indeed on the rise and that the emergence of post-materialist values was clearly related to intergenerational change (see Appendix 2-1).

Nearly all of the 1981 and 1990 WVS, including the Canadian surveys, contained the now-standard materialism/post-materialism battery of items, and so it is possible to ask: Have these same value shifts continued along the same trajectory? And is there evidence of any collateral value change in the Canadian setting? Figure 2-4 reports the aggregate value shifts for the ten European countries as well as the country-specific shifts for the United States and Canada. The evidence is clear: in both Europe and North America materialist orientations declined during the 1980s, while the number of citizens of the pure post-materialist value type grew. Not surprisingly, there is evidence of national variations among Europeans in the pace and scope of these value changes. The significant point, once again, is that in every national setting the direction of the trend is the same. And it turns out that by 1990 the overall balances of materialist, mixed, and post-materialist value orientations among European and North American publics are remarkably similar. Moreover, detailed analysis of the national responses to the individual items within the materialist/post-materialist scale reveals a striking degree of cross-national consistency in another respect: North Americans and West Europeans structure their responses to those items in almost identical ways (Appendix 2-2). That finding indicates that the materialist/post-materialist value dimension is robust, meaningful, and stable for all publics.

In the broad scheme of things, the Canadian–American results are in both the structure of responses to the post-materialism index and the changing levels of post-materialism. Much more fine-grained comparisons of the data for these two countries reveal another intriguing finding: they provide little support for the idea that Canadian orientations lag behind American ones or that Americans show Canadians the "picture of their own future," at least on this value dimension. In both 1981 and 1990 Canadians were both less materialist and more post-materialist than their American counterparts.[4] That finding is quite consistent with earlier explanations of cross-national variations in levels of post-materialism. The per capita income in the United States is higher than that in Canada, and wealthy people may tend to feel more secure than those who are not so well off. There is no simple one-to-one relationship between economic level and the prevalence of post-materialist orientations; post-materialism springs from a *subjective* sense of security. But a sense of security also

Figure 2-4 Value Type: Europe, U.S., and Canada (The Four-Item Battery)

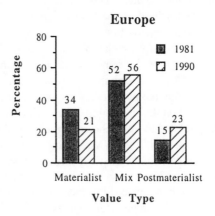

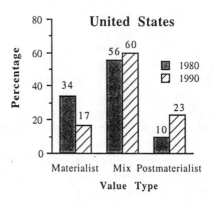

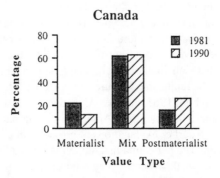

Source: 1980 NES Survey; 1981 and 1990 World Values Surveys.

Table 2-2 Materialist/Postmaterialist Orientations within Canada, 1981–1990 (Percentages)

Value Type	English Canada			French Canada			New Canada	
	1981	1990	Change	1981	1990	Change	1981	1990
Materialist	17	9	-8	35	21	-14	n.a.[a]	10
Mixed	66	68	+2	52	50	-2	n.a.	62
Postmaterialist	17	23	+6	13	29	+16	n.a.	28

Source: 1981 and 1990 World Values Surveys.
n.a. = data not available for 1981.

depends upon such other factors as the cultural setting and social institutions that surround individuals during their formative years (Inglehart et al., 1996).[5]

What about the third perspective on Canadian value change? Are there significant discrepancies between the value orientations of "new Canadians," those not born in Canada, and their francophone and anglophone counterparts who have lived in the country all their lives? It is not difficult to speculate about what the potential value differences between these groups might be. New Canadians, for example, might have been motivated to come to Canada to improve their economic situation. That line of reasoning produces the expectation that new Canadians might be more materialist than the other subgroups. Then again, if Max Weber's hypothesis relating Protestantism to the "spirit of capitalism" is any guide to the value orientations of contemporary publics, anglophone Canadians, who are mostly Protestant, might be more materialist than their francophone counterparts, who are mostly Catholic. How do these groups compare when it comes to materialist/post-materialist orientations?

On this point, the data reveal another intriguing finding. Anglophones turn out to be consistently less materialist than francophones; at least they were in 1981 and 1990. The 1981–1990 increases in post-materialist orientations were much sharper among francophones than their anglophone counterparts. Cross-time data for new Canadians are not available, but according to the 1990 data, new Canadians were not so very different from other Canadians; they were about as materialist as anglophones and about as post-materialist as francophones. Where crosstime data are available, the trend is again the same; post-materialist value orientations were on the rise among Canadians during the course of the decade.

In addition to predictions about the rising level of post-materialism, post-materialist theory also predicts that post-materialist values will be distributed unevenly across generations. Because of the effects of socialization, the expectation is that those who are in the younger cohorts—those who could not have experienced the Depression or the Second World War first hand and who enjoyed a climate of sustained economic prosperity during their formative years—are more likely than older cohorts to have these post-materialist orientations. With data from only a ten-year period, it is not possible to demonstrate decisively that the 1981–1990 shifts are a result of generational change alone. But if there are generational value differences, then there should be evidence of value differences across age groups. Once again, the WVS data provide clear support for that claim. Figure 2-5 unpacks the distribution of materialist/post-materialist orientations by age group for both 1981 and 1990. It shows that in 1981 materialist orientations clearly increase with age and post-materialist orientations are more prevalent among the younger age groups; the slopes are consistent. The same overall pattern holds for 1990. A comparison of the 1981 and 1990 results also shows that post-materialist orientations increased across all age groups, during the decade: in 1981 materialists outnumbered post-materialists in *all* age groups, but by 1990 post-materialists outnumbered materialists in three out of the six cohorts considered. The scope and extent of this secular shift towards post-materialism is clearly illustrated when we track the "same" age cohort across the two points for which we have data. For example, consider the 1981 data, and look at the balance of materialist/post-materialist orientations for the 35–44 age cohort. In that group, materialists far outnumbered post-materialists—by a ratio of about 2:1. By 1990, nine years later, most of that 1981 cohort would fall into the 45–54 age group, and in 1990 the balance between materialists and post-materialists had shifted to 1:1. In other words, although the rise of post-materialist orientations plainly is associated with intergenerational effects, generational replacement does not, by itself, account for the full extent of the value shift to post-materialism: this secular shift to post-materialism exceeds what we would expect from generational replacement alone by about 7 per cent.[6] Two important conclusions emerge from the data presented so far. First, the evidence clearly indicates that a general value shift towards post-materialism took place in all the advanced industrial states, including Canada, between 1981 and 1990. Second, this particular value shift does, as the theory predicts, appear to be linked to intergenerational change.

Public Priorities and Orientations towards Authority

Having established the basic trajectories of post-materialist value change, we can now set the stage in two other respects. First, the scope of analysis throughout this book is deliberately broad; the goal is to explore value change in the political and economic domains as well as in the area of primary relations. That line of analysis can be both launched and given perspective by exploring how much importance citizens in these states assign to each of these various domains. Second, the thread conceptually uniting much of the analysis is orientation towards authority. This theme has a familiar ring; a variety of observers have claimed that, among other things, Canadians "remain more

Figure 2-5 Value Type by Age Group: Europe and North America, 1981–1990

1981:

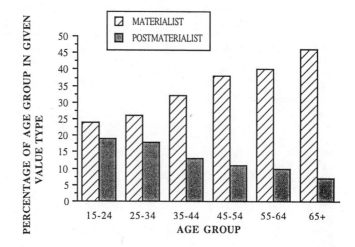

1990:

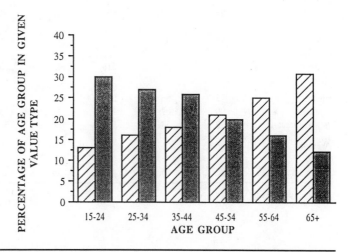

Note: Value type by age group, among the publics of France, Britain, West Germany, Italy, Netherlands, Denmark, Belgium, Spain, Ireland, Northern Ireland, U.S., Canada, and Mexico. (1981, $N = 16,043$; 1990, $N = 20,464$). Value type is not available for U.S. 1981.
Source: 1981 and 1990 World Values Surveys.

respectful of authority" than Americans, are more deferential, more elitist (Bell, 1992; Lipset, 1990). Lipset, for example, suggests that these Canadian–American differences flow from variations in founding circumstances and remain embedded in different basic organizing principles (1990: 8).

Table 2-3 Percentage of Respondents Saying that Family, Work, Leisure Time, Religion, and Politics are "Very Important," in 12 Advanced Industrial States

Country (Sample Size)	Family Important %	Work Important %	Friends Important %	Leisure Important %	Religion Important %	Politics Important %
France (1,002)	82	61	41	31	14	8
Britain (1,484)	89	49	48	44	18	10
West Germany (2,101)	71	35	37	40	13	9
Italy (2,018)	87	63	39	34	31	7
Netherlands (1,017)	81	50	59	50	21	12
Denmark (1,030)	88	51	53	48	9	8
Belgium (2,792)	84	56	47	40	17	6
Spain (4,147)	83	65	45	38	21	6
Ireland (1,000)	91	65	55	32	48	5
N. Ireland (304)	94	57	53	31	34	6
U.S. (1,839)	93	62	54	43	54	16
Canada (1,730)	92	59	51	42	30	15
English	92	56	53	42	29	14
French	90	69	49	44	28	13
New Canadians	92	58	51	37	38	19
Average	86.3	56.1	48.5	39.4	25.8	9.0
European Average	85	55.2	47.7	38.8	22.6	7.7

Source: 1990 World Values Survey.

The 1990 WVS contain a battery of questions designed to indicate the general priorities of publics, and they provide initial guidance on where Canadian priorities "fit" within the priorities of other publics. The 1990 surveys asked respondents in every country how much importance they attached to work, family, friends and acquaintances, leisure time, politics, and religion. Table 2-3 summarizes the aggregate results, reporting the percentage of the twelve publics replying "very important" in each of the six domains. The results are clear: in every country the family clearly ranks first. After that, national variations come into play. In nine out of the twelve countries work comes before friends and acquaintances: the exceptions are West Germany, the Netherlands, and Denmark. In eleven out of twelve countries "friends and acquaintances" comes next. Leisure was considered very important by close to 40 per cent of respondents. Religion typically rates as very important for about 30 per cent of respondents, and in all countries politics comes last; slightly less than 10 per cent of the publics see politics as being very important.

There is nothing here to indicate that the priorities of Canadians differ much from those of their counterparts in other advanced industrial states, and there are relatively few instances in which there are sharp differences between one public and the others. The West Germans are somewhat less likely than others to think of work as very important.[7] The Dutch stand out when it comes to the importance attached to friends. Canadians and Americans are more likely than Europeans to see politics as very important. Americans appear to be exceptional in that more than half see religion as very important. More striking than the outliers, though, is the cross-national consistency of the findings; taken together, the general priorities of citizens in all these states look very much alike.

Is there any evidence of sharp differences between the three groups within the Canadian community—new Canadians, anglophones, and francophones? The short answer is no. The largest proportion of each group thinks the family is very important. Work comes next, followed by friends and acquaintances, leisure, religion, and then politics. Francophone Canadians are more inclined to give higher priority to work, whereas new Canadians are least likely to see leisure as very important and are most likely to see religion and politics as very important. The striking finding, though, is that the overall order of priorities is precisely the same for each group; there is nothing to suggest that new Canadians have priorities that are fundamentally different from other Canadians, or that the general importance new Canadians attach to these different domains has the effect of tilting value priorities systematically in any particular direction.

The findings reported in Table 2-3 represent but a snapshot of responses to questions that were asked in 1990 only. By themselves they do not, and cannot, speak directly to the theme of value change. It is possible, of course, that the importance citizens attached to each of these six domains at the time of the 1990 surveys could have been the result of value shifts that took place during the 1980s. That possibility can be indirectly explored by investigating where materialists and post-materialists stand on each of the six value domains. Figure 2-6 uses the 1990 aggregate data to illustrate the differences between materialists and post-materialists. At the top end and at the bottom end, the differences between the two value groups are minor. Materialists are slightly more likely than post-materialists to think of the family as very important and a little less likely than post-materialists to think of "politics" as very important. After that, the differences across this value divide become sharper. As would be expected, for materialists work is clearly more important than friends and acquaintances or leisure. Not so post-materialists, for

Figure 2-6 Percentage of Respondents Saying that Family, Work, Friends, Leisure Time, Religion, and Politics Are "Very Important," by Value Type in 12 Advanced Industrial States, 1981–1990

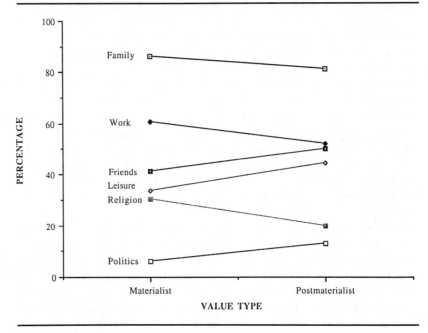

Source: 1990 World Values Survey ($N = 20,464$)

whom work is less important. In fact, post-materialists regard work, friends and acquaintances, and leisure as of about equal importance. Moreover, post-materialists are less likely than materialists to think of religion as very important. In general, then, the materialist/post-materialist value divide does seem to have some impact on what people think is important in life, and it is entirely possible that the general value priorities reported by publics in 1990 were the result of value shifts that took place in the 1980s.

What about orientations towards authority? Authority relations, and orientations towards authority more generally, is not just a theme that Lipset happens to stumble upon as a handy way of organizing observations about Canadian–American similarities and differences; it occupies a central place in both evaluations of democratic stability and speculations about transitions to advanced industrialism. Eckstein's pioneering work (1966, 1969, 1992), for example, holds that norms about authority—particularly the structure, shape, and congruence of authority patterns—are fundamental to understanding the dynamics of democracy. Indeed, they are so fundamental that Eckstein recommends the study of the political should be expanded to encompass authority relations "in any and all social units" (Eckstein & Gurr, 1975). Wildavsky (1987) and colleagues (Thompson, Ellis, & Wildavsky, 1990) make a similar case, arguing that the degree to which the individual is subordinated to the society of which he or she is a part is one of the two crucial dimensions along which cultures vary.

Particularly significant, from our standpoint, is that a variety of other analysts working from quite different perspectives see disturbances in authority relations as a central feature of the transition from mature to late industrialism. Rosenau (1992), for example, observes that it is a "crisis of authority" that lies at the heart of the "puzzle of the 1980's" (1992: 254–60). Rosenau is primarily concerned with the effects of this crisis of authority on the state system, and he sees a simultaneous reallocation of authority in two directions as involving "an upward shift towards transnational organizations and a downward shift towards subnational groupings" (1992: 256). Inglehart views shifting orientations towards authority as a recurrent theme, one of the patterns of change, *within* advanced industrial states. He interprets the growing disaffection with traditional hierarchical organizations as signifying a general shift from elite-directed to elite-directing behaviours (1990: 339–43). Flanagan (1982) still more directly associates the socioeconomic transformations underpinning the onset of advanced industrialism with a complementary shift in public attitudes "from a devotion to authority to cynicism and self-assertiveness" (1982: 408), a conclusion echoed by Ester and colleagues working with more recent European evidence (1993: 18). Variations in focus and terminology aside, a host of different observers characterize these transformations in remarkably similar ways.

Is there any *direct* evidence, including evidence from Canada, that citizen orientations towards authority have undergone any such change? As will become apparent, there are several indications that citizens' attitudes towards authority are changing. Before launching into that more detailed investigation, we can set the stage by considering, first, responses to a single broad indicator used in both the 1981 and 1990 WVS. Respondents in all twelve countries were presented with a list of "changes ... that may take place in the near future" and were then asked: "for each one, if it were to happen [do] you think it would be a good thing, a bad thing, or don't you mind?" Included in the list was the option "greater respect for authority."

According to the findings reported in Figure 2-7, deference appears to be on the decline: the percentages of Europeans, Americans, and Canadians responding that greater respect for authority would be a good thing dropped between 1981 and 1990, and the shifts are significant. Notice that by this measure, support for greater respect for authority is much higher in the United States than in Canada and the 1981–1990 decrease in Canada was sharper (about 11 per cent) than in the United States (about 8 per cent). It turns out that on this indicator, too, there is no evidence that Canadians lag behind the United States. In fact, American 1990 scores turn out to be about the same as Canadian 1981 scores.

A single decade is a relatively short time frame for changes as basic as orientations towards authority to take place. Even so, some changes are

Figure 2-7 Support for the General Principle of Deference

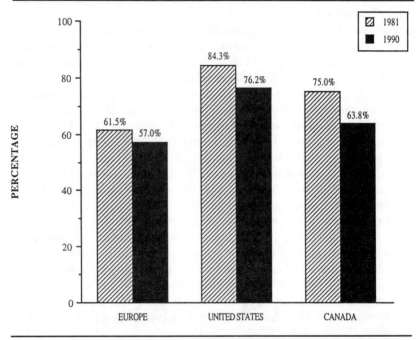

Question: "Here is a list of various changes in our way of life that might take place in the near future. Please tell me for each one, if it were to happen whether you think it would be a good thing, a bad thing, or don't you mind?" The above results report the percentages of respondents saying that greater respect for authority in the future would be a "**good thing**."
Source: 1981 and 1990 World Values Surveys.

detectable, and what is most striking is the overall consistency of the pattern; between 1981 and 1990 citizens became less deferential in ten out of the twelve countries—the exceptions are Britain (+3.5% to 73.2% in 1990) and France (+2.5% to 55% in 1990). It is not unusual to find a good deal of cross-national variation in responses to any single indicator. In this case, Americans do not score the highest on this measure of deference—the Irish do (82.4% in 1990)—nor do Canadians rank even close to the bottom—those positions are occupied by West Germans (29.4% in 1990) and Danes (33.7% in 1990). As it happens, the shifts within Canada have been especially dramatic among francophone Canadians. Of the three Canadian groups, it is francophones who were the most deferential in 1981, with 78.5% indicating that greater respect for authority would be a good thing, but those deferential responses dropped very sharply to 62.6% in 1990.[8]

Is there any indication that these shifts in orientations are connected to background factors? One might expect young people, who typically do not occupy positions of authority, to be less deferential than their older counterparts. In this instance, evidence of a consistent relationship between age and orientations towards authority could be interpreted in a variety of ways. They might indicate life-cycle effects—the idea that as people get older they are simply more "conservative" in this respect and more likely to think that "greater respect for authority" would be a "good thing." Figure 2-8 illustrates that there clearly is a link between age and orientations towards authority, and in every case the relationship is reasonably strong (gamma, Europe = .23; Canada = .15; United States = .23). But do these age differences indicate life-cycle effects only? Or is it possible that they signify period effects or deeper long-term generational change?

The plausibility of the generational change interpretation depends upon how much weight is given to the other evidence presented in Figure 2-8. As has already been demonstrated, one of the significant structural changes accompanying the shift to advanced industrialism is the emergence of a more highly educated public. If orientations towards authority are related to such an indicator of structural change, it is unlikely, though not impossible, that orientations towards authority could be easily reversed. In effect, once people experience higher levels of education, it is unlikely that they will become "uneducated," as it were, with the passage of time. Once again, the evidence indicates that in every country included in the study there is a clear and strong relationship between level of education and orientations towards authority: the higher the level of formal education, the less likely people are to respond that greater respect for authority in the future would be a good thing. Moreover, this particular relationship is *strongest* in Canada (gamma, Europe = -.26; United States = -.24; Canada = -.31).

What about the impact of the materialist/post-materialist value divide? This is a third perspective from which to evaluate whether orientations towards authority are undergoing long-term generational change. Of critical importance here, of course, is the interpretation that emerging post-materialist orientations are themselves generationally driven (see Appendix 2-2). From Figure 2-8, it is clear that there *is* a relationship between post-materialist orientations and orientations towards authority: post-materialists are consistently far less deferential than their materialist counterparts (gamma, Europe = -.37; United States =-.17; Canada = -.25). In this case, and regardless of national setting, materialists are about equally likely to support the idea that greater respect for authority would be a good thing. The differences between materialists and post-materialists are quite dramatic, but the impact of post-materialism appears to be refracted through national "prisms" to different effect. American post-materialists, for example, are twice as likely as their European counterparts to think that greater respect for authority is a good thing.

When all of these background factors are considered together, the cumulative evidence suggests that orientations towards authority are undergoing long-term generational change. For reasons discussed earlier, the data cannot *prove* that these shifts indicate generational change; but they are *consistent* with that interpretation. Other findings help to reinforce that interpretation.

Figure 2-8 Support for the General Principle of Deference by Age, Education and Value Type

Support for the general principle of deference by age:

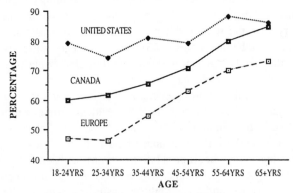

Support for the general principle of deference by level of education:

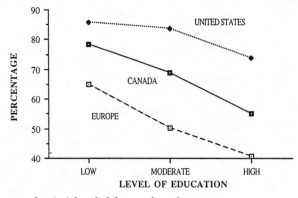

Support for the general principle of deference by value type:

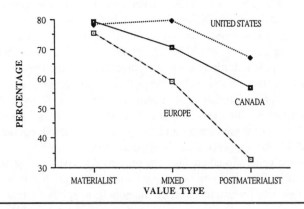

Source: 1981 and 1990 World Values Survey.

For example, the same background factors—age, education, and the materialist/post-materialist value divide—clearly work in equally powerful ways both within and between countries. In the case of Canada, for example, there are clear age effects within each of the three communities (gamma, francophones = .28; anglophones = .24; new Canadians = .17). The same holds for education (gamma, francophones = -.44; anglophones = -.27; new Canadians = -.28) and for post-materialism (francophones = -.33; anglophones = -.23; new Canadians = -.14). And both cross-nationally and within Canada, deference is also significantly higher among those in lower income groups and those in manual rather than nonmanual occupations.

The benchmark evidence presented so far raises a variety of intriguing questions about the scope and nature of value change in both Canada and other advanced industrial states. But it would be premature to take these initial findings as much more than a roadmap for further investigation. It might be tempting, for example, to take the data presented on changing attitudes towards authority as a convincing refutation of Lipset's claim that Canadians are more deferential than their American counterparts. But relying on single broad indicators as the basis for reaching firm conclusions is a very risky business. It could well be, for example, that Americans are responding to questions about greater respect to authority not on the basis of some shared absolute standard of authority orientations, but on the basis of contextual experiences peculiar to the contemporary American situation. Thus, Americans may be more enthusiastic about "more order" because they are more inclined than other publics to judge their own social order as chaotic. In fact, that interpretation gains momentum when all the data are considered together. Another stereotype is that German society is one of the most orderly of all European countries and, if anything, has too much respect for authority. If that stereotype has any merit, and if it shapes the answers German respondents provided to the same questions, then one might expect Germans to be the *least* likely to say more respect for authority would be a good thing. That is precisely what we do find. These interpretations are intuitively appealing. The problem is that they may also be unreliable, and this is a good reasons to be extremely cautious in using single, general indicators that lack common, cross-nationally reliable, benchmarks. To see whether these interpretations hold up, it is necessary to weigh all of the accumulated evidence together.

Conclusions

This chapter sets the stage for the rest of the book by underscoring three general themes. First, all advanced industrial states, Canada included, have experienced substantial structural transformations over the last twenty-five years. All of these states have experienced fundamental changes in their economic dynamics. One central feature of this change is reflected in the declining importance of primary resources and manufacturing as wealth-producing sectors and a growing emphasis on service sectors. The rise of knowledge-based and technologically driven economic sectors has been particularly rapid. Second, these shifts have been accompanied by changing social structures. Publics are better educated, levels of geographic and occupational mobility have increased, and these in turn are linked to such other shifts as the rise of two-income families, declining fertility rates, and other trends that have profound implications for primary relations. The phrase "advanced industrial state" implies that there are significant disjunctures in the industrializing process; it draws attention both to the interconnectedness of economic, social, and political forces and to the qualitative differences between the lives of contemporary Europeans and North Americans and those of their predecessors.

The uniqueness of Canadian values could undoubtedly be brought into sharp focus through a comparative survey of contemporary Canadians and, say, the citizens of some Third World state. But what would be learned by such an approach? And how relevant would those findings be? The alternative strategy, and the one adopted here, amounts to a tougher test; it approximates a most-similar-system design. Canadian values are compared with the values of publics in states sharing similar structural characteristics. This strategy assumes that the "structural situation" of publics matters, and the choice of countries for comparison deliberately attempts to take these common situations—advanced industrialism—into account.

The second theme that helps to set the stage comes from the benchmark evidence indicating that structural transformation has indeed been accompanied by systematic shifts in the values of these publics. By itself, that theme is not a novel one. The gradual evolution of post-materialist orientations among West European publics, for example, has been documented with Eurobarometer surveys for well over two decades. What is novel, and what the initial analysis of the benchmark data presented in this chapter plainly demonstrates, is that Canadian value shifts appear to be very much in step with the value shifts that have been amply documented in other advanced industrial states. They are in step in two respects. First, the balance of materialist/post-materialist orientations in Canada is remarkably similar to that found among West European publics. The two orientations are of about the same magnitude and, for the period for which we have direct data, the pace of value change is similar. Second, as with their European counterparts, the post-materialist orientations of Canadians are connected to such other factors as age, one possible proxy for generational change, and levels of education, an indicator of structural change. Indeed, cross-nationally, the basic patterns of these connections are truly striking: they are almost identical. In short, when it comes to one indicator of value change that is widely linked with the onset of advanced industrialism, Canadians do not appear to be exceptional. Nor, in this respect, do Canadians appear to lag behind their American counterparts. If anything, they lead them. That observation does *not* mean that all of the turmoil experienced by Canadians throughout the 1980s can be attributed *tout court* to the emergence of post-materialist orientations. As will become apparent, that is not the case. But it does suggest that these value shifts deserve careful consideration as a candidate explanation for some of these changes.

The third general theme that helps to set the stage comes from the overview indicating the relative priorities of Canadians and the publics in the other eleven states. These data (Table 2-3) have to be interpreted cautiously, but they help to establish an initial point that deserves careful consideration: there is nothing to indicate that the priorities of Canadians are radically different from those of any of these other publics. Indeed, there is not a single value dimension along which Canadians qualify as outliers. Certainly, Canadians are more likely than most others to say that politics is very important, and part of the explanation for that finding has to do with the priorities of new Canadians. But according to all of the general indicators considered so far, Canadian value orientations appear to be characteristic of those shared by publics in other advanced industrial states.

This introductory overview also sets the stage in another respect: it provides an initial glimpse of citizen orientations towards authority. This theme has not only been a template for a host of Canadian–American value comparisons, but is also a central preoccupation of contemporary empirical democratic theory. The preliminary indications are that orientations towards authority do seem to be in transition, and this transition does appear to be systematically connected to indicators of structural and value change.

General indicators are a starting point only; they provide just rough guidelines and are an inadequate foundation for firm conclusions about value change. They say nothing, for example, about which aspects of economic, social, or political values have shifted. What is called for, and what follows, is a far more detailed investigation of each of the general domains considered above. The next section, Part 2, delves into the theme of changing political values with more fine-grained evidence. It begins by examining the redistribution of political skills and interest in politics and then considers the question of confidence in governmental and nongovernmental institutions. It concludes by exploring changing levels of unconventional forms of political action. Part 3 explores themes relating to what might broadly be referred to as the changing economic culture. Central to that analysis is the question of whether a variety of economic values—attitudes to economic fairness, to explanations for poverty, to work, to decision-making in the workplace, and to leisure—have changed. Part 3 closes by asking: Are general shifts in attitudes to work and the workplace related to those shifts in political orientation considered in Part 2? In Part 4 primary relations are of central concern, and here the main focus is upon changing attitudes to marriage, the family, and children. The analysis probes shifting orientations towards religion, morality, and tolerance and concludes with a more comprehensive examination of authority relations: Are attitudes towards authority in the family connected to attitudes towards authority in the polity and the workplace?

In each section, the analysis relies primarily on direct evidence of cross-time value change or stability. Part 5, the final section, pulls the threads of the evidence together; it revisits the central questions raised in Part 1 and speculates about what the core findings mean. The single theme that most aptly unites the changes documented throughout the entire analysis is adopted as the title of this book: The Decline of Deference.

Appendix 2-1

The difficulty of proving generational (cohort) change is a subject of much debate. The problem is mostly technical; the point is that generational effects, period effects, and aging effects cannot be isolated statistically because each one is a perfect linear function of the other two (Glenn, 1977). At issue, then, is the plausibility of the evidence, and here, it seems to me, Inglehart is on firm ground. It is worth revisiting the basic evidence because some of the interpretation in this book rides on the generational change argument.

When it comes to post-materialist value change, the largest body of cross-time evidence comes from six European countries surveyed between 1970 and 1990. Consider Figure 2-9. It shows the *net* balance between materialists and post-materialists within given birth cohorts from 1970 to 1990; it uses pooled data from all six West European countries (over 200,000 interviews). The position of each cohort at each time point is calculated by subtracting the number of materialists in that cohort from the percentage of post-materialists. So the zero point on the vertical axis of the graph means that the two groups—materialists and post-materialists—are equally numerous. In this graph, for example, this is the case in 1970 for the cohort born in 1946–1955. As one moves up the vertical axis in the graph the proportion of post-materialists increases, and as one moves down the proportion of materialists increases. If age differences indicated life-cycle effects—people becoming more materialist as they get older—then we would expect the cohort lines to move downward with the passage of time. That is, scores should drop off towards the materialist pole as one moves from left to right across the twenty-year period. The first crucial point is that they do not. Notice that the younger birth cohorts remain more post-materialist across the whole twenty-year period; there is no evidence of life-cycle effects as this group ages by twenty years. In fact, as our own data show, most of these cohorts turn out to be slightly less materialist at the end of the period than they were at the start.

It is also clear that the ratio of post-materialist: materialist values experiences some "wobble"; there are downward spikes at various points. These spikes almost certainly indicate period effects. There was a major recession affecting all advanced industrial states in the mid-1970s and another in the early 1980s. These had an impact on all cohorts in about the same way and did so at the same time. Consequently, these downward troughs in the data are also consistent with the theory—people will tend to become *less* post-materialist in times of economic insecurity. Notice, too, that post-materialist orien-

Figure 2-9 Value Priorities of Six West European Publics, 1970–1990

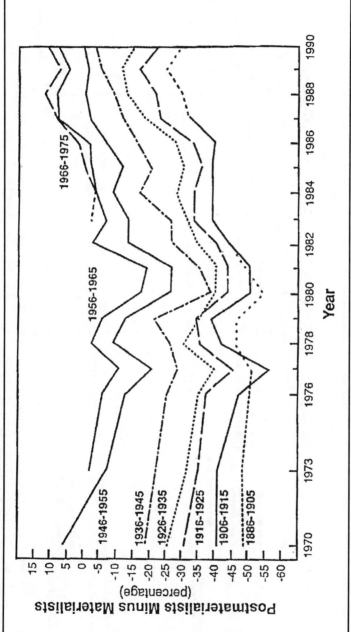

Source: Based on data from representative national surveys of publics of France, Great Britain, West Germany, Italy, Belgium, and the Netherlands, interviewed in European Community surveys of 1970, 1973, and Euro-Barometer surveys 6 through 33 (total *N* = 214,168)

Appendix 2-A The Materialist/Postmaterialist Dimension in the U.S., Canada, and Western Europe, 1990 (Factor Loadings in Principal Component Analysis)

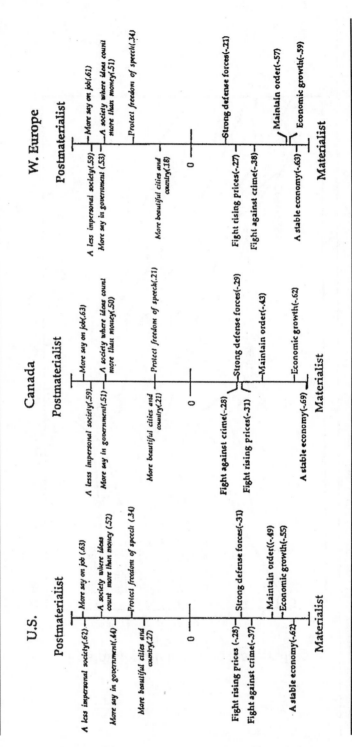

tations bounce back; the impacts of the period effect are relatively short-lived for all cohorts. It does not take very long for people to revert to their earlier levels of post-materialism. Consequently, what is impressive is the overall stability of the cohorts, and that stability also points to a generational change interpretation.

There are some wrinkles to these data. For example, not all of the cohort lines are precisely equidistant but it might be more remarkable if they were. Economic conditions are not entirely even, and socialization theory indicates that there are critical ages at which people are most susceptible to formative events. The youngest cohort shown in the graph (those born between 1966–1975) shows a unique pattern, and here the suggestion is that this group would have been young enough to be affected by the recessions of the mid-1970s (Inglehart et al., 1996).[9]

Appendix 2-2

The Materialist/Post-materialist Dimension in the U.S., Canada, and Western Europe, 1990 (Factor Loadings in Principle Components Analysis)

NOTES

[1] For a discussion of the distinction between values, attitudes and opinions see Vincent Price (1992) Public Opinion. Newbury Park, Ca: Sage.

[2] This is not to underplay the significant weaknesses of surveys. The presumption is that researchers are adept at asking the "right" questions; that the answers tap genuine values rather than "manufactured" ones; and that the research design reduces systematic error to acceptable levels. Cross-national survey research is plagued by problems of conceptual and measurement equivalence. For a lucid review of some of these problems and the methods for dealing with them, see Verba.

[3] A single decade is a relatively short time frame when it comes to tracking value change; here we confront a practical limit.

[4] Responses to the post-materialism index fall into three categories, of which "mixed" is the largest. Thus, evidence that Canadians are both less materialist and more post-materialist indicates sharper value differences than just differences at one end of the scale.

[5] Thus, regardless of differences in absolute levels of incomes, Canadians (and publics in other "mature welfare states") may exhibit higher levels of post-materialism because their more comprehensive social welfare arrangements produce a greater sense of security than the American arrangements.

[6] One explanation is that during the 1980s those holding post-materialist values had achieved a "critical mass" among publics in advanced industrial states and that post-materialists had moved to positions of influence in society, the economy, and the poli-

ty, and thus were positioned to project these values more broadly. This explanation is entirely consistent with the "new middle class" explanation of value change. Note, too, that one byproduct of this shift is that, in the long run, we would expect a gradual weakening of the statistical relationship between age and post-materialism. For 1981 the correlation between age cohort and post-materialism is .22, and for 1990 the Pearson correlation coefficient is .23. Both relationships are statistically significant at $p < .0001$.

[7] Notice that relative to the other publics, West Germans consistently score quite low; they are at the low end on five of the six categories considered here. This may indicate a systematic cultural difference in response to measurement categories.

[8] The figure is for anglo-Canadians are 73.6% in 1981 and 64.8% in 1990; 62.8% of new Canadians indicated that "greater respect for authority" would be a "good thing."

[9] For an accessible discussion of cohort analysis, see Glenn, 1977. A detailed analysis of the relative impacts of such economic factors as inflation and unemployment on post-materialist value orientations can be found in Inglehart and Abramson, 1994. An application of cohort analysis to post-materialist value change in the Canadian setting is explored in Bakvis and Nevitte, 1987. See also Abramson and Inglehart, 1987.

3: A Changing Political Culture?

The turmoil Canadians experienced during the 1980s was most evident in the political life of the country, and in some respects this comes as no surprise. After all, politics is about the open competition of ideas and interests. The constitution was, perhaps, the biggest single issue to dominate the political agenda during the 1980s, but to see Canada's political dynamics of the decade solely in terms of constitutional bickering has two limitations: it highlights what was probably most idiosyncratic about Canadian politics, and it deflects attention from other significant aspects of political change that had little to do with the constitution. As we have seen, one such change involved how citizens are connected to traditional political parties. During the 1980s the Canadian party system was clearly in a state of flux, though the full extent of that flux—the dramatic collapse of the Progressive Conservatives and the equally dramatic rise of the Reform Party and the Bloc Québecois—did not become evident until the 1993 federal election. The gradual weakening of citizen attachments to traditional mainstream political parties, partisan dealignment, is a well-documented trend that goes back to the 1970s. Significantly, though, that trend gained momentum during the 1980s. As Clarke and Kornberg (1993) demonstrate, the proportion of the Canadian public claiming "very strong" identification with longstanding federal political parties dropped from a high of 31% in 1980 to a low of 13% in 1991; over the same period the proportion of the electorate reporting "no" identification with any federal political party climbed from 10% to 30%.[1] But there is nothing peculiarly Canadian about these dynamics. A mounting body of evidence shows that during the same period party systems throughout the advanced industrial world were in a state of flux.

Patterns of shifting partisan attachment have been most amply documented in the United States. In that setting, election studies indicate that between 1952–1964 about 75% of American voters identified themselves as either Democrat or Republican. Since 1972 the proportion of voters identifying with the two major parties has dropped to about 64% (Dalton & Wattenberg, 1993). It has also been shown that the proportion of voters saying they neither liked nor disliked anything about the Republican and Democratic parties nearly tripled between 1952 and the 1980s (Wattenberg, 1990). One consequence of partisan dealignment in the United States has been the rise of "split-ticket voting": the tendency for voters to support one party at one level of government and a different party at another. According to Fiorina (1992), in 1988 only 40% of all American states had one party in control of both legislative houses and the governor's office. At the national level, ticket-splitting between presidential and House voting rose from 14% in 1960 to 34% in 1980. The levels rose even higher in 1992 (Dalton & Wattenberg, 1993).

Electoral politics in the United States is unique in many respects. American political parties are typically seen to be weaker than their counterparts in parliamentary-style systems: the American public has more opportunities than publics elsewhere to elect public officials (Crewe, 1981), and they are more likely than others to vote for the individual, to engage in candidate-centred voting, rather than party voting. Consequently, some have argued that the notion of the partisan independence of the American voter is simply a characteristic unique to that particular system and that the American experience cannot really be generalized to voters in other settings (Budge et al., 1976). Even so, a growing body of evidence indicates that very similar trends have been underway even in parliamentary systems, where partisan attachments have typically been more robust. In Britain, for example, over 40% of voters reported that they were "strong partisans" in the 1960s. By the late 1970s, however, that figure had dropped to about 20% (Abramson, 1992). Other, cross-time studies independently undertaken in Germany, France, Holland, Italy, the Scandinavian countries, and Australia produce very similar findings that all point to the same general conclusion: citizen attachments to traditional political parties have been weakening in nearly every advanced industrial state during the last decade or so (Dalton, 1992; Dalton et al., 1984; McAllister, 1992). The striking finding is that, despite significant differences in electoral systems and regardless of variations in other institutional arrangements, these transformations all appear to have been taking place at about the same time. Symptomatic of these same shifts are other such changes as gradually declining levels in voter turnout and the fracturing of long-standing party systems.

In some respects, the erosion of citizen attachments to mainstream political parties and declining levels of voter turnout are worrisome trends. They may even be seen as paradoxical. For decades researchers have demonstrated that higher levels of education are a powerful stimulus for a variety of forms of political participation, including voting (Almond & Verba, 1963; Lipset, 1960; Milbrath, 1965; Mishler, 1979). Educated citizens are more likely than the less educated to be aware of the impact of government on the individual; they are more likely to "follow politics," to know more about politics, and to spend more time discussing politics. They are, by definition, more sophisticated about politics (Luskin, 1987). One clear finding to emerge from the last chapter is that publics in every advanced industrial state have levels of education that far surpass those of preceding generations. Hence one might expect public levels of voter turnout to be higher and attachments to political parties stronger. Why, then, are citizens in advanced industrial states less attached to their mainstream political parties than before? And why are levels of voter turnout falling rather than rising, or no higher now than before?

One possibility is that these trends are just coincidental, that they reflect temporary shifts, or that they apply only to a very narrow range of political concerns. Another possibility is that Canadians, and publics in other advanced industrial states, are flinching from the increasing complexity of the political world, or that people are simply becoming increasingly preoccupied with other aspects of life and more apathetic about, and detached from, normal politics.[2] These apparently straightforward explanations, however, do not seem to hold up. As will become clear from this chapter and the next, striking changes are taking place across a wide variety of political domains, and the location, scope, and content of these changes, in Canada as elsewhere, are consistent with what others have conceptualized as a shift from "old" politics to "new" politics. These shifts do not just reflect changing values, though as we will see, that is part of the story. They are also accompanied by declining confidence in both governmental and nongovernmental institutions and the emergence of nontraditional forms of political participation. Two central themes repeatedly emerge throughout the analysis in the next two chapters: the erosion of institutional authority, and the rise of citizen intervention in politics. Taken together, these transformations reflect a systematic set of wide-ranging shifts that signify the political face of the decline of deference.

Interest in Politics

One characteristic that separates the generation of the 1980s from preceding ones is exposure to information. As a result of the technological revolution, few households in the advanced industrial world are now without television. Not only do most citizens have immediate access to information about world and domestic events, but publics also increasingly rely upon television as a source of political information (Dalton, 1984). Moreover, and again in contrast to preceding generations, contemporary publics have a much greater stake in what governments do; the role of government occupies an increasingly important place in the well-being of citizens of these states. Since the Second World War, for example, governments' share of the gross domestic product has increased and public reliance on government-inspired programs has expanded (Heidenheimer et al., 1983). In other words, publics in these states have both the opportunity and an incentive to be more concerned about the politics of government decision-making. Citizens are more sophisticated and have more reason to concern themselves with their political world, but that is no guarantee that they will be more interested in the stuff of politics; many things compete for the attention of busy publics.

There is some evidence that interest in politics has been gradually rising since the 1950s. Dalton (1984), for example, has shown that in four countries—Britain, France, West Germany, and the United States—citizens have

Figure 3-1   Percentage Saying They Are "Very Interested" in Politics, 1981–1990

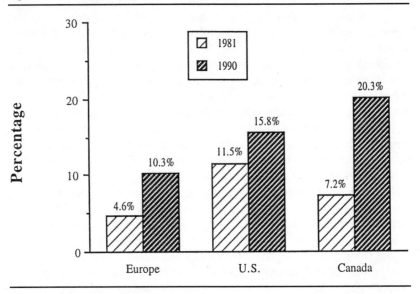

Source: 1981 and 1990 World Values Surveys.

become more interested in elections and other aspects of political life. But as Dalton himself points out, these data have to be read cautiously; they rely on a variety of indicators of "political interest," and they may not be generalizable to other settings. The World Values Surveys provide a far larger body of "even" data for many more countries. They do not speak to pre-1981 trends, but in both 1981 and 1990 the WVS asked citizens a now-standard question about political interest: "How interested would you say you are in politics?" Figure 3-1 reports the aggregate results, which point to a clear trend: the proportion of respondents saying they are "very interested" in politics has risen in both western Europe and North America. In fact, between 1981 and 1990 interest in politics increased in every country in which the surveys were undertaken. In some cases, as in France or Italy, the increases would have to be regarded as fairly modest; but in others, including Canada, they have been very substantial indeed. In 1981 just over 7% of Canadians said they were very interested in politics, and that figure increased sharply to just over 20% in 1990. Moreover, those increases are more or less uniform for both anglophone Canadians (6.9% in 1981; 19.3% in 1990) and francophones (8.1% in 1981; 19.4% in 1990), and in 1990 the level of interest in politics was actually higher among new Canadians (23.7%) than among others. Notice, too, that Canadian levels of interest in politics were lower than those for Americans in 1981 but higher by 1990. According to these measures, over the

Figure 3-2 Percentage Saying They Are "Very Interested" in Politics, by Education

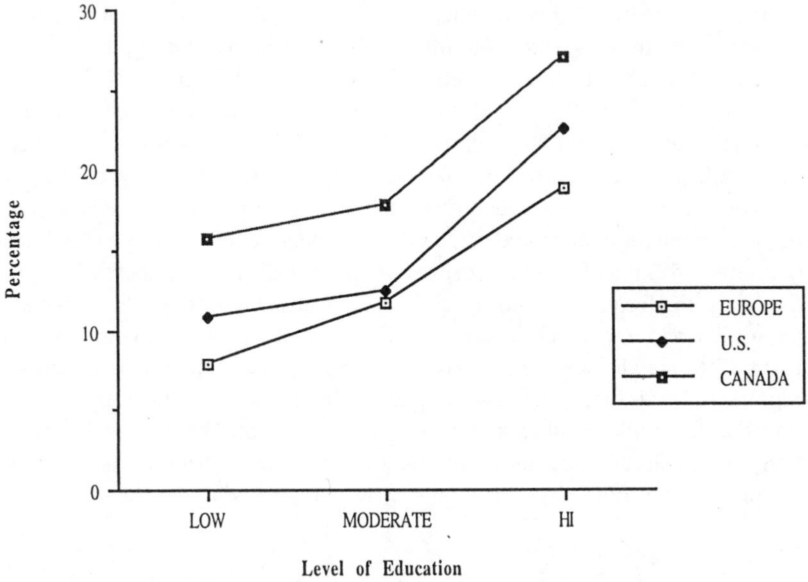

Source: 1990 World Values Survey.

same period levels of political interest doubled in the United States but tripled in Canada.

It is possible, of course, that the sharp increase in interest in politics among Canadians reflects a highly charged political climate: the presence of such contentious issues as free trade and the constitution. That interpretation would imply that the rate of increase in political interest in Canada was uniquely high, or perhaps between 1981 and 1990 was unusually rapid. Certainly, the levels of political interest in Canada rose faster, and to a higher level, than in *most* other advanced industrial states, but not all. In West Germany, the Netherlands, Northern Ireland, and Denmark levels of interest in politics increased even more sharply.[3]

More remarkable, perhaps, than the national differences in levels of political interest is the consistency of the general trend. There is nothing here to indicate that publics have become less attached to mainstream political parties *because* they are less interested in politics; they have become more interested in politics, and that trend is entirely consistent with what one would anticipate given rising levels of education. Indeed, as Figure 3-2 shows, the relationship between levels of education and interest in politics is quite strong.[4] Regardless of absolute level of political interest, the general relationship between education and interest in politics is stable; those with high levels of education are about twice as likely as those with low levels to be very interested in politics.

There are other indications that publics are becoming more, not less, concerned about their political environment. The 1981 and 1990 World Values Surveys also asked respondents how often they discussed political matters "when they got together with their friends." The evidence, once again, generally points in the same direction: in nearly every national setting, the proportion reporting that they discussed politics "frequently" increased between 1981 and 1990.[5] In 1981 slightly less than 10% of Canadians said they discussed political matters "frequently"; and by 1990 the proportion giving that same response had nearly doubled. Not surprisingly, interest in politics is closely related to how frequently people discuss politics. The relationship between political interest and discussion is stronger among European publics (gamma = .52) than Canadian (gamma = .22) or U.S. publics (gamma = .20). Similarly, the frequency with which people discuss politics, levels of interest in politics, and how much importance people generally attach to politics (see Figure 2-6) are all interrelated, and each is also related to levels of education. Significantly, all these indicators are connected to the materialist–post-materialist value divide. Publics in advanced industrial states have more information about politics, they are more attentive, and they are more interested in politics, but this does not mean that they are satisfied with the status quo.

Confidence in Governmental Institutions

If the emergence of more educated and interested publics increases the potential for citizen participation in public decision-making, why has public support for such representative institutions as political parties weakened? One possibility is that citizens have become increasingly disenchanted with their elected representatives. It is not difficult to identify possible country-specific examples to illustrate that point. In the Canadian case, for example, the timing of the 1990 round of the World Values Survey coincided with the slumping popularity of the government of the day. Prime Minister Mulroney's popularity ratings were in the process of plunging towards the 15% level, the lowest on record for any prime minister in Canadian history. Prime Minister Mulroney's flagging popularity may go some distance towards explaining dealignment in the Canadian setting, but this kind of explanation does not travel very far. The problem is that it fails to account for very similar transitions that were taking place in other advanced industrial states at about the same time. Cross-national shifts towards rising citizen competence and weakening attachments to mainstream political parties call for more general explanations. One such explanation, supplied by "new politics" theorists, is that conventional vehicles for citizen representation, such as traditional political parties, are losing their appeal because they operate from principles that satisfy a shrinking proportion of the public. It has been argued, for example, that

mass political participation emerges through two fundamentally different routes, one based on an older mode of participation, the other on a newer mode.

The institutions that mobilized mass political participation in the late nineteenth and early twentieth century—labor union, church and mass political party— were hierarchical organizations in which a smaller number of leaders or bosses led masses of disciplined troops. These institutions were effective in bringing large numbers of newly enfranchised citizens to the polls in an era when universal compulsory education had just taken root and the average citizen had a low level of political skills. But while these elite-directed organizations could mobilize large numbers, they produced only a relatively low *level* of participation, rarely going beyond mere voting. (Inglehart, Nevitte and Basanez, 1996).

With the expansion of education, and with the information explosion, the once-large skill gap between leaders and publics has narrowed. Consequently, organizations that invite little participation from "below," or that are premised upon low levels of citizen input, may be adequate for those satisfied with the older, elite-guided modes of participation. But such institutions carry little appeal for the increasing numbers of informed and interested citizens who occupy the expanding ranks of the new middle class (Lipset, 1979), and who hanker for newer modes of participation. Seen this way, the weakening attachment to mainstream political parties is but one aspect of a wider set of concerns that have little to do with evaluations of the particular people who hold elected office or even the government of the day. Instead, the trend embraces more general evaluations about the kinds of institutions political leaders occupy, how hierarchical the institutions are, and whether the institutions provide citizens with the opportunities for meaningful participation. This line of explanation contains other expectations; it anticipates generational differences in citizen preferences, with younger and better-educated cohorts—the advance guard of the transition—preferring the newer modes of participation and older generations being more supportive of institutions guided by traditional assumptions about organizational life.

The WVS contain a number of indicators that allow us to evaluate the broad claims suggested by this alternative explanation. Both the 1981 and 1990 surveys asked publics how much confidence they had in a variety of institutions. Respondent ratings of institutions cluster together: those who express high levels of confidence in any one of what might loosely be called "governmental institutions"—Parliament/Congress (or equivalent legislative body), the armed forces, the police, and the civil service—also tend to express high levels of confidence in the other governmental institutions. As a result, it is possible to combine the ratings for each of these institutions into a single broader and more reliable index of public confidence in the governmental institutions for each country.

If the weakening attachment to political parties is but one face of a more widespread phenomenon, then the World Values data should show a decline in public confidence towards this entire set of governmental institutions. The decade 1981–1990 is a relatively short time span for evaluating shifts in this kind of broad-scale system support, but it should reveal traces of any attitude

Figure 3-3   Percentage Expressing "High" Confidence in Government Institutions, 1981–1990

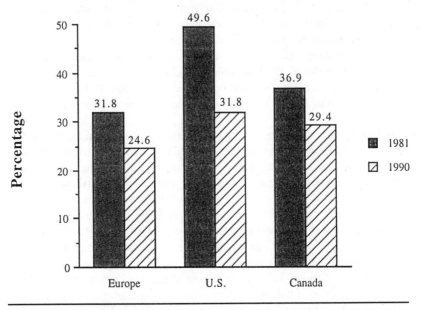

Source: 1981 and 1990 World Values Surveys.
Note: Respondents were asked how much confidence they had in their country's armed forces, police, parliament, and civil service. Shown above are the percentages with an average score of 2 or lower, when 1 = "a lot," 2 = "quite a lot," 3 = "not very much," and 4 = "no confidence at all."

change and whether the directions are consistent with the theory. As Figure 3-3 clearly shows, between 1981 and 1990 there has been a decline in public confidence in institutions in Canada, the United States, and Europe. Overall, the size of the decline is quite substantial, and it is remarkably consistent: citizen confidence in governmental institutions slipped in ten of the twelve countries. The only exceptions are Denmark and Northern Ireland.[6] Not surprisingly, there are significant cross-national variations in the scope of these changes. The shifts in levels of confidence have been particularly sharp in Spain and the United States. Notice that on this dimension there seems to have been some convergence between Americans and Canadians. At the beginning of the 1980s, American levels of confidence in governmental institutions were much higher than those in Canada; by the end of the decade, the differences had all but evaporated. And within Canada confidence in governmental institutions fell among both anglophones and francophones, although here there are consistent communal differences. At both time points, francophones expressed higher levels of confidence in these institutions (1981, 46.3%; 1990, 38.6%) than their anglophone counterparts (1981, 33.4%; 1990,

Figure 3-4 Percentage Expressing "High" Confidence in Government Institutions, by Age Group

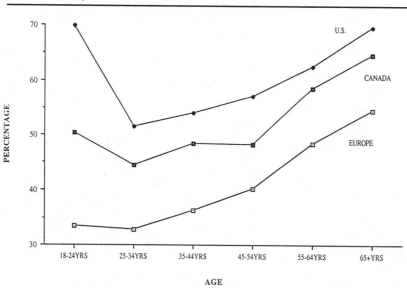

Source: 1981 and 1990 World Values Surveys.
Note: Respondents were asked how much confidence they had in their country's armed forces, police, parliament, and civil service. Shown above are the percentages with an average score of 2 or lower, when 1 = "a lot," 2 = "quite a lot," 3 = "not very much," and 4 = "no confidence at all."

26.7%), and the orientations of new Canadians in 1990 were more like anglophones (27.2%).

Equally important to the plausibility of the new politics explanation are the issues of whether this general decline of confidence in governmental institutions is related to generational differences and to value differences, or more specifically to the materialist–post-materialist value divide. It has already been shown that that divide is indeed driven by generational change. In the absence of longitudinal data, age differences can be used as a proxy for, and a symptom of, generational effects.[7] In fact, the World Values data show that there are age-related effects that operate in the direction the theory predicts. Overall, the relationship between age and confidence in government institutions is significant, and it is negative (for Europe the 1990 correlation is r = -.20; for the United States r = -.24, and for Canada r = -.15). Younger respondents have significantly lower levels of confidence in government institutions than older ones. The relationship, however, is not a simple linear one; as Figure 3-4 demonstrates, it is actually curvilinear. For the very youngest age group surveyed, those in the 18–24 group, levels of confidence are quite high.

Figure 3-5 Percentage Expressing "High" Confidence in Government Institutions, by Value Type

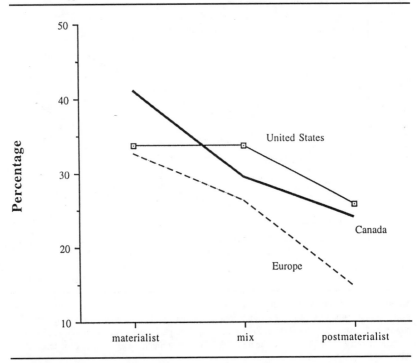

Source: 1990 World Values Survey.

Note: Respondents were asked how much confidence they had in their country's armed forces, police, parliament, and civil service. Shown above are the percentages with an average score of 2 or lower, when 1 = "a lot," 2 = "quite a lot," 3 = "not very much," and 4 = "no confidence at all."

But in all cases confidence in governmental institutions drops dramatically for the 25–34 group and then gradually increases again with each successive age group. In the Canadian and European samples, the oldest respondents express greater confidence in governmental institutions than the very youngest.[8]

The idea that declining confidence in governmental institutions could reflect genuine generational change gains credibility when other evidence is taken into account. Recall that earlier research has provided powerful evidence linking value shifts to generational change (Inglehart & Abramson, 1994), and data presented in Chapter 2 indicated a clear conjunction of age-related differences and value change (Figure 2-5) for the twelve publics examined here. The evidence from the World Values data is unequivocal on one point: for all the countries considered, post-materialists record much lower levels of confidence in government institutions than their materialist counterparts. According to the evidence in Figure 3-5, that pattern holds up regardless of national variations in absolute levels of confidence. These findings are both revealing and consistent with the general argument that people raised under circumstances of insecurity are more likely to prefer strong authority relations than those whose formative experiences occurred within an environment of physical and economic security.

Confidence in Non-Governmental Institutions

Eroding public confidence in governmental institutions might reflect citizens' increasing irritation with all things governmental. Keep in mind, though, that the explanation being explored here is a more general one. At issue is not just shifting public feelings about governments themselves, but the levels of citizen confidence in a particular kind of institutional framework—hierarchical institutions. Bureaucratic hierarchies, certainly, are a common feature of governmental institutions, but they are not unique to governments. Consequently, for the new politics explanation to hold up, we would also expect to find declining levels of public confidence in hierarchical organizations that lie outside the domain of government. The World Values Surveys probed attitudes about a variety of what might be called nongovernmental institutions—churches, educational institutions, the country's legal system, and the press. There are substantial variations in the structural configurations of these institutions. Some, like the legal system, plainly *are* organized along hierarchical principles, as, typically, are churches. The organizational structures of the press, on the other hand, are far more difficult to discern and to generalize about. Nonetheless, responses to questions about confidence in these institutions once again cluster together, and so there is some justification for relying on a simple index that reflects general orientation to these institutions. What does the evidence show?

The general pattern is a familiar one. On balance, our evidence indicates that public confidence in nongovernmental institutions has also declined over the period for which directly comparable data are available. As Figure 3-6 shows, the changes have been most dramatic in the two North American countries. Notice here that Canadian–American differences narrowed between 1981 and 1990 and, once again, Canadians seem to be leading the change: in 1990 American levels of confidence in nongovernmental institutions were about the same as 1981 Canadian levels.[9] By these standards, European levels of confidence were already quite low in 1981.

The general shift in public evaluations of nongovernmental institutions is neither as sharp nor as uniform as was the case for governmental institutions. In fact, in some instances, as in France and Denmark, public confidence in these institutions increased very slightly.[10] The "wobble" in these results may well reflect the fact that publics were being asked to evaluate a far more diverse set of institutions. Confidence in the church, for example, dropped quite sharply between 1981 and 1990, at least in all countries but two

Figure 3-6   Percentage Expressing "High" Confidence in Non-Government Institutions, 1981–1990

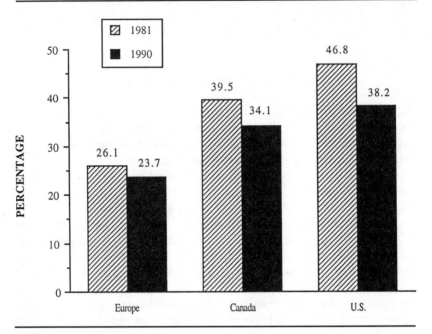

Source: 1981 and 1990 World Values Surveys.
Note: Respondents were asked how much confidence they had in their country's churches, educational system, legal system, and press. Shown above are the percentages with an average score of 2 or lower, when 1 = "a lot," 2 = "quite a lot," 3 = "not very much," and 4 = "no confidence at all."

(Northern Ireland and the United States).[11] By contrast, the shifts in public confidence in the press were generally quite small. More relevant than the size of these changes is the question whether the identifiable shifts are associated with the age and value differences that indicate possible generational effects.

Figure 3-7 tracks confidence in nongovernmental institutions by age group; the pattern of age variations is remarkably similar to that found in Figure 3-4. North Americans, once again, express much more confidence in these institutions than do their European counterparts, and the age effects, also as before, conform to a remarkably similar *J* curve in each case. Those in the very youngest age groups (18–24 years) express far more confidence in these institutions than those in the middle age groups, and thereafter levels of confidence increase almost uniformly with age. What about the impact of value differences? These findings, once again, are reminiscent of the results emerging

Figure 3-7 Percentage Expressing "High" Confidence in Non-Government Institutions, by Age Group, 1990

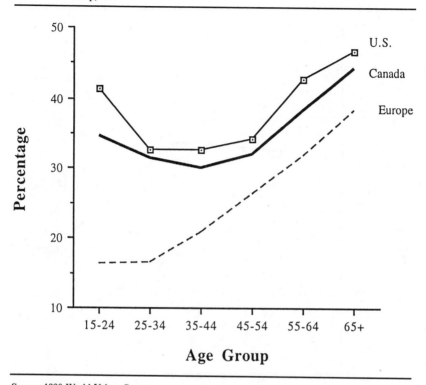

Source: 1990 World Values Survey.
Note: Respondents were asked how much confidence they had in their country's churches, educational system, legal system, and press. Shown above are the percentages with an average score of 2 or lower, when 1 = "a lot," 2 = "quite a lot," 3 = "not very much," and 4 = "no confidence at all."

from our analysis of governmental institutions (see Figure 3-5). According to Figure 3-8, post-materialists are much less likely than materialists to report high levels of confidence in nongovernmental institutions. Significantly, too, the value divide has about the same impact on levels of public confidence in each one of the twelve countries.

That confidence in both governmental and nongovernmental institutions has eroded throughout the advanced industrial world over the same time period has a number of implications. It is highly improbable, for example, that these results simply reflect people's irritations with specific political leaders. Moreover, given the nature of our data—covering the decade in twelve countries—it is also extremely unlikely that these findings could reflect citizen

Figure 3-8 Percentage Expressing "High" Confidence in Non-Government Institutions, by Value
Type, 1990

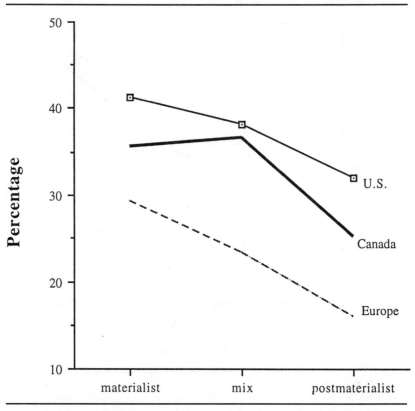

Source: 1990 World Values Survey.

evaluations of the particular performance of particular governments. Citizen
evaluations of one political leader, or a government of the day, undoubtedly
do spill over into momentary judgements about the political system. But those
feelings would be transient, short-term responses that are limited to the political lifespans of specific leaders and governments. Even if these findings are
taken to indicate a generalized rise in cynicism about governments, why
would attitudes towards governmental institutions be so powerfully related (r
= .49) to orientations towards *non*governmental institutions? The scope and
timing of these shifts suggests that deeper, long-term changes are involved.
On balance, then, the accumulated evidence lends credence to the new politics explanation, that there is a sustained, and possibly generationally driven,
public reaction against *all* hierarchical institutional arrangements that limit
the opportunities for meaningful citizen participation.

The Rise of Cosmopolitanism

Institutions serve an important function: they connect citizens to the state, and it is the state itself that is the primary source of authority in advanced industrial societies. Does the erosion of citizen attachments to traditional institutions mean, by extension, that people's more general loyalties to the state may also have weakened? Canadians perhaps more than citizens of any other advanced industrial state have been encouraged to reflect on the integrity and future of their state. Recent books analyzing the condition of the country bear such bleak titles as *Must Canada Fail?* (Simeon 1977), *The Roots of Disunity* (Bell 1992), and *The Collapse of Canada?* (Weaver 1993). Canadians perhaps can be forgiven for reaching the conclusion that theirs is a state in crisis, one wracked by division and in which citizens have unusually fragile attachments to the country. And both of the major political issues of the 1980s—the constitutional turmoil and free trade with the United States—may well have heightened that sense of crisis.

Canadians worry out loud about what "holds the country together," and they lament the absence of patriotism. Is there anything in the survey evidence, though, to indicate that Canadians are uniquely "unpatriotic"? The World Values Surveys indicate that in 1981 63% of Canadians reported they were "very proud" to be a Canadian. When that finding is placed in the context of other comparable data there is no hint that Canadians lack pride in their country, or that absence of patriotism has reached crisis proportions. In 1981 levels of national pride were higher in only two other countries: in the United States 76% of respondents said they were very proud to be American, and 68% of Irish respondents indicated they were very proud of their country. On average, 39% of Europeans said they were very proud of their country: levels of pride were particularly low in the Netherlands (18%), West Germany (21%), and Belgium (29%). National pride is a relatively stable attribute: as Table 3-1 shows, those countries with relatively high levels of national pride in 1981 also had relatively high levels of national pride in 1990; the cross-time variations are minor. Between 1981 and 1990 the proportion of Canadians saying they were very proud of their country dropped three percentage points, a change so slight that it can be attributed to measurement error.

Canadian judgements about pride in country are undoubtedly informed by comparisons with the United States. By that standard Canada falls short, but then, according to our findings, so do all the other countries. There are significant variations in how people express national pride: different publics find pride in different things. Americans, for example, are nearly twice as likely as Canadians to look to their scientific achievements (46% versus 26%) as a source of pride, and they are more likely to be proud of their political system (17% versus 4%) and their economic achievements (12% versus 5%). Canadians, on the other hand, express much greater pride than Americans in their health and welfare system (37% versus 7%), and they are slightly more likely to look to their sporting achievements (10% versus 5%) and their cul-

Table 3-1   Percente of Respondents Saying They are "Very Proud" to Be Canadian (American, Irish, etc.): Canada, U.S., and Europe, 1981 and 1990

Country	1981	1990	% Change (1981–1990)
United States	76.1	75.2	-0.9
Ireland	67.6	76.8	9.2
Canada	62.2	60.2	-2.0
Britain	52.9	52.5	-0.4
Spain	50.7	45.4	-5.3
Northern Ireland	49.3	53.5	4.2
Europe (average)	39.6	40.1	0.5
Italy	39.5	40.1	0.6
France	31.1	34.9	3.8
Denmark	29.7	42.2	12.5
Belgium	28.9	30.6	1.7
Germany	21.3	19.8	-1.5
Netherlands	18.3	22.8	4.5

Source: 1981 & 1990 World Values Surveys.

ture (10% versus 8%) as sources of pride.[12] Predictably too, the levels of pride in country differ from one Canadian community to the next.[13]

Quite aside from cross-national differences in sources of pride and the between-group differences within the Canadian setting, the overall stability of levels of national pride masks systematic individual-level variations across all of these populations. A more detailed probing of these data yields a key finding: in every country, levels of national pride are consistently related to education, age, and value differences—all of which are also related to declining confidence in governmental and nongovernmental institutions. Europeans with low levels of formal education, for example, are almost twice as likely as those with high levels of education (45% versus 27%) to be very proud of their country. The relationship is clear and significant for Europeans (gamma = -.26) as it is for Canadians (gamma = -.15) and Americans (gamma = -.21). Levels of pride systematically increase with age (Europe, gamma = .10; United States, gamma = .27; Canada, gamma = .13). The same holds for the value divide: post-materialists express much less pride in country than do their materialist co-nationals (Europe, gamma = -.3; United States, gamma = -.16; Canada, gamma = -.17).

One intriguing question that emerges from these findings is: How can we explain aggregate stability of levels of national pride when there is so much evidence of individual variability? Part of the answer seems to involve significant shifts in the bases of community identification: publics are becoming less parochial and more cosmopolitan. In both the 1981 and 1990 surveys, publics in all twelve countries were asked: "To which of these groups would you say you belong, first of all? And what would come next?" Respondents were presented with the following options:

1. The locality or town where you live.
2. The state (province) or region of the country in which you live.
3. Your country as a whole.
4. North America (or Europe) as a whole.
5. The world as a whole.

The question taps a parochialism/cosmopolitanism dimension, and in the vast majority of cases respondents' first and second choices are consistent with each other. For instance, those who select "town" as their first choice nearly always select a contiguous geographic unit, like "region," as their second choice. According to Figure 3-9 there have been modest but consistent shifts in the bases of communal identity: public horizons are expanding. The proportion of respondents identifying with the "locality or town where you live" has decreased while supranational identifications, the proportion of citizens expressing a sense of belonging with continent or beyond, have increased.

The shift is sharpest among North Americans. In the case of the United States, for example, the proportion of Americans identifying first with their town or region dropped from 71% to 50% between 1981 and 1990. During the same period, the proportion identifying with North America or the world doubled, increasing from 10% to 21%. The pattern is very similar in Canada. In 1981 62% of Canadians identified first with some subnational unit—town or region—compared with 49% in 1990. Meanwhile, the proportion identifying with some unit beyond "the country" increased from 9% to 13%.[14]

Communal identifications are in flux, and appear to be particularly mobile in Canada and the United States. In 1981 a majority of people felt they belonged to some subnational aggregate, but by 1990 community identifications appear to migrate from subnational aggregates *through* a middle ground—identification with the nation—towards cosmopolitanism. This movement produces absolute increases in the proportions of both Americans and Canadians identifying with the country between 1981 and 1990 with Canadians being more likely than Americans to identify with their country at both time points. Given the rising proportions of these "country-first" identifiers, one might expect to find corresponding increases in levels of national pride. But as we have already seen (Table 3-1), overall levels of national pride have actually been relatively stable, or in the case of both Canada and the United States have declined over the period.

These findings are particularly intriguing given the timing of the surveys. Publics in all three North American countries were becoming more cosmopolitan during the run-up to continental free trade.[15] But is there anything to suggest that these changes might reflect more sustained long-term trends? One possibility is that these expanding communal horizons are related to the

Figure 3-9   Percentage Belonging to Given Geographical Units, 1981–1990

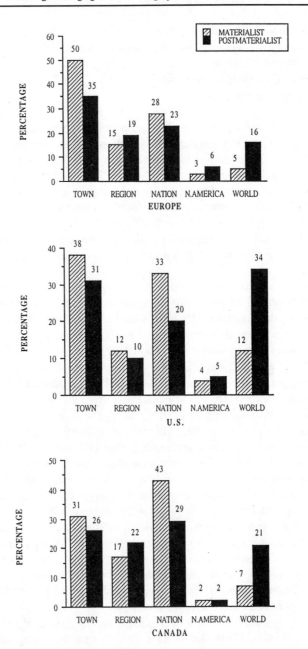

Source: 1981 and 1990 World Values Surveys.

same kinds of factors, like age and value orientations, that are symptomatic of generational change and that underpin the changing attitudes towards governmental and nongovernmental institutions. Once again, the evidence is entirely consistent with that interpretation. For example, young people (those in the 18–24 age group) are two to three times more likely than the old (those over 65 years of age) to take on supranational identifications. That finding holds in Canada and in *every other country* included in the analysis. The impact of the value divide on shifting communal horizons is equally impressive. As Figure 3-10 shows, post-materialists are about three times more likely than materialists to have these cosmopolitan identifications and are much less likely to have subnational identifications. The patterns are familiar ones, and they are stable: the impact of the post-materialist orientations is almost exactly the same at both time points in every country for which data are available.[16]

Conclusions

This chapter began by indicating that significant changes seem to have swept across the Canadian political landscape over the past decade or so. Citizen attachments to traditional political parties have been eroding; publics appear increasingly fickle, more willing to cast off their traditional partisan loyalties; and levels of voter turnout are not increasing to the extent one might expect given the increasingly educated publics. One thing is clear: these transformations do *not* appear to be symptoms of a peculiarly Canadian malaise. The WVS evidence clearly shows that these same transformations are taking place in most states throughout the advanced industrial world. One speculation was that these changes may apply only to a relatively narrow range of political phenomenon. Another is that they might reflect rising apathy about things political. None of the evidence coming from the World Values Surveys, however, provides any support for these particular interpretations. There is nothing to suggest that citizens are becoming increasingly apathetic about or disengaged from politics more broadly defined. As the last chapter demonstrated, citizens are certainly not preoccupied with politics, but they are more interested in political life than before. More importantly, there is nothing to indicate that partisan dealignment is an isolated phenomenon, a single shift confined to just one part of the political universe.

The progressive weakening of attachments to traditional political parties, declining levels of confidence in both governmental and nongovernmental institutions, and shifting bases of communal identifications all point to broadgauge changes in how citizens are connected to their states. Two observations help to underscore the extent to which these shifts are linked. First, it comes as little surprise to discover that levels of citizen confidence in governmental institutions are associated with how much pride people have in their country. These relationships are somewhat stronger in Europe than in either Canada or the United States, but they are all significant and they operate in the same

Figure 3-10   Percentage Belonging to Given Geographical Units, by Value Type

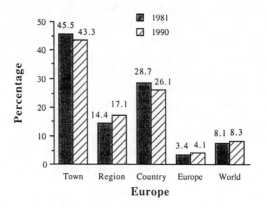

Europe

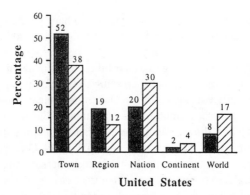

United States

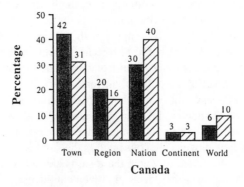

Canada

Source: 1990 World Values Survey.

Table 3-2 Multiple Classification Analysis: Predictors of Declining Confidence (in Governmental and Non-Governmental Institutions) and Cosmopolitanism; Europe, the U.S., and Canada, 1981–1990

	Institutions				State			
	Confidence in Governmental Institutions		Confidence in Non-Governmental Institutions		National Pride		Cosmopolitan	
Predictors	Eta	Beta	Eta	Beta	Eta	Beta	Eta	Beta
Interest in Politics	0.05	0.03	0.06	0.00	0.13	0.05	0.14	0.06
Post-materialism	0.26	0.22	0.22	0.19	0.29	0.22	0.24	0.18
Age	0.25	0.19	0.20	0.16	0.19	0.11	0.13	0.07
Education	0.15	0.04	0.11	0.00	0.19	0.07	0.17	0.08
R^2	0.108		0.073		0.104		0.072	

Source: 1981 and 1990 World Values Surveys.
Note: The postmaterialist index was not included in the 1981 U.S. data.

direction.[17] More surprising, perhaps, is the finding that pride in country (and cosmopolitanism) is also significantly and consistently related to confidence in nongovernmental institutions.[18]

The pervasiveness of these shifts is further underscored by the finding that *all* of these changes are related to the very same set of underlying factors—age, levels of education, interest in politics, and the materialist–post-materialist value divide—which in turn are related to each other. It is impossible, on the basis of simple correlations alone, to tell whether education, for example, is a more important determinant of these changes than, say, the materialist–post-materialist value divide. Table 3-2 helps to pull the threads of the analysis together and provides a comprehensive overview using a more powerful strategy. Basically, the results of this regression analysis tell us *which* of age, education, interest in politics, or the materialist–post-materialist value divide best predicts public confidence in institutions, national pride, and cosmopolitanism *after* the effects of all of the other factors have been taken into account. In reading these results, it is important to keep two sets of questions in mind: (1) How big is the coefficient? Is it statistically significant? (2) What is the direction of the relationship? Is the coefficient positive or negative?

One key finding is that, with but one exception (interest in politics as a predictor of confidence in nongovernmental institutions), all of the coefficients are significant. This means that age, education, interest in politics, and post-materialism all have a significant and independent impact on declining confidence in institutions. The same applies to national pride and cosmopolitanism. So, older people, for example, have greater confidence in governmental and nongovernmental institutions, higher levels of national pride, and are less like-ly than the young to be "cosmopolitan." Those with higher levels of education have less confidence in governmental institutions, more confidence in non-governmental institutions, lower levels of national pride, and are more "cos-mopolitan" than their less-educated counterparts.

Another key finding has to do with the relative importance of these predic-tors and the question whether these shifts indicate short-term fluctuations or more deep-seated generational shifts. It is important to emphasize, once again, that with data from a single decade it is not possible to be certain that the changes documented reflect genuine generational shifts. Recall, though, that new politics theory predicts that the changes sweeping across advanced indus-trial states are generationally driven. For that argument to hold water, the key indicators of generational change—age, education, and post-materialist orien-tations—would all have to emerge as significant predictors of these changes. The findings from the multivariate analysis indicate that they do so. The results reported in Table 3-2 demonstrate, in fact, that age and post-material-ist orientations are consistently the most powerful predictors of confidence in governmental and nongovernmental institutions. Those two indicators are also the most powerful predictors of national pride. Post-materialism is the strongest predictor of cosmopolitanism, and age, in this case, is about as pow-erful as interest in politics and education.

The shifts documented so far suggest an intriguing story: the changes that took place in the 1980s, both in Canada and in other advanced industrial states, conform to a general pattern. There is little to indicate that the Canadian changes followed those that took place in the United States or that, in these respects, the United States shows Canada the picture of its own future. More often than not, in fact, the reverse appears true. Equally intriguing is an apparent paradox: the potential for citizen participation in public life seems to have risen—people are better educated and more interested in politics—while citizen attachments to the traditional vehicles for participation have declined. As will become clear in the next chapter, citizens are not participating less in political life; they are participating more. What appears to have changed, in Canada and in other advanced industrial states, is that citizens are choosing different avenues and styles for their political participation.

NOTES

[1] The 1993 federal election study indicates that 18.4% of respondents claimed "very strong" party identification while 28.5% reported that they identified with "no federal party." Gallup surveys similarly show that respect for political parties has declined markedly over the last decade or so. The percentage of respondents saying that they had "a great deal" or "a lot" of respect for political parties are as follows: 1979, 30%; 1984, 22%; 1989, 18%; 1992, 9% (Jackson & Jackson, 1994). For a more detailed review of dealignment in the Canadian setting, see LeDuc, 1984.

2 For a discussion of nonvoting in Canadian federal elections see Pammett, 1991. For a useful comparative perspective on Canadian levels of voter turnout, see Black, 1991.

3 Percentage of Respondents Saying They Are "Very Interested" in Politics, by Country

Country	1981	1990
France	6.5	7.0
Britain	5.6	12.8
West Germany	6.4	25.2
Italy	4.9	6.0
Netherlands	2.8	13.6
Denmark	4.2	15.0
Belgium	3.3	6.9
Spain	4.4	5.7
Ireland	4.4	8.2
Northern Ireland	2.2	8.9
U.S.A.	11.5	15.8
Canada	7.2	20.3

Source: 1981 and 1990 World Values Surveys.

4 Overall, the relationship between interest in politics and education level, measured by years of formal education, is gamma = .32. In Canada, it is somewhat weaker (gamma = .20) than in Western Europe (gamma = .31).

5 Of the twelve countries included here, the exceptions are the Netherlands (15.7% said "frequently" in 1981; 14.7% said "frequently" in 1990) and Spain (15.7% in 1981 and 9.8% in 1990).

6 Percentage of Respondents expressing "High Confidence" in Government Institutions, 1981 vs. 1990

Country	1981	1990
France	32.2	26.9
Britain	43.5	40.3
Germany	26.9	22.7
Italy	21.8	16.8
Netherlands	22.8	18.0
Denmark	25.9	28.5
Belgium	23.5	18.9
Spain	33.5	19.3
Ireland	50.3	44.3
Northern Ireland	46.4	48.8
U.S.A	49.6	31.8
Canada	36.9	29.4

Source: 1981 and 1990 World Values Surveys.
Note: Both the Danish and Northern Irish results are well within the margins of statistical error.

[7] By themselves, age differences are not enough to demonstrate generational effects. The point is that without any evidence of age differences, it is unlikely that generational effects could be present.

[8] To determine precisely why the relationship is curvilinear rather than linear requires much more detailed investigation. Closer scrutiny shows differences between the 1981 and 1990 data; the 1981 pattern turns out to be almost perfectly linear, while the 1990 data clearly is more curvilinear. This indicates much higher confidence levels among the young, which implies that period or generational effects rather than life-cycle effects may be responsible for the shift.

[9] The shifts within the three Canadian subgroups are also consistent with the overall trend. The percentage of anglophones reporting "high" confidence in these institutions dropped from 37% in 1981 to 31.5% in 1990. For francophones it dropped from 46.3% to 39.2%, and in 1990, new Canadians occupied the middle ground at 35.6%.

[10] Percentage of Respondents Expressing "High" Confidence in Nongovernment Institutions, 1981 vs. 1990

Country	1981	1990
Europe	26.1	23.7
France	20.5	22.4
Britain	25.5	18.1
West Germany	20.7	19.2
Italy	22.9	20.5
Netherlands	19.4	15.7
Denmark	26.0	28.5
Belgium	34.3	24.4
Spain	28.6	28.0
Ireland	46.2	38.7
Northern Ireland	39.0	34.9
U.S.A.	46.8	38.2
Canada	39.5	34.1
English	37.0	31.5
French	46.3	39.2
Other	n.a.	35.6

Source: 1981 and 1990 World Values Surveys.
Note: Respondents were asked how much confidence they had in their country's churches, educational system, legal system, and press. Shown above are the percentages with an average score of 2 or lower, when 1 = "a lot", 2 = "quite a lot," 3 = "not very much," and 4 = "no confidence at all."

[11] Perhaps the most striking country-specific finding here is that in the Irish republic, confidence in the church dropped quite dramatically, from 50.7% in 1981 to 39.7% in 1990.

[12] Both the Canadian and American 1990 surveys used the menu format: they presented respondents with a list of "achievements" and then asked "Do any of these things make you proud of your country?"

[13] In 1981, for example, 66% of anglophone Canadians said they were "very proud"

to be Canadian, compared to 52% of francophones. In 1990 the proportion of anglophones saying they were "very proud" to be a Canadian remained virtually unchanged (68%); 63% of new Canadians gave that same response, while the proportion of francophones who were "very proud" fell to 39%. Closer analysis of these data reveals very striking age-related discontinuities. As one would expect, in general, levels of national pride increase with age. For both the anglophone and "new Canadian" communities the age-related increases in pride are gradual and incremental. In the anglophone community, for example, the proportion of those saying "very proud" rises from 61% for the youngest group to just over 78% for those over 65 years of age. For francophones, about 40% of *all* age groups except the oldest say they are "very proud." But among those over 65 years of age, 68% say they are "very proud." There are also consistent education and value differences. Those with high levels of education are less likely to be "very proud," and post-materialists express much lower levels of national pride than materialists.

[14] Not surprisingly, there are very significant differences between the three segments of the Canadian population, and the 1981–1990 shifts in the communal identifications of anglophone Canadians are particularly striking. For them the proportion of what might be called "parochials"—those identifying with the town and region—dropped from 58% in 1981 to 39% in 1990. Over the same period those identifying with "the country" increased from 33% to 48%, while the "cosmopolitans" increased from 9% to 15%. For understandable reasons, the patterns for francophones are very different. In 1981 72% of francophones identified first with "town" or "region," and that figure *increased* to 76% in 1990. In 1981 20% of francophones identified with "their country," and that dropped to just 14% in 1990. One would expect local or regional identifications to be weaker for new Canadians and they are: 31% identified with their "town" or "region," 44% identified with Canada, and 25% identified with either North America or "the world."

[15] A detailed analysis of the Mexican findings is provided in Inglehart, Nevitte, and Basanez, 1996. The evidence shows that Mexican identifications were also becoming more "continentalist" between 1981 and 1990.

[16] The exception, a significant one from the Canadian standpoint, is the case of Quebec. In this instance, post-materialist francophones (35%) are more likely than their materialist counterparts (27%) to identify with "their region." We note, too, that only 10% of post-materialist francophones identify with "the country" and 17% have supranational identifications.

[17] For Europe the correlation between pride in country and confidence in government is gamma = .32 compared to gamma = .24 and gamma =.23 for the United States and Canada, respectively.

[18] The correlations for the relationship between confidence in nongovernmental institutions and pride in country are Europe, gamma = .25; United States, gamma = .16; and Canada, gamma = .15.

4: Changing Patterns of Political Participation

Whether declining public confidence in institutions and weakening attachments to traditional political parties means that our twelve democracies are "in crisis" is a matter of perspective. There are long-standing debates about how much, what kind of, or indeed even whether, democracy is good for society, and the controversies hinge partly on the balance to strike between political leaders and citizens: How much say should citizens have in political decision-making? Proponents of elite versions of democracy, for example, claim that crucial to a smoothly functioning and stable democratic polity is the freedom of political leaders to make policy decisions. Political leaders, after all, are better informed than the average citizen, and are better positioned to see the whole picture and to make public decisions—even unpopular ones—in the interests of all; too much citizen participation can overload the political system and threaten stability. From this perspective, what is crucial is political leaders' commitment to democratic ideals and the public's acceptance of those leaders (Dye & Zeigler, 1970; Huntington, 1981). Others counter with a variety of arguments: that elite versions of democracy are fundamentally undemocratic (Barber, 1984); that the interests of leaders and publics are not always the same; and that if publics are too passive, if political leaders are not routinely "reined in" and held accountable by watchful publics, then leaders become aloof and less responsive to citizen demands. Others contend that these elite versions of democracy operate on faulty assumptions; they fail to take into account that the once large knowledge gap between elites and publics has narrowed. Proponents of elite versions of democracy, this argument runs, underestimate just how well-informed contemporary publics really are (Popkin, 1991; Zaller, 1992). For those averse to elite versions of democracy, the recent transformations are encouraging. The emergence of increasingly interested, informed, and even critical publics is a healthy sign; it indicates the potential for a more vital and more broadly participatory version of democracy. From this vantage point, democracy is not so much "in crisis" as in a state of transition. All that is in crisis is "old politics"—the traditional notion that democracies work best when publics are passive, disengaged, and relatively uninformed.

Interested and informed publics scrutinize their political systems more closely, and it is not difficult to find scattered evidence indicating that Canadians are critical of, and feel distant from, their government. The 1990 round of the WVS asked, "Would you say that this country is run by a few big interests looking out for themselves, or that it is run for the benefit of all the people?" Fully 70% of Canadian respondents (compared to 66% of Americans) held the opinion that the country is "run by a few big interests looking out for themselves." Nor, according to the results from the 1990 WVS, do Canadians express much trust in government. When asked how often "do you trust the government in Ottawa [Washington, for American respondents] to do what is right?" 42% of Americans said "always" or "almost always" compared to just 20% of Canadians. One in four Canadians replied "never," while only one in ten Americans gave that response. Furthermore, Canadians, it seems, feel relatively powerless. The 1990 surveys asked Canadians and Americans if they strongly agreed, agreed, disagreed, or strongly disagreed with the following statement: "If an unjust law were passed by the government I could do nothing at all about it." One in three (32%) Canadians either agreed or strongly agreed, compared to one in four (25%) of Americans.

At about the same time that Canadians were expressing these sentiments, the Canadian federal government was in the process of launching a royal commission the purpose of which was to examine Canada's electoral rules and the methods of party financing.[1] According to Pierre Lortie (1991), the chair of the commission, the need for such a review was "dictated largely by the major constitutional, social and technological changes of the past several decades, which have transformed Canadian society, and their concomitant influence on Canadians' expectations of the political process itself." "Parliament and the national government," Lortie argued, "must be seen as legitimate," and he went on to express the hope that "electoral reform can both enhance the stature of national political institutions and reinforce their ability to define the future of our country in ways that command Canadians' respect and confidence and promote the national interest" (1991: xiii–xiv). Electoral reform is one strategy for reconnecting citizens with such tradition-al representative institutions as political parties. Elections, though, provide only occasional opportunities for citizens to register their preferences. Certainly, voting is the most visible and widespread form of conventional political participation, but it is also only one form of political participation. Furthermore, it is far from clear that voting is the most effective way for citizens to register their preferences and to make demands on the political system. A host of other avenues of participation are available (Verba, Nie, & Kim, 1971), and it is becoming increasingly apparent that publics throughout the advanced industrial world are trying out the alternatives; they are turning to other forms of political participation, both conventional and unconventional, in growing numbers.

The Rise of Protest Behaviour

There is nothing new about unconventional political behaviour. Nearly all Western states have some experience with protest behaviours—rebellions, riots, uprisings, marches, strikes—the goals of which have ranged from feeding the hungry, resisting conscription, and protecting jobs to getting the vote. As Russell Dalton observes:

> In historical terms, protest and collective action were often the last desperate acts of citizens, arising from feelings of frustration and deprivation. Protest was concentrated among the socially disadvantaged, repressed minorities or groups that were alienated from the established political order. Unconventional political action was an outlet for groups that lacked access to politics through conventional participation channels. (1988(a): 60).

With increased access to politics, lower barriers to formal participation, and spreading affluence, one might expect the frequency of protest politics to have waned. There is striking evidence, however, that levels of unconventional behaviour have actually increased, not fallen (Barnes et al., 1979). Significantly too, protest behaviours turn out to be most prevalent in those states that are more affluent (Powell, 1982).

Despite such a long history of protest behaviour, systematic documentation of these outbursts is relatively recent; it was stimulated by the upsurge of protest activities in the 1960s. Contemporary analysts typically characterize unconventional, or protest, behaviours in terms of a hierarchy of activities (Dalton, 1988(a); Kaase & Marsh 1979; Marsh 1977; Verba, Nie, & Kim, 1978). As Figure 4-1 illustrates, the low end of the "protest hierarchy" is anchored by such actions as signing a petition, a relatively mild form of protest. At the other end the hierarchy is topped by much more extreme activities that include damaging property or even personal violence. Two features of this hierarchy are particularly relevant for our purposes. First, a substantial body of evidence (Barnes et al., 1979) demonstrates that these kinds of protest behaviour are *cumulative*. That is, individuals engaging in protest at, say, the mid-point of the hierarchy (Figure 4-1) are nearly always prepared to also engage in those milder forms of protest that are at lower levels of the hierarchy. Second, the hierarchy itself is not an entirely "smooth" continuum. In moving up the hierarchy, in engaging in increasingly intense kinds of protest activity, a protestor crosses a number of thresholds that involve qualitatively different kinds of activities (Dalton, 1988(a)). Signing a petition, for example, is an entirely legal and increasingly orthodox activity. Joining a boycott is also legal but is a less orthodox form of direct action. Joining a boycott requires a much greater investment of time and energy. Occupying a factory entails an even higher level of personal investment, but occupying factories is plainly an illegal form of direct action.

Figure 4-1 The Hierarchy of Protest Behaviour

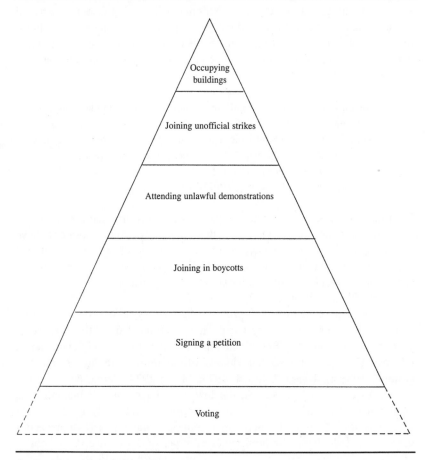

Source: Adapted from Dalton (1988(a): 65).

Several cross-national studies, the World Values Surveys included, now routinely use the same standard strategy for detecting the "protest potential" of publics. In both 1981 and 1990, respondents to the WVS were presented with a card listing the core set of protest activities and were asked "whether you have *actually done* any of these things, whether you *might do* it or would *never*, under any circumstances, do it?"[2] Two major findings emerge from the responses to these questions: First, no matter how one looks at the evidence (see Appendix 4-A for the complete findings), one result stands out: the protest potential of publics in these advanced industrial states increased significantly between 1981 and 1990. Second, and somewhat surprisingly,

Canadians turn out to be among the most protest oriented of all. Figure 4-2 summarizes the evidence in two ways. It first considers those reporting that they have done at least one of four activities that are in the middle of the protest hierarchy.[3] The second part reports the proportions of respondents who say they would never do any of those four activities "under any circumstances"; it provides an indication of how reluctant publics are to resort to these kinds of protest activity. Either way, the scope and direction of the 1981–1990 changes are absolutely clear. In every country except one (Spain), publics became *more* inclined to engage in protest behaviours, and in every case except two (Spain and Northern Ireland), citizens became *less* reluctant to rule out the idea of taking up one of these forms of protest. Viewed in a cross-national context, the levels of Canadian protest potential appear surprisingly high; this finding seems to contradict the stereotype that Canadians are "conformists." Nor do they indicate that Canadians are "more deferential to authority" than Americans (Lipset, 1990: 227). According to these measures, Canadians (at 23.6%) ranked fifth out of twelve in protest potential in 1981—slightly higher than the United States (21.1%), but well behind France (30.7%) and Italy (26.9%). By 1990 Canadians had moved up to fourth place (32.5%), behind Italy (37.2%), France (35.7%), and Denmark (35.4%). Canadians were actually *less* reluctant than Americans to engage in *any* form of protest behaviour. Nor do the trajectories of the 1981–1990 changes suggest that Canadians lag or follow Americans in these respects.[4]

These Canadian–American comparisons are intriguing in their own right, but there is a larger question: Is there any evidence that protest behaviour is associated with the same generationally related factors—post-materialist orientations and age—that have been linked to the other changes examined so far? These particular connections have been documented in great detail in such other countries as Norway (Lafferty & Knutsen, 1985) and Britain (Marsh, 1975), and have been generally demonstrated throughout Europe (Barnes et al., 1979). To the extent that Canadian attitudes and behaviours are typical of those found in the publics of other advanced industrial states, it would be remarkable if no such links were present in the Canadian setting. Figure 4-3 presents the aggregate findings from both 1981 and 1990; it shows that the relationship between protest potential and materialist/post-materialist orientations is reasonably strong (Canada, corr = .16; United States, corr = .17; Europe, corr = .23) and the relationships operate in the predictable direction. In fact, in *every* country post-materialists are somewhere between two and three times more likely than materialists to engage in at least one of these four protest behaviours. There is another significant finding. Notice that the Canadian–American differences in levels of protest behaviour cannot be explained simply by the fact that Canadians, proportionately, are more likely than Americans to be post-materialists. It turns out that Canadians have a higher protest potential than their American counterparts regardless of whether the focus is on materialists, post-materialists, or those of "mixed" value types.[5]

Figure 4-2   Those that "Have Done" at Least One of Four Protest Behaviours
Those that Would "Never Do" Any of the Four Protest Behaviours

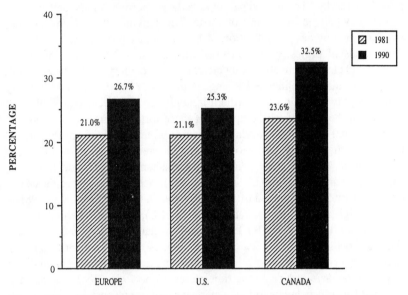

Those That Would "Never Do" Any Of The Four Protest Behaviours

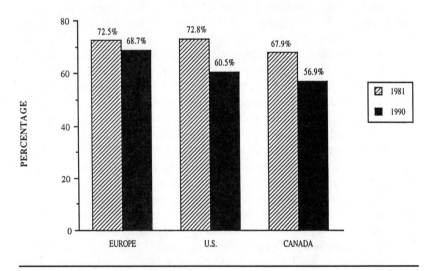

Source: 1981 and 1990 World Values Surveys.
Note: The four types of behaviours include (1) joining in boycotts, (2) attending unlawful demonstrations, (3) joining unofficial strikes, and (4) occupying buildings or factories.

Figure 4-3 Those Who Have Done at Least One of Four Protest Behaviours by Value Type

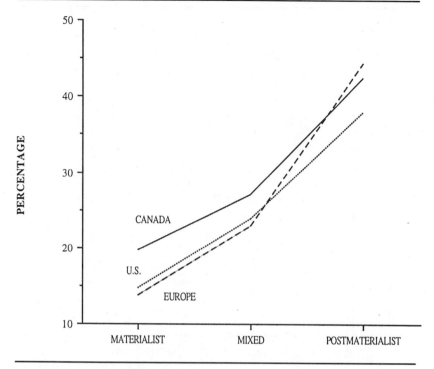

Source: 1981 and 1990 World Values Surveys.
Note: The four types of behaviours include (1) joining in boycotts, (2) attending unlawful demonstrations, (3) joining unofficial strikes, (4) and occupying buildings or factories.

What about age effects? As before, the linkages between age and readiness to engage in protest behaviour are consistent with the interpretation that protest potential may be related to generational change. In general, older respondents are less likely than the young to engage in protest. The relationships between age and protest potential are statistically significant in every country, although in Canada (gamma = -.07) and the United States (gamma = -.08) the associations turn out to be much weaker than in Europe (gamma = -.23). The reason for this finding becomes clearer when the data are unpacked and when one looks at the protest potential of each age group, as in Figure 4-4. The age-protest behaviour gradients are not linear; the patterns are plainly curvilinear. In fact, the age-protest potential patterns are remarkably similar to the earlier findings tracking the connection between age and confidence in governmental institutions (Figure 3-4). In no case is the highest protest potential found among the youngest age group. For Europeans, protest potential is highest among those in the 25–34 age group, whereas for Americans and

Figure 4-4   Those Who Have Done at Least One of Four Protest Behaviours by Age

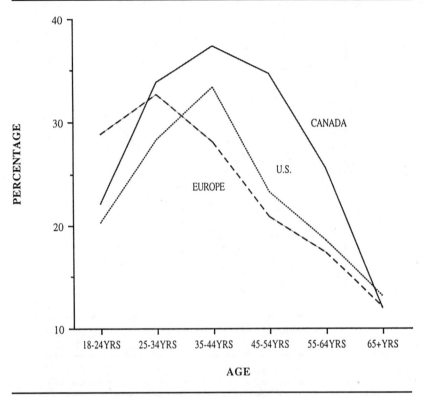

Source: 1981 and 1990 World Values Surveys.
Note: The four types of behaviours include (1) joining in boycotts, (2) attending unlawful demonstrations, (3) joining unofficial strikes, and (4) occupying buildings or factories.

Canadians those in the 35–44 age group have the highest protest potential. Notice, too, that Canadian levels of protest potential are higher than American levels for *every* age category except one, those over 65 years of age.

The consistency of these findings is striking. Regardless of which measures are used, the results all point to the same conclusion: in Canada, as in nearly every other advanced industrial state, publics have become *more* willing to engage in protest actions, and the proportion of these publics reporting that they would never do any of these protest behaviours under any circumstances has declined. The very same patterns hold for each of the three communities within Canada. On balance, francophone Canadians have a slightly higher protest potential than anglophones and new Canadians.[6] And in each case, the protest potential of each group is also associated with age and value type. The findings are consistent in yet another significant respect: in *every*

Table 4-1 Predictors of Protest Potential: a Multiple Classification Analysis

Predictors	Aggregate		Europe		United States		Canada	
	Eta	Beta	Eta	Beta	Eta	Beta	Eta	Beta
Interest in Politics	0.27	0.18	0.28	0.19	0.16	0.10	0.22	0.16
Post-materialism	0.31	0.19	0.32	0.18	0.26	0.20	0.24	0.15
Age	0.18	0.09	0.21	0.10	0.20	0.16	0.17	0.15
Education	0.23	0.10	0.25	0.10	0.25	0.15	0.24	0.15
Confidence in government	0.15	0.06	0.18	0.07	0.09	0.03	0.16	0.06
Confidence in non-government	0.14	0.05	0.15	0.05	0.03	0.01	0.10	0.02
R^2	0.161		0.176		0.139		0.144	
R	0.402		0.419		0.372		0.380	

Note: The postmaterialist index was not included in the 1981 U.S. data.
Source: 1981 and 1990 World Values Surveys.

country, the protest potential of publics increases with education and political interest.[7]

Table 4-1 pulls these results together and provides a more comprehensive overview of them; it reports the findings that come from a simple multiple classification analysis (MCA). The MCA, a more sophisticated multivariate technique, is useful because it isolates which factors, among all of those considered so far, best predict the protest potential of publics in Europe, Canada, and the United States. The *eta* coefficients provide baseline evidence; they are simply measures of the correlation between each predictor and protest potential. More important are the *beta* coefficients, which indicate the correlation between each predictor and protest behaviour after all the effects of the other variables have been taken into account. The results are quite uniform: all of the variables in Table 4-1 are correlated with protest potential. More importantly, the results provide further indication that the changing political orientations documented in this and the last chapter are part of a broad pattern. None of the relationships completely disappears when controls for other factors are introduced. Overall, the post-materialist value divide turns out to be the best single predictor of protest potential: this indicator has the largest beta value. Interest in politics, education, and age are also important predictors. In fact, in both Canada and the European countries interest in politics is a slightly better predictor of protest potential than is the value divide. Notice too, though, that confidence in governmental and non-governmental institutions also predicts protest potential. Plainly, it is not just value change, the rise of post-materialist orientations, that accounts for the rising protest potential of these publics. It is a combination of factors—increasing levels of education, higher interest in politics, declining confidence in institutions, age effects, and value change—that all work together to make publics less compliant, and more likely to resort to unconventional forms of political behaviour. In a nutshell, it is those with a higher participatory potential that are increasingly turning to non-traditional modes of political participation.

New Movements

A variety of explanations have been offered for the apparent rise in protest behaviours in advanced industrial states. Some argue that political protests are cyclical phenomena, responses to sudden economic transitions—sharp upswings or downturns (Brand, 1990). Others see the surge in protest behaviours as a reaction to new phases of technological change (Offe, 1985), part of the structural shifts associated with late industrialism (Touraine, 1981), or a consequence of an emergent new middle class faced with limited opportunities for upward mobility.[8] In all likelihood, a comprehensive explanation for the surge in unconventional behaviour would have to take into account economic conditions, shifts in the structural characteristics of these states, the impact of emerging technologies, institutional factors, and value change (Kaase, 1990).

While the precise causes for these rising levels of protest remain controversial, disputes typically revolve around how much of the rise can be explained by structural as opposed to value change. Regardless of differences of opinion, most observers do agree on one point: that the protests of the post-1960s era are qualitatively different from those that plagued the earlier histories of western states. According to Klandermans (1988), the new forms of protest differ from the old in at least three respects: (1) they involve different kinds of *issues*; (2) they attract different kinds of *actors*; and (3) they involve the use of different *strategies* of political action. As has already been pointed out, the older forms of protest were primarily concerned with such "distributional issues" as poverty, hunger, and lack of access to the political process (Dalton, 1988(a)). New protests focus less on redistributing wealth and instead emphasize issues of what might be broadly termed the "quality of life" in modern industrial societies. In effect, the concerns prompting the new protests amount to a critique both of the status quo and of many of the assumptions, such as the importance of profit-making, that probably helped to make the advanced industrial states so economically successful in the first place. Second, unlike the old protest movements, which attracted the support of the marginalized, the ranks of new protest movements are not filled with those who suffer from any personal deprivation. On the contrary, they are stacked with those of the post-war generation who are part of the educated new middle class and who are typically relatively well off. And unlike the spontaneous uprisings typical of old protests, new protests rely upon a more deliberate array of political tactics (Rucht, 1990), including media campaigns designed to mobilize public opinion, intensive lobbying of bureaucratic and legislative agencies, the use of the courts, and the formation of new political parties to mount electoral challenges to old-line parties (Dalton, Kuechler, & Burklin, 1990; Kitschelt, 1989).

Perhaps the most recognizable evidence of the political transformations experienced by advanced industrial states is the emergence of issue-driven political formations pushing a variety of "new" causes onto their respective national political agendas. The causes promoted by these new movements range from environmental protection, peace, human rights, and women's issues to animal rights. The goals pursued by these groups are plainly diverse, but the ideological bond uniting the movements, according to some analysts, hinges on two major traits: "a humanistic critique of the prevailing system and the dominant culture," and "a resolve to fight for a better world here and now with little, if any, inclination to escape into some spiritual refuge" (Keuchler and Dalton, 1990: 280).[9]

These generalizations seem to resonate with Canadian experience. The Canadian environmental movement appeared to flourish during the 1980s, women's issues became more prominent during that decade, and the country has a record of supporting human rights. It seems farfetched, then, to claim that Canadians remain aloof from, or untouched by, the kinds of issues that are so actively promoted by new social movements in other settings. The mere presence of groups pressing for environmental protection or women's rights, though, is no guarantee that these issue-driven movements enjoy widespread support; a handful of dedicated and sophisticated activists can give issues visibility. To what extent do the causes advocated by these groups preoccupy Canadians more generally? Is support for these issues both widespread and deep? And do Canadians embrace these causes with the same kind of enthusiasm that seems to be displayed by their European counterparts? On the whole, the answers seem to be yes. Systematic cross-national evidence of support for these new movements is in short supply, and the World Values Surveys are useful, once again, because they provide multiple benchmarks. The 1990 WVS asked respondents how strongly they approved, or disapproved, of a variety of "groups and movements looking for public support" and if they "belonged" to any. The list of groups included many commonly seen as the new, social movement variety: the disarmament/peace movement, the human rights movement, the women's movement, and the ecology/conservation movement.[10] Table 4-2 reports the percentages of respondents in each country saying that they approve strongly of each movement, as well as the proportion saying they belonged, and these data suggest that support for these new issues is as widespread in Canada as in most other advanced industrial states. In every category, Canadians rank at least in the top half of all countries considered, and Canadian support for the environment and women's rights is among the highest anywhere. Compare the level of Canadian support for each issue with both the American findings and the European average, and it becomes clear that Canadian orientations are in these respects far closer to those of Europeans than to Americans. Canadians are as enthusiastic as their European counterparts, and they are considerably more enthusiastic support-

Table 4-2 Percentage of Respondents Saying They "Strongly Support" (or Belong to) Each Group

Ecology (Conservation)		Peace (Disarmament)		Human Rights (Third World)		Womens' Rights	
Country	%	Country	%	Country	%	Country	%
West Germany	70.0 (4.6)	Spain	61.3 (0.7)	Spain	73.3 (0.9)	Ireland	37.1 (4.6)
Spain	66.8 (1.4)	Ireland	49.7 (0.6)	Italy	66.4 (1.1)	Canada	36.7 (6.6)
Canada	53.9 (7.6)	Italy	49.7 (1.2)	Ireland	63.1 (1.6)	United States	31.5 (8.5)
Netherlands	53.7 (23.8)	West Germany	47.6 (2.0)	France	61.9 (2.6)	Spain	30.2 (0.7)
Italy	51.1 (3.3)	Belgium	44.4 (1.9)	Canada	58.3 (4.6)	Belgium	24.8 (9.7)
Ireland	50.4 (2.3)	Canada	40.0 (2.0)	Netherlands	56.8 (14.3)	France	23.3 (1.0)
France	49.5 (2.3)	France	36.0 (0.5)	Belgium	54.2 (5.9)	West Germany	21.7 (5.6)
Britain	46.0 (5.0)	Netherlands	31.9 (2.9)	West Germany	54.2 (2.2)	Britain	19.2 (4.8)
Belgium	48.6 (6.6)	United States	26.5 (2.0)	Denmark	51.3 (2.8)	Northern Ireland	17.9 (5.3)
United States	46.4 (8.3)	Denmark	26.4 (2.1)	United States	50.6 (2.0)	Netherlands	17.8 (7.3)
Northern Ireland	37.8 (2.3)	Northern Ireland	17.4 (0.7)	Britain	41.8 (2.0)	Italy	13.9 (0.4)
Denmark	29.6 (12.5)	Britain	16.7 (1.1)	Northern Ireland	32.9 (2.6)	Denmark	12.2 (1.7)
European Aggregate	54.9 (5.3)	European Aggregate	44.5 (1.4)	European Aggregate	59.8 (3.1)	European Aggregate	23.3 (3.9)

Question: "There are a number of groups and movements looking for public support. For each of the following movements, ... can you tell me whether you approve strongly, approve, disapprove, disapprove strongly, or don't know?"

ers of new-movement kinds of issues than Americans. There are also variations within Canada's three communities: anglophone Canadians are consistently *more* likely than Americans to approve of these movements, but they
are always *less* enthusiastic in their support for all groups and movements
than either francophones or new Canadians.[11] Sympathizing with the general
goals of a movement is one thing; the notion that one "belongs" to a movement indicates a stronger commitment to the movement's goals, and so it
comes as no surprise to discover that sympathizers greatly outnumber "members."[12]

The 1990 survey questions about approval and disapproval of movements,
or whether people belong to those movements, were not asked in the 1981
WVS, and hence it is impossible to provide direct evidence of whether support for or membership in these movements rose or fell between 1981 and
1990. Most analysts agree that value change is at least partly responsible for
the growing popularity of these movements. Support for environmental movements, for example, has been linked to post-materialist orientations in Austria
and Denmark (Gundelach, 1991; Pelinka, 1991). And Inglehart (1990) has
demonstrated that these same value orientations are also connected to membership in various peace movements throughout Europe. But is the spread of
post-materialist orientations linked to growing support for all of these movements? And does the emergence of these values help to structure orientations
to these movements in North America, as they do in Europe? According to
Figure 4-5, post-materialists are far more likely than materialists to express
strong approval for all of these movements. The differences are significant and
striking in every single case. Once again, national variations come into play.
The important preliminary point, though, is that the differences in the value
orientations of supporters are consistent across all of the countries, and they
are consistent, yet again, within the three Canadian communities. A more
detailed analysis of support for and membership in these movements reveals
other familiar patterns. Levels of formal education and political interest—
indicators of participatory potential—are strong predictors of both approval
and membership. And in each case the indication is that generational changes
may be involved: in addition to age and education, post-materialist value orientations also predict approval of and membership in these movements.
Overall, post-materialism emerges as the best single predictor of support for
all these movements.

This overview falls far short of a comprehensive explanation for why these
new social movements emerge in the first place, but the findings are sufficient
to illustrate one general point: in all of the advanced industrial states considered, the very same background factors are associated with citizen approval of
and membership in a striking variety of new social movements. Each one of
the four movements considered above deserves a far more searching analysis
than has so far been provided. Given their diversity of goals, there is reason to
expect significant differences in levels of concern, variation in the motivations
of supporters, and unique organizational dynamics. A closer consideration of

Figure 4-5   Those Who "Strongly Approve" of Various Movements by Value Type

Europe:

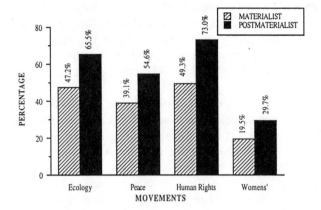

United States:

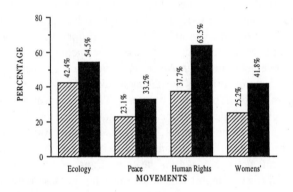

Canada:

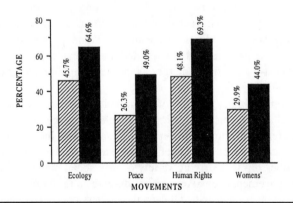

Source: 1990 World Values Survey.

just one case, the environmental movement, provides a glimpse of these nuances.

The Case of Environmentalism

Ecological degradation is unquestionably a global problem. But the politics of environmental activism seems to divide the world into two camps: the industrializing world and the advanced industrial states. The most comprehensive body of cross-national evidence available indicates that nearly everyone worries about the environment to some extent. The 1990 WVS was conducted in some forty-two countries, and an overview of all the data indicates that the overwhelming majority of respondents in all of those countries, 96% on average, said they approved of the ecology movement (62% reported strong approval and 34% indicated approval). When these countries are ranked according to the proportion of each population saying they "strongly approve" of the ecology movement, the clear finding is that approval of the ecology movement is higher in Eastern Europe and Latin America than in most advanced industrial states (Inglehart, 1993). One straightforward explanation for that finding is that it reflects a reasonable reaction to poor environmental conditions. People living in the most ecologically degraded environments, like Bangkok or Mexico City, have more reason to be concerned about the environment: the threat to their health is greater. More than that, conditions in the industrializing world have deteriorated dramatically, according to a recent World Bank report (1992): air quality has worsened, clean water is less available, and problems of waste disposal and sanitation have mounted; all this despite the ready availability of technologies to resolve these difficulties.

Publics in advanced industrial states, by contrast, enjoy a cleaner environment. Air and water quality in most of these states have actually improved quite dramatically over the last twenty-five years. If approval of the ecology movement is higher in the industrializing world than among advanced industrial states, why have conditions in these countries not improved? The answer to that question is not straightforward, partly because environmental problems pose dilemmas that are particularly acute in industrializing states that are trying to "catch up" economically. Newly industrializing states sometimes argue, perhaps with some justification, that the advanced industrial states paid little attention to environmental standards when they were in the early stages of their economic take-off. For these now-wealthy countries to turn around and try to foist their new-found standards upon others who are at earlier stages of development and are struggling with hunger, poverty, and high unemployment is unreasonable. A further difficulty is revealed by another finding from the 1990 WVS data. One analyst noticed that "the *highest* levels of support for environmental protection are found in those countries that have some of the *lowest* levels of pollution in the world" (Inglehart, 1993). The political will driving the politics of environmental protection, then, cannot be explained just as a reaction to objective levels of environmental degradation; it comes from publics that subjectively place a high priority on promoting and protecting the environment.

Environmental movements in advanced industrial states have received far more attention than their counterparts in the rest of the world. But even within these states, ecological movements are far from uniform. Best documented are the cross-national variations in the extent to which publics are mobilized, and differences in the organizational cohesiveness of the movements, their choice of tactics, and degree of success in effecting change. In some settings, like Austria, Belgium, Switzerland, and West Germany, environmentalists have formed their own political parties and some have enjoyed electoral success, particularly at the local level (Burklin, 1985; Hildebrandt & Dalton, 1978; Kitschelt, 1988; Muller-Rommel, 1985; Paehlke, 1989).[13] In others, such as Holland and Britain, environmentalists have focussed more on changing the priorities of existing parties. In yet other countries, ecology activists pursue their goals through vigorous lobbying efforts (Dalton, 1988(a); Kitschelt, 1989). By most accounts, Canada falls into the latter category. No ecology party has yet mounted a significant challenge to existing political parties, even though public sensitivities to ecological issues appear to have risen. By one calculation, some 2,500 interest groups have emerged to press a variety of environmental goals (Bakvis & Nevitte, 1990; Wilson, 1992).

National differences in ecology movements notwithstanding, policy-makers in advanced industrial states face similar dilemmas. Governments can be responsive to environmentally conscious citizens and bolster their public support by pushing though tough environmental legislation. The problem is that by imposing stringent environmental standards on polluters, governments disadvantage their own industries, particularly those seeking customers in the fiercely competitive international marketplace. From the strictly economic standpoint, governments have little incentive to become world leaders when it comes to setting high environmental standards for their own industries. Yet if they fail to appear decisive in protecting the environment, or if they neglect environmental issues entirely, they risk paying a heavy political cost, of losing the support of increasingly environmentally conscious electorates. How "environmentally conscious" are these electorates? One unequivocal finding is that support for the objective of a clean environment is nearly universal. It is not so difficult to support strict environmental standards when there are no costs. A more telling indication of the depth of support for a clean environment is what kind of trade-offs people are prepared to make. How much are publics willing to sacrifice to achieve that objective?

The 1990 WVS probed the depth of environmental concern by asking respondents if they agreed or disagreed with four statements about the environment. Table 4-3 summarizes the findings; it shows that in nearly every case the Danish and Dutch publics have the strongest commitment to environmental protection. More than 80% of the Danes and the Dutch agreed to give up

Table 4-3 Environmental Concern in Advanced Industrial Countries

| Strongly Agree and Agree | | | | Strongly Disagree and Disagree | | | | Public Support for Environmental Concern | |
| Would Give Part of Income (1) | | Would Agree to Increase in Taxes (2) | | Should Not Cost Me (3) | | Environment Less Urgent than Suggested (4) | | (Percentage Scoring "High" on Environmental Concern Index)* | |
Country	%	Country	%	Country	%	Country	%	Country	%
Denmark	84.3	Denmark	69.5	Netherlands	81.1	West Germany	88.1	Denmark	64.5
Netherlands	81.7	Netherlands	68.4	Denmark	71.0	Italy	83.6	Netherlands	63.5
Northern Ireland	74.9	Britain	67.6	Canada	47.7	Netherlands	82.6	Canada	42.0
United States	74.2	Northern Ireland	65.2	United States	46.2	Denmark	82.0	West Germany	41.5
Canada	73.4	Canada	63.5	West Germany	43.1	France	81.3	United States	40.4
Ireland	69.5	United States	63.2	Britain	42.0	Belgium	80.5	Britain	39.1
Italy	69.1	Spain	57.0	Ireland	40.3	Canada	78.1	Northern Ireland	36.4
Spain	68.2	Italy	55.2	Northern Ireland	37.1	Britain	77.6	Ireland	33.5
Britain	66.6	France	54.4	Belgium	36.8	Spain	74.2	Belgium	31.0
France	61.3	Ireland	50.6	France	26.4	Ireland	74.2	Spain	30.1
Belgium	54.7	West Germany	49.1	Spain	24.4	United States	71.5	France	30.1
West Germany	52.6	Belgium	39.7	Italy	18.6	Northern Ireland	70.1	Italy	28.2
								European aggregate	36.9

Note: Statements read:
  1. I would give part of my income if I were certain that the money would be used to prevent environmental pollution. [% agreeing]
  2. I would agree to an increase in taxes if the extra money is used to prevent environmental pollution. [% agreeing]
  3. The Government has to reduce environmental pollution but it should not cost me any money. [% disagreeing]
  4. Protecting the environment and fighting pollution is less urgent than often suggested. [% disagreeing]

*Respondents are classified as "high" on the environmental concern index if they *"agree"* or *"strongly agree"* that (1) "I would be willing to give part of my income if I were sure that the money would be used to prevent environmental pollution," AND who *"disagree"* or *"strongly disagree"* with these statements: (1) "The government should reduce environmental pollution, but it should not cost me any money" and (2) "Protecting the environment and fighting pollution is less urgent than often suggested."

Source: 1990 World Values Survey.

income, and 70% agreed to an increase in taxes, "if the money is used to prevent environmental pollution." The Dutch (81%) and the Danes (71%) were
also the most likely to disagree with the idea that reducing environmental pollution "should not cost me any money." A clear majority of respondents in
every country disagreed with the statement that "protecting the environment
and fighting pollution is less urgent than often suggested," and here, too, the
Danes and Dutch rank close to the very top.

Some observers argue that the European experience with environmental
activism is no benchmark for evaluating environmentalism in Canada, or the
new world more generally (Hay & Haward, 1988). West European states, they
note, have a long historical record of "deep industrialism," and as a result the
main goal of European environmentalists is "recuperative." By contrast,
because new world countries lack any equivalent experience with "smoke-
stack industrialism," the environmental movements of the new world should
be characterized as "protective"; they aim to protect relatively unsullied
wilderness settings. This may be so; but publics in the new world, or at least
those in Canada and the United States, turn out to be just as committed as their
European counterparts to preventing environmental pollution. Notice that
Canadians, and Americans, rank relatively high on environmental concern on
three out of the four measures. Nearly three out of four Canadians, and about
the same proportion of Americans, agreed to give up income, and about two-
thirds indicated that they would agree to an increase in taxes. The only significant difference between Canadians and Americans lies in responses to the
last item: Canadians were more likely than Americans to disagree with the
idea that environmental concerns are "less urgent than often suggested."[14]
Furthermore, according to evidence from the broader WVS data, publics in
those countries that unquestionably did have long experience with "smoke-
stack industrialism"—Britain, West Germany, France, and Belgium—turn out
to be no more concerned about the environment than are Canadians or
Americans.[15]

If the surge of interest group activity over the last twenty or so years is any
indication, it would appear that public concern about the environment has
grown in tandem with the gradual spread of post-materialist value orientations.
It is possible, of course, that these two trends are merely coincidental. It is also
possible that environmental considerations have become increasingly salient
because publics in advanced industrial states have become less preoccupied
with their physical security and material gain and more concerned about their
quality of life. There is some empirical support for this line of interpretation.
As Figure 4-6 indicates, post-materialists are twice as likely as materialists to
score high on the environmental concern index, the composite measure of the
four items presented in Table 4-3. The correlation between post-materialist
value orientations and concern for the environment is remarkably consistent;
it holds in all of the European countries (gamma = .29) as well as in Canada
(gamma = .34) and the United States (gamma = .26). At the same time, it is
clear that structural factors play a role. Education is just as strongly related to

Figure 4-6   Concern for Environmental Protection by Value Type

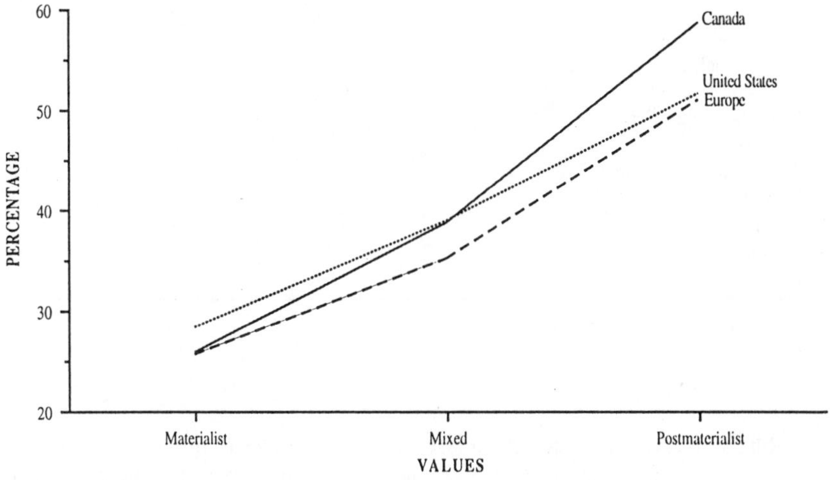

Source: 1990 World Values Survey.

environmental concern as is the value divide: the higher the level of education the more concerned people are about the environment (Europe, gamma = .31; Canada, gamma = .25; the United States, gamma = .31). Age is also related to environmental concern: younger people express greater concern than their older counterparts, but surprisingly, perhaps, the age effects are weaker than one might expect (Europe, gamma = -.11; United States, gamma = -.10), and in Canada there is almost no evidence at all of age effects (gamma = -.01).[16]

Which factors best explain environmental concern? Once again, multiple classification analysis helps to answer that question. As before, keep in mind that MCA indicates both the simple correlations between the various predictors of environmental concern (eta coefficients) and also shows the independent effect of each individual predictor after the effects of all the other predictors have been controlled for (beta coefficients). The results of the MCA, reported in Table 4-4, indicate that the value divide and education are the best predictors of environmental concern. Political interest is also relevant; those who are more interested in politics express greater concern about the environment. But other factors are also important. Levels of financial satisfaction and income level come into play: those who earn more and are more satisfied with their financial position score higher on the environmental concern index. Those living in urban centres, those working in non-manual occupations, and women score significantly higher than the rural populace, manual workers, and men. Post-materialist value orientations do have a significant impact on

Table 4-4 Multiple Classification Analysis (All 12 Countries):
Predictors of Concern for Environment

Predictors	Eta	Beta
Postmaterialism	.16	.12
Interest in Politics	.11	.08
Financial Satisfaction	.09	.06
Education	.18	.12
Age	.06	.03
Income	.13	.06
Occupation	.14	.06
Urban/rural	.04	.04
Male	.04	.05

Source: 1990 World Values Survey.

public sensitivities to ecological issues, but so too do structural factors. In this instance, age turns out to be a much less important factor, but interest in politics, the value divide, and education—each of which is demonstrably linked to the pervasive changes already described—are all linked to environmental concern.

To conclusively demonstrate that there is a connection between the structural and value changes and *all* of the various causes taken up by new social movements would require a separate analysis for each and every group. The case of environmentalism, though, is sufficient to illustrate the central point: what separates citizens in advanced industrial states from publics elsewhere is not the extent to which people care about the environment; it is the greater willingness of publics in advanced industrial states to give up something in order to halt ecological degradation. Certainly, these publics are far better positioned to make these sacrifices. People who have more can give up more; most citizens in advanced industrial states do not live at, or even close to, the subsistence level. But what explains the differences between people within advanced industrial states? Why is it that some are more likely than others to make these sacrifices? Part of the answer, it seems, has to do with the emerging value divide. Post-materialists are somewhat more likely than materialists to express their approval of the environmental movement, by a ratio of about 1.4 to 1. The truly striking finding is that post-materialists are *seven times* more likely than materialists to be *active* members of an environmental group (Nevitte & Kanji, 1995).

Civil Permissiveness

The declining confidence in governmental and non-governmental institutions, the rising levels of protest potential among publics, and the spread of new social movements collectively point to fundamental changes in the political cultures of advanced industrial states. Do these changes mean that traditional standards of acceptable conduct are disappearing, and that publics have turned in increasing numbers to an "anything goes" attitude towards public life?

The 1981 and 1990 WVS shed some light on that question. Both surveys presented publics with a list of "permissive" actions and asked respondents to indicate whether they thought each action could "always be justified," was "never justified," or "something in between." As is often the case with this grab-bag format for questions, responses tend to cluster into a variety of groups. In this case, one such coherent cluster reflects attitudes to "civil permissiveness," the idea that people will "free ride" at public expense, or put their own interests before the public welfare if they think they can get away with it.[17] Specifically, this civil permissiveness cluster combines responses to five questions: claiming government benefits that you are not entitled to; avoiding a fare on public transport; cheating on taxes if you have the chance; keeping money that you have found; and lying in your own interest.

If the rise of protest potential, the spread of new social movements, and the erosion of confidence in institutions is symptomatic of an underlying collapse of traditional norms—a rise in civil permissiveness—then one would expect to find evidence of corresponding changes in the levels of civil permissiveness. These changes would have to be consistent in both direction and scope with the shifts that are demonstrably taking place in these other domains. The basic findings, reported in Table 4-5, fall short of that explanation. It is true that, on average, there has been *some* change and the overall direction of change is towards greater civil permissiveness. But it is also clear, on closer inspection, that this average figure is somewhat inflated by two idiosyncratic cases (Italy and Belgium). Regardless of whether one relies on stringent or relaxed criteria, there is little evidence of *uniform* across-the-board increases in civil permissiveness of the magnitude that one would expect. In seven of the twelve cases, the scope of the changes can only be described as minuscule; they are so small that they might be attributable to measurement error. And in three of the twelve cases (Britain, Northern Ireland, and Denmark), the direction of the changes turns out to be the opposite of what one would expect. More striking than the changes is the cross-time stability of levels of civil permissiveness.

It is entirely possible, of course, that attitudes towards civil permissiveness really are a part of the syndrome of changes that has already been documented, despite the apparent ambiguity of the results reported in Table 4-5. Orientations to civil permissiveness, for example, could be lagging behind the other changes. Then again, the connections between civil permissiveness and changes in other domains may simply be indirect ones, with not enough done to flesh out precisely where those connections lie. Civil permissiveness, for example, could still be related to education or the post-materialist value divide, the structural and value shifts that are more directly connected to protest potential, confidence in institutions, and the other benchmarks of polit-

Table 4-5 The State Of Civil Permissiveness in 12 Advanced Industrial States (Percentages)

Country	One or More Behaviours Is Justified			Two or More Behaviours Are Justified		
	1981	1990	% Change	1981	1990	% Change
France	45.7	47.5	+1.8	25.7	26.2	+0.5
Britain	29.2	22.5	-6.7	14.8	9.6	-5.2
W. Germany	31.2	32.7	+1.5	15.4	17.5	+2.1
Italy	27.4	38.7	+11.3	9.9	17.5	+7.6
Netherlands	32.9	37.9	+5.0	14.4	17.8	+3.4
Denmark	22.2	19.7	-2.5	9.2	6.6	-2.6
Belgium	37.4	52.5	+15.1	18.9	29.1	+10.2
Spain	40.4	43.3	+2.9	20.4	21.3	+0.9
Ireland	20.7	23.4	+2.7	13.7	8.6	-5.7
N. Ireland	18.4	17.7	-0.7	6.6	6.0	-0.6
European aggregate	33.6	37.9	+4.3	15.5	18.2	+2.7
United States	32.5	32.7	+0.2	12.3	12.3	—
Canada	40.9	44.2	+3.3	18.6	19.1	+0.5

Note: The "civil permissiveness" scale is operationalized using the following five items (items that cluster together as one dimension when factor analyzed using varimax rotation with principle components analysis): cheating on tax if you have the chance (factor loading = .65) + avoiding a fare on public transport (factor loading = .63) + keeping money that you have found (factor loading = .58) + lying in your own interest (factor loading = .58) + claiming government benefits which you are not entitled to.

Each item on the civil permissiveness scale ranges from a low of 1, indicating that such an action is *never* justified, to a high of 10, indicating that such an action is *always* justified. Before creating the latent variable—civil permissiveness—each individual indicator is coded into a dummy variable (i.e., 1 to 5 = 0 and 6 to 10 = 1).

Source: 1981 and 1990 World Values Surveys.

ical change. The problem is that a far more detailed search for these possibilities comes up empty; there is no evidence of *any* indirect connections. When it comes to education, for example, the correlations between civil permissiveness and level of education are weak at best (Europe, gamma = .12), and are weaker still in Canada (gamma = .05) and the United States (gamma = .05). The connections between civil permissiveness and the value divide are similarly limp for the North American publics (Canada, gamma = .09; United States, gamma = -.01), though there is some evidence that they might be more relevant to the value divide in Europe (gamma = .18). Civil permissiveness, however, plainly is related to age; the young are much more permissive than the old (Europe, gamma = -.3; Canada, gamma = -.31; United States, gamma = -.26). Identifying long-term generational shifts is difficult under any circumstances. Here, though, the *presence* of powerful age effects and the *absence* of clear links with both education and the value divide suggest a life-cycle rather than generational interpretation: as people get older they become less permissive in these particular respects.

Even if civil permissiveness is not an integral part of the long-term changes in political orientations, Table 4-5 nonetheless indicates remarkable cross-national variations in absolute levels of civil permissiveness. The French, Belgian, and Spanish publics, for example, plainly exhibit much higher levels of civil permissiveness than do the Danes or the British. If received wisdom is any guide, there is reason to suppose that law-abiding, deferential, traditional Canadians, people with a history of collectivist orientations, would rank relatively low on the dimension of civil permissiveness. There is certainly some expectation that they would rate lower than Americans (Lipset, 1990). Such traits may have accurately characterized Canadians in the past, but there is no evidence whatsoever to indicate that contemporary Canadians are less permissive than most of their European counterparts. If anything, Canadian levels of civic permissiveness are *higher* than those found in most European countries, and they are significantly higher than in the United States.[18]

Orientations towards Change

The indications are that the values of Canadians and of publics in other advanced industrial states are changing, but this does not mean that people like facing the uncertainties that changes bring. Nor does it mean that everyone is equally accepting of change. Indeed, it is sometimes argued that part of the collective Canadian psyche is a distaste for change. Lipset, for instance, suggests that Canadians "are more hesitant than Americans to experiment and to introduce change in political, economic and moral affairs" (1963: 530). Is there any direct evidence of significant cross-national variations in attitudes to change? Are some publics more accepting of change than others? The WVS do not provide any cross-time data that make it possible to track such shifts directly, but the 1990 survey did ask respondents about both their general orientations to the idea of change and their attitudes to political change.

Table 4-6 pulls together a great deal of evidence based on responses to three different questions about change. Each one presented respondents with contrasting statements anchored at the opposite ends of a ten-point scale; respondents were asked to select the position (choose a number on the scale) that best reflected their own view.[19] The first asked about reactions to change: "When changes occur in my life I ... *worry* about the difficulties they may cause [1 on the ten-point scale] ... or ... I *welcome* the possibility that something new is happening [at the 10 end of the ten-point scale]. The first two columns in Table 4-6 report the cross-national responses to that question, they provide no support whatsoever for the stereotype that Canadians are averse to the general idea of change. In fact, Canadians seem to be more likely than other publics, including Americans, to "welcome" change, and they are less likely than most to "worry about the difficulties that changes may cause." The

Table 4-6 Attitudes towards Change in 12 Advanced Industrial Countries (Percentages)

Country	When Changes Occur, I ... (1)		Which Ideas Are Better? (2)		With Change, Be ... (3)	
	Welcome	Worry	New	Old	Bold	Cautious
France	30.5	19.2	12.8	23.1	22.5	28.6
Britain	28.7	17.6	15.1	21.2	27.4	20.5
West Germany	27.7	24.9	15.8	28.9	38.1	21.4
Italy	33.6	18.9	20.4	25.2	40.3	16.6
Netherlands	32.9	9.2	13.7	9.2	37.0	9.6
Denmark	35.5	12.9	17.6	14.0	33.0	12.9
Belgium	29.6	21.8	18.4	25.7	30.2	26.5
Spain	21.9	24.9	23.8	22.0	18.8	32.3
Ireland	28.0	26.1	19.2	31.9	21.2	32.5
N. Ireland	22.1	17.8	12.6	24.9	16.9	26.5
European aggregate	28.3	20.9	18.6	23.2	28.8	24.1
United States	27.6	16.3	11.9	26.2	19.5	27.2
Canada	41.9	15.0	19.1	22.6	25.7	33.0
English	40.4	14.1	18.3	23.1	25.7	28.9
French	43.8	18.1	15.3	22.0	21.3	47.4
New Canadians	44.8	14.9	26.0	22.7	30.2	30.5

Note: These data are based on three separate ten point scales:
1. Those that scored 8 or higher and 3 or lower on a scale ranging from 1 to 10, where 1 indicates that "when changes occur in one's life, they worry about the difficulties they may cause" and 10 indicates that "when changes occur in one's life, they welcome the possibility that something new is beginning."
2. Those that scored 8 or higher and 3 or lower on a scale ranging from 1 to 10, where 1 indicates that "ideas that have stood the test of time are generally best" and 10 indicates that "new ideas are generally better than old ones."
3. Those that scored 8 or higher and 3 or lower on a scale ranging from 1 to 10, where 1 indicates that "one should be cautious about major changes in life" and 10 indicates that "one will never achieve much unless one acts boldly."
Source: 1990 World Values Surveys.

middle two columns of Table 4-6 indicate preferences about new and old ideas: do people think "ideas that have stood the test of time (*old ideas*) are generally best" or "*new* ideas are generally better than old ones"? On balance, more respondents are attracted to old ideas than to new ones, but Canadians, once again, turn out to be more like Europeans. They are significantly less conservative in this respect than Americans. The data from the third question about change—"one should be *cautious* about major changes in life" or "one will never achieve much unless one acts *boldly*"—are slightly more equivocal. In this case, more Canadians (19%) than Americans (12%) chose the "bold" response. At the same time, more Canadians (33%) than Americans (27%) give the "cautious" response. The explanation for this apparent paradox seems to have to do with the very substantial variations between the three Canadian communities. Francophone Canadians are far more likely (47%) than either anglophones (29%) or new Canadians (31%) to say that one "should be cautious." On this dimension, the differences between anglophone Canadians and Americans are trivial, and are not statistically significant.

The absence of 1981 benchmark data is problematic, of course, but there is powerful indirect evidence that attitudes to change are themselves related to the other pervasive shifts. Further, openness to change may well play a supporting role in the generationally driven transformations that have already been described. Recall that the plausibility of the generational shift argument hinges on at least three minimal conditions being met: (1) there must be evidence of a strong tie with age, because generational effects should leave an age-related footprint; (2) there must be some link with an indicator of structural change like education; and (3) there should be a connection with the post-materialist value divide that others have shown to be generationally driven. There is no guarantee, of course, that the long-term generational change interpretation necessarily applies even if all three conditions are met. The point is rather that the generational interpretation is harder to sustain if the evidence falls short of these conditions.

A closer analysis of responses to all three of the attitudes to change indicators reveals a striking and stable pattern: attitudes to change are clearly and significantly related to age, to education, *and* to the materialist/post-materialist value divide. For instance, on the item concerning new ideas versus old ideas, post-materialists are far more likely to prefer new ideas and materialists to prefer ideas that have stood the test of time. This basic relationship between new ideas/old ideas and the value divide holds in every country. The strength of the relationship varies (Europe, gamma = .16; Canada, gamma = .12; United States, gamma = .09), but the direction is always the same. Similar findings emerge for age effects: the young are always significantly more likely than the old to prefer new ideas (Europe, gamma = -.24; Canada, gamma = -.14; United States, gamma = -.10). And those with higher levels of formal education are significantly more likely to prefer new ideas (Europe, gamma = .11; Canada, gamma = .17; United States, gamma = .07).

Replicating that same analysis with the other two indicators of attitudes towards change, the welcome/worry and bold/cautious items (see Table 4-6), produces the same patterns yet again. In every case there is clear evidence of consistent age effects, education effects, and value divide effects.[20] The strength of these relationships varies from one setting to the next, but the important point is that all of the relationships are in the same direction. It is likely, then, that the increasing willingness of publics to accept change is part and parcel of the other long-term transformations.

We can take this exploration of the theme of change one step further by asking: Is this greater general willingness to embrace change accompanied by any specific preferences about the direction or scope of *political* change? The WVS do not contain questions that allow us to disentangle the nuances

Table 4-7 Attitudes towards Political Change in Twelve Advanced Industrial Countries

Country	Government Should Be More Open (% Strongly Agreeing)	Political Reform Is Too Rapid (% Disagreeing)	Society Must Be Defended against All Subversive Forces
France	33.3	44.6	21.1
Britain	43.6	45.5	13.8
West Germany	40.2	37.6	31.8
Italy	37.9	55.0	9.8
Netherlands	19.8	63.5	23.9
Denmark	47.7	38.8	21.6
Belgium	31.3	35.8	20.9
Spain	45.6	39.7	6.1
Ireland	46.2	61.0	19.9
Northern Ireland	44.9	51.4	20.6
European aggregate	39.2	44.6	16.9
United States	34.6	46.6	17.8
Canada	49.6	44.1	13.2
English	52.4	44.3	14.9
French	41.6	39.1	9.4
New Canadians	48.9	48.8	12.3

Source: 1990 World Values Surveys.

of political change in any great detail, but the 1990 surveys provide some data that help to shed light on the issue. Respondents were asked to indicate whether they agreed or disagreed with two statements both of which seem to resonate with the kinds of issues Canadians were engaged in throughout the 1980s and beyond: (1) "Our government should be made much more open to the public," and (2) "Political reform in this country is moving too rapidly." The WVS also asked a standard battery of questions tapping preferences about the *style* of social change. Respondents were presented with four options and asked to select the one coming closest to their own opinion:

1. The entire way our society is organized must be changed by revolutionary action.
2. Our society must be gradually improved by reforms.
3. Our present society must be valiantly defended against all subversive forces.
4. Don't know.

The aggregate responses are summarized in Table 4-7. The statement that "our government should be more open to the public" gets nearly unanimous support from citizens in each of the twelve countries; 86% of Europeans agreed with it, as did 91% of Canadians and 83% of Americans. The first column of

Table 4-7 reports the proportion of each public indicating they *strongly agree* with the statement, and these data are revealing: about half of all Canadians, a larger proportion than for any other public surveyed, expressed strong support for more open government.

The other results reported in Table 4-7 are less clearcut, but they are nonetheless worth considering. Canadians are about evenly divided when it comes to judgements about the *rate* of political reform. They are less likely than the Dutch or the Irish to think that "political reform is too rapid"; Canadian responses are close to the European average, and the Canadian–American differences are trivial. On the third indicator, however (the question asking respondents if they want radical reform, gradual reform, or to defend society against all "subversive forces"), the cross-national variations are far sharper. Few respondents (about 4%) in any country express much enthusiasm for radical reform; a clear majority want gradual reform (Europe, 79%; Canada, 82%; United States, 76%). Publics differ most on the "defend against subversive forces" item, the response indicating how strongly people feel about the status quo. Here, Canadians seem to be significantly *less* troubled than either Americans or the majority of Europeans about defending society against "subversive forces."

Are these orientations to *political* change related to age, education, and the value divide, the same factors that have repeatedly been shown to be linked to the other, more general, attitudes to change? On the whole, the answer is yes, they are. Regardless of nationality, those with higher levels of education are much more likely than others to want more open government, they are less likely to think that political reform is too rapid, and they are less likely to express concern about defending society from subversive forces. The impact of the value divide, the differences between materialists and post-materialists, conforms to the same predictable pattern: post-materialists want more open government, are less likely to think reform is too rapid, and it is materialists who are far more likely to want to defend society against subversive forces.[21] The relationships between age and orientations to political change are somewhat weaker and less stable. But in general these, too, operate in the direction one would predict: the young, more than the old, want more open government, are less opposed to rapid change, and are less worried about defending society against subversive forces.

Two essential conclusions emerge from this analysis. First, Canadians are *not* uniquely resistant to change. In general, they are as open, and in many instances more open, to change than most other publics, including Americans. That finding applies to both general orientations towards change and attitudes about political change. Second, orientations towards change are consistently connected to the same background factors: age, education, and the value divide. The implication is that the increasing willingness to embrace change is itself a part of the broader political transformations that have been detailed to this point.

Challenging Political Authority

This investigation of shifting political orientations has identified two dimensions that seem to be particularly central, and there are indications that each may be a part of a long-term, generationally related transformation. Chapter 3 demonstrated a systematic decline in public confidence in a variety of institutions, particularly governmental ones, and this chapter has presented evidence that citizens are increasingly inclined to engage in unconventional forms of political participation. One interpretation of these synchronized changes is that, together, they signify fundamental shifts in orientations towards different aspects of political authority. The first shift seems to represent the institutional face of these changes. Waning public confidence in institutions is not indiscriminate; it does not apply to any and all institutions. It is directed more at those institutions whose role it is to mediate authority relations within the state: the police, parliament, the civil service, and the military. The rising levels of unconventional political behaviours signify the participatory face of citizen challenges to political authority. Is there any way to verify this interpretation?

Chapter 2 suggested that citizen orientations towards authority are important for at least two general reasons: because they are fundamental to understanding the dynamics of democratic societies; and because disturbances in them are symptomatic of the rhythms of advanced industrialism. Some initial cross-time empirical findings seem to support the claim that advanced industrial states have been experiencing "disturbances in authority orientations." In both 1981 and 1990, respondents were asked if "greater respect for authority" in the future would be "a good thing," "a bad thing," or "don't you mind?" Recall that those data indicated a *decline* in the number of citizens responding that greater respect for authority was a good thing. If the *rising* levels of unconventional behaviour and the rising levels of non-confidence in governmental institutions really are two faces of shifting orientations towards authority, then it should be possible to determine whether each of these dimensions is empirically related to the general indicator of orientations towards authority used in Chapter 2. To be more precise, the expectation is that these relationships should be negative: as non-confidence in governmental institutions *rises*, respondents should be *less likely* to say that greater respect for authority is a good thing. Similarly, those with *high* levels of support for unconventional political participation should be *less likely* than others to say that greater respect for authority is a good thing. Some of the key findings concerning these connections are summarized in Figure 4-7.

Does the evidence provide any support for this general line of speculation? Plainly, yes. First, protest behaviour is *negatively* related to the general indicator of orientations towards authority: the more inclined people are to engage in protest behaviour, the less likely they are to say that greater respect for authority in the future is a good thing. And second, non-confidence in governmental institutions is also *negatively* related to the general indicator of

Figure 4-7   The Congruency between General and Political Orientations toward Authority

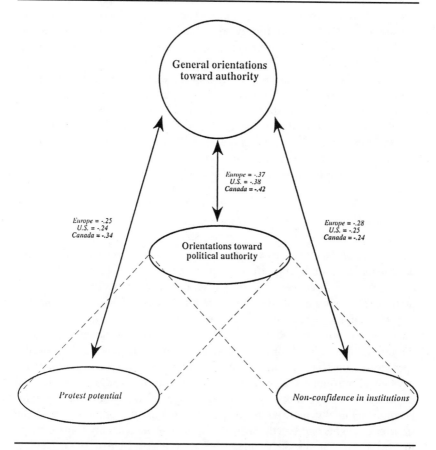

Source: 1981 and 1990 World Values Surveys.
Note: The above figures represent merged gamma coefficients for 1981 and 1990.

respect for authority. The findings are statistically significant, and the consistency of the patterns is truly striking. The very same pattern holds in every single country in both 1981 and 1990. Out of the forty-eight pairs of relationships examined—twelve countries at two time points—all forty-eight work in the predicted way (see Appendix 4-A). When the institutional and participatory indicators are combined into a single measure of political orientations, the results are, not surprisingly, even stronger. The clear implication, and one that will become central to this analysis, is that both non-confidence in governmental institutions and protest behaviour really do appear to capture different aspects of orientations towards political authority.

Aside from this extremely powerful and intriguing result, there are other noteworthy findings. There is cross-time stability; where there are strong associations in 1981 there are typically also strong associations in 1990. As always, there are some significant cross-national variations. The results for Ireland, for instance, are uniformly powerful. Results are also strong in Spain. On balance, the Canadian results are stronger than those in the United States, and within Canada the francophone results are most powerful. These variations raise other questions. Why, for example, are the relationships stronger in some countries than others? One candidate explanation might be that authority orientations are particularly coherent in Catholic countries. But a more detailed probing of the data indicates that the Catholic–Protestant divide does not seem to explain these differences. As will become apparent in the analysis that follows, shifting orientations to political authority form only one part of a more comprehensive pattern of change.

Conclusions

The weight of the evidence assembled in these last two chapters points to the conclusion that significant shifts in political values have taken place in the last decade or so. It is conceivable, of course, that there are quite specific, even unique, reasons Canadians have become more assertive, less compliant, and why they appear to be less confident in their governmental institutions, more interested in politics, and more willing than before to pursue their goals through unconventional forms of political action. There may also be Canada-specific reasons for the surging interest in new issues, growing support for new social movements, as well as for the erosion of parochial identities and the emergence of cosmopolitan ones. One suggestion is that Canadians have become politically more combative as a result of the introduction of the Charter of Rights and Freedoms in 1982. There is undoubtedly some merit to that argument (Brodie & Nevitte, 1993(a), 1993(b); Cairns, 1993; Nevitte, 1991). Unquestionably, the introduction of the Charter has opened up new avenues for a qualitatively different form of political participation, avenues that rely less on the rugged political arithmetic of majoritarianism and give Canada's courts a more prominent role in resolving policy disagreements. It is difficult to argue, however, that the Charter could have unleashed all of the shifts that have been documented in the last two chapters, not least of all because of the sheer scope of those shifts. It is unlikely, for example, that the introduction of the Charter could be responsible for rising public interest in politics, and even less likely that it could be linked to the decline of parochial identities and the emergence of cosmopolitan orientations. There is also the problem of timing. There is evidence of low confidence in governmental and non-governmental institutions, high protest potential, and high participatory potential *before* the Charter of Rights and Freedoms came into effect. Presumably, the Charter could not explain events, or cause dynamics, that preceded it. But even if we wanted to attribute the rise of protest potential to the

Charter, there is other awkward evidence to be dealt with. If the Charter contributed to the protest potential of Canadians, then one would expect Canadians' protest potential to have risen in the period immediately following the Charter. It did. But what is also evident is that protest potential increased even faster in other countries, countries that had no intervening constitutional event equivalent to the introduction of the Charter.

The more compelling interpretation, perhaps, is that the changes Canadians experienced in their political world over the last decade or so are a part of a broad transformation that is taking place throughout all advanced industrial states. Most persuasive here is the consistency of the patterns of change. The cross-time evidence indicates that citizens in nearly every advanced industrial state are becoming more interested in politics. Confidence in institutions is falling not just in Canada but in other states too. Publics throughout these advanced industrial states are increasingly inclined to turn to unconventional forms of political action. And in all of these areas the shifts are empirically related in the same ways to the same set of background factors. Even where no cross-time data are available, as with support for new movements, those background indicators have the same effect in different national settings. Such an interpretation emphatically does *not* mean that there is nothing unique about the dynamics of Canadian political life. Citizens in every country face issues that are peculiar to their own setting, and idiosyncratic institutional arrangements and inherited practices give common dynamics a particular twist and a unique public face. Moreover, the pace and scope of these changes clearly do vary. What the evidence does suggest is that Canadians, like publics elsewhere, are exposed to the broader political rhythms of advanced industrialism, and their political life is shaped by the combination of structural and value changes that is common to those states.

One theme that helps to bring order and coherence to this complex pattern of multiple shifts is that Canadians, like their counterparts in other settings, are experiencing turbulence in authority relations. Moreover, at least two key benchmarks of the political face of this turbulence—declining confidence in hierarchical institutions and rising levels of protest potential—are both linked to age effects, education effects, and the materialist/post-materialist value divide. If the logic of generational change outlined in Chapter 2 has any weight at all, the implication is that the value changes documented so far are less likely to be short-term blips on the political landscape, transient shifts, and more likely to be signals of a longer-term, generationally related transformation.

What do these results tell us about Canadian–American value change? Several things: first of all, some of the evidence presented in the last two chapters challenges the stereotype that Canadians are a passive lot, wedded to the status quo or peculiarly deferential. Canadians are more interested in politics than Americans, and a higher proportion of Canadians subscribe to the post-materialist value orientations that Inglehart (1990(a)) suggests signal directions of future change. And when it comes to the institutional and participatory faces of political authority—confidence in political institutions and protest potential—there is nothing to indicate that Canadians are more likely than Americans to trail along willingly, and passively concede to the demands of their traditional political leaders. Significantly, too, there is no evidence indicating that Canadian orientations lag those of their American counterparts, at least when it comes to the aspects of political life examined so far. If anything, Canadian orientations appear to *lead* in several categories. Certainly, Canadian levels of national pride are lower than those found in the United States, but Canadians' levels of national pride are higher than those of publics in nine other advanced industrial states. More importantly, perhaps, there is nothing to indicate that Canadians are particularly averse to new ideas. Canadians are more likely than Americans to say that they "welcome change" and to think that "new ideas are better than old ones," at least they were in 1990.

This analysis of changing political values could undoubtedly be taken much further. The data could be analyzed in greater detail, subjected to more fine-grained statistical evaluations, and sliced in different ways. Even so, the results tell an important story as they stand. The primary goal now is to take the analysis in a different direction: to expand the *scope* of the investigation into value change and to explore the possibility that value changes in one domain, the polity, may be related to value changes in others. Our focus now switches away from the analysis of political values and towards an exploration of economic values.

NOTES

[1] This was the Royal Commission on Electoral Reform and Party Financing, struck in November 1989.

[2] The 1981 World Values Surveys found that only extremely small proportions of publics in any of the twenty-two countries surveyed said that they had, or might, engage in "personal violence" or "damage windows." Consequently, the 1990 World Values Surveys dropped these items from the standard battery.

[3] Not surprisingly, another finding is that the vast majority of Europeans (76% in 1981) and North Americans (Americans, 88%; Canadians, 87% in 1981) report that they either "have" signed, or "might" sign a petition. By 1990, willingness to sign a petition increased slightly; in that year only 8% of Canadians and 8% of Americans said that they would "never" sign a petition. In fact, some suggest that the signing of petitions is now so widespread that it no longer qualifies as a useful indicator of protest behaviour (see Van den Broek & Heunks, 1993). Our analysis uses a more stringent standard of protest potential.

[4] As the following data indicate, the aggregate protest potential of Canadians is not skewed by large variations within the Canadian population:

Protest Behavior within Canada (Percentages)

Type of Behavior	English 1981	English 1990	% Change	French 1981	French 1990	% Change	New Canadians 1990
Those who would never:							
Join in boycotts	38.8	32.6	-6.2	44.3	36.9	-7.4	34.8
Attend unlawful demonstrations	40.9	37.4	-3.5	42.3	30.7	-11.6	35.6
Join unofficial strikes	78.6	66.0	-12.6	75.1	62.6	-12.5	65.2
Occupy buildings or factories	83.2	80.4	-2.8	75.2	67.8	-7.4	74.7
Those who would do at least 1 of 4 protest behaviours	23.3	30.7	+7.4	24.3	38.2	+13.9	32.5

Note: The 1981 data for new Canadians were not available.
Source: 1981 and 1990 World Values Surveys.

[5] When it comes to reluctance to engage in protest behaviour, though, a quite different picture emerges. The proportions of Canadians and Americans who would "never do" any of these actions "under any circumstances" are virtually identical for each value type.

[6] These differences hold across a variety of categories, and the age and value type effects are also consistent. For example, just over half (52%) of the francophone post-materialists, compared with 41% of anglophones and 40% of new Canadians, indicate that they "would do" at least one of the four protest behaviours. And just 31% said they would "never do" any of these four actions, compared to 53% of their anglophone and 44% of their new Canadian post-materialist counterparts.

[7] In fact, for both the Canadian and American publics, the simple correlations between education and protest potential—Canada, gamma = .24; United States, gamma = .21—are stronger than for value type and protest potential—Canada, gamma = .16; United States, gamma = .17.

[8] For useful overviews of these different explanations see Dalton, Kuechler, and Burklin, (1990), and Klandermans (1991).

[9] The extent to which these movements are genuinely new, and a precise characterization of the ideological core of these new movements, are matters of debate. Some claim, for instance, that the origins of many of these movements reach back into the nineteenth century (Brand, 1990; Rochon, 1990). Others contend that they are new in the sense that they can be better described as post-ideological, as they lack the clear prescriptive characteristics of doctrines associated with earlier protest movements. As Keuchler and colleagues point out, the new protesters' "concept of the future society is largely negatively defined. They know what they do not want, but they are unsure and inconsistent with respect to what they want in operational detail," and "they do not picture a better future just for themselves, for their group. They envision a better soci-

ety for all" (Dalton et al., 1990: 281). Alternatively, Offe (1987) argues that the new movements stand for "integrity, recognition and respect."

[10] People were asked to choose between five answers indicated on a response card: "Strongly disapprove," "Disapprove," "Approve," "Strongly approve," and "Don't know."

[11] "Strong" Approval Rates for Various Movements Ranked in Descending Order within Canada

Ecology (Conservation)		Peace (Disarmament)		Human Rights (Third World)		Womens' Rights	
Group	%	Group	%	Group	%	Group	%
French	58.3	French	50.3	French	65.8	French	50.0
New		New		New		New	
Canadians	56.8	Canadians	37.0	Canadians	62.3	Canadians	36.7
English	51.8	English	37.0	English	54.6	English	31.9

Note: The question read: "There are a number of groups and movements looking for-public support. For each of the following movements, … can you tell me whether you Approve strongly, Approve, Disapprove, Disapprove strongly, or Don'tknow."

Source: 1990 World Values Survey.

[12] In fact, there are some overlapping memberships. A significant proportion of respondents, about one in ten, report that they "belong" to more than one group.

[13] As Kuechler and Dalton (1990) note, it is difficult to isolate which particular contextual factors explain why ecological parties have been successful in some national settings but not in others. Differences in electoral systems may be important, they suggest, because those countries in which "green" parties have been successful all have proportional representation.

[14] Within Canada's three communities the results are as follows. Percentage agreeing to "give up part of my income": new Canadians 76%; anglophones 76%; francophones 66%. Percentage agreeing to "increase taxes": francophones 67%; new Canadians 65%; anglophones 62%. Percentage disagreeing with "should not incur any cost": anglophones 49%; new Canadians 48%; francophones 43%. Percentage disagreeing with "the environment is less urgent problem than sometimes suggested": new Canadians 82%; anglophones 80%; francophones 69%.

[15] For an intriguing analysis of the role of institutional factors in the politicization of environmental issues in the United States and Canada, see Hoburg and Harrison (1991).

[16] When we break out the data by age cohort, it becomes apparent that in Canada concern about the environment follows a bell curve that peaks with the 45–54 age group.

[17] The "clusters," or dimensions, are empirically identified through standard factor analytic procedures—varimax rotation with principal components extraction. Respondents were asked to use a ten-point scale to indicate whether they felt the actions were "always justified" (score of 1 on the ten-point scale), "never justified" (10 on the scale), or something in between. The factor loadings were as follows: claiming

government benefits .56; avoiding a fare on public transport .63; cheating on taxes .65; keeping money found .58; lying in your own interest .58. Responses to all items form a reliable additive scale, alpha = .66.

[18] There are significant differences in levels of civil permissiveness found in Canada's three communities. There have also been changes in those levels between 1981 and 1990.

The State of Civil Permissiveness within Canada (Percentages)

Group	One or More Behaviours Is Justified			Two or More Behaviours Are Justified		
	1981	1990	% Change	1981	1990	% Change
English	34.8	40.9	+6.1	13.5	18.5	+5.0
French	57.4	57.3	-0.1	32.2	23.6	-8.6
New Canadians	—	39.9	—	—	16.0	—

[19] This question format can be difficult to interpret because it is not always clear whether respondents are attracted to one end of the scale or repelled by the other. For that reason, we omit those responses that fell in the middle range of the scale, that is, scored 4, 5, 6, or 7 on the 10-point scale; these mid-range responses are the most difficult to interpret. We also report on both polarities. The reader should keep in mind that respondents had the option of answering that they "didn't know."

[20] The data for these other relationships (gammas) are as follows: welcome/worry with materialist/post-materialist value change (Europe = .23, U.S. = .08, Canada = .02); welcome/worry with age (Europe =- .24, U.S. =- .06, Canada =- .12); welcome/worry with education (Europe = .20, U.S. = .10, Canada = .03); bold/cautious with materialist/post-materialist value change (Europe = .22, U.S. = .10, Canada = .18); bold/cautious with age (Europe = -.21, U.S. =-.08, Canada =-.07); bold/cautious with education (Europe = .14, U.S. = .12, Canada = .21).

[21] These data have to be interpreted with some caution because there is almost certainly some artificial inflation of the post-materialist/open government correlations owing to autocorrelation; recall that one component of the the post-materialism index has to do with preferences about having "more say in government."

Appendix 4-A Protest Behaviour in Advanced Industrial Countries

Type of Behaviour	% Change (1990–1981)											
	France	Britain	West Germany	Italy	Nether-lands	Denmark	Belgium	Spain	Ireland	Northern Ireland	United States	Canada
Those who would never:												
Join in Boycotts	-3.0%	-9.4%	-6.1%	-21.4%	-5.5%	0.9%	-10.0%	5.8%	0.3%	3.2%	-11.3%	-6.4%
Attend Unlawful Demonstrations	-7.0%	-4.0%	-11.7%	-20.9%	-17.8%	-2.0%	-5.7%	-1.2%	-4.4%	-3.5%	-7.0%	-5.5%
Join Unofficial Strikes	1.5%	-3.4%	-0.4%	-12.7%	-8.0%	-2.6%	-6.6%	0.8%	1.6%	-1.1%	-13.7%	-12.7%
Occupy Buildings or Factories	0.2%	2.5%	3.0%	-8.8%	-1.6%	5.4%	-4.6%	-6.3%	-4.2%	0.9%	-7.4%	-4.5%
Those who would do at least 1 of 4 protest behaviours	5.0%	6.8%	5.9%	10.3%	12.7%	11.5%	9.9%	-1.6%	4.4%	4.5%	4.2%	8.9%

Source: 1981 and 1990 World Values Surveys.

Appendix 4-B The Links between General and Political Orientations toward Authority

Country	Links between General and Political Orientations towards Authority			Links Between General Orientations towards Authority and Protest Potential			Links between General Orientations towards Authority and Non-confidence in Institutions		
	1981	1990	Merged	1981	1990	Merged	1981	1990	Merged
France	-.37	-.31	-.34	-.32	-.30	-.31	-.27	-.12	-.21
Britain	-.39	-.36	-.37	-.32	-.28	-.29	-.26	-.27	-.26
W. Germany	-.32	-.29	-.31	-.29	-.22	-.25	-.21	-.19	-.20
Italy	-.41	-.27	-.34	-.28	-.17	-.24	-.34	-.22	-.27
Netherlands	-.38	-.33	-.35	-.29	-.34	-.30	-.22	-.07	-.16
Denmark	-.21	-.15	-.18	-.19	-.14	-.17	-.08	-.06	-.07
Belgium	-.23	-.31	-.29	-.12	-.18	-.16	-.19	-.21	-.20
Spain	-.45	-.41	-.42	-.34	-.30	-.31	-.38	-.32	-.34
Ireland	-.52	-.64	-.57	-.34	-.44	-.39	-.45	-.44	-.45
N. Ireland	-.58	-.36	-.47	-.24	-.13	-.19	-.51	-.39	-.44
United States	-.40	-.30	-.38	-.27	-.18	-.24	-.26	-.20	-.25
Canada	-.46	-.38	-.42	-.35	-.32	-.34	-.32	-.18	-.24
English	-.44	-.40	-.42	-.33	-.33	-.34	-.29	-.18	-.23
French	-.52	-.44	-.49	-.42	-.34	-.39	-.39	-.26	-.32
New Canadians	—	-.32	—	—	-.32	—	—	-.15	—

Note: The above figures are gamma coefficients.
Source: 1981 and 1990 World Values Survey.

5: Changing Economic Cultures?

Very substantial changes have taken place in the political values of publics in the advanced industrial states, but have these changes been accompanied by shifts in other domains? Part 3 shifts the focus and considers economic values. It begins with the broad view: Chapter 5 starts by considering citizens' orientations towards such general economic matters as the free market, competition, and support for the principle of meritocracy, and then explores conceptions of economic fairness and justice. The preliminary findings are that some changes in economic values have taken place, and these conform to a general pattern: public support for the idea of "meritocracy" is rising, and there are indications that citizens in these states are increasingly likely to attribute poverty to social injustice. None of these changes is as dramatic as those that have taken place in the realm of political values, but the direction of the shifts is consistent from one country to the next. Furthermore, detailed probing of the evidence suggests that these shifts in economic orientation are a part of the complex set of long-term value changes documented in the preceding chapters. Chapter 5 concludes by exploring in greater detail one issue that preoccupied Canadians for much of the decade: free trade. Are these broad-gauge economic values connected to support for continental integration?

Support for the Free Market

McClosky and Zaller identify capitalism and democracy as the principal components of the American ethos (1984: 17). These two themes, they contend, are grounded in complementary values and ideas: both emphasize the virtues of competition and freedom of exchange. As has already been indicated, most advanced industrial states subscribe to those general principals; all support to some degree the idea of free markets and the principles of liberal democracy, although the breadth and depth of these ideas varies from one public to the next. European countries, typically, give the state a larger role in the economy than Americans: Europeans are less tolerant of wide income disparities, they provide citizens with a more expansive set of social supports, and they spend more on the welfare state (Andrian, 1980). Public values in different countries, even ones as similar as these advanced industrial states, set different benchmarks for what is fair. Those values establish different standards for citizen rights: they strike different balances between collectivism and individualism, group and individual rights, and they reflect varying preferences about how much the state should help both business and the destitute (Heidenheimer, Heclo, & Adams, 1983).

The American experience is sometimes held out as the beacon of free enterprise in the Western world, but a closer examination of that case illustrates that attitudes about the distribution of wealth and entitlements are frequently contentious and not entirely stable. In the 1920s, for example, the free market ethos prevailed and issues of social, economic, and political equality captured little public interest. That changed with the depression of the 1930s; public control over the economy gained momentum with the New Deal and the Roosevelt administration. In the 1950s the pendulum swung back in the other direction in the United States, as in many other countries, and in the 1960s and 1970s seemed to reverse once again. Free market values retreated in the face of rising American public concern about the rights and equality of minorities. In the 1980s there was yet another reversal. The Reagan administration cut taxes, reduced government regulation of the economy, and justified the change of course by claiming that the administration had a mandate to revive individual initiative and reinforce the work ethic (Glazer, 1988; McClosky & Zaller, 1984). The patterns in some other countries, including Canada, roughly parallel the American experience. The conservatism of the Mulroney government, for example, claimed common cause with the Reagan administration and the Thatcher government in Britain (King, 1987; Kreiger, 1986). In the 1990s, public controversy about the proper scope of government involvement in the public economy has been prompted as much, perhaps, by government debt loads and high taxes as by ideology.

The economic values of Canadians are often judged against the American standard. According to Lipset, for example, Canadians "are less friendly than Americans to private enterprise" (1990: 134). Canadians certainly do have a history of placing greater reliance on direct state involvement in the economy, and there is no denying that levels of public ownership are higher in Canada, that welfare programs are more expansive, and that taxes are correspondingly higher (Lipset, 1990). In *Continental Divide*, Lipset assembles a great deal of evidence suggesting that Canadians are "economically more cautious and conservative than Americans" (1990: 127). "Americans," he suggests, "are more prone to take risks. The differences show up with respect to investment strategies, savings, insurance purchases, use of credit, and consumer behaviour" (1990: 123). For example, he observes that "Americans have been more disposed [than Canadians] to put their money in stocks" (1990: 123); "more Canadian capital is invested in the United States than is being invested by Americans in Canada" (1990: 125). Americans are also more likely than Canadians to use credit to make "a major purchase"; they are more likely to "borrow money from a bank," and less likely to "pay cash for everything" they buy (1990: 127).

The Canadian–American differences itemized by Lipset are undoubtedly genuine ones. Lipset's explanation for these variations is plausible, but the evidence raises complicated interpretive issues. To what extent, for example, do these variations reflect fundamental differences in the economic *values* of Canadians and Americans? Are there not other plausible explanations for these behavioural differences? Canadians and Americans live within different economic frameworks, frameworks with different rules, that can make the same economic behaviour rational in one setting but irrational in the other. Consider the case of taxes. Americans enjoy tax relief for interest on mortgages; Canadians do not. Thus, unlike Americans, Canadian homeowners have a stronger incentive to pay off their mortgages as quickly as possible. Consequently, differences in income levels aside, Canadians are likely to have less disposable income than their American counterparts, at least early on. If Canadians are relatively "house poor," they will have less discretionary income, less money available to invest in the stock markets. Arguably, then, it could be differences in tax rules, rather than different orientations towards risk-taking, that explain why "investment is a much more significant source of personal income in the United States than in Canada" (123).

Consider another example: why do Canadians invest outside of the country? More particularly, why do they invest so heavily in the United States? One explanation, again suggested by Lipset, is that Canadians have less faith in themselves and in the Canadian market. But there are other possible interpretations. Canadians might have a realistic assessment of the relative advantages and disadvantages of Canada and the United States as places to invest. The American market is bigger; it is the lifeline of the Canadian economy; the United States recovers more quickly from recessions; and the American dollar holds its value better in international money markets. Canadians may be more "risk averse," but the fact that they "send more money south than Americans send north" also means, surely, that Canadians and Americans are increasingly investing in the same places. The implication of that line of speculation is not that Canadians and Americans have different evaluations of risk and returns to capital, but that they have similar ones. Then again, does the fact that Canadians are more likely to pay for goods in cash, rather than use credit, really mean they are more cautious than Americans? Perhaps, but those different behaviours may also be a consequence of Canadian–American differences in the cost of borrowing money. Interest rates on loans are significantly lower in the United States. That being so, the fact that Canadians save more than Americans becomes less of a mystery: Canadians need to save more to avoid the relatively punitive rates of borrowing money to make big purchases.[1]

These examples emphatically do not mean Lipset is necessarily wrong in his assessments of economic values north and south of the border. He may well be right. But these examples do help to illustrate three general points that

Lipset himself raises. First, economic behaviours may or may not be a reliable indicator of basic differences in economic values. It is entirely possible that behavioural differences between Canadians and Americans flow from "structural variations"—the different economic situations in which Canadians and Americans find themselves. If Americans found themselves in Canada, they might behave in the same way as Canadians. Second, economic values, like other values, can change, and as Lipset points out, Canadian and American values may be less different now than they once were. In the past, there may have been genuine and sharp differences between the economic values of Canadians and Americans. But that does not mean that contemporary Canadians' and Americans' economic values are still different, or as different as they once were. Third, two-country comparisons tend to emphasize differences. When Canadian and American economic values are viewed in the broader perspective provided by the WVS twelve-country comparisons, the variations may seem less dramatic and less stark.

Where do Canadian, and American, economic values "fit" when they are placed in the larger context of publics in the other advanced industrial states? Consider, first, the findings from responses to two very broad sets of questions asked in the WVS. The first, reported in Table 5-1, indicates support for five items that, together, reflect what might be called "free-market" orientations. They come from a battery of questions in which respondents were presented with pairs of contrasting statements each of which anchored the opposite ends of a ten-point scale. Respondents were asked to choose a number, assign a score, indicating their views. A score of 10 meant that the respondent completely agreed with the option on one end of the scale, and a score of 1 indicated complete agreement with the statement at the other end (see Appendix 5-A for the full text of the questions).[2]

Overall, these findings show that Americans and Canadians are the most supportive of free markets. Of the twelve publics considered, Americans or Canadians rank either first or second in their free-market orientations, and in most cases the gap between the second and third countries is statistically significant. For example, the first column in Figure 5-1 indicates the proportion of each public choosing the item "Competition is Good. It stimulates people to work hard and develop new ideas" (as opposed to "Competition is harmful. It brings out the worst in people."), and on this dimension Canadians score highest. On the second item, "Individuals should take more responsibility for providing for themselves," Canadians and Americans rank well ahead of publics in *any* of the European countries. The same holds for the responses to Items 3 and 4, which deal respectively with support for private ownership and views about the rewards for work. The only exception to this general pattern emerges on the final item, "There should be greater incentives for individual effort." In this instance it is the Northern Irish who are slightly more likely than Americans to support greater incentives.

The consistently high clustering of the responses on these items can perhaps best be interpreted as indicating North American exceptionalism rather

Table 5-1 Support for Free Markets (percentages)

Country	Competition is good		Individuals should take more responsibility for providing for themselves		Private ownership of business and industry should be increased		In the long run, hard work usually brings a better life		There should be greater incentives for individual effort	
	Support	Don't	Support	Don't	Support	Don't	Support	Don't	Support	Don't
France	48.0	11.4	45.8	13.2	38.8	11.6	38.0	13.1	27.9	31.9
Britain	50.5	11.6	29.4	25.2	31.8	17.3	37.9	21.2	43.0	15.3
W. Germany	61.9	4.9	49.1	15.9	51.8	5.5	44.6	15.3	41.3	20.9
Italy	46.4	14.1	29.7	31.8	41.2	12.6	35.5	23.8	38.4	25.2
Netherlands	36.5	8.1	32.7	12.5	31.8	4.2	23.0	18.3	28.5	13.0
Denmark	48.9	9.5	42.5	10.7	49.9	5.9	15.1	31.1	40.5	14.7
Belgium	46.4	11.0	38.9	21.7	46.5	9.5	37.8	21.5	38.5	25.0
Spain	43.7	13.1	22.8	33.6	26.2	19.1	28.8	25.9	23.8	34.0
Ireland	56.0	9.0	37.4	22.8	45.0	9.5	44.7	21.4	46.3	20.7
N. Ireland	53.5	10.0	30.1	26.3	35.2	13.6	44.1	14.1	50.7	11.4
U.S.	64.4	6.9	60.6	8.9	62.7	4.8	60.3	8.8	47.0	13.0
Canada	66.0	6.8	51.4	13.8	57.9	6.6	55.5	13.3	53.4	17.2
English	65.3	6.1	50.7	12.8	57.4	6.2	58.0	10.7	56.7	13.7
French	72.4	6.2	61.0	11.4	63.9	5.5	48.9	17.7	42.2	28.4
New Canadians	59.9	8.7	42.3	20.3	51.3	9.1	53.7	16.8	57.2	14.7

Free market issues

Note: On a scale of 1 to 10, support = 8, 9, 10 and don't support = 1, 2, 3.
Source: 1990 World Values Survey.

than just American exceptionalism. Americans and Canadians are systematically different from their European counterparts. There are also some within-Canada variations, and these are intriguing for two reasons. First, francophones appear to be somewhat more supportive of the free-market items than anglophones or new Canadians, at least on three of the five items. Second, the within-country variations are relatively small, typically smaller than the variations between Europeans and North Americans, a finding that also suggests a coherent North American economic ethos. The responses reported in Table 5-1 come from questions that were asked only in 1990, so it is not possible to determine directly whether there have been significant cross-time changes in these orientations. But a background analysis of the connection between support for these items and age, post-materialist value orientations, and education suggests that if there have been cross-time shifts they are probably not a result of generational change. Older people and the better educated typically are slightly more likely than the young and the less well educated to favour free markets. But the correlations are all weak, and they are unstable, varying from one setting to the next. The same applies to post-materialist value orientations.

The second WVS indicator providing a glimpse of general economic values has to do with "meritocracy," and for this item cross-time data are available. In both 1981 and 1990, respondents were presented with the following scenario: "Imagine two secretaries, of the same age, doing practically the same job. One finds out that the other earns $50 a week more than she does. The better paid secretary, however, is quicker, more efficient and more reliable at her job. In your opinion, is it *fair* or *not fair* that one secretary is paid more than the other?"

The orientation tapped by this question is clear: those supporting the principle of meritocracy, the idea that more efficient people who do more work should get paid more, will be more likely to believe that, all else being equal, it is fair for more productive people to get paid more than those who are less productive. It is reasonable to suppose that people who believe in the free market will also be likely to express strong support for the principle of meritocracy. The findings reported in Table 5-2 seem to support that speculation. In 1981 Americans and Canadians were more likely than other publics to say that it is fair for the quicker, more efficient, more reliable secretary to be paid more than the other. Notice, too, that between 1981 and 1990 there is a sharp and consistent increase in the proportions of all publics saying that this is a fair division of rewards: the shifts are particularly dramatic in Italy, Denmark, France, and West Germany. The more telling point is that *all* of the changes are in the same direction and all are significant: the cross-time differences are well beyond anything that could be attributed to measurement error. In economic terms, it appears that all the advanced industrial states experienced a shift to the right. In fact, when one looks at the left–right self-placement of these publics on the traditional indicator of ideological location, there is no evidence of such a shift to the right; the 1981 and 1990 mean left–right scale

Table 5-2 Support for "Meritocracy"

Country	1981	1990	% change
France	63.0%	78.5%	+15.5%
Britain	67.9%	76.4%	+8.5%
West Germany	70.3%	84.5%	+14.2%
Italy	47.9%	79.3%	+31.4%
Netherlands	61.5%	71.2%	+9.7%
Denmark	59.4%	76.3%	+16.9%
Belgium	63.4%	72.7%	+9.3%
Spain	69.7%	74.5%	+4.8%
Ireland	59.4%	72.7%	+13.3%
Northern Ireland	64.1%	71.1%	+7.0%
United States	80.0%	85.1%	+5.1%
Canada	73.9%	82.6%	+8.7%
English	76.4%	84.1%	+7.7%
French	66.6%	79.3%	+12.7%
New Canadians	—	82.2%	—

Question: "Imagine two secretaries, of the same age, doing practically the same job. One finds out that the other earns $50 a week more than she does. The better paid secretary, however, is quicker, more efficient and more reliable at her job. In your opinion, is it fair or not fair that one secretary is paid more than the other?"

The above data report the percentages of each public saying that it is *fair*.

Source: 1981 and 1990 World Values Surveys.

scores for publics in each country are relatively stable. By this measure, some countries appear actually to have shifted to the left. Intriguingly, for those who saw themselves as being on the left support for meritocracy jumped more sharply than for those on the right. Even more striking is evidence indicating that, in 1990, levels of support for meritocracy are the same for Canadians on the left as for those on the right. The very same finding applies to Americans on the left and right.[3]

It turns out that support for meritocracy is systematically related to support for all five of the free-market items examined in Table 5-1. The connections are not always robust, but they are in the expected direction. That being so, one might speculate that support for free-market ideas also grew over the 1981–1990 period. The more important question, however, has to do with whether the sharp increases in support for meritocracy are just short-term changes, or whether they signify longer-term shifts associated with generational change. In this instance the signals are somewhat mixed. A detailed analysis of the connections between support for meritocracy and age, education, and post-materialist value orientations indicates that the rising levels of meritocratic orientations may be consistent with the generational change explanation. Figure 5-1 shows that when it comes to age effects, older people are more supportive of meritocracy than the young. Taken alone, that finding

Figure 5-1   Support for Meritocracy by Age, Education, and Value Type

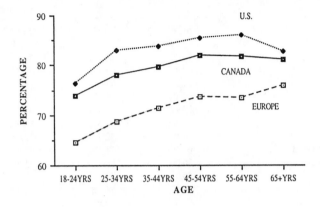

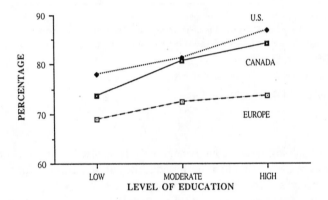

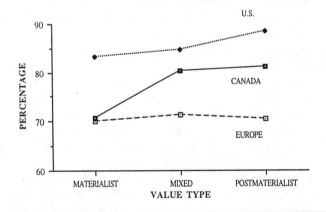

Source: 1981 and 1990 World Values Surveys.

is *not* consistent with a generational change explanation. But there are nuances that shape these results. When these data are probed in greater detail, it becomes clear that between 1981 and 1990 support for meritocracy grew faster among the young than the old, which suggests that the shifts may be partly driven by generational change. Education and value effects are also consistent with generational change as the explanation: those with higher levels of education and post-materialists are generally more likely to support the principle of meritocracy.

The broad-gauge cross-national empirical findings reviewed so far place the stereotypes about Canadian–American economic value differences in a slightly different perspective. These indicators do not cover the entire terrain of economic values. Even so, the basic finding is that Canadians do *not* fall short on some key entrepreneurial values, and the broader cross-national perspective brings into focus North American–European rather than Canadian–American differences. Americans *and* Canadians are more likely than Europeans to believe that competition is good, individuals should take responsibility for themselves, and there should be greater incentives for individual effort. Both groups of North Americans are also more supportive than Europeans of increasing private ownership, and they are more likely to believe in rewarding hard work. In 1981 Americans were slightly more inclined than Canadians to be meritocratic, but the gap between the two North American publics is closing and, on balance, North Americans are more meritocratic than their European counterparts.

Why do people live in need?

Support for free markets and meritocracy addresses but one aspect of economic values. Free-enterprise ideas are easy to endorse in principle; in practice, however, the rigours of economic competition can bring human cost, for in the competitive marketplace there are economic winners and losers. What about the other side of the picture? An equally important and in some respects complementary aspect of economic values has to do with *why* these publics think some "win" and some "lose." The 1990 WVS included a battery of questions probing public assessments of why some people lose, asking

> Why are there some people in this country who live in need? Here are four possible reasons. Which one do you consider to be most important? And which reason do you consider to be the second most important?
> Because they are unlucky
> Because of laziness and lack of willpower
> Because of injustice in our society
> It's an inevitable part of modern progress
> None of these

Table 5-3 Why Are There People Who Live in Need?

Country	Because they are unlucky		Because of laziness and lack of willpower		Because of injustice in our society		Because it is an inevitable part of modern progress	
	1st choice	2nd choice	1st choice	2nd choice	1st choice	2nd choice	1st choice	2nd choice
France	18.3%	21.6%	15.4%	17.8%	42.1%	26.7%	21.0%	29.6%
Britain	14.1%	23.4%	26.8%	21.6%	36.8%	21.9%	19.6%	27.8%
W. Germany	14.7%	22.6%	22.3%	23.0%	31.3%	23.0%	26.8%	24.3%
Italy	12.4%	17.3%	27.8%	26.7%	45.1%	27.5%	12.0%	23.9%
Netherlands	25.1%	34.0%	15.6%	15.9%	36.5%	21.3%	15.9%	19.4%
Denmark	18.4%	25.4%	14.4%	17.0%	29.2%	22.4%	34.8%	30.6%
Belgium	29.8%	29.4%	23.1%	21.5%	31.5%	24.1%	10.6%	19.1%
Spain	18.4%	23.7%	24.4%	21.5%	43.9%	25.9%	10.4%	21.6%
Ireland	18.5%	24.7%	21.2%	22.9%	35.6%	22.2%	23.3%	28.0%
N. Ireland	12.4%	21.5%	31.5%	18.7%	24.8%	26.3%	29.9%	30.1%
U.S.	7.9%	16.2%	38.7%	22.5%	32.8%	27.4%	17.1%	28.7%
Canada	8.8%	18.3%	31.5%	24.4%	32.2%	25.0%	22.6%	26.8%
English	7.8%	15.5%	32.9%	26.6%	30.4%	24.6%	24.0%	26.7%
French	10.8%	25.1%	24.2%	18.4%	39.8%	26.8%	19.9%	27.1%
New Canadians	9.5%	19.9%	36.7%	23.0%	27.5%	23.7%	21.6%	26.8%

Question: a) Why are there people in this country who live in need? Here are four possible reasons. Which one reason do you consider to be the most important?
    b) And which reason do you consider to be the second most important?

Because they are unlucky	1
Because of laziness and lack of willpower	2
Because of injustice in our society	3
It's an inevitable part of modern progress	4
None of these	5

Note: The percentages in bold indicate the most popular first choice for publics in each country.
Source: 1990 World Values Survey.

The alternative responses do not capture all of the nuances and complexities of the real world, nor do they exhaust the reasons why people live in need. They say nothing, for example, about the problem of structural unemployment, of sickness, or of the possible effects of such other factors as sexual discrimination. But there is little indication that respondents had any difficulty in attributing poverty to one of the four causes listed: few supplied the "none of these" response.

Begin with the overall findings reported in Table 5-3. Here, the numbers in bold type highlight the most popular option chosen by publics in each country. Notice that in eleven out of the twelve countries, publics attribute poverty, "living in need," to the second and third options; a plurality of publics in nine countries attribute poverty to social injustice and in two others to "laziness and lack of willpower." Danes are the outlier in this instance; more Danes select the fourth option—people live in need "because it is an inevitable part of modern progress"—than any other. Conceptually, the second and third options are the most intriguing ones. Attributing poverty to laziness and lack of willpower is an orientation that places the responsibility on the shoulders of the individual. The implication is that individuals are the authors of their own plight, they could escape poverty if they were just willing to work hard. Where this option places the blame for poverty on factors *internal to the individual*, those selecting the "injustice in society" alternative attribute poverty to factors that are *external to the individual*. From this standpoint it is not just luck, the first option, or even modern progress, the fourth option, that are the primary culprits; it is *society* that carries the blame for poverty. There are two implications of this response: that people would not live in need if society were more justly ordered, and that if the causes of poverty are rooted in factors beyond the control of the individual, then individual effort will have little impact on one's economic success or failure. Both the second and third options, then, like support for meritocracy, say something about the achievement orientations of these publics.

According to Table 5-3, Americans are more likely than others to attribute poverty to laziness and lack of willpower, and Canadians, along with Northern Irish respondents, rank second. That finding is entirely consistent with the other evidence of general economic orientations presented earlier. Furthermore, there is no significant difference between Canadians and Americans when it comes to attributing poverty to social injustice. Canadians and Americans are less likely than publics in six other countries to think that poverty is the result of social injustice. But there are, clearly, very significant differences within Canada. New Canadians, for example, are the most inclined to think that people live in need because of laziness and lack of willpower, and francophone Canadians are significantly more likely than others to blame poverty on injustice in society.

Is there any evidence that these achievement orientations are undergoing long-term changes? A close background analysis points to evidence of generational differences in achievement orientations. The data come from only one time point, and the relationships between these achievement orientations and age, education, and value type are not entirely straightforward, but they are worth exploring in some detail. First, there are clear, consistent patterns indicating that level of education *and* value type are related to both "laziness" and "social injustice" as explanations for why people live in need. Materialists and those with lower levels of education are more inclined than their well-educated and post-materialist counterparts to say that people live in need because of laziness and lack of willpower. Furthermore, those with more education and post-materialists are *more likely* than the less well educated and materialists to think poverty is the result of injustice in society. This much is absolutely

Figure 5-2   Why People Live in Need, by Level of Education

Europe:

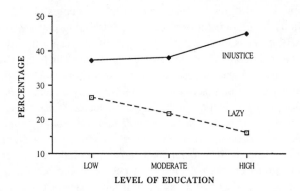

United   States:

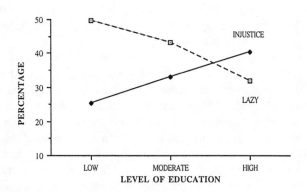

Canada:

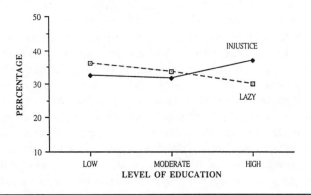

Source: 1990 World Values Survey.

Figure 5-3 Why People Live in Need, by Value Type

Europe:

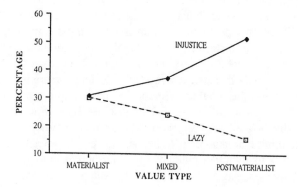

United States:

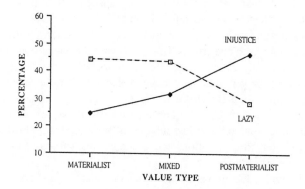

Canada:

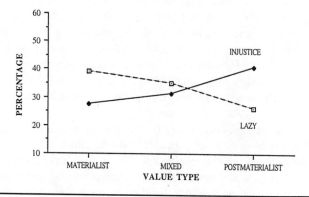

Source: 1990 World Values Survey.

clear from the background statistical evidence (see Appendix 5-B) and from the summary data reported in Figures 5-2 and 5-3.

Figures 5-2 and 5-3 also illustrate striking differences between the aggregate European results and the North American findings. Figure 5-2 shows that, regardless of level of education, Europeans are always more likely to volunteer "social injustice" than "laziness" as the most important reason for poverty. The keener perception of injustice in Europe could reflect the residue of societies that, historically, were highly stratified and in which opportunities for upward mobility were far more limited. For Americans and Canadians, however, only those with high levels of education are more likely to attribute poverty to injustice than laziness. The basic findings presented in Figure 5-3 replicate those in Figure 5-2 almost precisely. European materialists are equally divided between those who attribute poverty to injustice and those who think that laziness is to blame, whereas American materialists are about twice as likely to attribute poverty to laziness than to injustice. The Canadian findings, once again, are closer to the American results.

If structural change (rising levels of education) and value change (rising levels of post-materialism) continue apace, and if they signify long-term change, then important shifts in public reasoning about economic fairness may be underway. Generationally driven long-term shifts should also be detectable from age effects. But in this case the background evidence suggests only weak age effects. Age effects do operate in the direction that is consistent with the generational change explanation, but they are somewhat uneven (see Appendix 5-B). However, the age effects are particularly weak in North America, and in Canada they are actually perverse—quite the opposite of what one would expect.[4] As it happens, the aggregate statistical summary data mask interesting variations across age groups, variations that are brought into full view in Figure 5-4.

As with education and value type, the relationship between age and "injustice" and "laziness" appears to be roughly inverse: the top half of each graph in Figure 5-4 looks like an unfolded version of the bottom half. From this vantage point, the European age effects look quite different from those in either the United States or Canada. In the European case there is little indication of age effects among those under 44 years, but in older groups the age effects are almost linear. By contrast, it becomes clear why the connections between Canadian and American publics age effects and "injustice" and "laziness" are statistically weak: in those two cases the relationships are not linear, but curvilinear, like a flattened or inverted ∪ curve.

What are the likely explanations for these findings? For European publics, *all* of the indicators are consistent with the explanation that significant long-term generational changes are under way: people are becoming progressively more likely to attribute poverty to *external causes*, social injustice, and they are correspondingly less inclined to attribute poverty to *internal causes*, or laziness. One possibility is that those socialized in an environment of relative affluence find it difficult to understand why some people live in need, and so

Figure 5-4   Why People Live in Need, by Age

Europe:

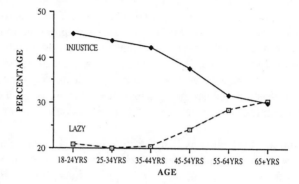

United   States:

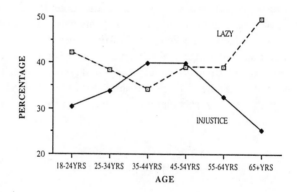

Canada:

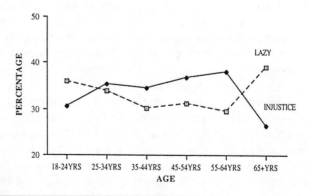

Source: 1990 World Values Survey.

they are more inclined to believe there is something wrong with "the system." But what about the North American findings? The evidence for North Americans captured in Figures 5-2 and 5-3 is entirely consistent with the same kind of generational change explanation; it is the age-related differences that are harder to interpret. For North Americans, the curvilinear age differences could signify the presence of life-cycle effects. The difficulty here, however, is that such a life-cycle explanation seems counter-intuitive; it implies that those most likely to be closest to poverty—the young and the old—are also most likely to attribute poverty to laziness. And the older respondents are precisely those who are least likely to be able to do anything about their own condition. It is the middle-aged groups, those who are most likely to be in their prime earning years, who are most inclined to attribute poverty to social injustice.

Another possibility is that the different ends of the North American ∪ curves require slightly different explanations. In effect, the direction of the changes for all respondents over 55 years of age, both European and North American, is the same. And in all cases, the explanation for this segment of the North American public could also be the same: this age "tail" reflects the imprint of a generational shift. But what this particular line of interpretation leaves unexplained is the young tail of the North American data. It is possible, of course, that younger North Americans are in the forefront of a reverse intergenerational trend in which *internal* factors are beginning to replace *external* factors as the primary explanation for poverty. To establish the credibility of that line of speculation, however, requires evidence from a much longer time frame.[5]

When jobs are scarce

The two trends so far documented—rising public support for the merit principle and increasing attribution of poverty to such external causes as social injustice—reflect substantively important shifts in the economic values of publics in advanced industrial states. But it is not at all clear whether these two shifts are entirely complementary. In many advanced industrial states, for example, contemporary policy debates appear particularly fractious and difficult to resolve when the principle of merit crashes headlong into questions of social justice. At issue is whether the merit principle is genuinely fair. Minority groups contend, for example, that it is but a thin veil masking discriminatory practices on the part of majorities. Women complain, with some justification, of the "glass ceiling" that prevents them from reaching the pinnacles of organizational authority. Comparable frustrations are expressed by racial minorities, linguistic minorities, and others who find themselves outside of the social mainstream. Policy-makers struggle with questions of whether historically disadvantaged groups should be given an edge, or any special consideration, in hiring decisions. The gatekeepers of law schools and medical schools ponder admissions "quotas" for their institutions, institutions that provide students with opportunities for upward mobility. Philosophers grapple with a variety of related questions: What balance should be struck between group rights and individual rights? Do groups that were discriminated against in the past have a justifiable claim for compensation in the present? When is preferential treatment reverse discrimination? Under what circumstances is it permissible, and justifiable, to depart from the merit principle?[6]

Questions of fairness and justice, plainly, are not just the concern of philosophers, lawyers, and policy-makers; there is every indication that citizens have quite refined notions of what is fair.[7] Convictions about fairness or unfairness, and about distributive justice, do not have to be explicitly grounded in sophisticated abstract reasoning to be deeply held. How divisive these issues are undoubtedly depends on a variety of factors. Preferential hiring policies, for example, may be less controversial when economies are expanding and jobs plentiful. A tougher test of public standards of fairness comes not when economies are expanding, but when jobs are scarce.

The 1990 WVS contain some questions that help to flesh out standards of justice and fairness. Respondents were asked if they agreed, or disagreed, with the following four statements:

When jobs are scarce, men have more right to a job than women.
When jobs are scarce, people should be forced to retire early.
When jobs are scarce, employers should give priority to Canadian people (co-nationals) over immigrants.
It is unfair to give work to handicapped people when able-bodied people can't find jobs.

Each statement invites responses to a variety of scenarios that, technically, involve departures from the merit principle. Each brings different groups into consideration and taps preferences in an environment where jobs are scarce. Respondents were not presented with a "forced-choice" question format; they had the opportunity to say "neither" or "don't know," although, as the findings reported in Table 5-4 indicate, relatively few respondents selected those options. Not surprisingly, the basic finding is that people are not equally sympathetic to all groups. An overwhelming majority of every public, for example, *disagrees* with the idea that it is unfair to give work to handicapped people when able-bodied people can't find work. On the other scenarios, opinion is more divided, and the cross-national variations are more pronounced. In the case of the first scenario, for example, Italian, Belgian, Irish, and British respondents are about twice as likely as Canadians to agree that when jobs are scarce "men have more right to a job than women"; only Danes are more liberal than Canadians on this scenario. The basic findings point to more evidence of North American versus European differences. Not only do relatively few North Americans subscribe to the idea that gender differences confer different rights to access to the workplace; they are also less inclined than most

Table 5-4 What Should Be Done "When Jobs Are Scarce ..."
(Percentages)

Country	Men have more right to a job than women		People should be forced to retire early		Give priority to "co-nationals" over immigrants		It's unfair to give work to handicapped people when able-bodied people can't find jobs	
	Agree	Disagree	Agree	Disagree	Agree	Disagree	Agree	Disagree
France	32.9	58.9	48.9	42.7	63.0	31.2	9.5	82.1
Britain	35.0	58.6	43.1	50.4	53.4	41.5	7.8	88.1
W. Germany	30.7	58.5	50.0	38.3	61.5	29.7	15.7	73.5
Italy	39.8	47.7	55.0	31.1	71.2	17.8	15.7	68.2
Netherlands	24.8	69.9	42.0	53.1	33.3	62.0	11.6	85.0
Denmark	10.5	86.0	24.3	66.0	52.8	37.9	8.6	81.8
Belgium	37.4	51.5	49.2	36.5	62.6	26.9	15.9	68.1
Spain	29.0	63.1	57.5	31.2	76.5	16.6	20.3	66.4
Ireland	35.5	59.0	47.0	47.5	68.8	28.5	8.8	86.9
N. Ireland	33.8	60.6	43.0	53.3	62.4	33.6	6.3	92.0
United States	23.8	71.1	15.9	79.6	52.2	42.7	10.0	85.3
Canada	18.5	74.6	30.9	62.0	52.5	42.3	8.1	87.9
English	17.3	75.8	25.0	67.9	56.1	38.3	6.7	88.5
French	23.6	71.3	46.6	46.3	62.1	34.6	10.8	87.5
New Canadians	16.8	73.8	30.1	62.4	29.2	64.0	9.5	86.2

Question: "Do you agree or disagree with the following statements?
  a) When jobs are scarce men have more right to a job than women
  b) When jobs are scarce people should not be forced to retire early
  c) When jobs are scarce employers should give priority to co-nationals over immigrants
  d) It is unfair to give work to handicapped people when able-bodied people can't find jobs"

Note: The percentages do not add up to 100% because responses to other alternatives, "neither" and "don't know," are omitted from the table.
Source: 1990 World Values Surveys.

Europeans to support either "early retirement" or "giving priority to 'co-nationals' " over immigrants as strategies for parcelling out access to jobs.

If narrow self-interest counts for anything, there is reason to suppose that citizen reactions to these various alternatives might well be shaped by respondents' own personal characteristics. One might expect women, for example, to be more opposed than men to the idea that men have more right to a job than women. The striking finding in this particular instance, however, is the *absence* of any consistent empirical evidence of gender effects. There are gender differences in the expected direction among West Germans, French, and Italian respondents. In these countries, men are significantly more likely than women to believe that they have more of a right to a job. Remarkably, however, there are almost as many instances of gender effects in exactly the opposite direction. Danish and Dutch women, for example, are more likely than their male counterparts to believe that men have more of a right to a job than women. For similar reasons, one would expect immigrants to be less sympathetic than others to the idea that native-born nationals should be given preference over immigrants in the job market. The Canadian data give substance to this line of speculation. Native-born Canadians, for example, are about twice as likely as new Canadians to give priority to co-nationals when jobs are scarce.

There are good reasons to examine the effects of other background factors as well. The WVS asked questions about economic fairness in 1990 only. But if orientations to economic fairness are part and parcel of the other value changes that have been documented, then there should also be systematic variations in these orientations reflecting consistent age, education, and value type effects. Overall, there is impressive evidence of a basic underlying pattern. The indication is that *all* of these economic fairness orientations are consistent with the generational change explanation. The detailed statistical evidence illustrating the consistency of the patterns for all countries is reported in Appendix 5-C. As with our analysis of why people live in need, the basic structure of the findings can be summarized schematically.

Figure 5-5 illustrates the impact of education on orientations to each aspect of economic fairness. In every case, the direction of education effects is the same. Those with more formal education are *less* apt than others to agree that some groups should be favoured over others when jobs are scarce. That finding holds in *every* country, and it holds regardless of which particular groups are under consideration. Figure 5-5 also shows that there are some cross-national variations in the amount of sympathy people have for the various groups. All publics have relatively little sympathy for immigrants and a great deal of sympathy for handicapped people. After that, differences come into view. Europeans and Canadians, for example, are much more inclined than Americans to target early retirement as a preferred policy for dealing with high unemployment.

The effects of value type are almost precisely the same as those for education. A comparison of Figures 5-5 and 5-6 plainly shows that the direction and gradient of these slopes are almost identical. Post-materialists are significantly *less* likely than their materialist counterparts to think that particular groups should get favourable treatment when jobs are in short supply. Once again, there are no exceptions; education effects and value type effects are both strongly associated with these orientations towards economic fairness (see Appendix 5-C). The implication is that, other things being equal, if publics continue to enjoy increased access to higher education and if post-materialist value orientations continue on the same trajectory that has been tracked over the last three decades, then publics will become progressively *less* supportive of group-based distinctions as criteria for solving unemployment problems.

Figure 5-5 "When Jobs Are Scarce ... ," by Level of Education

Europe:

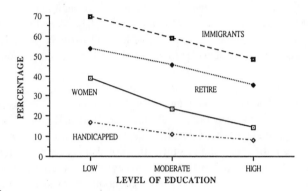

United States:

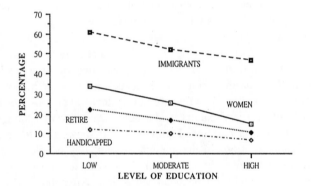

Canada:

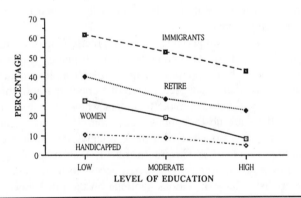

Source: 1990 World Values Survey.

Figure 5-6   "When Jobs Are Scarce ... ," by Value Type

Europe:

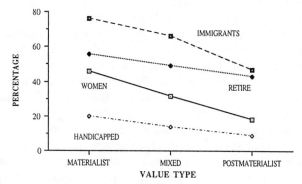

United   States:

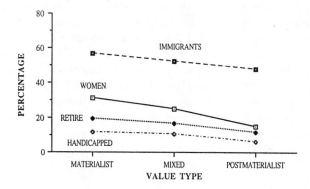

Canada:

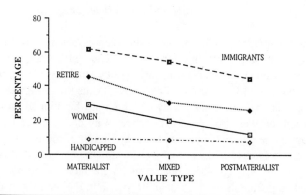

Source: 1990 World Values Survey.

What about age effects? These results are less straightforward; there is greater age-related variation, but the important initial point is that these findings are also consistent with the idea that gradual generational shifts may be driving orientations towards economic fairness. The age effects are reported in Figure 5-7. In some respects the European findings are the most arresting. As has already been suggested, there are reasons to suppose that some background characteristics of respondents will be more important than others in shaping public reaction to the four alternative strategies for job scarcity. One such example has been illustrated above: new Canadians are much less supportive than native-born nationals of the idea that employers should give native-born nationals preference over immigrants. The idea that "people should be forced to retire early" targets older people in the workforce, and for that reason one might speculate that age effects would have a quite different impact on public reactions to this alternative. It comes as no surprise, then, to discover that age effects are much weaker on the "people should be forced to retire early" alternative than for any of the other alternatives. Far more surprising, perhaps, is the finding that in every country except one, West Germany, the overall relationship between age and support for the idea that "people should be forced to retire early" is positive. On balance, older people are *more likely* to support this proposal than the young.

The initial indications are that in matters of broad economic orientation, Canadians and Americans have more in common with each other than with publics in other advanced industrial states. Both publics express similar levels of support for the principle of meritocracy, they share similar beliefs about why people live in need, and they appear to be similarly enthusiastic about free markets. Do these shared economic orientations have anything to do with the emergence of continental free trade?

Free Markets and Free Trade: The Case of NAFTA

Continental free trade was one of the giant issues that preoccupied Canadians during the late 1980s and early 1990s. The North American free trade agreement (NAFTA) represents a historic policy shift that was particularly divisive for publics in Canada and Mexico. NAFTA also raises a variety of theoretical and practical questions, many of which are familiar to those who have followed the West European experience: Why do countries pursue greater economic integration? What explains the timing of these policy shifts? And can countries work together effectively within the new frameworks? The economic reasons why countries pursue such agreements as NAFTA are multiple: free trade agreements are a strategic response to the realities of globalization and the emergence of vigorous new trading blocs; controlled access to large markets helps countries reap the joint benefits of comparative advantage and economies of scale. From the North American perspective, NAFTA has also

Figure 5-7 "When Jobs Are Scarce ... ," by Age

Europe:

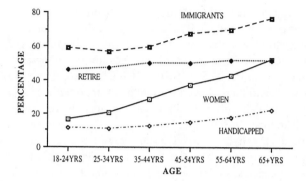

United States:

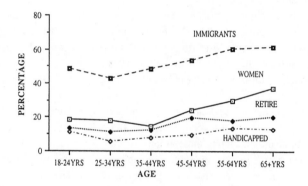

Canada:

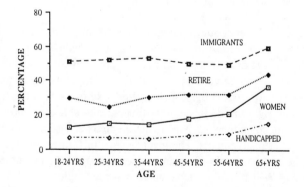

Source: 1990 World Values Survey.

been interpreted as the logical extension of evolving patterns of closer com-mercial cooperation (Smith, 1988). From that standpoint the puzzling questions, perhaps, are not why NAFTA was signed but why such an agreement was not formalized decades ago, and why it was so divisive.

The economic case for free trade is powerful, and economic interests undoubtedly are vital to the dynamics of continental integration. Economists, however, were among the first to recognize that economic explanations, taken alone and viewed narrowly, fail to provide a convincing account of why, and when, countries take such decisive steps towards integration (Johnson, 1965; Milner & Yoffie, 1989). In the 1970s, more comprehensive explanations emerged, and these drew attention to the importance of such political factors as leadership, levels of institutional coordination, and styles of decision-making (Lindberg & Scheingold, 1970; Nye, 1968; Puchala, 1968). More recently, others highlight the role the state plays in the dynamics of integration, seeing the connection between the state, society, and interest groups and the interdependence of international and domestic decision-making as vital to understanding the process (Gourevitch, 1986; Milner, 1988; Nye, 1988; Rogowski, 1989).

Public values do not feature very prominently in any of these perspectives. Even so, there are two kinds of explanations of why values might matter to the dynamics of expanding markets. The most forceful contemporary account is supplied by Putnam (1988) who observes that international negotiations, such as those leading up to NAFTA, can be thought of as "two-level games":

> At the national level, domestic groups pursue their interests by pressuring governments to adopt favorable policies, and politicians seek power by constructing coalitions among these groups. At the international level, national governments seek to maximize their own ability to satisfy domestic pressures, while minimizing the adverse consequences of foreign developments. Neither of the two games can be ignored by central decision-makers, so long as their countries remain interdependent yet sovereign.

From this standpoint, Putnam indicates that public values may count, first, because those sitting at negotiating tables trying to strike trade deals like NAFTA do not have independent policy preferences (1988: 436); and second, because if such agreements are to "fly," negotiators must steer a course that satisfies two groups: the hard bargainers sitting across the negotiating table and the relevant domestic constituencies that each bargainer represents. Domestic constituencies have to be satisfied because publics are positioned to ratify these agreements. The mechanisms for ratification, Putnam points out, can be either formal or informal depending upon the institutional rules of the game (436–40). In the Canadian case, for example, the 1988 Canadian federal election can be seen as the opportunity Canadian citizens had to ratify the Canada–United States free trade agreement (Johnston et al., 1992). Presumably, too, those who count as the "relevant" domestic constituencies may also differ with a variety of factors, such as how open or closed governing regimes are.

The second, and more general, explanation for why public values may matter comes from a much earlier set of speculations about integration. Forty-five years ago a number of scholars joined forces to explore a common question: could a lasting peace in Western Europe be secured by greater cross-national integration and through strategic institution-building? From those coordinated efforts, and informed by a variety of comparative European case studies, there emerged a variety of theoretical perspectives about the dynamics of integration. Haas (1958), for example, developed a functionalist interpretation holding that economic integration has an inherent tendency to "spill over" into political integration, an idea that appealed to the founders of the European Common Market.

As it turned out, the process of European integration was much less automatic than functionalists supposed. Determined opposition by Charles de Gaulle blocked most early attempts to forge an expanded community, and recalcitrant publics in the smaller European partner states stalled the process later on. But in the long run the European experience illustrates, yet again, that economic forces are difficult to disentangle from political ones. Successful economic integration did lead to regular intergovernmental consultations and eventually to a Europe with a common currency unit, the beginnings of a common foreign policy, and the development of a wide range of coordinated domestic policies.

The most comprehensive account of the role values play in the dynamics of regional integration springs from, and builds upon, the early work of Karl Deutsch (1952, 1957, 1968). Deutsch's (1957) social learning perspective involves a four-step chain of reasoning. He begins by arguing that high volumes of transactions between peoples (communications flows, trade, and the movement of peoples) encourages greater similarities in the main values of publics in adjacent states. Second, similarities in main values are in turn conducive to greater trust between peoples. Trust is the expectation that another's behaviour will be predictable and friendly (Pruitt, 1965). Third, higher levels of trust encourage greater cooperation and economic integration. And economic integration, Deutsch concludes, is conducive to greater political integration. The essential logic of the Deutsch line of reasoning is schematically represented in Figure 5-8.

Deutsch's account of the dynamics of regional integration is plausible, and the essential elements of that perspective can still be found in contemporary versions of integration theory (Diebold, 1988; Keohane, 1977; Lindberg & Scheingold, 1970).[8] Furthermore, some of the basic links between key elements of the Deutsch model have been empirically verified in a number of settings. It has been shown, for example, that interpersonal trust plays an important role in economic and political cooperation (Abramson, 1983; Almond & Verba, 1963; Banfield, 1958; Luhmann, 1979; Wylie, 1957). Systematic empirical research about trust between nationalities is more scarce, but the

Figure 5-8   Values and the Dynamics of Integration

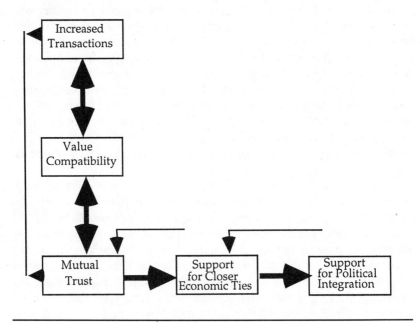

general finding is that cross-national trust is a stable attribute (Buchannan & Cantril, 1953; Deutsch, 1952; Deutsch et al., 1957; Merrit & Puchala, 1968; Nincic & Russett, 1979), though there are important exceptions (France and Germany, 1945–1988). The weight of the accumulated evidence seems to work in ways that are consistent with expectations contained within the Deutsch model. Even so, Deutsch's perspective remains speculative. The kinds of data that might have provided the foundations for a direct test of the theory's central propositions were simply not available when the theory was first developed and since then no attempt has been made to mount such a test. With the WVS data, it becomes possible to ask: Do public values matter in the way Deutsch supposes they do? And more generally, does his theory, which was developed on the basis of European experience, hold up when applied to the North American setting?

The North American context is a promising site for examining the Deutsch model, not least of all because a number of Deutsch's critical preconditions are in place. First, the signing of NAFTA provides *prima facie* evidence that greater economic integration between Canada and the United States, and indeed Mexico, has been formalized. Second, it is possible to demonstrate that the volume of cross-border transactions has increased. For example, the volume of Canada–United States two-way border crossings (the movement of peoples) rose from seventy-two million visits in 1980 to ninety-four million visits in 1989 (Statistics Canada, 1991). As Deutsch's theory predicts, trade in goods and services also increased sharply in the decade immediately prior to the signing of the free trade agreement (Schott & Smith, 1988). The very same trends are mirrored in U.S.–Mexican cross-border transactions over the same period. Finally, Deutsch himself claims that the dynamics of integration work in the same ways in different places.

There is no simple strategy for empirically connecting multiple indicators of individual-level value change either with such aggregate national variations as shifts in cross-border transactions, or even with single indicators such as feelings of mutual trust. Nor are there any cross-time data available that allow direct comparisons of how mutual trust among the three North American publics may have changed during the 1990s. But we do know that, compared to publics in other advanced industrial states, the level of mutual trust between Canadians and Americans is relatively high (Inglehart, 1990(a)). According to the WVS, nearly two-thirds of Americans (64%) said they "trust Canadians" while only 4% reported not trusting Canadians very much or not at all. Similarly, more than half of Canadian respondents (55%) said they trust Americans, and only 15% did not trust Americans. Trust of Mexicans is higher among American respondents (52%) than Canadians (37%), but American trust of Mexicans is not reciprocated; only 20% of Mexicans reported that they trusted Americans, and more than half of the Mexican sample (52%) said they did not trust Americans. Absolute levels of trust are undoubtedly important, but from the Deutschian perspective, they are not the critical issue; what is, is whether higher levels of trust vary systematically with support for closer economic ties, and that question can be explored with our data. The 1990 surveys asked respondents in all three countries whether their own country should have closer or more distant economic ties with the other NAFTA countries. Here, Deutsch's theory produces a clear prediction: respondents with higher levels of trust for other nationalities should be more likely than their non-trusting counterparts to support closer economic ties. On this point, the findings reported in Figure 5-9 are unequivocal: In every country and for every set of relationships higher levels of mutual trust always correspond to greater support for closer economic ties. All of the relationships are robust and none is weaker than gamma = .39.

Support for closer economic ties is one thing, support for political integration quite another. The 1990 surveys asked respondents a variety of questions about political integration, including one question that tapped attitudes to what, arguably, is the most radical and unambiguous variant: "All things considered, do you think that we should do away with the border between … Canada and the United States [Canadians]/ the United States and Canada [Americans]/ Mexico and the United States [Mexicans] …?"

The idea that Canadians, or Mexicans, would seriously consider doing away with the borders between their own country and the United States is a radical one: it flies in the face of long-standing policy efforts aimed at resisting the economic, political, and socio-cultural influences of the United States.

Figure 5-9   Support for Closer Economic Ties with a Given Nation, by Trust in that Nationality (Percentage in Favour of "Much Closer" or "Somewhat Closer" Economic Ties)

Attitudes of the American Public:

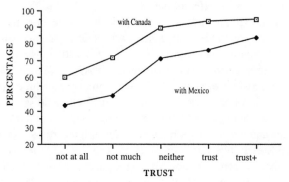

Attitudes of the Canadian Public:

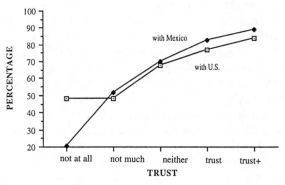

Attitudes of the Mexican Public:

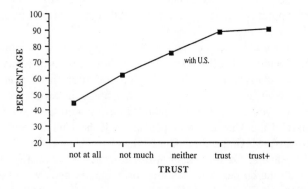

Source: 1990 World Values Survey.

From this historical standpoint it would be surprising if more than a handful of Canadians or Mexicans supported such an alternative. The basic finding from the WVS is truly striking: nearly one in four Canadians (24%) and just less than half (46%) of Americans indicate they would favour doing away with the Canada–U.S. border. Remarkably, too, one-quarter of Mexicans favoured abandoning the border between Mexico and the United States.

Not surprisingly, support for doing away with borders is connected to a variety of factors.[9] Of more concern to an evaluation of Deutsch's theory, though, is the "slippery slope" question: Is support for political integration systematically related to support for closer economic ties, as Deutsch predicts? Are the supporters of closer economic ties also political integrationists, and are they more likely to support doing away with borders? Once again, the evidence provides support for Deutsch's line of speculation. As Figure 5-10 shows, support for closer economic ties *is* related to support for doing away with borders. The relationship is consistent in all three countries and, as before, all of the relationships are reasonably strong.

When we step back from the details of each particular set of linkages and consider the broader pattern of findings, the weight of the evidence provides more support for the Deutsch perspective on integration. Cross-border transactions increased during the period preceding NAFTA. There have been significant changes in the political and economic values of Canadians and Americans between 1981 and 1990—the period leading up to NAFTA.[10] As Deutsch predicts, levels of mutual trust are indeed related to support for closer economic ties. Furthermore, support for political integration is significantly and positively related to support for closer economic ties. Figure 5-11 provides further grist for Deutsch's theory. Notice that the *direct* relationship between mutual trust and support for political integration actually turns out to be quite weak. That is, if Deutsch's theory is re-specified, for example, taking a link out of his chain of reasoning, the results are far less robust. That finding implies that, by itself, mutual trust between people is not a sufficient condition for greater political integration; mutual trust works *through* support for closer economic ties. It is the interaction of mutual trust between people and support for closer economic ties that jointly work to encourage support for greater political integration.

To empirically investigate Deutsch's line of grand-scale theorizing calls for a certain kind of broad value evidence. The WVS findings reported above certainly suggest that North American value change *may* have shaped public opinion about NAFTA for the kinds of reason Deutsch speculated about. By the same token, the evidence considered so far does not exhaust all of the possible ways in which values might shape attitudes to expanding trade environments. It provides no indication, for example, of whether those economic values considered at the beginning of this chapter are related to orientations about free trade. The broad-gauged data shed no light on how robust public support is for closer economic ties or political integration. Nor do they go any distance towards supplying any evidence for Putnam's (1988) claim that pub-

Figure 5-10   Support for Political Integration by Support for Closer Economic Ties

American support for abolishing border with Canada:

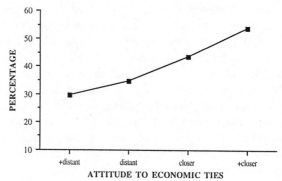

Canadian support for abolishing border with the U.S.:

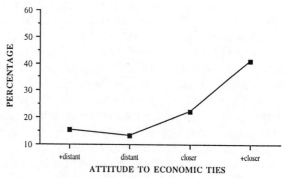

Mexican support for abolishing border with the U.S.:

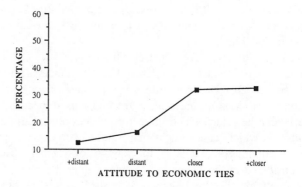

Source: 1990 World Values Survey.

Figure 5-11 The Deutsch Model of Integration

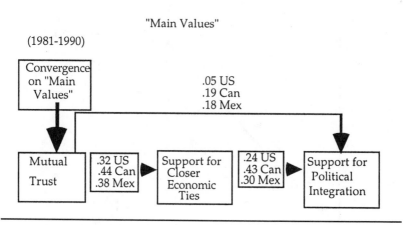

"Main Values"

(1981-1990)

| Convergence on "Main Values" | | | .05 US
.19 Can
.18 Mex | | |

| Mutual Trust | .32 US
.44 Can
.38 Mex | Support for Closer Economic Ties | .24 US
.43 Can
.30 Mex | Support for Political Integration |

Source: 1990 World Values Survey.

lic support for expanding trade environments is significantly shaped by domestic policy preferences. The Canadian, American, and Mexican 1990 surveys contained some questions specifically dedicated to the issues of continental free trade, and the findings help to flesh out important nuances and sources of variation in attitudes to continental trade, and to integration more generally.

Recall the evidence presented at the beginning of the chapter: the cross-time findings indicating both that Canadians and Americans rank high on the principle of meritocracy and that support for meritocracy increased among publics in all of the advanced industrial states, Canadians and Americans included. Canadians and Americans also rank high on the five indicators of support for free markets each of which, not surprisingly, turns out to be related to the meritocracy indicator. It is reasonable to suppose that support for the principle of free markets and meritocracy might be related to support for freer trade, and the WVS data support that line of speculation, at least in the Canadian case. Support for the principle of meritocracy, and for each of the five free-market items reported in Table 5-1, is consistently related to support for free trade with the United States. All of the relationships are in the expected direction; the more Canadians support meritocracy, endorse private ownership, believe that competition is good, and so on, the more inclined they are to express support for free trade with the United States.[11]

These findings indicate that publics do connect the principles of free markets to the idea of freer trade and that shifting preferences about free markets have consequences for the public acceptability of free trade. But free trade is not an all-or-none proposition, and in practice levels of public support for free trade may be contingent on more nuanced understandings of what a particu-

Figure 5-12   Support for Three Ways of Dealing with Trade Issues

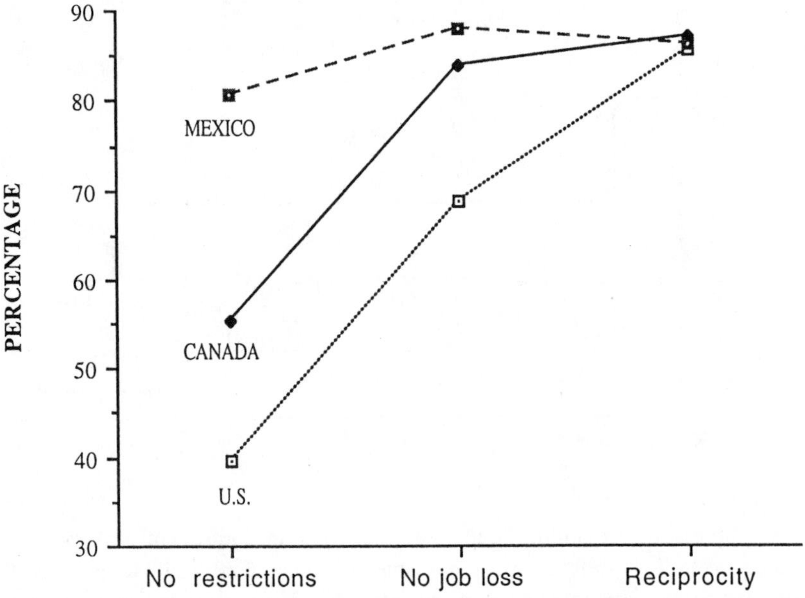

Source: 1990 World Values Survey.

lar free trade proposal entails. Principled support for the idea of free trade, for example, does not necessarily mean that publics would be willing to endorse a free trade deal under any conditions. When the Canadian, Mexican, and American publics were asked about different versions of free trade, the responses indicated significant shifts in opinion. The WVS put the following to respondents in all three NAFTA countries:

> Most countries like our own depend on trade. Here is a list of various ways of dealing with trade issues. Please tell me how much you agree or disagree with each of the following statements:
>
> 1. There should be no restriction on the free flow of goods and services across international borders.
>
> 2. We should allow goods and services to flow *more* freely across our borders as long as [Americans/Canadians/ Mexicans] don't lose jobs.
>
> 3. We should give countries free access to our markets only if they give us free access to theirs.

The national responses, the proportions of each public agreeing with each option, are reported in Figure 5-12. Notice the substantial national differences in responses to the first option, the one that taps the principled "no-strings-attached position" on free trade. Mexicans are most inclined to support no restrictions on free trade: four out of five support this option, while just over half of Canadians (55%) support it, and only two out of five Americans. With the second option, public support for free trade increases quite dramatically, particularly in Canada and the United States. The possibility that with free trade jobs would be lost was a powerful public concern in both countries. Organized labour in Canada, for example, vigorously opposed the Canada–United States free trade agreement on the ground that lower levels of unionization, and thus lower wage rates, in the United States would tempt Canadian business, particularly labour-intensive enterprises, to relocate to the United States. Ross Perot made precisely the same argument to "America's working people" during the run-up to NAFTA; the colourful metaphor of "the great sucking sound" successfully fixed attention on the potential loss of jobs to the Mexican low-wage environment. Figure 5-12 also clearly shows that public support for free trade increases yet again when the third option, which focuses on reciprocity, is introduced. Regardless of national setting, more than 80% of all three North American publics support free trade when it means "we should give countries free access to our markets only if they give us free access to theirs." With this formulation, cross-national differences in support for free trade completely disappear and only 15% of each public opposes the idea of free trade. These findings demonstrate that support for free trade is not simply an extension of free-market orientations, but is also contingent on the particulars of free trade agreements.

It would be surprising if public support for an expanding trade environment were only a matter of the expansiveness and depth of a free-market ethos. As Rogowski (1989) impressively demonstrates, the prospect of expanding trade environments produces predictable coalitions in both support for and opposition to opening borders. To be sure, proponents of NAFTA made the case for free trade by emphasizing the aggregate advantages to the publics in the three national economies. Overall, the argument went, the people as a whole stood to gain because of the complementary comparative advantages that flow from having secure access to large markets. Large markets mean economies of scale; economies of scale result in lower unit costs; and lower unit costs yield lower prices to consumers and improve the competitive position of North American products—they improve chances of gaining a larger share of world markets. All the same, expanding trade environments have quite different impacts on different sectors of the three national economies. According to Rogowski, what counts are *interests*, and the competitive position of different sectors vis–à–vis opposing sectors in the other parts of the proposed free trade zone. This perspective predicts that support for and opposition to free trade will be shaped by the gains or losses anticipated from a trade deal.

A more detailed analysis of the WVS data indicates that "interests" do matter. In the American case, for example, the strongest support of closer economic ties with Canada comes from respondents employed in big and small business. Big business employees were also the strongest supporters of closer ties with Mexico. With those in the agricultural sector, the anticipated gains and losses looked different. A stable climate, cheap land, low labour costs, reforms in communal farms, and a surge in the application of technology to Mexican agriculture have resulted in dramatic increases in Mexican food production. Between 1985 and 1990 Mexican food exports to the United States doubled; Mexico is now the United States' largest foreign source of food, accounting for 25% of all the food Americans eat. Mexican agriculture presents a competitive challenge to American farmers and unskilled labour, and it is these two groups who are the strongest opponents of closer economic ties with Mexico.

The same kind of analysis yields similarly predictable results in both Canada and Mexico. The sectoral distribution of advantages and disadvantages of free trade in the Canadian setting looks different. Canadians business confronts a severe domestic disadvantage: a small market. Closer economic ties with the United States and Mexico held out the promise of access to markets fifteen times the size of their own. Not surprisingly, those employed in the Canadian business sector support closer economic ties with both the United States and Mexico. The service sector accounts for a very substantial, and growing, proportion of Canadian–U.S commercial transactions. But here, Canadian professionals face a challenge. American service enterprises enjoy the advantages of greater size and greater specialization, and they are well positioned to reap major gains in the Canadian service sector—at the expense of Canadian professionals. Canadian professionals, it turns out, are the *least* supportive of closer economic ties with the United States. Mexico presents no such challenge to this group, and the Canadian professional class, along with big and small business employees, are very supportive of closer economic ties with Mexico. The Canadians who are least enthusiastic about closer ties with Mexico? Canadian farmers and unskilled workers. Per capita income in Mexico is about one-ninth as high as in Canada and the United States. Bringing the Mexican economy even approximately into line with those of her northern neighbours would be a massive accomplishment, so it is little wonder that Mexican support for closer economic ties with Canada and the United States is much higher—among business, among farmers, and among skilled and unskilled labour.

Support for free trade and closer economic ties, then, is not entirely attributable to values. Values play a role, but so do interests. Does the same apply to closer political relations? More specifically, does support for integration vary with domestic policy preferences as Putnam (1988) contends? The short answer is: yes.

In considering Deutsch's theory of the role of values, we based the analysis of support for political integration exclusively upon responses to a single "bottom-line" question: "All things considered, do you think that we should do away with the border ...?" There is reason to be cautious about travelling too far with those initial results: the question is a blunt one, and the sentiments it taps certainly go far beyond the kind of arrangement that governments envisioned when they negotiated NAFTA. But it is possible to add texture to those findings because, in addition to the question about integration, the 1990 Canadian, American, and Mexican surveys used other strategies to probe attitudes towards political integration. The additional evidence helps both to flesh out the initial findings and to identify what sorts of considerations shape support for integration.

One set of open-ended questions probed what people thought the advantages and disadvantages might be if Canada and the United States (or the United States and Canada/ Mexico and the United States) were to form "one country." The responses to this battery reflect a fundamental dilemma faced to varying degrees by publics in all three countries—the tension between anticipated economic gains and potential socio-cultural trade-offs. One-third of Americans, for example, cite economic advantages to forming one country with Canada, and another third see socio-cultural problems coming from such a union. In the Canadian case, 44% of respondents see economic advantages while 60% oppose forming one country for socio-cultural reasons. The figures for Mexico are about the same. Moreover, 32% of Americans, 42% of Canadians, and 32% of Mexicans see "no advantages" to any political union.[12] If these responses are genuine indicators of the outer limits of opinion, the striking implication is that some 68% of Americans and Mexicans and about 59% of Canadians could conceivably be moved to support political union under the right circumstances. What might these right conditions be?

All three of the 1990 surveys presented the American, Mexican, and Canadian publics with seven equivalent "scenarios" or "vignettes," each of which spelled out a possible policy consequence of political union. Respondents were asked whether they would favour or oppose Canada and the United States (the United States and Canada/ Mexico and the United States)

forming one country if it meant—
(1) that you would enjoy a higher standard of living?
(2) losing Canada's/Mexico's cultural identity [Canada and Mexico]/having a large French speaking minority [U.S.]
(3) that we would deal more effectively with environmental issues like acid rain and pollution?
(4) Canada would form 12 new states in the U.S.?/Mexico would form 32 new states?
(5) a better quality of life?
(6) having a government-funded (rather than private) health care system [U.S.]/having a privately funded rather than a government-funded health care system]Canada]
(7) slightly higher taxes and more government services [U.S.]/slightly lower taxes and fewer government services [Canada and Mexico]

Figure 5-13 reports responses to each of these scenarios against two benchmarks. It indicates the extent to which the policy scenarios move support from the bottom-line position in each country (i.e., support for doing away with borders), and also indicates which of the scenarios could produce a majority support for political union. Overall, the evidence suggests just how fluid public attitudes to political union are. Notice that a majority of Canadians[13] appear to support political union with the United States under two conditions: if it meant a better quality of life, and if it meant that we could deal more effectively with environmental issues. The "better quality of life" scenario is difficult to interpret for obvious reasons; it taps an imagined "best of all possible worlds" outcome and serves the purpose of signalling an upper limit. The environmental scenario, as has already been demonstrated (Chapter 4), is a relatively concrete and increasingly salient concern. The promise of a higher standard of living has the effect of boosting Canadian support for political union with the United States, but that scenario is not sufficiently attractive to produce a majority in favour of forming one country. Significantly, *all* of the other scenarios have the effect of depressing support for political union.

In the case of the United States, the scenarios produce majorities for political union in five of the seven vignettes. The promise of government-funded health care, an issue that is divisive in American domestic politics, boosts support for political union. The prospects of getting twelve new states also boosts that support. At the same time, Americans are less enthusiastic about the idea of adopting a francophone minority.

Mexican responses also indicate fluidity. The quality-of-life and environmental scenarios produce majority support for political union with the United States, as in the Canadian case. For understandable reasons, the promise of a higher standard of living has a very substantial impact on Mexican support for political union. But as in Canada, the potential loss of cultural identity depresses support for political union. Together, these data indicate that domestic policy preferences do have a significant impact on support for integration. But they also suggest that opposition to political integration may be less robust than has previously been supposed.

Conclusions

Three main findings emerge from the evidence considered in this chapter. First, the general economic orientations of Canadians—their views about free markets and meritocracy—differ less from those of their American counterparts than is sometimes implied. Perspective is critical to any evaluation of differences and similarities, and when the economic orientations of Canadians are viewed in the context of the economic values held by publics in other advanced industrial states, it is Canadian–American similarities that come into focus. As Innis (1956), Clark (1968), Lipset (1990), and others have rightly pointed out, there are very persuasive institutional, historical, and

Figure 5-13 Scenarios of Moving Public Opinion

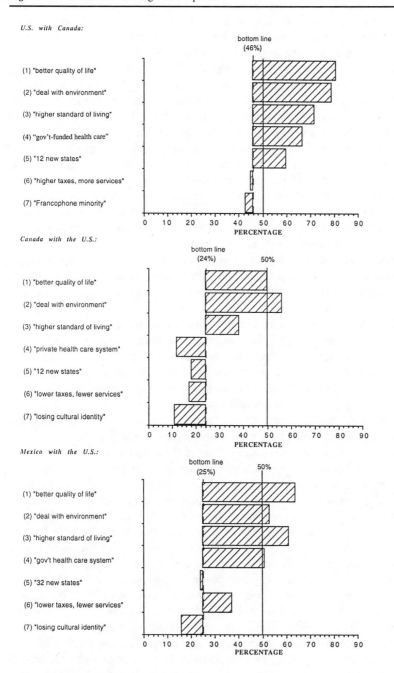

Source: 1990 World Values Survey (Canada and U.S.).

structural reasons why Canadians may have been more communal, less individualist, more reliant on the state, and "less friendly to capitalism" than Americans. But structural conditions change, and so do values. Canadian–American structural differences have narrowed, and a smaller proportion of the Canadian workforce is engaged in extractive and other primary economic activities than it once was. The WVS evidence spans too short a time period to give a historical perspective to the findings or to usefully inform speculations about the pace of value change. But for the period for which directly comparable survey data are available, the striking findings have to do with the *consistency* of similarities in Canadian and American economic orientations. That consistency is evident not only in levels of support for free-market ideas and the principle of meritocracy, but also from the effects of background factors. And where there are cross-time changes, the magnitude of the shifts is similar. The theme of North American similarities in economic values, or even North American "exceptionalism," is underscored by the second set of findings—those relating to explanations for poverty and what should be done when jobs are scarce. The effects of such background factors as education and age on "why people live in need," for example, are almost identical in Canada and the United States. Where the impact of age produces a curvilinear relationship among Americans, it also produces a curvilinear relationship in Canada.

Second, the most striking direct evidence of economic value change, clearly, is the rising support for the principle of meritocracy. All of the other indications of shifting economic values have to be inferred from the consistency of the correlations with key background factors. But some of these, particularly the possibility that poverty has less to do with laziness and more with "social injustice," are substantively intriguing.

The WVS produce findings that illustrate a connection between values and free trade but are also striking for other reasons. There is sufficient evidence here to make the case that values count in the dynamics of integration from three different vantage points. The first vantage point, informed by Deutsch's model, withstands the plausibility probe informed by the WVS data; the basic chains in Deutsch's line of speculation hold up under closer scrutiny, with the implication that the lessons drawn from West European experience apply to the North American setting. The evidence falls short of a conclusive "proof" that Deutsch was right, but it is plainly consistent with his speculations. Second, and quite aside from Deutsch's elegant theory, there is other basic empirical evidence indicating that economic values matter: economic orientations as support for meritocracy and the free-market ethos are demonstrably related to support for free trade. Third, and as Putnam (1988) maintains, domestic policy preferences also matter. That as many as one in four Canadians is prepared to entertain the idea of forming one country with the United States is a striking finding, which reflects, perhaps, that state boundaries are less relevant than they once were. One reading of that finding is that

Canadians supported free trade with the United States and NAFTA because they had little choice (Stairs, 1994). Another is that Canadians are less reluctant continentalists than has sometimes been supposed. More central to the contention that domestic policy preferences affect attitudes to integration, however, is the unmistakable evidence indicating that public support for integration moves in response to various experimental scenarios—many of which capture the substantive policy concerns raised by publics during the course of the NAFTA debates. The conclusion to be drawn from all of this is not that economic values determine orientations to free trade. If anything, the indications are that political factors, particularly mutual trust, are more powerful determinants of orientations towards continental integration.[14] We should instead conclude that values do play a role in the dynamics of integration; they play a more prominent role than contemporary renditions of integration theory allow.

The main concern of this chapter has been to examine some broad economic orientations. The task now is to fill in the picture, to turn away from general economic orientations and to add important details with a more fine-grained investigation of other economic values. This is the task of the next chapter.

NOTES

[1] One could reasonably counter that this alternative interpretation simply shifts the explanatory problem onto other ground. What, for example, explains Canadian–American differences in tax regime? One possibility is that the differences between the Canadian and American tax frameworks are themselves just another measure of differences in basic economic values. This, of course, may be true. Then again, it is not at all clear that the ground rules of tax regimes are more likely to reflect elite values than public ones.

[2] On questions that have this format, it is difficult to assign precise meaning to the scores in the mid-range of the scales. For that reason, only the responses at the extreme ends of the scales—8, 9, and 10 or 1, 2, and 3—are reported here.

[3] These findings provide yet another example of the difficulty of assigning precise and stable content to the notions of "left" and "right." For an early general discussion of the issue, see Laponce (1972). A contemporary empirical investigation is provided by Fuchs and Klingemann (1990). A discussion of the impact of "new politics" on left–right orientations is taken up in Kitschelt and Hellemans (1990). For empirical evidence of North American variations, see Gibbins and Nevitte (1985), and Nevitte and Gibbins (1990).

[4] According to the correlation coefficients (Appendix 5-B), the aggregate Canadian age effect on "laziness" is negative and weak. This, though, almost certainly reflects the impact of new Canadians. Notice too, that new Canadians are very different from others when it comes to injustice. I have no ready explanation for these variations.

[5] The complication here, of course, is that these North American data become candidates for country-specific explanations. In the Canadian case, for instance, the data in Appendix 5-B unequivocally show that new Canadians are very different from others; they are much more inclined to attribute poverty to laziness. These differences introduce statistical "noise" in any analysis of the aggregate Canadian data. When new Canadians are left out of the analysis, the evidence of generational change becomes far more compelling. One contributing factor to the ∪ curve in the Canadian case stems from the fact that age effects work in precisely the opposite direction for new Canadians and francophone Canadians. It turns out that anglophone Canadians are relatively immune from age effects. This leaves the American data open to "exceptional" explanation.

[6] A useful collection of essays that captures the spirit of these vigorous philosophical debates is Cohen, Nagel, and Scanlon (1977). See also Letwin's (1983) collection of essays. Some Canadian context to these issues is provided in Nevitte and Kornberg (1985).

[7] See Hochschild (1981) and Sniderman, Brody and Tetlock (1991).

[8] Typically, the focus on the role of values has been limited to elites. Schmitter, for example, suspects that "the more complementary elites come to acquire similar expectations and attitudes towards the integrative process, the easier it will be to form transnational associations and to accept regional identities" (1971: 253).

[9] For instance, one in three Québecois support doing away with the Canada–U.S. border, compared to one in five in the rest of Canada. More detailed analysis also shows that such factors as patriotism, partisanship, and where respondents are located in their domestic economics come into play. (For a more detailed analysis of these aspects see Inglehart, Nevitte, and Basanez, 1994).

[10] The patterns of Mexican, Canadian, and American value change are summarized elsewhere; the essential finding is that in most, but not all, instances North American values seem to have converged. See Nevitte (1995), Inglehart, Nevitte and Basanez (1994), and Nevitte and Inglehart (1995). For an analysis of how geographic contiguity with the United States may shape Mexican and Canadian public opinion towards the United States, see Nevitte (1994).

[11] The gamma coefficients for support for free trade with the United States and each of these items are: meritocracy = .2; incentives for individual effort = .17; private ownership should be increased = .23; individuals should take more responsibility for themselves = .19; competition is good = .23; hard work usually brings a better life = .18.

12 Abolishing Borders: Advantages* and Disadvantages** (Percentages)

Advantages	U.S. with Canada	Canada with U.S.	Mexico with U.S.
Economic	33	42	41
Political	17	11	3
Social/Cultural Relations	9	3	7
General/Other	9	4	18
No Advantages	32	41	32
Disadvantages			
Economic	10	11	5
Political	28	10	5
Social/cultural relations	34	60	52
General/other	–	6	30
No Disadvantages	28	13	7

*The question reads: "What do you think would be the main advantages of the U.S. and Canada [U.S. and Canada]/the U.S. and Mexico [Mexico] forming one country?" **The question reads: "And what do you think would be the main disadvantages?" *Source*: 1990 World Values Survey.

13 The very same analysis of value change was replicated for two groups within Canada: francophone and anglophone. In that analysis, there is value convergence on eight out of thirteen value domains. Anglophone Canadians appear to have political and economic values that are more similar to American orientations. Anglophone and francophone Canadians are closer on social values.

14 This conclusion flows from a regression analysis of the determinants of orientations towards "closer economic ties" and "doing away with borders."

Appendix 5-A Questions tapping general economic orientations

Question prompt: Now I'd like you to tell me your views on various issues. For each pair of contrasting issues, 1 means you agree completely with the statement on the left (or in this case, the first statement presented); 10 means you agree completely with the statement on the right (or the second statement given), or you can choose any number in between. How would you place your views on this scale?

Competition is harmful. It brings out the worst in people. vs. **Competition is good. It stimulates people to work hard and develop new ideas**.

The state should take more responsibility to ensure that everyone is provided for. vs. **Individuals should take more responsibility for providing for themselves**.

Government ownership of business and industry should be increased. vs. **Private ownership of business and industry should be increased**.

Hard work doesn't generally bring success—it's more a matter of luck and connections. vs. **In the long run, hard work usually brings a better life**.

People who are unemployed should have the right to refuse a job they do not want. vs. **People who are unemployed should have to take any job available or lose their unemployment benefits**.

People can only accumulate wealth at the expense of others. vs. **Wealth can grow so there's enough for everyone**.

Incomes should be made more equal. vs. **There should be greater incentives for individual effort**.

Source: 1990 World Values Survey.

Appendix 5-B Those Saying that People Live in Need because They Are Lazy or Because Society is Unjust, by Age, Value Type, and Level of Education (Gamma Coefficients)

	Lazy			Injustice		
Country	Age	Value Type	Level of Education	Age	Value Type	Level of Education
France	.11	-.27	-.13	-.08	.14	-.02
Britain	.22	-.17	-.20	-.15	.28	.09
W. Germany	.18	-.35	-.19	-.16	.36	.16
Italy	.06	-.21	-.11	-.03	.20	.06
Netherlands	.16	-.36	-.23	-.14	.25	.12
Denmark	.01	-.43	-.15	-.11	.37	.03
Belgium	.15	-.19	-.11	-.24	.25	.19
Spain	.10	-.21	-.14	-.17	.29	.20
Ireland	.24	-.11	-.24	-.12	.27	.27
N. Ireland	.37	-.30	-.64	-.39	.39	.02
U.S.	.08	-.21	-.24	-.07	.28	.22
Canada	-.002	-.18	-.09	-.01	.19	.07
English	.0004	-.15	-.11	-.05	.17	.02
French	.10	-.26	-.30	-.27	.28	.29
New Canadians	-.11	-.26	.03	.13	.21	.03

Source: 1990 World Values Survey.

Appendix 5-C "When jobs are scarce ..." by Country (Gamma Coefficients)

Country	Men have more right to a job than women			People should be forced to retire early			Employers should give priority to co-nationals over immigrants			It is unfair to give work to handicapped people when able-bodied people can't find jobs		
	Age	Education	Value Type	Age	Education	Value Type	Age	Education	Value Type	Age	Education	Value Type
France	.25	-.39	-.40	.07	-.24	-.17	.30	-.39	-.45	.24	-.32	-.33
Britain	.48	-.40	-.25	.21	-.25	-.08	.23	-.32	-.26	.33	-.50	-.33
W. Germany	.38	-.38	-.46	-.07	-.14	-.15	.22	-.44	-.48	.18	-.33	-.33
Italy	.37	-.35	-.40	.10	-.10	-.15	.27	-.37	-.36	.19	-.20	-.24
Netherlands	.41	-.43	-.49	.06	-.23	-.21	.29	-.29	-.50	.19	-.17	-.31
Denmark	.59	-.43	-.40	.09	-.14	-.20	.21	-.35	-.51	.23	-.24	-.33
Belgium	.26	-.38	-.30	.02	-.22	-.16	.20	-.22	-.32	.15	-.26	-.28
Spain	.33	-.38	-.35	.04	-.18	-.11	.14	-.17	-.26	.15	-.31	-.16
Ireland	.46	-.45	-.14	.19	-.28	-.14	.15	-.29	-.16	.26	-.45	-.09
N. Ireland	.46	-.46	-.20	.20	-.41	-.11	.37	-.24	-.24	.39	-.16	-.25
U.S.	.24	-.28	-.24	.14	-.25	-.16	.17	-.16	-.10	.13	-.18	-.16
Canada	.25	-.34	-.23	.14	-.23	-.18	.02	-.23	-.20	.18	-.19	-.11
English	.23	-.33	-.22	.15	-.21	-.18	.01	-.20	-.15	.13	-.17	-.09
French	.30	-.42	-.36	.001	-.18	-.29	.10	-.34	-.37	.21	-.36	-.07
New Canadians	.27	-.36	-.08	.21	-.31	-.15	.12	-.08	-.06	.26	-.07	-.31

Source: 1990 World Values Survey.

6: A Changing Work Culture?

Attitudes to competition, meritocracy, economic fairness, free trade, and the like all concern general, and in some senses quite abstract, economic orientations. Far less abstract is the work world that most people confront from day to day. Chapter 2 introduced some evidence on people's attitudes to work indicating that people generally give it high priority. When asked about "the most important things in life," respondents ranked work second, albeit a distant second, behind the family. Chapter 5 also touched on work-related values, and indicated that there is some cross-national variation in what rewards people think "hard work" will bring. But these were isolated results; they relied on single indicators and on data from just one time point. Orientations towards work are a part of economic culture, and this chapter brings work-related values from the margins to the centre of investigation. It delves into attitudes about the work world in much greater detail, and fleshes out the theme of economic value change with much more cross-time evidence.

Five broad questions guide the investigation. The first three probe issues that directly tap workplace attitudes: How do people feel about the work ethic and the place that work occupies in their lives? What reasons do people give for working? And, relatedly, what is it that people want in a job? The fourth question moves the analysis much closer to the kinds of issues raised in the preceding chapters. It asks: What kind of participation do people want in the workplace? Has there been any change in people's orientations regarding participation in workplace decision-making? The fifth question involves an explicit search for conceptual and empirical common ground between workplace participation and participation in the political world more generally: Are attitudes to workplace participation systematically related to attitudes to political participation?

The fundamental finding from the WVS data is that attitudes to work have changed in nearly every one of the twelve states examined. As before, the changes in these economic values are not nearly as dramatic as the political value changes, but consistent patterns are detectable; some shifts clearly are significant, and nearly all are in the same direction. Particularly striking are changes in workplace motivations and shifts in attitudes to workplace participation; there is evidence of emerging support for a new work ethos and, along with that, shifting public preferences towards greater participation in workplace decision-making. The concluding part of the chapter embarks upon a

Table 6-1 Percentage Saying a Decrease in the Importance of Work in Our Lives
is a "Bad Thing"

Country	1981	1990	% Change
Britain	57.3	48.5	-8.8
West Germany	52.2	50.6	-1.6
Italy	65.1	58.9	-6.2
Netherlands	45.0	42.4	-2.6
Denmark	57.3	63.9	+6.6
Belgium	41.6	32.0	-9.6
Spain	48.6	36.1	-12.5
Ireland	66.0	68.2	+2.2
Northern Ireland	62.2	55.8	-6.4
United States	67.0	62.4	-4.6
Canada	59.6	52.8	-6.8
English	64.9	57.0	-7.9
French	45.2	43.0	-2.2
New Canadians	—	50.8	—
European Average (without France)	55.0	50.7	-4.3

Question: "If 'a decrease in the importance of work in our lives' were to happen, would it be a good thing, a bad thing, or don't you mind?"
Note: The above results reflect the views of those respondents who indicated "a decrease in the importance of work in our lives" would be a bad thing.
Source: 1981 and 1990 World Values Surveys.

more sustained analysis of the theme that is central to this book: it becomes absolutely clear that attitudes towards workplace participation are systematically related to views and preferences about political participation. Now to the evidence itself.

The Work Ethic and Pride in Work

The World Values Surveys contained a variety of questions about work, many of which were asked in both 1981 and 1990. One such general question about work turns out to be quite closely related to the "important things in your life" battery the findings of which were introduced at the very beginning. It asked: "If a decrease in the importance of work in our lives were to happen, would it be a good thing, a bad thing, or don't you mind?" Here, one would expect strong supporters of the work ethic to evaluate a decrease in the importance of work as a "bad thing." According to the aggregate cross-time results reported in Table 6-1, there appears to be some erosion of the work ethic among publics in advanced industrial states: the proportion of respondents indicating that a decrease in the importance of work is a bad thing is on the decline.[1] The decline is not sharp, nor is it entirely even; there are very substantial national variations in support for the work ethic even among this group of states. Dutch and Belgian respondents, for example, seem relatively unconcerned about a decline in the work ethic; they score low on this indicator in both 1981 and 1990. Irish and American respondents, by contrast, score considerably higher at both time points. Notice, too, that the gap between Canadians and Americans is quite substantial; there are significant variations between Canada's three groups, and the decline in the Canadian work ethic is relatively sharp. In general, however, the overall trend is one of declining support for the work ethic. With the exception of Denmark, which experienced a 1981–1990 increase in support for the work ethic of just over 6%, all of the other shifts that are beyond the margin of error (plus or minus 3%) are in the same direction.

Why are these changes taking place? One possibility is that shifts in the work ethic are shaped by contextual factors. A defence of the work ethic, for example, could be a more urgent matter for those who live close to the margins of subsistence than for those, like citizens of advanced industrial states, who typically enjoy a relatively high standard of living. According to this line of speculation, people with relatively high incomes should exhibit higher levels of financial satisfaction, and this in turn might lead them to place less emphasis on work. The findings reported in Table 6-2 suggest that there is probably something to that line of reasoning. When citizens in the objectively wealthy twelve advanced industrial states are considered alongside publics in twelve relatively poor states and the two groups are compared by levels of financial satisfaction and attitudes to the work ethic, there are some fairly clear differences. Levels of financial satisfaction typically are much higher in advanced industrial states, and these publics are much less likely than their counterparts in the less developed countries to say that the decrease in the importance of work is a bad thing.

A full explanation for cross-national differences in support for the work ethic, however, is almost certainly more complex than that. Indeed, the very same data (Table 6-2) also point to a number of important exceptions to such a general explanation. Consider the cases of Ireland, Denmark, and the United States on the one hand and Poland, Hungary, and Mexico on the other. Publics in the first three countries plainly are much wealthier than those in the other three: the aggregate income gap is quite substantial. That being so, why would an almost identical proportion of each of these publics say that a decrease in the importance of work is a bad thing? That stark finding turns attention to other tantalizing possibilities. Regardless of the precise explanation for the variations between publics in high- and low-income countries, pursuing that line of enquiry is a detour from issues that are more central here: Why has support for the work ethic eroded *within* advanced industrial states? And what explains the differences between this set of countries?

One place to begin looking for an answer to that question is to consider what impact such contextual factors as people's attitudes about their own economic circumstances and their jobs might have on their work ethic. At least

Table 6-2 Attitudes towards Declining Importance of Work and Financial Satisfaction in 24 Countries (1990)

Country	GDP/Capita (World Bank, 1992)	Decrease in importance of work is a bad thing	High level of financial satisfaction
Advanced Industrial States:			
France	$16,090	—	24.9%
Britain	$12,810	48.5%	40.4%
W. Germany	$18,480	50.6%	42.4%
Italy	$13,330	58.9%	46.0%
Netherlands	$14,520	42.4%	58.4%
Denmark	$18,540	63.9%	54.8%
Belgium	$14,490	32.0%	50.0%
Spain	$7,740	36.1%	26.7%
Ireland	$7,750	68.2%	44.0%
N. Ireland	$8,000	55.8%	41.8%
United States	$19,840	62.4%	46.9%
Canada	$16,960	52.8%	52.1%
Average	$14,046	52.0%	44.0%
Less Developed Countries:			
Nigeria	$290	82.1%	28.1%
China	$330	79.3%	33.5%
India	$340	87.1%	33.8%
Turkey	$1,280	74.5%	12.0%
Mexico	$1,760	64.2%	34.1%
Poland	$1,860	62.3%	18.1%
Brazil	$2,160	74.4%	26.6%
Chile	$2,250	76.1%	28.4%
S. Africa	$2,290	82.9%	32.4%
Hungary	$2,460	61.1%	20.4%
Argentina	$2,520	72.8%	20.1%
S. Korea	$3,600	75.4%	24.2%
Average	$1,762	74.4%	26.0%

Note: The 12 advanced industrial states are the same states that are the focus of analysis throughout the first 5 chapters. The 12 developing countries include those countries, with low levels of GDP/Capita (ranked in ascending order), that were included in the 1990 round of the World Values Surveys.
Question: "How satisfied are you with the financial situation of your household?" (Responses range from a low score of 1, meaning "dissatisfied," to a high score of 10, meaning "satisfied." The responses shown in the table above represent those that scored either an 8, 9, or 10.)
Source: 1990 World Values Survey; World Bank (1992).

three testable possibilities come to mind. One line of speculation has already been suggested: it could be that publics in advanced industrial states are becoming less preoccupied about the work ethic simply because they are financially better off. Then again, support for the work ethic may have eroded because people are less satisfied with the workplace and the jobs they do. People's expectations of the workplace might be higher than they once were, workplace conditions could be deteriorating, or there may be some combination of these kinds of factors. Yet another possibility, one that captures the reservations that older generations have about the young, suggests that generational effects may be important if "young people nowadays just don't have any pride in their work."

Is there any substance to these speculations? Both the 1981 and 1990 WVS asked respondents about financial satisfaction, job satisfaction, and pride in their work. Not surprisingly, most of these factors are strongly related to each other and to feelings about the work ethic. It turns out that these factors are connected in very similar ways in each of the twelve countries: people with high levels of job satisfaction, for example, typically express a great deal of pride in their work (gamma = .43). Again, the higher people's level of financial satisfaction the more satisfied they are with their job (gamma = .32). The importance people attach to the work ethic is more weakly related to pride in work (gamma = .17) and to job satisfaction (gamma = .15). Significantly, however, support for the work ethic does not appear to be related to financial satisfaction (gamma =.08).

Figure 6-1 summarizes the aggregate cross-time findings for those in the full-time paid workforce in Canada and the United States and for publics in the ten European countries. The evidence is somewhat uneven. Aggregate levels of financial satisfaction, for example, have shifted hardly at all; they have inched down both in Europe and Canada and risen very slightly in the United States. Nor is it clear that variations in financial satisfaction reflect only variations in income level. Two pieces of evidence underscore that point. First, the aggregate data show that it is the Dutch (59.9%), Danes (55.5%), and Canadians (50.8%) who rank at the top in their subjective assessments of job satisfaction, but by most objective indicators it is Americans who enjoy the highest aggregate income levels. Second, while there plainly is a relationship between individual levels of income and reported financial satisfaction (Europe, gamma = .28; United States = .14; Canada = .36), there are also significant cross-national variations in the strength of those relationships, and they are not as strong as might be expected.

Figure 6-1 also demonstrates that the aggregate cross-time changes in levels of job satisfaction are again quite small. On average, job satisfaction has fallen by about 7 percentage points in the European countries. It has risen by about the same amount among Americans and remained stable for Canadians. Over the course of the decade, the gap between Canadians and Americans narrowed somewhat, but Canadians still scored significantly higher than Americans in their job satisfaction ratings in 1990.

Figure 6-1   Financial Satisfaction, Job Satisfaction, and Pride in Work, 1981–1990

High levels of financial satisfaction:

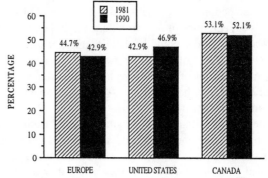

High levels of job satisfaction:

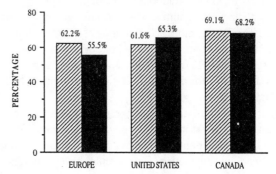

High levels of pride in work:

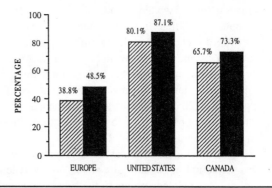

Source: 1981 and 1990 World Values Surveys.
Note: High levels of household financial satisfaction (percentage scoring 8, 9, or 10 on a scale ranging from 1 to 10); high levels of job satisfaction (percentage scoring 8, 9, or 10 on a scale ranging from 1 to 10—employed only); and high levels of pride in work (those saying they take a great deal of pride in work—employed only).

Figure 6-2 Percentage Saying that a Decrease in the Importance of Work in Our Lives Is a "Bad Thing," by Age

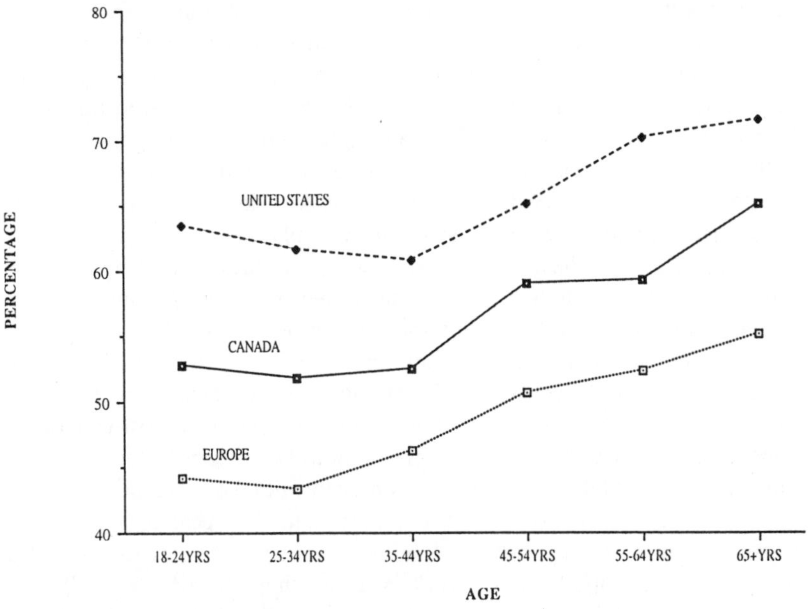

Source: 1981 and 1990 World Values Surveys.

The clearest evidence of a consistent trend comes from the findings dealing with pride in work. Between 1981 and 1990, the proportions of respondents expressing "a great deal of pride in their work" increased in every single country, and on this dimension the American respondents are clearly the outliers (see Appendix A for the full results). Once again Canadians are also at the high end of the rankings, but they still sit well behind the Americans (87.1%), the British (83%), and, to a lesser extent, the Irish (80.8% and 76.8%) and the Danes (76.4%).

The preliminary indications are that none of these contextual factors seem to supply an entirely satisfactory explanation for the cross-national variations. It is hardly plausible that stable levels of financial and job satisfaction can account for a declining work ethic, and it is even less likely that rising levels of pride in work can explain declining support for the work ethic. It is possible, perhaps, that those areas where shifting economic orientations are detectable—the shifts in the work ethic and pride in work—might be related to the same underlying factors (age, post-materialist value orientations, and education) that are connected to changing political orientations. When it comes to the work ethic, for example, Figure 6-2 provides clear and consistent evidence of the presence of age effects in every single country. Generally, the young tend to be less worried than the old about the decline of the work ethic. The relationship between age and support for the work ethic, however, is not entirely straightforward. According to the data presented in Figure 6-2, there is hardly any relationship between age and work ethic orientations for those in the 18–44 age group; the line is flat and age effects only seem to kick in for respondents 45 years and older. That same pattern holds in every one of the twelve countries. Figure 6-2 also provides yet another illustration of American exceptionalism: American respondents in every age group consistently score higher than other publics on this work ethic measure, and that finding is as good an indication as any that the American public is exceptional and that nationally specific factors come into play.

It is possible that these age differences indicate life-cycle effects; people may give higher priority to the work ethic as they get older. Or they may indicate that genuine generational shifts are taking place. As before, the plausibility of the generational change interpretation hinges partly on whether the key indicators—age, post-materialist orientations, and education level—are *all* related to attitudes to the work ethic in the same way. Post-materialist value orientations and education have somewhat different effects in each national setting, but they are generally consistent with the generational change explanation. The strongest evidence comes from the European data: European post-materialists are significantly *less* likely than materialists to say that a decrease in the importance of work is a bad thing (gamma = -.17), and Europeans with higher levels of education are *less* likely than those with low levels of education to be worried about a declining work ethic. In the two North American countries, however, the evidence is less clearcut. For Canadians and Americans, the direction of the relationship between post-materialist orientations and the work ethic is consistent with the generational change interpretation (Canada, gamma = -.09; United States, gamma = -.06), but the relationships are much weaker than for Europe. Education effects are even murkier. In Canada, the impact of education level on support for the work ethic is similar to that in Europe; those with higher levels of education are *less* worried about the declining work ethic. For American respondents, however, higher levels of education seem to have the opposite effect. The higher the level of education, the *more* support there is for the work ethic (gamma = .03). On balance, the generational change explanation for an eroding work ethic appears to apply to the European and Canadian settings. But the findings are too weak and inconsistent to supply clear support for generational shifts in the work ethic in the United States.

How do the shifts in pride in work square with these results? Recall that the basic finding concerning the relationship between support for the work ethic and pride in work produces a seemingly awkward, even counterintuitive piece of evidence: support for the work ethic appears to be *declining* while pride in work is *increasing*. What explanation can there be for such a paradoxical finding? Making inferences about individual level change on the basis of aggregate shifts is risky, and so one possibility is that the apparently anachronistic aggregate results mask more subtle country-specific variations: a few "outliers," rogue results, could be skewing the overall pattern. There is no evidence, however, that this is the case: the very same relationship between pride in work and the work ethic holds in each one of the twelve countries. Moreover, the country-specific results are not weak, but quite robust (Europe, gamma = .22; United States = .22; Canada = .29). Another, more complicated possibility is that levels of pride in work and attitudes to the work ethic are *both* in transition, but that each is affected by *different* underlying factors. Is there any evidence that such factors as age, post-materialist value orientations, and education have a different impact on pride in work and the work ethic? And what about the effects of all of the other economic orientations considered so far? Are these related to pride in work and the work ethic in the same way?

One way to explore such a possibility is to run a whole series of tests that consider, in turn, the impact of each single background factor on pride in work and then on the work ethic. That approach is cumbersome, and it would reveal nothing about any possible interactions between the various factors. More to the point, it would be extremely difficult to construct a meaningful synthesis from such a laborious item-by-item analysis. An alternative and more revealing approach relies on a more powerful strategy, multivariate analysis. The advantage of multivariate analysis is that it indicates the relative importance of all of these factors taken together while isolating the independent effects of each factor. By using the same background factors (predictors), a multivariate strategy helps to identify which predictors are the most important determinants of the two sets of attitudes—support for the work ethic and pride in work—that appear to have undergone changes between 1981 and 1990. The results of that multivariate analysis, summarized in Table 6-3, underscore three key findings.

The first has to do with the *scope* of the changes. It has already been established that support for the work ethic has declined between 1981 and 1990. Notice, however, that the estimates for the variable "time" indicate that the overall changes in attitudes to the work ethic are *not* statistically significant. By contrast, the increased levels in pride in work are statistically significant. Are the shifts in pride in work a result of generational change? Probably not. In this instance, the estimates indicate that both age and post-materialist orientations are significantly related to pride in work, but education is not. Moreover, post-materialist orientations are *negatively* related to pride in work, which means that the rise of post-materialist values would be expected to produce a decline, not an increase, in pride in work.

Second, the most powerful predictor of pride in work clearly is job satisfaction. The more satisfied people are with their work, the more likely they are to express a great deal of pride in it. Job satisfaction is also the best predictor of support for the work ethic, but is a far weaker predictor of the work ethic than pride in work. Notice, too, that other important predictors come into play. Family income is one: the more families earn, the more likely they are to

Table 6-3   Regression Analysis: Predictors of Pride in Work and the Work Ethic

Predictors	Pride in Work	Declining Importance of Work Is a "Bad Thing"
Time (1981 to 1990)	.10**	-.02
Job Satisfaction	.42**	.12**
Financial Satisfaction	.01	.04**
Postmaterialism	-.05**	-.08**
Age	.03*	.02*
Male	.02	.01
Income	.12**	-.02*
Education	.02	-.01
Non-manual occupation	.0003	.03**
Catholic	-.02*	-.06**
Canadians	.08**	.01
Americans	.17**	.05**
Constant	1.34	1.84
R-squared	.28	.03

Note: * significant at $p < .05$; ** significant at $p < .01$.
Source: 1981 and 1990 World Values Surveys.

express pride in their work.[2] One speculation is that the increases in pride in work could also be related to underlying shifts in the character of the work-force. As has already been indicated, women came into the paid workforce in unprecedented numbers, and the relative balance of manual and non-manual occupations has also changed. Indeed, structural and occupational shifts in the economy are one of the defining features of advanced industrialism. These transformations are undoubtedly of great significance, but there is nothing in the WVS data to suggest they have anything to do with the increases in pride in work, at least in these states. There is also some support for the classic theory (Weber, 1958) that religion matters: Protestants express more pride in their work than Catholics and are stronger supporters of the work ethic.

What about national differences?[3] The evidence is clear: both Canada and the United States are significantly different from Europe; Canadians fall in between Europeans and Americans. A more detailed probing of these data shows that anglophone Canadians are almost indistinguishable from Americans, at least on the pride in work dimension. On support for the work ethic, however, Canadians are indistinguishable from Europeans, and it is on this dimension that Americans are most clearly exceptional.

That such a high proportion of the American public expresses a "great deal of pride in work" provides yet further evidence of how central notions of "diligence, toil, and exertion" are to the American ethos (McClosky & Zaller, 1984). But when that finding is placed in a broader context, other fascinating questions arise. Hard work, of course, may bring greater financial rewards, and in terms of aggregate per capita income the United States ranks first among the twelve countries considered. But when it comes to financial *satis-faction* Americans rank fifth (46.9% saying they are "very satisfied") out of twelve. They rank significantly behind the Dutch (58.4%), Danish (54.8%), Canadians (52.1%), and Belgians (50.0%).[4] An alternative interpretation might be that Americans attach greater importance to work because they derive other kinds of satisfaction from the workplace. The difficulty with that explanation is that American respondents (65.3%) also rank well behind their Danish (74.3%) and Canadian (68.2%) counterparts in their self-reported assessments of job satisfaction.

It is entirely possible that pride in work is simply an idea, or phrase, that carries enormous symbolic weight in the American context.[5] But then why are there echoes of these same awkward discrepancies in the Canadian setting? Anglophone Canadians are significantly more likely than their francophone counterparts to express "a great deal of pride in work" (84.1% versus 46.2%, 71.8% for new Canadians), but francophone Canadians score significantly higher than others on both job satisfaction (75.1%, versus 65.9% for anglo-phones and 67.5% for new Canadians) and financial satisfaction (61.3% versus 49.1%, and 51% for new Canadians).[6]

Why Do People Work?

It is useful to take stock of the findings to emerge so far. According to the results of the multivariate analysis, different background factors are responsi-ble for the slight decline in the work ethic and the sharper increase in pride in work. But two other findings—that job satisfaction is the single best predic-tor of pride in work and that there are significant cross-national and cross-time variations in the pride people take in their work—provide particularly valuable clues. Considered together, these two findings suggest that the para-dox of rising levels of pride in work and declining levels of support for the work ethic might have something to do with the reasons why people work. People's motivations for working, and the expectations they have of the work-place, may themselves be in transition, and these dynamics could in turn in different ways be affecting attitudes both to pride in work and to the work ethic.

That orientations to work can shift and that they have undergone significant changes has been amply documented elsewhere. In *The World at Work*, for example, Yankelovic and others (1985) identify three main value orientations towards work, each of which, they suggest, tends to predominate during dif-ferent economic eras. In agrarian economies, they speculate, *sustenance* val-ues prevailed: people were preoccupied with putting bread on the table and clothes on their backs. With the transition from an agrarian to an industrial economy, sustenance values retreat and orientations that give greater priority to *material success* come to the fore. Similarly, the transition from smoke-stack industrialism to technologically driven late industrialism brings another shift: *expressivism* replaces material success as the prevailing work value. Different schemas have been proposed. Some suggest, for example, that the dominant work values corresponding to each of the three economic eras should more properly be labelled "need-driven," "outer-directed," and "inner-directed" (Cherrington, 1980; Zanders, 1993).

Contemporary survey evidence, such as the WVS, can for obvious reasons say little about the long history of work values. But they can shed some light on contemporary work values; in this the 1981 and 1990 WVS are a remarkably rich source of data because they contain some thirty questions investigating various aspects of work motivation. An item-by-item analysis of cross-national responses to each single question would be unwieldy, to say the least. A background analysis of responses to all these questions, however, shows that such a cumbersome strategy is not necessary. People's work motivations, according to factor analysis, are consistently structured around the four basic dimensions shown in Figure 6-3. These dimensions are labelled "instrumental," "comfort," "self-actualization," and "terminal" (See Appendices 6-B and 6-C). Some of these factors correspond fairly closely to dimensions that have been empirically identified by others.

The two items contained in the "instrumental" dimension, for example, reflect orientations that are similar to Furnham's (1990) category. They reflect the view that work is not intrinsically valuable, but rather involves some calculation of the balance between effort and reward. From this perspective, work is considered a means to an end (Zanders, 1993). The items contained in the "terminal" dimension, by contrast, correspond to one part of Cherrington's (1980) typology reflecting the view that work is a desirable activity in and of itself. It is this dimension, according to Zanders, that comes closest to "the classic work ethic in which work is seen as a calling that has to be followed" (1993: 134). The third dimension, "comfort," corresponds almost exactly to the dimension uncovered by Zanders' own empirical investigations; it contains those items that have to do more with work conditions.[7] The fourth dimension, "self-actualization," clearly refers to those aspects of work that hold out possibilities for personal development. From this perspective, people work not because they have to, nor because they see work primarily as providing a source of material comfort, but because the workplace fulfills other goals, such as the opportunity to express their abilities. This is the dimension usually identified as the key emerging value orientation within the contemporary work world.

Because public attitudes to work are consistently organized into four reliable dimensions, it is possible to analyze orientations to work by using scales that summarize respondents' positions on each of four dimensions identified by the background analysis.[8] The WVS do not provide cross-time evidence for all of the scales; the items contained in the "instrumental" and "terminal" dimensions, for example, were asked only in the 1990 surveys, so it is not possible to provide direct evidence of any changes on these two dimensions. But we can still look for indirect traces of change by checking to see if "instru-

Figure 6-3 Four Reasons Why People Work

Instrumental[1]	Comfort[2]	Self-Actualization[2]	Terminal[1]
Work is like a business transaction. The more I get paid, the more I do; the less I get paid, the less I do. Working for a living is a necessity; I wouldn't work if I didn't have to	Good hours Generous holidays Not too much pressure Good pay Good job security	An opportunity to use initiative A job in which you feel that you can achieve something A responsible job A job that is interesting A job that meets one's abilities	I enjoy my work; it's the most important thing in my life I will always do the best I can, regardless of pay

1. Question: Here are some statements about why people work. Irrespective of whether you have a job, or not, which of them comes closest to what you think?

   (a) Work is like a business transaction. The more I get paid, the more I do; the less I get paid, the less I do.
   (b) I will always do the best I can, regardless of pay.
   (c) Working for a living is a necessity; I wouldn't work if I didn't have to.
   (d) I enjoy my work; it's the most important thing in my life.

2. Question: Here are some aspects of a job that people say are important. Please look at them and tell me which ones you personally think are important in a job.

   (a) Good Pay
   (b) Not too much pressure
   (c) Good job security
   (d) Good hours
   (e) An opportunity to use initiative
   (f) Generous holidays
   (g) A job in which you feel that you can achieve something
   (h) A responsible job
   (i) A job that is interesting
   (j) A job that meets one's abilities

mental" and "terminal" work motivations vary systematically with age, post-materialist values, and education level.

First, there are significant national differences in citizen responses to both dimensions. Americans are far more likely than Europeans, for example, to say that they work for "instrumental" reasons: they are more inclined to indicate that "work is like a business transaction" or "working for a living is a necessity." As Figure 6-4 shows, Canadians occupy a middle ground, but are closer to the European than to the American score. When it comes to "terminal" work motivations, however, the gap between North America and Europe disappears, which is somewhat surprising. If this dimension really does reflect the "classic work ethic," as Zanders contends, and the classic work ethic really is a distinguishing feature of the American ethos, then one would expect Americans to score much higher than other publics on this particular dimension. In fact, Irish (58.7%), Dutch (52.1%), Belgian (47.7%), and Danish (47.4%) respondents all score significantly higher than their American counterparts on the "terminal" dimension.

The impact of background factors is also quite different for each dimension. Figure 6-5 illustrates one such contrast by showing the age differences behind both sets of orientations at the same time. For the most part, the age effects on instrumental work orientations indicate that, in every age group, Americans have a more "instrumental" orientation than other nationals, and regardless of nationality, younger respondents are more likely than older ones to express instrumental reasons for working. The older people become, the less likely they are to think of work as a "business transaction" or "a necessity." With the exception of those Americans over 65 years of age and Canadians in the 35-to-44 age group, the age-instrumental orientations gradient is fairly even (gammas: United States = -.10; Canada = -.13; Europe = -.07). Compare that pattern with the age effects on "terminal reasons." The two patterns in these graphs are quite different. For Europeans, the proportion of these publics recording "terminal" work motivations increases gradually with age, and the gradient is quite even. But in the American case, there is a clear ∪ curve and there are traces of a similar ∪ curve for Canadians. Even if one sets aside the findings for those under 25 years and over 65 years on the ground that these two groups are least likely to be in the full-time paid workforce, Europeans and Canadians are both *more* likely than Americans to say that "work is the most important thing in my life" and/or "I will always do the best I can, regardless of pay." By this measure, there is nothing to indicate that Canadians or Europeans are less likely than Americans to be motivated by the classic work ethic.

What about the impact of the background indicators—post-materialist value orientations and education—on terminal and instrumental work motivations? There is no evidence that either post-material values or education has any consistent effect on "terminal" motivations for working.[9] But there is some evidence, which is summarized in Figure 6-6, that post-materialist values and education do have consistent effects on instrumental work values.

Figure 6-4   Instrumental and Terminal Motivations for Working, in 1990

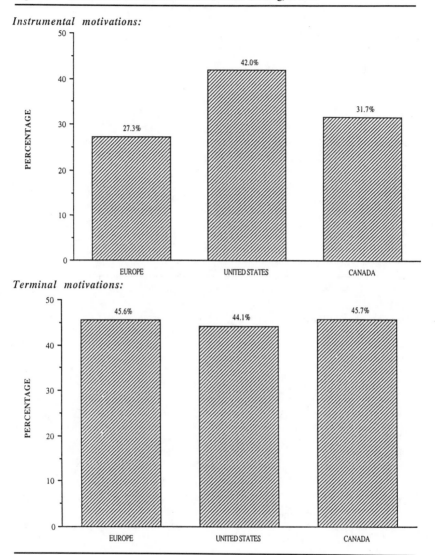

Instrumental motivations:

Terminal motivations:

Source: 1990 World Values Survey.

Regardless of national setting, post-materialists are always *less* likely than materialists to say they work for instrumental reasons. The differences are quite significant. In every national setting, those with higher levels of education are consistently less likely than their compatriots with low levels of education to supply instrumental reasons for working. Both of these findings sug-

Figure 6-5   Instrumental and Terminal Motivations for Working, by Age

Instrumental motivations:

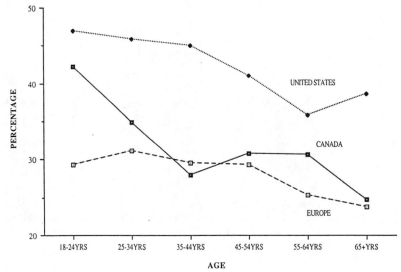

Terminal motivations:

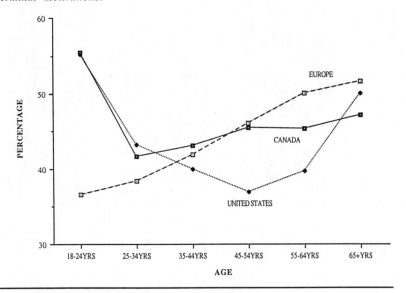

Source: 1981 and 1990 World Values Surveys.
Note: Both the instrumental and terminal scales range from a low of 0 to a high of 2. The above results represent those that scored 1 or more on either scale.

Figure 6-6 Instrumental Motivations for Working, by Value Type and Level of Education

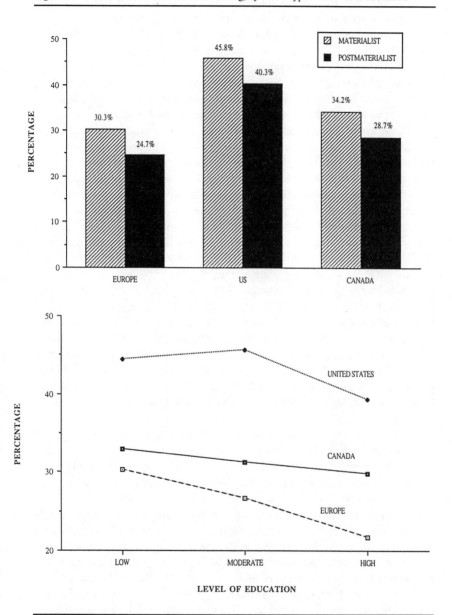

Source: 1990 World Values Surveys.

gest that instrumental work motivations may be undergoing some gradual generational shift. But that interpretation implies that the young should be less likely to subscribe to an instrumental view of work, and we have already seen (Figure 6-5) that in fact the reverse is the case: the young are *more* likely to score high on the instrumental dimension. Regardless of value type or education, the young have more reasons, perhaps, to view their work motivations in instrumental ways: typically, they have less disposable income, have been in the workforce for a shorter length of time, and have had less opportunity to transcend what might be viewed as the short-term considerations for working.

The scope and direction of shifts in the other two dimensions—"self-actualization" and "comfort" work motivations—should be easier to identify for two reasons. First, the background analysis shows that, of the four work-related dimensions, "self-actualization" and "comfort" are clearly the most robust: respondents' orientations are much more sharply structured around these dimensions. Second, it is possible to explore cross-time changes directly because the items pertaining to both of these dimensions were asked at both time points. If self-actualization, or expressiveness, is indeed the emerging work value associated with late industrialism, as Zanders (1993) and others claim, then there should be evidence of an increase in the proportion of these publics subscribing to that motivation. When it comes to comfort the predictions are more ambiguous. On the one hand, there is the argument that comfort, the desire for a "soft job," is a traditional work value, in which case one would predict a decline in comfort-orientated motivations. On the other hand, if the work world is becoming progressively less central to people's lives, people may be placing ever greater emphasis on good hours, generous holidays, and the like. It is these kinds of perks that give workers greater opportunity to focus their energies and attention on more rewarding activities outside of the workplace.

There have been changes on both of these dimensions. As Zanders (1993) and others predict, the WVS data show a shift *towards* self-actualization motivations and a slight shift *away* from comfort motivations. The changes are modest, but that is not so surprising; shifts in basic value orientations are typically incremental. The important point is that the changes are mostly in a consistent direction. Table 6-4 presents the aggregate findings and, in this instance, it is important to draw attention to the very conservative criteria used in constructing the table. For these items, the question format invites respondents to select their responses from a list of fifteen options, and it is left to the respondent to decide how many options to select.[10] The background factor analysis indicated that five options are grouped into the self-actualization dimensions and another five fell into the comfort dimension (see Appendix 6-C). Table 6-4 reports only the percentages of each public who selected *all five* of the self-actualization items, and *all five* of the comfort items as "important in a job."[11]

There are three key findings that deserve particular attention. First, when asked what is most important in a job, respondents are far more likely to

Table 6-4 Percentage of Publics Selecting All Five Items in the Self-actualization Scale and Percentages of Publics Selecting All Five Indicators in the Comfort Scale

Country	Self-actualization (1981)	Comfort (1981)	Self-actualization minus comfort (1981)	Self-actualization (1990)	Comfort (1990)	Self-actualization minus comfort (1990)
France	7.9	2.5	+5.4	12.1	2.1	+10.0
Britain	20.1	10.2	+10.1	17.9	8.5	+9.4
W. Germany	28.6	19.2	+9.4	28.6	14.0	+14.6
Italy	9.3	4.8	+4.5	15.5	9.1	+6.4
Netherlands	9.8	10.6	-0.8	22.2	14.2	+8.0
Denmark	14.9	7.7	+7.2	13.6	3.7	+9.9
Belgium	13.7	12.1	+1.6	13.5	8.4	+5.1
Spain	17.0	19.8	+2.8	15.6	17.2	-1.6
Ireland	13.6	9.5	+4.1	19.3	12.2	+7.1
N. Ireland	13.5	8.7	+4.8	12.8	7.9	+4.9
European Average	14.8	10.5	+4.9	17.1	9.7	+7.4
United States	33.0	16.6	+16.4	30.7	16.2	+14.5
Canada	31.1	13.0	+18.1	28.9	12.4	+16.3
English	31.6	13.0	+18.6	30.4	14.6	+15.8
French	29.7	12.9	+16.8	23.4	7.3	+16.1
New Canadians	—	—	—	29.3	11.4	+17.9

Source: 1981 and 1990 World Values Surveys.

choose self-actualization reasons than comfort reasons. There are only two exceptions to that general pattern, Dutch respondents in 1981 and Spanish in 1990, and in neither of these cases are the differences statistically significant. Second, the gap between self-actualization and comfort motivations increased between 1981 and 1990 in eight of the twelve countries, all of them European. Third, there are subtle variations that appear to indicate some convergence in self-actualization motivations. Notice that in 1981 there was a very substantial gap between North Americans and others on the self-actualization dimension: North Americans scored much higher. By 1990 North Americans still ranked at the very top of the self-actualization scale, but the North American—European gap had narrowed. One reason for the closing of this gap is the slight drop in the proportion of North Americans giving self-actualization responses in 1990. Another reason is the significant increases in the self-actualization scores from those countries that ranked relatively low on the scale in 1981.

Do the key background factors—age, post-materialist value orientations, and education—have any impact on self-actualization and comfort work motivations? And is there any evidence of generational change? The short answers are yes and yes. Figures 6-7 and 6-8 present the aggregate findings; in each case, the consistency of the patterns is truly striking. With self-actualization motivations (Figure 6-7) there is evidence of age effects in Canada, the United

Figure 6-7 Self-actualization, by Age, Education, and Value Type

Self-actualization by age:

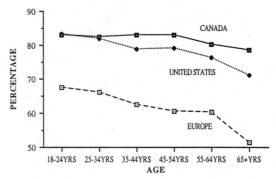

Self-actualization by education:

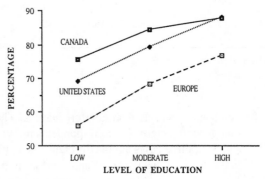

Self-actualization by value type:

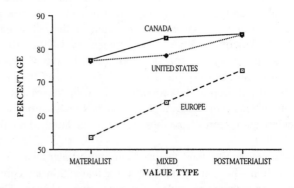

Source: 1981 and 1990 World Values Surveys.
Note: The self-actualization scale ranges from a low of 0 to a high of 5. The results above reflect those that scored 2 or more.

Figure 6-8 Comfort Work Motivations, by Age, Education, and Value Type

Comfort by age:

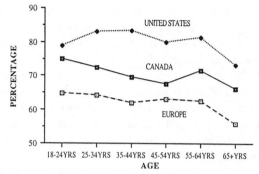

Comfort by education:

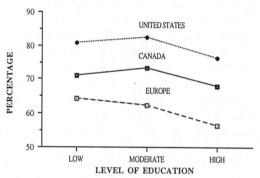

Comfort by value type:

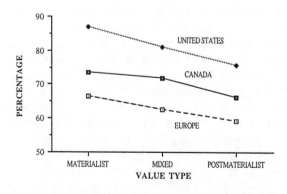

Source: 1981 and 1990 World Values Surveys.
Note: The comfort scale ranges from a low of 0 to a high of 5. The results above reflect those that scored 2 or more.

States, and Europe, and they are in a consistent direction: the young are *more* likely than the old to give self-actualizing reasons for working, though the impact of age is somewhat weaker in Canada (gamma = -.06) than in the United States (gamma = -.16) or Europe (gamma = -.14).

The impact of education is even sharper. In every single country, those with higher levels of formal education are more likely than others to indicate that self-actualization reasons are "important in a job." Again, there is evidence of national variations. At low and moderate levels of formal education, for example, Canadians are more likely than Americans to give self-actualization responses. But at the very highest levels of education these national differences disappear. The implication is that with the continued expansion of formal education, significant shifts in worker motivations will continue to take place. Publics throughout the advanced industrial states will be less concerned with comfort and more concerned with such goals as using their initiative in the workplace and having jobs that allow them to achieve something and do something that is interesting. The findings are robust in every country; the connection between higher education and self-actualizing work motivations is powerful (gammas: Europe = .33; United States = .37; Canada = .28).

Similarly consistent patterns emerge when it comes to value orientations: in *every case* post-materialists are significantly more likely than materialists to indicate that they care more about self-actualizing reasons. Once again, the differences between materialists and post-materialists are sharpest in Europe (gamma = .25; versus United States = .15; Canada = .14). When all of the evidence is considered together, the indication is that the shift towards self-actualization work motivations may well reflect long-term generational changes. The young, the well educated, and post-materialists are consistently and significantly more likely than the old, the poorly educated, and materialists to want responsible, interesting jobs that match their abilities, jobs that present them with opportunities to use initiative and to "achieve something."

In some respects, the impact of the same background factors on the "comfort" dimension (Figure 6-8) are a mirror image of the findings for "self-actualization," at least concerning education and value type. These data also underscore, once again, significant differences between American, Canadian, and European respondents: Americans always score higher on the comfort dimension regardless of age group, level of education, and value type. The impact of the background factors is of about the same magnitude in every setting: those who have more education are less concerned about comfort, and post-materialists are less concerned than materialists. There is some indication that the young are slightly more concerned about comfort than the old. None of these "comfort" results, however, are as striking as those that emerge from analysis of the effects of the same background factors on "self-actualization." The impact of the background factors, simply put, is much weaker: the association between age and "comfort" in Europe, the United States, and Canada, for example, is very weak (gamma = -.06, -.07, and -.08, respectively). The same holds for education and comfort (gammas: Europe = -.10;

Table 6-5 Regression Analysis: Predictors of Why People Work.

Predictors	Instrumental	Comfort	Self-actualization	Terminal
Time (1981–1990)	—	.01	.05**	—
Declining importance of work is bad	-.06**	-.02**	.06**	.14**
Pride in work	.02	-.05**	.06**	.06**
Job satisfaction	-.09**	.002	.03**	.02
Financial satisfaction	-.04**	-.02	.01	.04**
Postmaterialism	-.002	-.05**	.07**	.02
Male	.01	.05**	.04**	.003
Age	-.02	-.03**	-.04**	.08**
Education	-.04**	-.03*	.06**	.01
Income	-.07**	-.03**	-.003	-.11**
Non-manual occupation	-.05**	-.06**	.12**	.05**
Catholic	.03**	-.03*	-.12**	.14**
United States	.21**	.10**	.01	.001
Canada	.11**	.03**	.04**	.06**
Constant	0.57	1.02	0.31	-0.22
R-squared	.08	0.03	0.08	0.07

Note: * significant at $p < .05$; ** significant at $p < .01$.
Source: 1981 and 1990 World Values Surveys.

United States = -.10; Canada = -.04) and for value type and comfort (gammas: Europe = -.09; United States = -.20; Canada = -.11). Moreover, the age effects work in the opposite direction from education and value type, which suggests that while concern about comfort may be declining very slightly, it is unlikely that this shift is being generationally driven.

This chapter began by considering general orientations to work. The WVS data indicate that the work ethic is eroding; they also show that support for the work ethic is related to pride in work and to job satisfaction. But none of these initial findings revealed anything about the role deeper work motivations might play: they gave no indication of *why* people have more or less pride in their work, nor did they indicate *what* accounts for higher or lower levels of job satisfaction. With all of the evidence on the table, it is now possible to step back from the details and to provide a more comprehensive interpretation of how all of these factors work together. Table 6-5 relies on more powerful multivariate techniques to bring the two strands of the analysis together. What emerges is a much sharper picture of cross-time changes in work motivations of cross-national differences, and of the most important predictors of work motivations.

First, the direct evidence of cross-time changes is absolutely clear: there is only one instance in which statistically significant cross-time shifts are detectable, and these have to do with increases in self-actualization motivations for working. Furthermore, the results coming from the multivariate analysis provide more compelling reasons for believing that the increases in self-actualization motivations really are related to generational change: age, post-materialist value orientations, and education level all turn out to be significant predictors of "self-actualization," and all predictors operate in the expected direction. By contrast, the results for the other three sets of work motivations are far more mixed. Certainly there are hints that comfort work motivations may be generationally driven: age (the young), education (low), and materialist value orientations are all significant predictors. By the same token, there have been no significant cross-time shifts in the levels of comfort motivations. The evidence of generational change is even more flimsy when it comes to the "instrumental" and "terminal" dimensions. Neither age nor value type is a significant predictor of instrumental motivations, and value type and education are unrelated to terminal motivations.

Second, the patterns coming from the other predictors are revealing in other respects. Instrumental and comfort work motivations, for example, predominate in clearly identifiable segments of these populations: those in low-income and low-education groups and among manual occupational groups. Those working for instrumental reasons, typically, are less satisfied financially and less satisfied with their jobs. Furthermore, those who subscribe to comfort motivations are significantly *less likely* to express high levels of pride in work. Those working for self-actualization motives could hardly be more different. Self-actualizers express greater pride in their work, they report higher levels of job satisfaction, and they are more likely to be in non-manual occupations. Significantly, three predictors seem to differentiate self-actualizers from those who see work as an end in itself (as "terminal"). First, both income and financial satisfaction are significant predictors of terminal work motivations, but job satisfaction is not. But for self-actualizers, income and financial satisfaction turn out to be *unrelated* to their work motivations. For them, job satisfaction, which is a significant predictor, comes from other things. Second, age effects work in opposite ways: it is older respondents who subscribe to terminal work orientations and younger respondents who subscribe to self-actualizing work motivations. Then there is the religious factor. Catholic respondents are significantly more likely to subscribe to terminal work values and Protestants to support self-actualization motivations.

The main conclusion that emerges from all of the combined evidence is that self-actualization appears to qualify as the "new work ethic." People subscribing to this new ethic emphasize not material gain but self-development. Terminal work motivations, by contrast, seem to capture more traditional work orientations. According to Zanders, "for those who hold this value, dedication to work is a virtue, much like honesty or loyalty. Implicit in this value is an ethical demand that a person be diligent and industrious" (1993: 134). Notice too, that two factors—pride in work and declining importance of work—are significant predictors of both self-actualization and terminal work orientations. That finding goes some distance towards resolving the apparent paradox with which we began, the fact that the work ethic appears to be on the decline while levels of pride in work are rising. The conclusion to emerge from this more detailed analysis is that people take pride in work for both traditional and "new" reasons.

Third, the evidence presented in Table 6-5 draws attention to important sources of cross-national variation. It is tempting to try to rank publics according to whether they score high or low on some indicator of "the" work ethic. The preceding interpretation suggests, however, that the issue is more complex than that; there are different work ethics. American respondents score significantly higher than other citizens on both the "instrumental" and "comfort" dimensions. But it is Canadians who score significantly higher than others, including Americans, on both the traditional (terminal) and new (self-actualization) dimensions. Whether Canadians or Americans have a stronger work ethic becomes a matter of perspective; the conclusion depends more precisely on which work ethic is under consideration. The clear finding to emerge from the preceeding analysis is that Canadian and American work motivations are structured differently.

The bulk of this analysis of workplace motivations has relied on examining dimensions, which is a useful strategy for exploring broad themes. But dimensional analysis sacrifices detail. The exploration of comfort and self-actualization workplace motivations, for example, relied on dimensions derived from responses to just ten of the fifteen available questions tapping the reasons why people work. A more detailed picture of Canada–United States differences and similarities, and variations within and between Canada's three communities, can be sketched by returning to the basic evidence.

Elaborating Canada–United States Comparisons

There is no shortage of received wisdom about the ways in which Canadian and American economic values differ. Some of these were put to the test in the last chapter, and the WVS data can help to shed light on others. Lipset (1990), for example, approvingly cites one observer's judgement that "Americans are greater risk takers, they put more emphasis on making money," and he seems to agree with others who suggest that both Canadian corporate and public cultures are more averse than American ones to "pressure" in the workplace (1990: 121). Lipset also argues that Americans have a greater achievement drive in the workplace (1990: 128), and he cites another study indicating that Canadians place greater value than Americans on social relations (1990: 128).

The WVS data provide systematic support for some of these claims. As Table 6-6 shows, in both 1981 and 1990 a significantly higher proportion of Americans than Canadians said that "good pay" is "important in a job." But other findings are less clear. If the American economic culture is more oriented towards taking risks, for example, one might suppose that American respondents would be less concerned than Canadians about job security. On average, though, Canadians are *less* likely than Americans to say that "good job security" is important.

Table 6-6 Important Attributes of a Job (Percentages)

	Good pay		Pleasant people		No pressure		Job security		Promotions		Respect		Good hours		Use initiative		Useful		Holidays		Meet people		Achievement		Responsibility		Interesting		Meets abilities	
	81	90	81	90	81	90	81	90	81	90	81	90	81	90	81	90	81	90	81	90	81	90	81	90	81	90	81	90	81	90
Europe	65	70	65	66	28	28	56	55	32	33	29	35	40	41	42	44	35	35	28	27	41	44	44	49	35	40	53	58	47	53
US	80	85	75	79	38	33	72	73	59	58	45	43	58	56	54	52	43	42	31	31	53	38	74	72	59	57	72	69	59	58
Canada	72	76	74	73	29	28	66	67	51	49	39	37	48	52	58	55	39	40	28	26	51	42	73	74	55	57	73	72	61	57
English	74	78	78	80	30	29	66	71	53	52	39	40	48	55	61	57	38	43	25	30	51	47	75	74	55	58	76	78	61	56
French	68	72	63	57	29	26	66	61	45	41	38	27	49	50	49	48	42	31	35	16	52	33	67	72	52	52	66	55	63	59
New Canadians	—	74	—	71	—	29	—	62	—	46	—	37	—	46	—	54	—	44	—	25	—	38	—	73	—	56	—	75	—	54

Note: For the text of the question, see Figure 6-3.
Source: 1981 and 1990 World Values Surveys.

Nor is it clear that Canadians are more averse than Americans to pressure in the workplace. Canadians are *less* likely than Americans to volunteer that "not too much pressure" is "important in a job." What about "achievement"? On this indicator, there is hardly any difference: a slightly higher proportion of Canadians than Americans said that having a job "in which you feel you can achieve something" is important. There are reasons to be cautious about drawing firm conclusions about cross-national variations from evidence provided by single indicators; but the image of Canadians as, in comparison to Americans, half-hearted, risk-averse workers who show up at their jobs for social reasons finds little support in these data. Americans are *more likely* than Canadians to attribute importance to "good hours," "generous holidays," "pleasant people to work with," "job security," and "no pressure." Americans are also more likely than Canadians to want "good pay," "good chances for promotions," and "a job that is respected by people."

Lipset claims that on work-related values, anglophone Canadians sit about halfway between Americans and francophones (1990: 127) and, on balance, the data provide some support for that claim. A comparison of the three Canadian communities with the American indicates that anglo-Canadians are closer to Americans than francophone or new Canadians on ten of the fifteen work indicators. Americans score significantly higher on "good pay," "no pressure," and "chances for promotion," while anglophone Canadians score significantly higher on "using initiative," "meeting people," and having "a job that is interesting."

What about the within-Canada variations? Are the work motivations of new Canadians significantly different from those of other Canadians? In thirteen of the fifteen motivations included in Table 6-6, new Canadians fall somewhere between the aggregate responses of anglophone and francophone Canadians, and they are closer to anglophone than francophone Canadians on ten of those indicators. Of the just two instances in which new Canadians are outliers, they are significantly *less likely* than other Canadians to look for "good hours" in a job and significantly *more likely* to want "a useful job for society."

Reporting only aggregate scores for respondents in European countries masks substantial cross-national variations. Generally, however, Canadian work motivations come closer to those of Europeans than to those of Americans. A more detailed country-by-country analysis of each of the indicators provides further support for American exceptionalism. For example, of all twelve publics, Americans rank highest on four indicators: "good pay," "job security," "promotions," and "good hours." They come second on two others: "a job respected by people" and "pleasant people to work with," and third on the "no pressure" indicator. Lipset may well be correct in his assessment that Americans have a "greater absorption of values characteristic of the business-industrial system" (1990: 127). But as has also been demonstrated, the orientations on which Americans rank highest are also those that fall mostly within the "comfort" dimension, a dimension that is not undergoing any significant shift and that may be characterized as having more to do with *tra-*

ditional work values. As we have noted, the more significant and novel systematic shifts are taking place on the "self-actualization" dimension, and it is on this dimension that Canadian work values come into sharper focus. Of all countries considered, Canadians rank at the very top on two indicators: "a job that is interesting" and " a job in which you can achieve something"—and, significantly, *both* of these indicators form part of the self-actualization dimension, the emerging new work ethic.

Workplace participation

That levels of self actualization are rising implies that people are not just more willing to shoulder greater individual responsibility in the workplace, but also that they increasingly prefer to do so. Are these shifts isolated ones? Or are they connected to broader transitions in norms about the workplace? These questions can be explored from two distinct but related perspectives. The first has to do with general orientations towards the management of business and industry, the second with more specific attitudes and preferences about workplace decision-making.

One of the most spectacular and, for some, unexpected trends of the last two decades has been the widespread erosion of public support for state-controlled political economies. The collapse of the Soviet Union is probably the single most dramatic illustration of the political face of those trends. Less spectacular, though equally significant, has been the dwindling enthusiasm for state-run economies. Such global transformations might be interpreted as a vindication of liberal democracy as a political force and capitalism as an economic force. But, as has been argued elsewhere, to see the demise of communism as signifying a public embrace of the *traditional* capitalist order is almost certainly mistaken (Inglehart, Nevitte and Basanez, 1996). Most contemporary western advanced industrial states, for example, hardly qualify as "capitalist" in the pure sense of the term, not least because state expenditures on a wide variety of social supports take up somewhere between a third and a half of the gross national products. With more or less enthusiasm, nearly all of these states embraced incremental and cumulatively sweeping reforms involving the state in social and economic intervention in order to both regulate and protect citizens from the sharp upswings and downturns that typified the economic rhythms of the early twentieth century. There are, of course, very significant variations in the extent to which western states are involved in economic enterprises. But even where enthusiasm for the "big government" of the 1960s and 1970s may have waned, it is not at all clear that publics see a return to traditional capitalism as the most attractive alternative.

Both the 1981 and 1990 WVS asked citizens a variety of questions probing their preferences about the management of business and industry. Respondents were presented with four options, one representing the traditional capitalist position ("the *owners* should run their businesses or appoint the

Figure 6-9   How Should Business and Industry Be Managed?

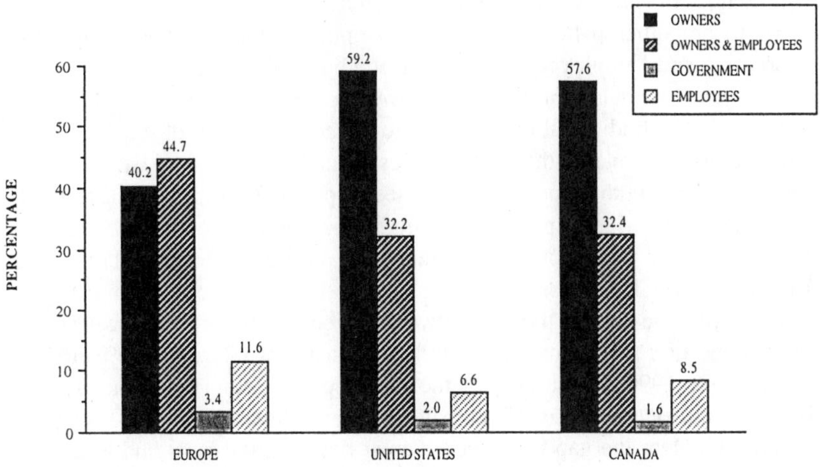

Source: 1981 World Values Survey.

managers"), another representing the classic state-centred viewpoint ("the *government* should be the owner and appoint the managers"), and two other alternatives, one giving employees a voice in selecting managers ("the *owners and employees* should participate in the selection of managers") and the other giving employees ownership and control ("the *employees* should own the business and should elect managers"). Figure 6-9 presents the aggregate response profiles for European, American, and Canadian responses in 1981; these data illustrate some fundamental differences between European and North American publics. First, Canadians and Americans are clearly more favourably disposed to the traditional capitalist alternative; they are more likely to support the idea that owners should run their businesses and appoint the managers. Europeans are much stronger supporters of the notion that owners and employees should participate in the selection of managers. In 1981 only a handful of Europeans and North Americans supported the state-centred alternative, and Europeans were significantly more supportive of employees owning and electing managers.

What about the shifts between 1981 and 1990? None were very large, but there is some evidence of a consistent pattern of change. In 1981, 3.4% of Europeans thought the government should be owners and appoint managers, and that dropped to less than 2% by 1990. Significantly, the declines have been sharpest in those countries, like Italy and Spain, that have longer traditions of state intervention (Italy declined from 8.2% in 1981 to 4.2% in 1990, and in Spain the figures are 8.2% and 4%, respectively). Support for the state-centred view also dropped in Canada (from 1.6% to 0.7%) and the United States (from 2% to 1%). For North Americans, the state-centred option was unattractive in 1981 and even less popular in 1990.

There are other patterns too. On two options—the traditional capitalist alternative and "employees should own the business and elect managers"—there is clear evidence of attitudinal *convergence*. Between 1981 and 1990, support for the traditional capitalist option *declined* in each of the five countries—Northern Ireland, the United States, Canada, Ireland, and Britain—that ranked *highest* on that option in 1981 (see Appendix 6-D for the full results). Over the same period, support for the traditional capitalist option *increased* in each of the five other countries—France, Spain, Italy, the Netherlands, and Denmark—which had ranked *lowest* in support for that option in 1981. In other words, the size of the gap between the countries with the greatest and least support for the traditional capitalist option narrowed from 42.2% in 1981 to 32.9% in 1990. In the case of the other option, "employees should own business and elect managers," the pattern of attitudinal convergence is equally striking. Here the gap between the countries with the most and least support for this idea narrowed from 20.5% in 1981 to 11.2% in 1990 (see Appendix 6-D).

The clearest evidence of 1981–1990 change is a general *increase* in support for joint owner-employee participation in the selection of managers. Out of the twelve countries, there is only one obvious exception to that trend, the case of Italy. What do these shifts collectively mean? Plainly, they do not mean that Western publics have turned away from traditional state control of the economy in order to throw their support behind the traditional capitalist model. The aggregate levels of support for *both* of these alternatives declined. Instead, the aggregate increases are found in the growing support for options "owners and employees should participate in the selection of managers" and "employees should own the business and should elect the managers." Between 1981 and 1990 publics became *less* attracted to economic structures that give employees little or no say in decision-making and *more* attracted to arrangements that give employees more say in the workplace.

There is other direct evidence that underscores that interpretation of the data. Both the 1981 and 1990 WVS asked publics specifically about workplace decision-making. Respondents were told:

> People have different ideas about following instructions at work. Some say that one should follow instructions of one's superiors even when one does not fully agree with them. Others say that one should follow one's superior's instructions only when one is convinced that they are right. With which of these two opinions do you agree?

Respondents could choose from three answers: 1 "should follow instructions," 2 "must be convinced first," and 3 "it depends."

Figure 6-10 reports the aggregate responses for 1981 and illustrates sharp

Figure 6-10 Following Instructions at Work

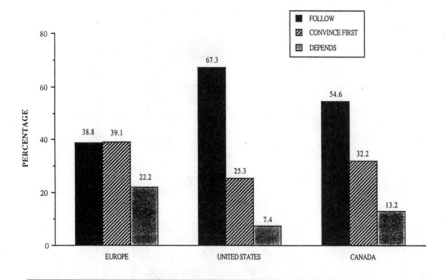

Source: 1981 World Values Survey.

differences, once again, between the European and North American response profiles: two-thirds of Americans and just over half of Canadian respondents said they would "follow instructions," whereas more than 60% of European respondents said that they would have to be "convinced first" or "it depends." The country-specific 1981–1990 changes are detailed in Appendix 6-E, and the pattern of change reported here is reminiscent of the shifting attitudes towards workplace structures. More impressive than the aggregate shifts, in this case, is the evidence of attitudinal convergence: the 1981–1990 *decreases* on the "follow instructions" response were sharpest among those countries—Denmark, United States, Britain, Canada, Northern Ireland—that ranked highest on that response in 1981. Obversely, the sharpest 1981–1990 *increases* are found in those countries, like France and West Germany, that scored lowest on "follow instructions" in 1981.

The changing preferences towards both workplace structures and workplace decision-making can be seen as different faces of the same underlying phenomenon—people want more meaningful participation in the workplace. The patterns of convergence are schematically represented in Figure 6-11, which uses a single scale to represent shifting public preferences about *both* workplace decision-making and workplace structures. The intriguing empirical finding here is that, for publics in these advanced industrial states, attitudes towards workplace participation seem to be converging towards a common threshold, which appears to be somewhere around the 40% mark. Notice that

Figure 6-11 Cross-time Changes in Worker Participation

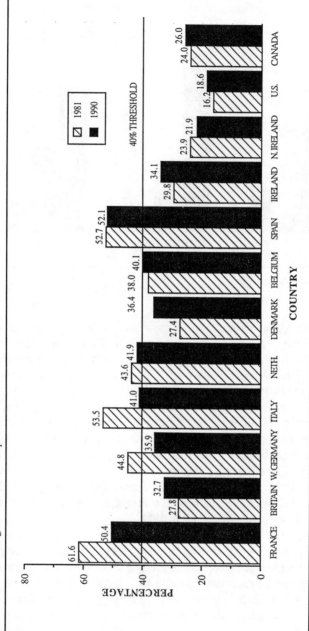

Source: 1981 and 1990 World Values Surveys.

Note: The worker participation index includes those that agreed with at least one of the following:
1. Business and industry should be managed by having owners and employees participating in the selection of managers
2. Business and industry should be managed by employees alone. Employees should own the business and elect the managers
3. One should follow one's superior's instructions only when one is convinced that they are right
4. It depends whether one should or should not follow one's superior's instructions before being convinced first

in each of the five countries scoring above the 40% threshold in 1981, workplace participation scores declined by 1990. And of the seven countries scoring below the 40% threshold in 1981, workplace participation inclinations increased in six. The case of Northern Ireland is the only exception to the pattern.

These findings are consistent with the idea, one widely held in management circles, that workplace hierarchies are becoming flatter and that work environments become more efficient when the distance between workers and decision-making managers is reduced. That particular interpretation, however, seems only a partial account of the transition. The evidence presented so far in this chapter draws attention to another aspect of workplace relations: workers are becoming less deferential. North Americans, it seems, are "catching up" to their European counterparts in these respects. As has already been demonstrated, they are:

1. increasingly motivated in the workplace by *self-actualization* kinds of reasons: the opportunity to use their initiative, to do a job that meets their abilities, a responsible job;

2. less inclined than before to simply follow instructions in the workplace;

3. less satisfied with working within those kinds of economic structures, be they of the traditional capitalist or state-centric variety, that give workers little room for meaningful participation in workplace decision-making.

Are these shifts in workplace participation in any way connected to those indicators—age, education, and post-materialist value orientations—that underpin the increases in self-actualization work motivations and the other transformations that have taken place? As it happens, they are, and the consistency of the findings is impressive. As Figure 6-12 shows, very clear age effects are present in every country: the young are significantly more likely than the old to want greater workplace participation (Europe, gamma = -.17; United States, = -.15; Canada, = -.13). Seen in isolation, those age-related variations could be interpreted as indicating life-cycle effects, but there are also consistent findings for the effects of education and value type. In every single country, those with higher levels of formal education score significantly higher on the worker participation item than those with less education (Europe, gamma = .12; United States = .13; Canada = .17). Moreover, the worker participation scores for post-materialists are, on average, double those of materialists (Europe, gamma = .27; United States = .17; Canada = .20). The very same findings emerge in country after country. The impact of background factors is also crystal clear. What makes these findings all the more remarkable is the absence of any clear connections between worker participation preferences and other socio-demographic indicators. For example, it might be argued that the changes in workplace participation are a result of broader structural changes in these economies, particularly the expansion of the service sector. That being so, one would expect to find corresponding differences between those in manual and non-manual occupations. There is no evidence of such differences. Another possible interpretation is that the

Figure 6-12   Worker Participation, by Age, Education, and Value Type

Worker participation by age:

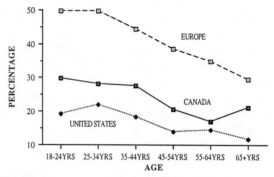

Worker participation by education:

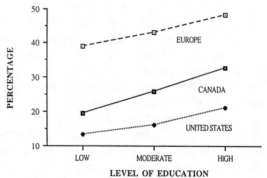

Worker participation by value type:

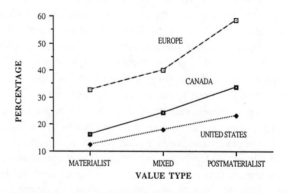

Source: 1981 and 1990 World Values Surveys.
Note: The worker participation scale ranges from a low of 0 to a high of 2. The results above reflect those that scored 2.

changes reflect the very substantial shifts in the gender balance within the workforce; but there is no evidence to substantiate this line of speculation. There are no statistically significant differences in workplace participation inclinations between men and women, manual and non-manual workers, or even high- and low-income groups. Despite the fact that the aggregate 1981–1990 shifts are quite modest, these findings collectively suggest that the shifting orientations towards workplace participation are both broad-gauged and related to generational change.

All of these changes in economic orientations are important in their own right and undoubtedly deserve far more detailed probing. But the central question here has to do with whether shifts in one domain are connected to shifts in others.

Chapter 2 proposed that shifting orientations towards authority might be a theme that provides the common thread uniting the wide-ranging value shifts identified with the WVS data. The findings from Chapter 4 add plausibility to that interpretation; that chapter identifies two dimensions of *political* value change. One of those dimensions, falling levels of confidence in governmental institutions, represents the institutional face of shifting orientations to political authority. The other, protest behaviour, represents the participatory face of orientations towards political authority. Recall, too, that the background analysis of those data not only shows that both of these value shifts are consistent with the generational change explanation, but also shows that *both* are empirically linked to an indicator of general orientations towards authority. What emerges as central from this chapter is evidence of two dimensions of shifting *economic* values: self-actualization and worker participation. Furthermore, according to the criteria consistently applied throughout this investigation, these too appear to be undergoing generational change.

Both self-actualization and worker participation can be seen as different aspects of orientations towards authority in the economic domain. Hannah Arendt (1959) was among the first to recognize that work serves an expressive function. Subsequent investigations (Yankelovic et al., 1985) identify more precisely the components of this expressive function and suggest that the expressive aspect of work is becoming increasingly important in advanced industrial states. Our own data provide further evidence of the same trend. Empirically, the key elements of this expressive dimension turn out to correspond almost precisely to the self-actualization dimension that emerges from our data: they include the opportunity to use initiative, a responsible job, an interesting job, a job that meets one's abilities, and one in which the worker feels he/she can achieve something. But what do these mean for authority relations in the economic domain? According to one observer, people who hold to these self-expressive, or self-actualizing, values are "emphasizing that creativity and autonomy be expressed in their jobs; they are rejecting authority and placing self-expression ahead of status" (Zanders, 1993: 130). Furthermore, our combined indicator of workplace participation also concerns orientations to authority in the workplace; it reflects preferences for a working environment both that is *less* centralized and in which workers have *more* *say* in workplace decision-making.

That citizens in advanced industrial states increasingly want both a more egalitarian political environment and a more egalitarian working environment are striking findings. More importantly, they are findings that raise important questions the answers to which could suggest a more sweeping interpretation of these value changes. Are orientations towards authority in the political and economic domains connected? Even more broadly, to what extent are people's orientations towards authority generalizable from any one domain to others? It is precisely this line of speculation that prompted such pioneering theorists as Eckstein (1966) to argue that authority orientations *in any and all* social relations are inherently political, and consequently traditional conceptions of the political should be expanded to encompass other domains, such as the workplace and the family, because these, too, are sites in which authority is exercised.

Eckstein's primary concern is with the congruence of authority patterns and he makes a persuasive case that uncovering the structure, shape, and congruence of authority patterns is an important clue that goes some distance towards explaining democratic stability. "A government will tend to be stable," Eckstein and Gurr propose, "if its authority pattern is congruent with the other authority patterns of the society of which it is a part" (1975: 234). Significantly, Eckstein never claims that *all* patterns of authority have to be democratic to arrive at democratic stability. Nor does he think it realistic, or even necessary, that authority patterns in one domain exactly imitate those in others. "Some social relations," he argues, "simply cannot be conducted in a democratic manner" (1966: 237), and Eckstein seems to have two particular examples in mind: the family and the economy. In Eckstein's estimation, there are practical constraints: "We have every reason to think that economic organizations cannot be organized in a truly democratic manner, at any rate not without consequences that no one wants" (1966: 237). He also suspects that "capitalist economic organizations and even certain kinds of public ownership militate against a democratization of economic relations" (1966: 237).[12]

Carole Pateman (1970), in a penetrating and persuasive analysis of the links between participation and democratic theory, takes issue with Eckstein's evaluations. Like Eckstein, Pateman is concerned with democratic stability, and she too sees other domains such as the workplace as "political systems in their own right" (83). But she challenges Eckstein's claim that the genuine democratization of such other domains is impossible for the practical reasons that he cites. Drawing on case studies of selected industries in Britain, and particularly the worker self-management experience in Yugoslavia, Pateman offers two important arguments. First, greater participation in the workplace is not necessarily at odds with economic efficiency. Second, and more generally, she sees worker participation in industry as enhancing democratic stability because it promotes political efficacy, the feeling that people can "do something" about their political situations. According to Pateman, "it is only if the individual has the opportunity to directly participate in decision-making and choose representatives in the alternative areas that, under modern conditions, he can hope to have any real control over the course of his life or the development of the environment in which he lives" (110). Consequently, "the necessary condition for the establishment of a democratic polity," she claims, "is a participatory society" (102). Pateman suspects, then, that such democratic values as joint decision-making and participation are vital to democratic citizenship, that these values can be learned in the workplace, and that they can be generalized to the polity.

Eckstein's and Pateman's investigations of some twenty-five years ago still stand as pioneering contributions to democratic theory; they are conceptually rich, but their empirical reach was confined, mostly, to well-chosen case studies. Pateman, for example, had few working examples of "industrial democracy" other than Yugoslavia from which to draw. And Eckstein saw his configurative case study of Norway and his explorations of Britain and Germany not as validating his theory, but as platforms for illustrating some central ideas. Remarkably, these far-reaching lines of speculation stalled. They did not stall because they were pre-empted by some devastating critique, nor were they replaced by a more compelling or more elegant theory; what they lacked was any broad empirical verification. Both Eckstein and Pateman supply convincing reasons for supposing that orientations towards authority are generalizable. The WVS data provide an opportunity to investigate whether there is any systematic support for these important general claims.

Figure 6-13 presents a more elaborate schema than the ones proposed by either Eckstein or Pateman; it folds the ideas advanced by Eckstein and Pateman together with some of the central findings coming from our own analysis. Protest potential and non-confidence in governmental institutions are subsets of orientations to political authority, and self-actualization and worker participation feature as two aspects of orientations toward authority in the workplace. Two significant findings emerge from this general overview of the empirical connections among these dimensions. One is that orientations toward workplace authority do seem to be related to the general indicator of orientations towards authority, the indicator introduced in Chapter 2. The relationship is not very strong, but it operates in the expected direction: those who want *more egalitarian* workplace arrangements are also *less* likely to say that greater respect for authority in the future would be a "good thing." Compare the workplace–general orientation coefficients (gamma = -.09), for instance, with those for the political–general authority coefficients (gamma = -. 35). Second, and more significantly, the WVS evidence provides clear support for Pateman's speculations: workplace authority orientations *are* directly related to orientations to political authority. Moreover, that basic relationship unequivocally holds for publics in every country: the more people support the idea of greater egalitarianism in the workplace, the less deferential they are when it comes to politics (see appendix 6-F). And precisely the same pattern is found within each of Canada's three communities.

Figure 6-13   The links between orientations toward general, political, and workplace authority in 12 advanced industrial states

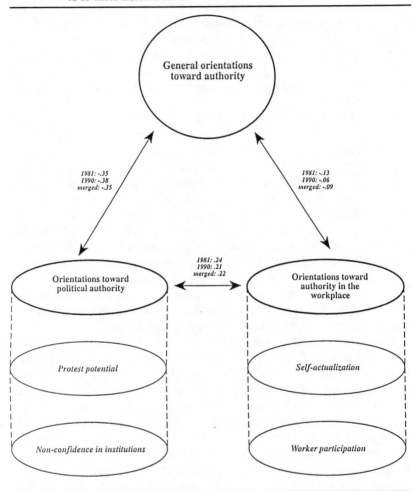

Source: 1981 and 1990 World Values Surveys.
Note: The above figures are gamma coefficients.

That workplace authority orientations are empirically linked to orientations to political authority is an important substantive finding, and it is possible to say much more about the underlying structure of these orientations by unpacking these results. Some dimensions of workplace and political authority orientations may be more powerfully connected than others. Figure 6-14 specifies the structure in greater detail by considering all of the possible connections at once; it builds on the earlier results and places them in the context

Figure 6-14 The Linkages between Dimensions or Orientations towards Political and Workplace Authority

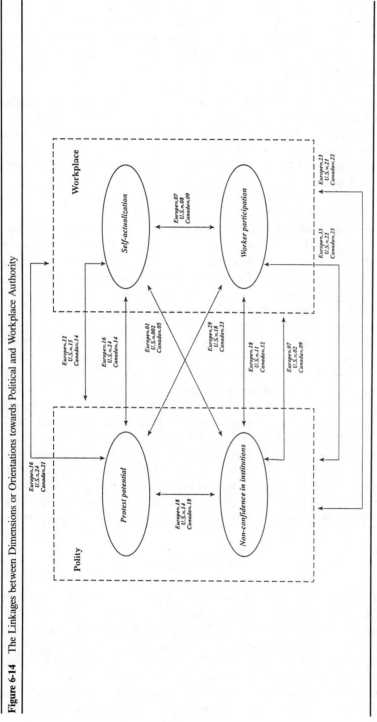

Source: 1981 and 1990 World Values Surveys.

Note: The above figures are gamma coefficients for the merged 1981 and 1990 data.

of the entire structure. At first glance, the picture looks to be a complicated one; the easiest place to begin is with the basic links between the four elipses in the middle of the figure: each elipse represents one dimension of workplace or polity authority orientations. Critical to an understanding of the structure are the relative strengths of these connections. Where are the relationships (gamma coefficients) strong? And where are they relatively weak?

First, the most powerful links are between "protest potential" and "worker participation." That finding provides yet further support for Pateman's hunch that workplace participation may be crucial to attitudes towards political authority more narrowly construed. Indeed, "workplace participation" is more strongly related to "protest potential" than anything else. In effect, these findings indicate that "workplace participation" is an even better predictor of "protest potential" than "non-confidence in institutions", the other indicator of orientations to political authority.

Second, it turns out that "self-actualization" work motivations are only very weakly connected to "worker participation" and also to "non-confidence in institutions." "Self-actualization", however, is clearly not irrelevant because it is consistently connected to the structure of orientations towards authority via "protest potential." In fact, these gamma coefficients are almost as strong as those for the "protest potential"–"worker participation" dyad; they are stronger in the case of American respondents.

If there is a single conclusion to be distilled from this somewhat complex set of findings, it is this: as both Pateman and Eckstein suspect, orientations towards authority do seem to be generalizable. More particularly, there is convincing evidence that attitudes towards participation in the workplace are connected to orientations towards political authority. Attitudes to worker participation, for example, are consistently linked to protest potential in every one of the twelve countries in both 1981 and 1990. In other words, out of twenty-four possible cases—twelve countries at two time points—there are absolutely *no exceptions* to this general pattern (see Appendix 6-G). Consequently, there are powerful reasons for believing that the generationally driven changes in attitudes to the workplace we have identified in this chapter are systematically connected to the generationally driven changes in attitudes towards the polity.

Conclusions

The results presented in Part 3 cover a great deal of ground. They demonstrate that significant changes have taken place in the economic orientations of publics in the twelve advanced industrial states, that these changes conform to identifiable and consistent patterns, and that some of the most significant shifts are systematically related to background indicators in ways that suggest the shifts are long-term ones that signify generational change.

At one level, the findings help to illuminate some aspects of the debate over the similarities and differences in Canadian and American economic values.

When it comes to free-market orientations and support for meritocracy, for instance, the balance of the evidence certainly does indicate that, in some respects, there is a strong case to be made for American exceptionalism. But another case, perhaps an even more compelling one, can be made for North American exceptionalism. The broader perspective provided by the analysis of values in twelve countries brings North American distinctiveness into bolder relief. According to the findings reported in Chapter 5, Americans *and Canadians* are strong supporters of free-market ideas and meritocracy. Chapter 6 demonstrated that Americans *and Canadians* also rank relatively high on such other indicators as pride in work and support for the work ethic. And when one fixes on just Canadian–American comparisons to evaluate specific claims about orientations towards competition, risk-taking, or attitudes to work, it is not at all clear that Canadians always fall short of American orientations.

Do these value changes have anything to do with orientations towards free trade? Yes, they do, for at least three different kinds of reasons. Free-market orientations are relevant. But economic values alone are not decisive in shaping attitudes towards integration. Other non-economic values are relevant because they play a prominent role in shaping domestic policy preferences and such orientations to others as levels of mutual trust between peoples. The purpose of drawing attention back to the role that economic and other values may play in expanding trade agreements was to make the case that interpretations of the dynamics of integration should provide some room for value change. Shifts in public values may decrease the level of public opposition to free trade agreements between countries. This does not mean, however, that other factors should not occupy a more prominent place in comprehensive explanations for the expansion of trading environments. Interests matter, and the shifting global trading environment, as well as domestic interest group responses to those shifts, are probably decisive for the reasons others have outlined (Lustig, 1994; Rogowski, 1989).

The findings presented in Chapter 6 shed new light on other aspects of significant shifts in economic value change. The initial findings presented seem to suggest a paradox: the work ethic is in decline but people's pride in work is increasing. By American standards, Canadian adherence to the work ethic is less robust. But the value of a broader reference group, once again, helps to place that finding in a more nuanced context. Canadian support for the work ethic is higher than the average for all advanced industrial states in the study. And there is a great deal of evidence suggesting that "the work ethic" is a part of the American ethos (see McClosky and Zaller, 1984). The more significant finding, however, comes from the evidence indicating why it is that the work ethic is on the decline while pride in work is rising. The resolution to the apparent paradox emerges with a clearer understanding of the reasons people have for working. Workplace motivations are shifting, and they are changing in consistent ways; there is not just one work ethic. The data suggest, instead, that it is useful to distinguish the "traditional work ethic" from a new and emerging work ethic. That distinction accomplishes two things. It helps to explain why Americans rank so high on simple indicators of the work ethic; they rate high on the *traditional* work ethic, the one that emphasizes instrumental and comfort orientations. And it sharpens our understanding of a key value difference that does separate Canadian from American workplace orientations: Canadians demonstrably rank much higher than their American counterparts on the new and emerging work ethic.

Are these shifts in economic values of limited interest because their effects apply to the economic domain? The answer to that question is emphatically no: important and sustained shifts in such values as workplace participation and decision-making have far-reaching effects on much broader concerns. Demonstrating the empirical connection between orientations towards authority in the workplace and the polity represents an important advance. This is so for reasons that other analysts, particularly Eckstein and Pateman, understood very clearly. The WVS break new ground because they provide clear support for Pateman's contention that workplace authority orientations are connected to political authority orientations more narrowly understood. They also provide consistent support for the broader claim, that orientations towards authority are generalizable.

It is tempting, perhaps, to take these findings and reach for a radical interpretation: Will workers be satisfied only when workplace authority structures are completely flat? Will the process stop only when workers have complete control over the economic structures of their workplace and over workplace decision-making? Such dramatic conclusions are fascinating to contemplate, but they are probably unwarranted. Nowhere, for example, does Pateman ever claim that workplace authority relations either should be or can be completely egalitarian. Pateman's challenge to Eckstein's analysis turns partly on the question of what the "practical constraints" to egalitarianism in the workplace are. In contrast to Eckstein, who contends that economic organizations cannot become democratic without bringing on "consequences that no one wants," Pateman holds that workplace authority relations can become more egalitarian without sacrificing organizational coherence and profitability. Pateman's other departure from Eckstein's formulation is more a matter of emphasis: Eckstein suspects that people learn about authority relations in the family and then generalize from the family to other domains, whereas Pateman suspects that people may also generalize from their workplace experiences to the polity.

Ruminations about practical constraints raise a variety of other intriguing questions. For example, is there some optimal balance between authority and egalitarianism in the workplace? And how would such an optimum be identified? The WVS data emphatically do *not* indicate that publics are clamouring for a completely egalitarian workplace. What they do indicate is something more subtle. The emerging work ethic gives increasing prominence to such work values as responsibility, achievement, engagement, and initiative. These values are not so different from those of ideal citizen of the democratic polity. Increasingly well-educated, interested, responsible, and informed workers are unlikely to be satisfied with hierarchical work environments that stifle these values or give them little opportunity to flourish. The very same people are citizens of democratic polities. What our data show is that long-term shifts in basic economic orientations, like the rise of self-actualization and work-place participation, are demonstrably connected to other orientations that have a direct bearing on the functioning of the democratic polity. The issue that now becomes relevant is whether comparable shifts in primary relations have occurred, and whether orientations to primary relations are also related to the broad-gauged changes in economic and political orientations.

NOTES

[1] The results for France are not included in this table. On this particular question, the coding of the French data may have been reversed. Because we were not able to confirm that, we have omitted the French data from this part of the analysis.

[2] Notice that for the work ethic the reverse finding emerges: the *lower* the level of family income, the *stronger* their support for the work ethic.

[3] To test for national differences, this summary equation introduces "nationality" as a dummy variable. So, the indicator "Canada" tests whether there are statistically significant differences between Canadian respondents and Europeans, and "United States" tests for differences between American and European respondents. Each analysis was also conducted separately for Canada, the United States, and Europe, though these results are not reported in full here.

[4] These results are from the 1990 WVS data. When the same question was asked in 1981, American respondents ranked even lower, ninth out of the twelve countries.

[5] There is other evidence of American exceptionalism in this regard. Since the 1970s, the average number of hours worked by those who are employed full time has increased in the United States but decreased in Europe. The typical American now works 15% longer than his/her German counterpart. Other survey evidence indicates that Americans prefer to work more not fewer hours. One speculation is that the real earnings of Americans have fallen, not risen, and the American people have to work harder just to maintain their standard of living. The difficulty here is that high-skill workers who have had large real increases in their standard of living are also working harder. Another line of speculation is that the falling marginal tax rates in the United States make it more profitable to work longer hours. That may be true, but levels of financial satisfaction in the U.S. are not higher than elsewhere. See *The Economist*, October 22, 1994: 20.

[6] These data are from 1990 only, but the same pattern holds for 1981.

[7] The key difference between Zanders' dimension and ours is that our dimension contains two elements—good pay and job security—that do not appear in his. Zanders' dimension also contains one item—respect—that does not feature in our results. The reasons for the differences are that Zanders derives his results from a slightly different set of countries, and he uses a slightly different factor-analytic procedure.

[8] Technically, these are additive factor scales.

[9] All of the correlations are very weak and their directions are inconsistent. For example, the gammas for value type and terminal orientations are: Europe = -.06; United States = .002; Canada = .01. For education and terminal reason, the gammas are: Europe = .03; United States = -.10; Canada = -.07. The only sharp results come from within the francophone Canadian subgroup, where education is strongly and negatively related to terminal work motivations: those with *low* levels of education are significantly *more* likely than others to subscribe to terminal work values, gamma = -.30.

[10] The issue of question format is not a trivial one, particularly in cross-national survey research. It has been argued that there are significant variations in how different publics respond to the kind of open-format question used here, particularly in the number of responses that different nationalities volunteer. One way to control for these sources of measurement variation is to compare scores on different scales *within* each country, as in Table 6-4. The number of responses given, of course, can also depend upon the interviewer.

[11] Because such stringent criteria are applied, the proportion of each public that "qualifies" for inclusion is relatively low, and so are the cross-time shifts. When these criteria are relaxed, when lower thresholds are used, the substantive interpretation remains essentially the same.

[12] Recall that our own data show that public support is declining for *both* traditional capitalist economic structures and state-controlled structures. Workers are, however, expressing an increased preference for economic structures in which they have greater opportunity for joint control in the selection of managers and greater say in workplace decision-making. Eckstein's analysis pays less attention to these alternatives.

Appendix 6-A Percentage Saying They Take a "Great Deal of Pride" in Their Work (1981–1990)

Country	1981	1990	% Change
France	12.4	15.2	+2.8
Britain	75.9	83.0	+7.1
West Germany	14.8	15.5	+0.7
Italy	24.7	29.7	+5.0
Netherlands	18.5	29.7	+11.2
Denmark	34.6	76.4	+41.8
Belgium	29.2	33.1	+3.9
Spain	37.9	44.6	+6.7
Ireland	71.9	76.8	+4.9
Northern Ireland	68.4	80.8	+12.4
United States	80.1	87.1	+7.0
Canada	65.7	73.3	+7.6
English	73.2	84.5	+11.3
French	49.7	46.8	-2.9
New Canadians	—	74.4	—

Question: "How much pride, if any, do you take in the work that you do?
  1. None
  2. Little
  3. Some
  4. *A great deal*"
Source: 1981 and 1990 World Values Surveys.

Appendix 6-B Factor Analysis: Why People Work
(Using principle components extraction and varimax rotation procedures on 1990 data for 12 advanced industrial democracies)

Variable	Instrumental	Terminal	Communality
Work is like a business transaction. The more I get paid, the more I do; the less I get paid, the less I do.	.70318	.11274	.50717
Working for a living is a necessity; I wouldn't work if I didn't have to.	62799	-.10598	.40560
I enjoy my work, it's the most important thing in my life.	.27485	.73927	.62206
I will always do the best I can regardless of pay.	-.31865	.67628	.55890
Eigenvalue	1.07	1.03	
% of variance explained	26.6%	25.7%	52.3%

Source: 1990 World Values Survey.

Appendix 6-C Factor Analysis: Important Attributes in a Job
(Using principle components extraction and varimax rotation procedures on merged data [1981 & 1990] for 12 advanced industrial states)

Indicators	Self-actualization	Comfort	Communality
An opportunity to use initiative	.74442	.09806	.56
A job in which you feel that you can achieve something	.70702	.09324	.54
A responsible job	.67067	.17214	.48
A job that is interesting	.62956	.19456	.43
A job that meets one's abilities	.62539	.18517	.43
Good hours	.13461	.74354	.57
Generous holidays	.15703	.72133	.54
Not too much pressure	.16588	.61761	.41
Good pay	.06571	.58148	.34
Good job security	.18794	.54029	.33
Eigenvalue	3.26	1.35	
% of variance explained	32.6%	13.5%	46.1%

Source: 1981 and 1990 World Values Surveys.

Appendix 6-D How Should Business and Industry Be Managed?
(Percentages)

Country	Owners 1981	Owners 1990	Owners % change	Owners & Employees 1981	Owners & Employees 1990	Owners & Employees % change	State 1981	State 1990	State % change	Employee 1981	Employee 1990	Employee % change
France	20.5	23.8	+3.3	56.4	61.2	+4.8	3.2	1.7	-1.5	20.0	13.3	-6.7
Britain	49.7	43.1	-6.6	39.7	44.8	+5.1	2.4	1.9	-0.5	8.2	10.3	+2.1
West Germany	47.0	47.1	+0.1	43.3	43.3	—	1.9	0.9	-1.0	7.7	8.7	+1.0
Italy	30.1	43.9	+13.8	54.8	45.3	-9.5	8.2	4.2	-4.0	6.8	6.6	-0.2
Netherlands	32.1	35.4	+3.3	54.9	55.6	+0.7	1.6	0.6	-1.0	11.4	8.3	-3.1
Denmark	41.7	47.3	+5.6	46.1	46.4	+0.3	1.7	0.7	-1.0	10.6	5.7	-4.9
Belgium	42.9	44.4	+1.5	45.6	44.3	-1.3	3.3	2.2	-1.1	8.2	9.2	+1.0
Spain	25.1	30.0	+4.9	39.7	48.1	+8.4	8.2	4.0	-4.2	27.1	17.8	-9.3
Ireland	50.5	43.3	-7.2	38.2	42.2	+4.0	3.0	1.5	-1.5	8.2	13.0	+4.8
Northern Ireland	62.7	55.3	-7.4	28.7	35.8	+7.1	0.7	1.4	+0.7	7.9	7.5	-0.4
United States	59.2	56.7	-2.5	32.2	34.7	+2.5	2.0	1.0	-1.0	6.6	7.6	+1.0
Canada	57.6	53.2	-4.4	32.4	37.0	+4.6	1.6	0.7	-0.9	8.5	9.1	+0.6
English	60.1	55.6	-4.5	30.1	36.6	+6.5	1.3	0.4	-0.9	8.4	7.5	-0.9
French	50.6	47.4	-3.2	38.7	37.5	-1.2	2.2	1.1	-1.1	8.5	14.0	+5.5
New Canadians	—	51.9	—	—	38.6	—	—	1.0	—	—	8.5	—
European (average)	40.2	41.4	+1.2	44.7	46.7	+2.0	3.4	1.9	-1.5	11.6	10.0	-1.6

Question: "There is a lot of discussion about how business and industry should be managed. Which of these four statements comes closest to your opinion?
1. The owners should run their own business or appoint the managers
2. The owners and employees should participate in the selection of managers
3. The government should be the owner and appoint the managers
4. The employees should own the business and should elect the managers"

Source: 1981 and 1990 World Values Surveys.

Appendix 6-E Following Instructions at Work (Percentages)

Country	Should follow instructions			Must be convinced first			Depends		
	1981	1990	% change	1981	1990	% change	1981	1990	% change
France	24.3	35.7	+11.4	60.9	47.5	-13.4	14.8	16.8	+2.0
Britain	48.7	44.6	-4.1	36.7	43.1	+6.4	14.7	12.3	-2.4
West Germany	26.3	40.7	+14.4	54.6	23.8	-30.8	19.1	35.5	+16.4
Italy	22.1	28.5	+6.4	41.8	46.9	+5.1	36.1	24.6	-11.5
Netherlands	40.8	38.4	-2.4	36.6	47.3	+10.7	22.6	14.3	-8.3
Denmark	61.4	35.4	-26.0	24.6	53.7	+29.1	14.0	10.9	-3.1
Belgium	37.0	30.7	+0.7	36.1	45.0	+8.9	26.9	24.3	-2.6
Spain	31.5	31.6	+0.1	45.2	50.4	+5.2	23.4	18.0	-5.4
Ireland	46.5	47.1	+0.6	26.9	41.3	+14.4	26.6	11.6	-15.0
Northern Ireland	49.3	55.4	-6.1	27.3	37.6	+10.3	23.4	6.9	-16.5
United States	67.3	62.0	-5.3	25.3	23.1	-2.2	7.4	14.9	+7.5
Canada	54.6	52.5	-2.1	32.2	28.6	-3.6	13.2	18.9	+5.7
English	57.8	52.6	-5.2	28.7	27.4	-1.3	13.5	20.0	+6.5
French	45.6	56.5	+10.9	41.9	28.4	-13.5	12.5	15.1	+2.6
New Canadians	—	49.4	—	—	31.6	—	—	19.0	—
European (average)	38.8	38.8	—	39.1	43.7	+4.6	22.2	17.5	-4.7

Question: "People have different ideas about following instructions at work. Some say that one should follow instructions of one's superiors even when one does not fully agree with them. Others say that one should follow one's superior's instructions only when one is convinced that they are right. With which of these two opinions do you agree?
1. Should follow instructions
2. Must be convinced first
3. Depends"

Source: 1981 and 1990 World Values Surveys.

Appendix 6-F   The Links Between Orientations toward General, Political, and Workplace Authority, by Country

Country	General orientations and political orientations	General orientations and workplace orientations	Political orientations and workplace orientations
France	-.34	-.17	.27
Britain	-.37	-.18	.11
West Germany	-.31	-.07	.23
Italy	-.34	-.11	.26
Netherlands	-.35	-.06	.25
Denmark	-.18	-.11	.32
Belgium	-.29	-.04	.23
Spain	-.42	-.13	.25
Ireland	-.57	-.08	.19
Northern Ireland	-.47	-.03	.11
United States	-.38	-.11	.21
Canada	-.42	-.17	.22
English	-.42	-.16	.24
French	-.49	-.25	.20
New Canadians	-.32	-.002	.20

Note: The above figures are gamma coefficients for the merged 1981 and 1990 data.
Source: 1981 and 1990 World Values Surveys.

Appendix 6-G Linkages between Worker Participation and Other Orientations towards Authority

Country	Worker Participation and General Orientations towards Authority			Worker Participation and Orientations towards Political Authority			Worker Participation and Orientations towards Protest Potential			Worker Participation and Non-confidence in Institutions			Worker Participation and Self-actualization		
	1981	1990	merged	1981	1990	merged	1981	1990	merged	1981	1990	merged	1981	1990	merged
France	-.30	-.25	-.28	.41	.33	.36	.34	.31	.32	.28	.20	.23	.15	.13	.12
Britain	-.27	-.20	-.23	.25	.27	.27	.23	.17	.20	.13	.18	.16	.03	-.003	.01
W. Germany	-.27	-.14	-.18	.46	.38	.40	.39	.30	.32	.29	.25	.26	.10	.07	.08
Italy	-.27	-.17	-.19	.39	.21	.26	.41	.20	.24	.16	.11	.12	.13	.11	.10
Netherlands	-.20	-.15	-.18	.36	.31	.34	.30	.31	.31	.23	.08	.17	.03	.06	.06
Denmark	-.20	-.11	-.17	.41	.40	.40	.40	.35	.37	.11	.15	.11	.15	.09	.13
Belgium	.03	-.12	-.08	.28	.22	.26	.34	.21	.26	.11	.09	.11	.19	.09	.13
Spain	-.28	-.22	-.24	.40	.35	.37	.40	.34	.35	.28	.17	.21	.14	.11	.12
Ireland	-.22	-.20	-.21	.36	.20	.30	.35	.19	.28	.19	.08	.14	.02	.00	.03
N. Ireland	-.35	-.19	-.27	.37	.20	.29	.33	.20	.26	.16	.14	.15	-.04	-.04	-.04
U.S.	-.23	-.22	-.24	.22	.20	.22	.18	.15	.18	.11	.10	.11	.08	.10	.08
Canada	-.32	-.17	-.23	.28	.23	.25	.22	.24	.23	.17	.08	.12	.05	.12	.09
English	-.31	-.20	-.26	.25	.25	.26	.18	.25	.22	.19	.07	.13	.07	.11	.09
French	-.38	-.12	-.21	.42	.17	.28	.33	.25	.28	.22	.07	.14	.06	.16	.11
New Canadians	—	-.11	—	—	.23	—	—	.26	—	—	.12	—	—	.11	—

Note: The above figures are gamma coefficients.
Source: 1981 and 1990 World Values Surveys.

7: Moral Outlooks

Demonstrating that political and economic value changes are connected opens up the possibility that comparable value shifts have taken place in other domains. Part 4 expands the range of the investigation yet again; it explores social values. Chapter 7 focusses on what might broadly be called "moral outlooks"; it begins by considering religious orientations. Traditionally, religious orientations have provided guidelines about good and evil, right and wrong, and to the extent that these guidelines are shared and deeply held, they serve as a moral cement for communities (Durkheim, 1961). The emergence of advanced industrialism is associated with the progressive secularization of these societies, and as religious values lose their social force world views become more pluralized and fragmented (Turner, 1991). Declining church attendance rates is the best-documented face of this trend, and our own WVS data provide further individual-level evidence. They also show that publics have become more secular in other important, non-institutional respects: between 1981 and 1990 there was a significant decline in the proportions of people saying that God was "important" to their lives. Over the same period, the moral authority of churches eroded: people became less inclined to believe their churches were providing adequate answers to questions about morality and the family. As will become apparent from the evidence presented in this chapter, these shifts are connected to other changes: publics became more permissive. Certainly, there is some indication that standards of *public* morality have shifted. Findings reported in Chapter 4 document rising levels of "civil permissiveness": people are becoming less likely to condemn as wrong such behaviours as avoiding fares on public transport, cheating on taxes, and lying in their own interest. But what about other, personal, standards of morality? According to the WVS data, people are also becoming more permissive about other aspects of morality. They are more likely than before to regard such once-proscribed behaviours as divorce and homosexuality as "justifiable." One interpretation of these findings is that they signify the rise of permissiveness. But there is another interpretation available; they may also signify that publics are becoming more tolerant. The concluding part of Chapter 7 considers the question of tolerance in some detail. Canada is sometimes described as a tolerant society, although remarkably little cross-national evidence has been produced to substantiate that claim. As will become clear, there is compelling evidence indicating that support for the *principle* of tolerance is widespread and is growing in all of the advanced industrial states. Less clear, however, is whether this expanding support for the principle of tolerance has any impact on how people make judgements about their daily affairs.

Values about the family are the focus of Chapter 8. If people are becoming less traditional and more "permissive," as Chapter 7 shows, then it is conceivable that other orientations, such as those surrounding the traditional family, may also be in transition. To what extent have core values about the family changed? And in what direction? Have people's priorities shifted when it comes to what values children should learn? The evidence emerging from this line of inquiry moves the investigation of social orientations back into the orbit of one of the central conclusions to emerge from our analysis of political and economic value shifts: the issue of authority orientations. The central question is a simple one, but it has broad ramifications. If orientations towards political and economic authority relations have changed, then similar shifts may well have taken place within the family itself. Two aspects of authority orientations in the family are of special relevance: authority relations between adults in the traditional family setting, or spousal relations, and parent-child relations. It turns out that there *are* detectable shifts in orientations towards authority within the family on both of these dimensions, and the direction of the shifts is consistent with those that have taken place in the polity and the workplace. Chapter 8 concludes by returning to a more expansive view of authority orientations. It picks up the threads of our earlier findings reported at the end of Chapters 4 and 6, and turns to an explicit empirical investigation of whether orientations towards authority in the family are connected to authority orientations in the polity and the economy, the central finding of which is that, unequivocally, they are.

Shifting religious orientations

People living under uncertain circumstances where the margin for error is small and any unexpected turn of events can have disastrous consequences have a much greater need for predictable rules and absolute norms. In traditional settings, religious norms were central because they provided a measure of certainty amid insecurity. With the transitions associated with emergent industrialism, many of the functions once performed by the church have been taken over by the state. Some traditional religious norms retained their significance by gaining secular-legal sanction, and for very good reason. For example, the commandment "Thou shalt not kill" restricts the scope of violent behaviour, and it is hard to imagine how any society could survive for very long without that kind of norm being widely embraced. Other religious norms, such as those that prohibit adultery or encourage honoring one's parents, are directed towards maintaining the traditional family unit.

But there are a number of reasons to expect traditional religious norms and practices to play a less pivotal role in the lives of publics in advanced industrial states. In instrumental terms, the traditional family unit is now less central to people's economic and physical survival than it once was. In advanced industrial states, for example, most people work outside the home and are typically educated outside the home. To a large extent, the emergence of the welfare state has taken some of the risk and uncertainty out of people's lives. By providing a comprehensive array of such social supports as unemployment benefits, health care, state-sponsored education, and care for the aged, the welfare state has reduced the levels of insecurity in people's lives. Because of such supports, children in these states can now survive outside of traditional two-parent family structures, and childless parents can survive in their old age without the "insurance" that children once provided. The breadth and depth of the welfare safety net varies from one country to the next, but people's most basic survival needs are now met in all of these states. But though individual welfare has become progressively less dependent on churches, it does not follow that religious values have changed very quickly or have become irrelevant. Life may now be less risky, but people still face fundamental questions about the meaning of human existence, about life and death.

We have already encountered one very general piece of evidence indicating where religion fits in the general priorities of our twelve publics. According to findings reported in Chapter 2, religion typically ranks behind family and work in people's priorities: about one in four respondents indicates that religion is "very important in their lives" (see Table 2-3). The WVS are an extremely rich source of data concerning religion; they contain more than thirty questions about different aspects of religious life. Of these, two questions turn out to be particularly useful, broad indicators: one taps personal subjective religiosity and the other probes church attendance rates. These two indicators have repeatedly been shown to be powerful and reliable summary indicators of religiosity, and both are closely related to a variety of other indicators of religiosity. The question about subjective religiosity simply asked, "... how important is God in your life?" Respondents answered using a ten-point scale on which "10 means very important" and "1 means not at all important." The other question tapped a well-tested behavioural benchmark of religious practice: "Apart from weddings, funerals and christenings, about how often do you attend religious services these days?" Here, respondents were given a variety of options ranging from "more than once a week" and "once a week" to "once a year" and "never, or practically never."

These questions were asked in every country in both 1981 and 1990. There is no reason to expect dramatic changes to have taken place on either of these dimensions: welfare states were entrenched in all of these countries well before 1981, shifts in basic values take place only gradually, and the WVS data cover only a relatively short time span. Table 7-1 presents the cross-time results for all publics on both of these indicators; it reports the proportions of each public scoring high on the subjective religiosity indicator—those indicating 8, 9, or 10 on the ten-point scale—and on the church attendance indicator—those reporting that they attend church at least once a week. As expect-

Table 7-1 The Importance of God and Church Attendance in 12 Advanced Industrial Countries (Percentages)

Country	Importance of God in One's life*			Weekly Church attendance**		
	1981	1990	% change	1981	1990	% change
France	22.4	19.5	-2.9	10.7	10.2	-0.5
Britain	31.3	28.3	-3.0	13.8	14.2	-0.4
W. Germany	31.1	29.6	-1.5	18.8	17.9	-0.9
Italy	48.7	52.6	+3.9	32.4	37.9	+5.5
Neth.	28.4	27.1	-1.3	25.5	20.2	-5.3
Denmark	17.6	13.1	-4.5	2.8	2.5	-0.3
Belgium	31.7	29.8	-1.9	30.6	26.6	-4.0
Spain	38.1	36.3	-1.8	40.1	29.2	-10.9
Ireland	68.4	64.7	-3.7	82.4	80.8	-1.6
N. Ireland	56.9	63.0	+6.1	51.6	50.0	-1.6
Europe avg.	36.5	34.9	-1.6	30.2	27.2	-3.0
U.S.	73.4	70.1	-3.3	43.3	44.1	+0.8
Canada	55.1	50.6	-4.5	30.8	26.8	-4.0
English	52.9	46.7	-6.2	29.2	26.5	-2.7
French	61.4	60.0	-1.4	35.1	25.0	-10.1
New Canadians	—	51.8	—	—	28.8	—

* The question read "And how important is God in your life? (10 means very important and 1 means not at all important.)" High = those indicating 8, 9, or 10 on the 10 point scale.

**The question read: "Apart from weddings, funerals and christenings, about how often do you attend religious services these days?
   1. More than once a week
   2. Once a week
   3. Once a month
   4. Christmas/Easter day
   5. Other specific holidays
   6. Once a year
   7. Less often
   8. Never, practically never."

Source: 1981 and 1990 World Values Surveys.

ed, none of the 1981–1990 changes are very large, but they are mostly in the same direction: the proportions of these publics saying that "God is important in my life" dropped in ten of the twelve countries; the only exceptions are Italy and Northern Ireland. And weekly church attendance rates have also declined in ten of the twelve countries. Here, the exceptions are Italy, once again, and the United States.

The cross-national variations in responses to these basic indicators are quite striking. On the personal religiosity dimension, for instance, there are sharp differences between publics in the northern European countries—mostly Protestant ones—and those in southern Europe and North America. Moreover, there is clear evidence, once again, of another well-documented face of American exceptionalism. In the United States levels of personal religiosity are remarkably high. Not surprisingly, responses to the behavioural and subjective indicators of religiosity do not correspond precisely; church attendance rates are nearly always somewhat lower than self-reported levels of personal religiosity. There is one intriguing exception to that pattern: self-reported church attendance rates in Ireland far exceed the self-reported levels of religiosity. That finding might be attributable to the pressures of social conformity in communities that are religiously homogeneous, although this interpretation does not seem to explain the discrepancy between subjective religiosity and church attendance rates in other settings, such as Italy, that are also religiously homogeneous. Nor does it explain the findings for Quebec francophones within Canada. In that setting, levels of personal religiosity have been relatively stable while church attendance rates have declined quite dramatically.[1]

There is every indication that these shifts, the slight declines in personal religiosity and church attendance rates, are part of the complex set of long-term transformations that have been repeatedly documented throughout this book. As Figures 7-1 and 7-2 show, both our behavioural and subjective indicators of religiosity are systematically related to each one of the background factors: age, education, and post-materialist value orientations. Furthermore, in every case the direction of these relationships is consistent with the generational change interpretation. Notice that Canadian levels of subjective religiosity are significantly higher than the European average. European and Canadian church attendance rates are indistinguishable from each other, and both clearly differ from, are lower than, those found in the United States. That religiosity is related to age comes as no surprise whatsoever, and viewed in isolation that finding could easily be interpreted as indicating life-cycle effects: older people are more likely than their younger counterparts to go to church. Life-cycle effects undoubtedly are a part of the explanation, but they are only one part. Levels of education also come into play, a finding that is somewhat more surprising because people with higher levels of education typically are more likely than others to be "joiners" and to have higher levels of participation in all kinds of organizations. When it comes to church attendance, however, the clear finding is that those with high levels of education participate significantly *less* than those with lower levels. That post-materialists are significantly less religious than their materialist counterparts is again not surprising, and is precisely what post-materialist theory would lead one to expect: post-materialists, after all, were socialized under conditions of relative security.

As has already been pointed out, church attendance rates and subjective religiosity are but two of the many available indicators of religious orientations contained in the WVS. An analysis of a variety of other indicators of religious orientations produces similarly consistent results. One finding is that people's attachments to traditional churches and main-line denominations are weakening. Personal non-institutional religious practices are also changing. Between 1981 and 1990, for example, there was a decline in the proportions

Figure 7-1 Importance of God in One's Life, by Age, Education, and Value Type

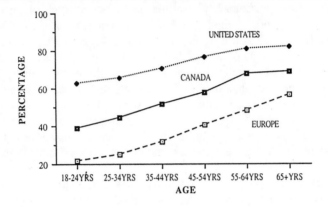

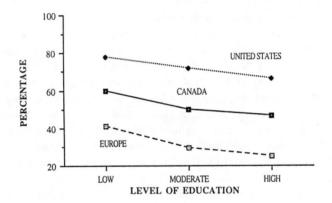

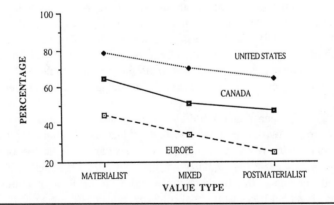

Source: 1981 and 1990 World Values Surveys.

Figure 7-2 Weekly Church Attendance, by Age, Education, and Value Type

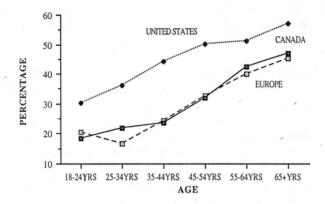

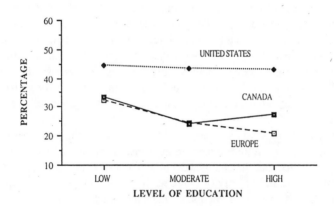

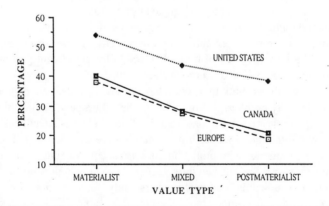

Source: 1981 and 1990 World Values Surveys.

of these publics saying that they "pray to God outside of religious services." The impact of background factors on this indicator turns out to be almost exactly the same as their effects on personal religiosity and church attendance.[2] The proportions of people saying that they gain "comfort and strength from religion" were lower in 1990 than in 1981. The trend is in the same direction for those saying they took some moments of "prayer, meditation or contemplation."[3] The percentages of respondents indicating that they thought of themselves as "religious," "independently of whether they go to church or not," also declined between 1981 and 1990. Across a whole set of indicators the basic structure of the findings reemerge again and again. In every case, the effects of background factors conform to virtually the same pattern, and they consistently point to the interpretation that these shifts are generationally driven.

Publics are gradually becoming more secular in a number of important respects, but they are not becoming more secular at the same rate. Nor does this widespread erosion of religious orientations necessarily mean that people are in the process of entirely abandoning all aspects of religious life. Some social theorists contend that collective participation in religious ceremonies and rituals is more important for social integration than is a consensus on religious beliefs. According to the WVS data, attachments to some ritualistic aspects of religious practice remain remarkably high. When asked, "Do you personally think that it is important to hold a religious service" for such events as birth, marriage, and death, a huge majority in nearly every public responded yes.[4]

One concern expressed by some social theorists is that the processes of secularization have a profound impact on the sense of moral order in society. Is there any evidence that the changes documented above are accompanied by a decline in the moral authority of churches in these societies? Do people see their churches as providing adequate leadership on the moral issues of the day? The 1981 and 1990 WVS asked two questions that help to illuminate this issue. Respondents were asked, "Generally speaking, do you think that your church is giving, in your country, adequate answers to (a) the *moral problems* and needs of the individual? And, (b) the problems of the *family*?" The replies to these questions, reported in Table 7-2, are revealing in two respects. First, churches still retain positions of moral leadership for significant proportions of these publics: some 40% of Europeans, two-thirds of Americans, and more than half of Canadians think their churches are giving "adequate responses" to moral and family problems. Among the northern European publics, the differences between levels of personal religiosity and church attendance rates and views about the moral leadership of churches are truly striking. The proportions of these publics who think churches are adequately answering moral and family problems are substantially *higher* than those reporting that they attend church or indicating that they are personally "very religious."

Nonetheless, the cross-time changes reported in Table 7-2 do suggest that churches have been losing some ground in this respect. The proportions of

Table 7-2 Is the Church Giving Adequate Responses to Moral and Family Problems (Percentage Saying Yes)

Country	Moral problems			Family problems		
	1981	1990	% change	1981	1990	% change
France	45.0	38.1	-6.9	36.5	28.1	-8.4
Britain	37.6	35.9	-1.7	39.8	38.0	-1.8
W. Germany	40.8	39.9	-0.9	38.3	34.1	-4.2
Italy	48.2	51.5	+3.3	47.6	44.7	-2.9
Neth.	38.3	36.3	-2.0	37.6	33.2	-4.4
Denmark	21.7	19.9	-1.8	13.6	13.0	-0.6
Belgium	47.7	41.7	-6.0	41.5	36.5	-5.0
Spain	45.9	42.6	-3.3	40.2	42.6	+2.6
Ireland	54.8	42.1	-12.7	51.0	35.9	-15.1
N. Ireland	54.5	55.1	+0.6	55.7	59.2	+3.5
Europe avg.	43.4	40.8	-2.6	39.3	37.0	-2.3
U.S.	72.2	67.2	-5.0	74.5	69.7	-4.8
Canada	62.9	54.5	-8.4	62.9	55.2	-7.7
English	62.3	55.2	-7.1	64.8	56.9	-7.9
French	64.4	49.6	-14.8	57.9	46.8	-11.1
New Cananadians	—	58.7	—	—	61.3	—

Question: "Generally speaking, do you think that your church is giving, in your country, adequate answers to:
    A. the moral problems and needs of the individual?
    B. the problems of family life?"
Source: 1981 and 1990 World Values Surveys.

these publics saying that the churches are giving adequate responses to moral and family problems declined between 1981 and 1990. As on the other dimensions, the shifts are far from uniform, and in the cases of Italy, Spain, and Northern Ireland there have actually been detectable increases. But on balance, it appears that people are less satisfied than before with the moral leadership provided by churches; the declines are particularly sharp in Ireland in France and among francophones in Canada.

One possibility, consistent with our earlier findings, is that the moral authority of these churches may have waned for the same kinds of reasons that seem to explain eroding public confidence in other institutions. Like they do other traditional institutions, people may regard churches as hierarchical and unresponsive. Another is that churches are viewed as being increasingly out of touch with the kinds of moral and family problems that people routinely confront. Regardless of the precise explanation, it is clear that perceptions about the adequacy of churches' responses to those problems are significantly and consistently shaped by the same background factors that are related to nearly all of the other broad changes so far documented. For example, the young, the well educated, and those with post-materialist orientations are *less* likely than their older, less well educated, and materialist counterparts to see the church as providing adequate leadership. These aggregate results are not skewed; nor do they overlook any national exceptions. The very same pattern holds up in every European public, in the United States, and in Canada; it also applies within each of Canada's three communities. Furthermore, the same background factors have the same impact on perceptions about the adequacy of the churches' responses to family problems in every single setting.[5]

There is nothing very dramatic about the scope of any of these shifts in religious orientations; many might even be described as marginal. Far more impressive than the scope of the shifts is their consistency of direction. Regardless of whether one relies on subjective indicators, like personal religiosity, on behavioural indicators such as church attendance, or on attitudes towards the adequacy of the churches' moral leadership, nearly all the changes are in the same direction: towards greater secularization. But given that these orientations are all connected to the same background factors in very much the same way, these changes seem also to be a part of the complex pattern of long-term shifts that are reshaping the political and economic values of publics in these states. Are declining church attendance rates, levels of personal religiosity, and the moral authority of churches collectively symptomatic of broader shifts in the moral axes of these communities? It is to this issue that we now turn. From one perspective, such changes might be interpreted to mean "the collapse of moral standards." From another, they might be construed as the emergence of "different" standards of conduct.

Moral Permissiveness

Chapter 4 presented a good deal of evidence indicating that standards of *public* conduct are shifting. Between 1981 and 1990, for example, publics became increasingly likely to indicate that cheating on taxes or avoiding fares on public transport, actions that involve some calculation of personal gain at public expense, were justified behaviours. These findings may signify rising frustration with the status quo, irritations with city hall, or general disaffection with government. From these perspectives, rising levels of civil permissiveness could simply indicate the small ways in which citizens want to "get back at the system." Another possibility is that these shifts are symptomatic of broader and deeper changes in personal standards of conduct. It could be, for example, that similar shifts are taking place in private standards of what is acceptable. The 1981 and 1990 WVS contained a variety of questions that probed how permissive, or restrictive, citizens are on matters of personal morality.[6] People were presented with a list of statements about a variety of behaviours and were asked to use a ten-point scale to indicate "whether you think that [the behaviour] can always be justified ['1'], never be justified ['10'], or something in between." Eight of the twenty-five items included in the larger battery of questions cluster into a single moral permissiveness dimension.[7] An exhaustive exploration of attitudes to each and every one of these items would be cumbersome,[8] but three of them—homosexuality, divorce, and euthanasia—deserve close attention because it is on these particular items that public opinion is most dynamic as well as most divided.

Table 7-3 summarizes the aggregate responses for each public on each of these three items at two time points; it reports the percentages of each public indicating that homosexuality, divorce, and euthanasia are justified (scoring 8, 9, or 10 on the ten-point scale). The columns to the right of the table group the summary responses into a single composite "moral permissiveness" index.[9] The overall patterns illustrated in Table 7-3 are unmistakable: the general trend is towards rising levels in moral permissiveness, or declining restrictiveness. The only exception to that pattern is Denmark. Notice, though, that the Danes exhibited very high levels of permissiveness in both 1981 and in 1990.

Consider, first, the findings for homosexuality. On this dimension, as on the others, there are very substantial cross-national variations in the proportions saying that homosexuality is justifiable. The Dutch and Danish are clearly the least restrictive: more than half of these publics said homosexuality is justifiable. They stand in sharp contrast with the American or Irish publics. In 1980 Canadian responses (13%) fell well below the European average (22.5%). By 1990, however, that gap had narrowed: levels of moral permissiveness increased in Canada at about twice the European rate with the shifts being particularly rapid among francophone Canadians. By 1991 Canadians were twice as likely as Americans to say that homosexuality was justified. Once again, the trajectory of change is in the direction of *declining* restrictiveness, and the data indicate that on this dimension, too, Canadian orientations appear to lead American ones: in 1990, American orientations towards homosexuality (13%) were at essentially the same level as Canadian orientations in 1981.

Orientations towards divorce follow a similar pattern: with the exception of Denmark, all publics became progressively *less* restrictive in their views about divorce. These results are intriguing not least of all because they seem to suggest that there is a significant gap between behaviour and preferences. As has already been demonstrated (Figure 2-3), American divorce rates are the highest in the western world; they are three times higher than those in Europe and nearly twice as high as Canadian rates. Given the sheer scope of these objective differences, one might surmise that Americans would be more permissive when it comes to divorce. The evidence does not support that line of interpretation. In 1990, for example, Americans ranked tenth of the twelve countries in voicing the opinion that divorce is justified. And in this respect Americans (37%) once again turn out to be *more* restrictive than Canadians (52%).

Homosexuality and divorce are contentious issues, and so is euthanasia. Policy debates about euthanasia become entangled in a complex web of ethical, medical, and legal questions, and nearly every country included in our analysis can offer wrenching examples of the tragic dilemmas surrounding the issue. At the time that the WVS were conducted, active euthanasia was a crime in every country included in the surveys, and in nearly every country the

Table 7-3 Changing Moral Permissiveness, 1981–1990 (Percentages)

Country	Homosexuality			Divorce			Euthanasia			Moral permissiveness index		
	1981	1990	% change	1981	1990	% change	1981	1990	% change	1981	1990	% change
France	18.5	25.2	+6.7	54.8	58.1	+3.3	40.3	47.1	+6.8	21.2	25.9	+4.7
Britain	21.1	15.4	-5.7	42.8	43.7	+0.9	32.4	33.5	+1.1	16.3	10.2	-6.1
W. Germany	23.7	34.6	+10.9	45.1	57.0	+11.9	34.0	27.5	-6.5	17.5	18.7	+1.2
Italy	12.2	23.6	+11.4	45.7	48.4	+2.7	18.5	21.9	+3.4	7.4	14.9	+7.5
Netherlands	58.0	78.6	+20.6	38.0	66.2	+28.2	53.0	59.9	+6.9	38.9	60.4	+21.5
Denmark	51.1	38.5	-12.6	77.4	62.3	-15.1	63.6	53.9	-9.7	50.8	29.7	-21.1
Belgium	12.7	21.9	+9.2	15.6	34.5	+18.9	19.3	41.1	+21.8	2.1	19.1	+17.0
Spain	12.6	24.7	+12.1	38.2	55.0	+16.8	16.2	28.6	+12.4	8.4	23.1	+14.7
Ireland	9.3	14.0	+4.7	14.0	23.0	+9.0	5.2	5.0	-0.2	1.1	2.4	+1.3
N. Ireland	2.8	4.0	+1.2	8.7	18.9	+10.2	8.4	10.5	+2.1	0.8	3.2	+2.4
Eur. avg.	22.5	27.9	+5.4	40.6	49.3	+8.7	28.0	32.3	+4.3	16.5	20.8	+4.3
U.S.	7.1	12.9	+5.8	34.1	36.8	+2.7	22.5	23.6	+1.1	3.7	9.0	+5.3
Canada	12.9	24.0	+11.1	38.0	51.8	+13.8	28.3	40.4	+12.1	7.8	21.3	+13.5
English	11.4	20.3	+8.9	39.5	53.1	+13.6	27.2	39.3	+12.1	7.3	17.3	+10.0
French	17.5	34.0	+16.5	34.0	57.9	+23.9	31.3	45.2	+13.9	8.8	34.2	+25.4
New Canadians	—	25.1	—	—	40.7	—	—	38.4	—	—	21.8	—

Question: "Please tell me for each of the following statements whether you think it can 'always be justified,' 'never be justified,' or 'something in between' using this card?"
Source: 1981 and 1990 World Values Surveys.

issue was becoming increasingly controversial. Publics mobilized, legislators were lobbied, reports were solicited, and commissions were struck to investigate the legal, ethical, and practical aspects of the question. Courts have been used to test the law on euthanasia, and in every country a variety of bodies such as churches, law societies, and physicians' associations have volunteered, or been invited to render, their opinions on the matter (Baron, 1981; Finlay, 1985; Gevers, 1987; Koop & Grant, 1986; Lucyk, 1985; Winkler, 1985; Younger, 1987). Contentious though the issue has become, cross-time opinion data about attitudes towards euthanasia are rare and cross-national evidence is rarer still. There is scattered evidence, some of it going back to the late 1940s, indicating that the American public has become less restrictive on the question (Ostheimer, 1980). The WVS data span a more limited time frame, but they include more countries, and these data indicate that there have been incremental shifts in the same direction among most advanced industrial states. The only exceptions are Denmark, once again, and Britain; the changes in Ireland are well within the margins of error. In this case as in others, however, American respondents turn out to be atypical: they are well below the European average and Canadians are well above it. Notice, too, that the rate of opinion change in the United States has been relatively slow, while in Canada the 1981–1990 shifts were quite dramatic.

Homosexuality, divorce, and euthanasia, of course, are quite different issues that raise quite different moral questions. The striking finding is, however, that the shifts on each of these dimensions of private morality are remarkably consistent; publics have become less restrictive in their assessments of each. Moreover, Canadians are significantly more permissive than their American counterparts, and on every dimension the Canadian 1981–1990 changes have been more rapid than those in the United States. Within Canada, the changes have been most rapid among francophone Canadians. Are these shifts in private morality also linked to age, post-materialist value orientations, and education? There is every indication that they are.

Figure 7-3 reports the similarities and differences between Canadian, American and European orientations using a single moral permissiveness index, the additive scale summarizing respondents' attitudes to all three items. The first observation is that the age effects are not entirely linear. Europeans, Americans, and Canadians in the very youngest age group (18–24 years) are actually *less* permissive than their counterparts in the next oldest groups (25–34 years). After that, the pattern becomes more straightforward. Older people tend to be *more* restrictive than the young, and the cross-national differences also narrow as people get older. Canadian–European differences, for example, evaporate after respondents reach 45 years of age, and beyond 55 years there are no longer any discernible differences in moral outlook between Americans and other respondents.

Education effects are also evident. Those with high levels of formal education score twice as high on the moral permissiveness index as those with low

Figure 7-3   Moral Permissiveness, by Age, Education, and Value Type

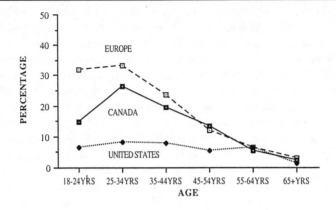

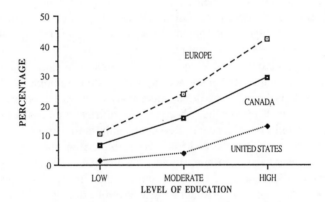

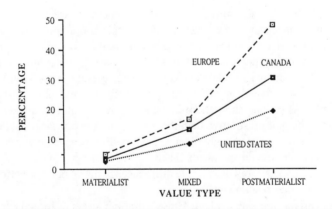

Source: 1981 and 1990 World Values Surveys.

Table 7-4   Regression Analysis: The Determinants of Moral Permissiveness

Predictors	12 Advanced Industrial Countries	Europe	United States	Canada
Religious outlook:				
High church attendance	-.29**	-.29**	-.33**	-.39**
High importance of God	-.32**	-.30**	-.32**	-.28**
Values:				
Postmaterialism	.17*	.19**	.13**	.04
Socio-Demographics:				
Age	-.09**	-.10**	-.01	.02
Male	-.06**	-.06**	-.07	-.07
Income	.01	.004	-.05	.05
Education	.14**	.14**	.13*	.25**
Nationality:				
American	.04*	—	—	—
Canadian	.004	—	—	—
Constant	.55**	.55**	.57**	.53**
R-squared	.53	.56	.35	.46
Adjusted R-squared	.53	.56	.34	.45

*significant at $p < .05$; **significant at $p < .01$.
Source: 1981 and 1990 World Values Surveys.

levels, a finding that holds up in every country. The impact of value type is equally impressive. Like education, value type seems to have a prismatic effect: the outlooks of materialists are almost identical regardless of nationality. The national variations become sharper for those in the mixed value type category, and sharper still for those who qualify as post-materialists. Most significant, age, education, and value type all work in the same direction: the old, those with lower levels of formal education, and materialists are all significantly more restrictive in their moral outlooks than the young, those with higher levels of formal education, and post-materialists.[10]

The argument is not that emerging post-materialist value orientations are solely responsible for shifting moral outlooks. In fact, changing moral outlooks appear to have more to do with the retreat of traditional religious orientations than was documented at the beginning of this chapter. The essential point can be demonstrated quite easily. Multivariate analysis allows us to compare the effects of both the religious orientations considered above and of value type as predictors of moral permissiveness. Keep in mind that the regression results reported in Table 7-4 isolate the separate effects of each of the predictors *after* the effects of the other predictors have been taken into account. For the combined data, the aggregate results from all twelve countries, the findings are absolutely clear. The coefficients for the two indicators of religiosity—church attendance and subjective religiosity (importance of God)—are higher than any others. In other words, these two items are the best predictors of orientations towards moral permissiveness. In both cases, the coefficients are negative, which means that respondents with low church attendance rates, or who attach little importance to God in their lives, score higher on the moral permissiveness scale. Notice too, though, that for the pooled data, post-materialist orientations, age, and education are also all significantly related to moral outlooks. That is, these indicators are also significant predictors of moral permissiveness even *after* religious orientations are taken into account.

There is also evidence of national differences. Americans are significantly different from Europeans, and the picture becomes more complicated, and more nuanced, when we shift our focus from the pooled data to the national aggregates. Not surprisingly, the European results reported in the second column replicate almost exactly the aggregate results. Only when the American and Canadian data are considered separately do the national variations come into clear focus. As before, both of the indicators of religious outlook are powerful and statistically significant predictors of moral permissiveness in every setting. Notice, however, that for American and Canadian respondents age effects disappear, and the impact of post-materialist orientations becomes much weaker in the Canadian setting. In Canada, education is a much stronger predictor of moral outlooks. (It is a significant predictor in every setting, but the coefficient is twice as strong in Canada.) These findings suggest that, for the most part, the shifts in moral outlooks have more to do with secularization than anything else. Rising educational levels are also part of the explanation, but so are post-materialist orientations, at least in most countries. There is no particular reason to expect post-materialist value change to be directly responsible for greater secularization. Post-materialist theory contains little direct commentary concerning secularization, although both the rise of post-material values and declining religious orientations may be complementary shifts each of which, in turn, might be related to individual feelings about security. Are these changing orientations towards moral permissiveness linked to the rising levels of civil permissiveness that were documented in Chapter 4? Are the shifts in private morality connected to the changes in civil permissiveness? They are, and the statistical evidence of such a linkage is overwhelming: where respondents stand on the moral permissiveness scale is associated with orientations towards civil permissiveness. The same basic finding holds up in every single country, and it does so at both time points. Moreover, in every case the relationship is very robust.[11] As it happens, post-materialist orientations turn out to be a much stronger predictor of civil permissiveness than of moral permissiveness. Value type, it seems, plays a more central role in shaping orientations to issues that engage questions of public rather than private morality.

It seems but a short leap from the observation that publics are becoming less restrictive, or more permissive, in their civil and moral orientations to the conclusion that publics are increasingly willing to adopt an "anything goes" stance to all questions of private or public morality. But there are reasons to be cautious about taking that leap. For example, people may have become more inclined than before to see divorce as justifiable, but that does not necessarily mean that they themselves approve of it. People may regard divorce, homosexuality, or euthanasia as *personally* objectionable but find fewer justifications for imposing their own preferences on others. The idea that people are more willing than they once were to "put up" with actions, attitudes, or people that they personally dislike brings the analysis closer to one value, tolerance, that is sometimes heralded as one of Canada's national traits. Is there any direct evidence to indicate that Canadians really are more tolerant than their counterparts in other advanced industrial states?

Tolerance

Hardly anyone disagrees with the idea that tolerance, or the willingness to put up with others, is an important value in free and open societies. In the realm of politics, for example, there are powerful reasons for believing that people ought to be tolerant: the more tolerant citizens are of the rights of others, the more secure are the rights of all, their own included (Gibson, 1992; McClosky & Brill, 1983; Sniderman et al., 1989). An equally persuasive case can be made for tolerance in other realms. Quite aside from matters of principle, pragmatic reasons come into play: tolerance undoubtedly promotes peaceful coexistence between diverse groups. To the extent that societies are becoming more diverse, and greater social diversity increases the potential for group conflict, it is reasonable to suppose tolerance will become an even more important value in the future.

Making the general case for tolerance is not difficult, then, particularly where political rights are concerned. Certainly most advanced industrial states have little difficulty in demonstrating some formal commitment to the idea of tolerance; they can point to an array of institutional and constitutional mechanisms intended to promote tolerance and to place severe constraints on public expressions of intolerance. Some forty years ago, Samuel Stouffer concluded his classic empirical study of tolerance, *Communism, Conformity and Civil Liberties*, with the confident prediction that publics would become more tolerant in the future:

> Great social, economic and technological forces are operating slowly and imperceptibly on the side of spreading tolerance. The rising level of education and the accompanying decline of authoritarian child-rearing practices increase independence of thought and respect for others whose ideas are different. The increasing geographic movement of people has a similar consequence as well as the vicarious experiences supplied by the magic of our ever-powerful media of communications. (1955: 236)

Despite Stouffer's optimism, it is not at all obvious that publics in advanced industrial states really have become more tolerant with the passage of time. There are several arguments to consider. First, the expansion of constitutional protections, legislative guidelines, and public policies dealing with the treatment of minorities and the prohibition of discrimination on the basis of race, political beliefs, religion, and other criteria may well have been intended to promote tolerance and discourage the practice of overt discrimination. The introduction of such provisions may even have assumed that standards of tolerance are increasingly widely shared and more highly valued. But to what extent do the launching of government policies, crafting of institutional guidelines, and introduction of constitutional guarantees provide reliable benchmarks of the attitudes of general publics? Constitutional and legislative manoeuvrings, typically, are elite-driven activities, and as such they may provide a better measure of elite values and conceptions of the public good than those held by publics at large. Indeed, it has been repeatedly demonstrated that elite orientations to such values as tolerance are quite different from those held by publics at large (Jackman, 1972; McClosky & Zaller, 1984; Sniderman et al., 1989 ; Sullivan, Piereson, & Marcus, 1982).

Second, it is fairly easy to assemble impressionistic evidence suggesting that public levels of tolerance may not have progressed along the trajectory Stouffer predicted. In the last decade, for example, rising levels of transborder movement of peoples in Europe and elsewhere seem to have sparked a variety of domestic reactions, ranging from "immigrant bashing" and racially motivated violence to the emergence of political formations opposing immigration and insurgent "multiculturalism" on a variety of grounds. If we take this anecdotal evidence at face value, we might conclude that publics have become less rather than more tolerant. To these perspectives one might also want to consider a more nuanced position that contends that public reactions to immigrant communities do not indicate declining levels of tolerance and that, in fact, public support for tolerance may be quite stable. The argument is that in the past intolerance was present but was quiet and institutionalized, and for the most part levels of citizen tolerance remained untested. Relying on evidence of increased outbreaks of communal conflict to make claims about changing levels of tolerance among publics is clearly a risky enterprise, one that invites friendly assumptions and unwarranted inferences. To what extent, for instance, are outbreaks of communal conflict the work of a few "bad apples"? Or do they reflect the concerns of the public at large? There are other considerations too. In one of the few explicitly cross-national analyses of the connection between immigration and racial conflict, Reitz (1988) makes a convincing case that cross-national variations in levels of communal conflict may have less to do with differences in citizen attitudes to tolerance and more with the structural and institutional conditions under which immigration takes place. It is not even clear if such explicit outbreaks of communal conflict are the most serious face of intolerance.

How tolerant are publics in Europe and North America? Have those publics become more or less tolerant in the course of the last decade? In what respects are these publics more or less tolerant? And what factors may account for differences in levels of tolerance? These are central and very basic questions.

The empirical study of tolerance has been a cumbersome enterprise for a variety of reasons. One difficulty is conceptual. As philosophers rightly point out, people willingly acknowledge that tolerance is an important value and one deserving support, but there is also a sense in which tolerance is not an absolute value. According to Crick, tolerance "is a value to be held among other values—such as liberty, and justice itself, but also order and truth"; but he then goes on to warn that "it can never always be right to be tolerant; there are occasions on which we should be intolerant" (1973: 64). Following the same line of reasoning, Sullivan and colleagues identify a "paradox of tolerance," namely, that "a defense of tolerance may require some degree of intolerance" (Sullivan, Piereson, & Marcus, 1982: 9). From this standpoint, there is little reason to suppose that publics will, or should, always become more tolerant. There is a threshold to tolerance, that is, there are proper limits to what should be tolerated, though precisely what those limits should be, or how they can be recognized, remain matters of vigorous debate.

Second, and particularly relevant for the analysis that follows, the cumulative research on tolerance has not produced any clear consensus about its dynamics for a variety of reasons. One problem is that the available studies of tolerance do not work from a single common framework. Attitudes to tolerance, for example, could well be multidimensional, which is to say that citizens might be tolerant in some respects but not others. Consequently, there are significant variations in the objects and levels of analysis. Another problem is that the vast bulk of the research on tolerance involves single-country studies. Explicitly cross-national analyses are few and far between, and cross-national explorations that bring in a cross-time dimension are very rare indeed (Weil, 1982). It is extremely risky to base generalizations about the dynamics of tolerance on the basis of single-country studies, ones that typically focus on a single dimension of tolerance—the political or the social—examined at one time point. Related to these difficulties are unresolved controversies about how tolerance is best measured (Abramson, 1983; Gibson, 1992). Some analysts focus on group antipathies, evaluations of how much members of one group like or dislike members of other groups (Davis, 1975; Nunn, Crockett, & Williams, 1978). Others prefer to examine tolerance from the standpoint of support for such important procedural norms as free speech (McClosky, 1964; Prothro & Grigg, 1960). Yet others target basic attitudes towards specific minorities. Fundamental differences in conceptualizing tolerance, significant variations in the objects to be analyzed, disagreements about measurement, and the absence of sustained cross-national evidence have combined to hobble the development of a cumulative body of research on which generalizable conclusions can be confidentally based.

In a most general sense, tolerant societies can be defined as those whose publics place a high value on the idea of tolerance.[12] From this vantage point,

Table 7-5 Support for the General Principle of Tolerance
(Percentages)

Country	1981	1990	% change
France	58.9	78.0	+19.1
Britain	62.1	79.6	+17.5
West Germany	43.1	76.7	+33.6
Italy	43.3	66.9	+23.6
Netherlands	59.4	87.1	+27.7
Denmark	58.4	80.5	+22.1
Belgium	45.2	67.2	+22.0
Spain	44.2	73.3	+29.1
Ireland	56.0	76.4	+20.4
Northern Ireland	59.9	79.9	+20.0
European Average	49.1	76.6	+27.5
United States	52.4	72.4	+20.0
Canada	53.0	80.2	+27.2
English	54.5	80.8	+26.3
French	48.6	79.8	+31.2
New Canadians	—	78.5	—

Question: "Here is a list of qualities which children can be encouraged to learn at home. Which if any do you consider to be especially important? Please choose up to five." (The above results reflect those respondents that selected "tolerance and respect for other people" as being an important quality to teach children.)
Source: 1981 and 1990 World Values Surveys.

the critical question becomes: To what extent do citizens in these advanced industrial states support the general principle of tolerance? And relatedly, has citizen support for the principle of tolerance increased or decreased, widened or deepened, in the course of the last decade? The 1981 and 1990 surveys presented all publics with a common list of ten qualities "which children can be encouraged to learn at home," and respondents were asked: "Which, if any, [of the following qualities] do you consider to be especially important?" One of the ten items included in the list was "Tolerance and respect for other people."[13] The question taps general orientations towards tolerance, and relies on projective techniques. The assumption is that the values people deem to be important for children are the same ones they themselves regard as important. As Table 7-5 shows, in 1981 about half of all respondents mentioned "tolerance and respect for other people" as an important value to teach children. Once again, there is clear evidence of cross-national variation in citizen support for principled tolerance. Far more striking than these differences, though, is the extent to which support for principled tolerance shifted between 1981 and 1990. On average, support for the principle of tolerance jumped by some 27%, with the increases being particularly sharp in West Germany, Spain, the Netherlands, and Canada.

Figure 7-4   Support for the Principle of Tolerance, by Age, Education, and Value Type

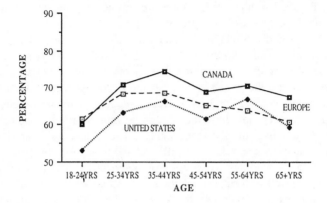

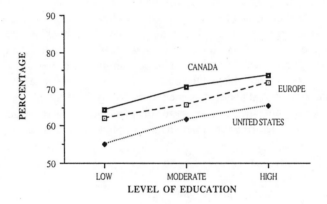

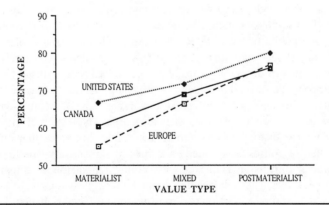

Source: 1981 and 1990 World Values Surveys.

Can these shifts be explained in terms of generational change? The evidence is uneven, and the most significant wrinkle has to do with the age-related effects. As Figure 7-4 shows, the relationship between age and support for the principle of tolerance is far from uniform. The youngest cohorts, typically, are *less* supportive of the principle of tolerance than others, and that finding applies to Europeans and North Americans alike. Those 35–44 years old tend to be the most tolerant, but thereafter the age effects are somewhat uneven. The pattern is curvilinear, and as a result the overall statistical association between age and tolerance is relatively weak.[14] Education and post-materialist orientations, however, both have the anticipated impact on tolerance orientations. Post-materialists and the more highly educated are significantly more likely than materialists and the less well educated to support the principle of tolerance, with the findings consistent cross-nationally.[15] The implication is that expanding levels of formal education and the continued rise of post-materialist orientations have precisely the kind of effect Stouffer predicted, but those effects do not leave, according to these data, a clear age-related imprint.

In one sense, this widespread and striking increase in levels of support for principled tolerance is a heartening discovery. It suggests that there are expanding reservoirs of good will among these publics. In other respects, however, these findings do not travel very far, not least because their practical implications remain murky. People seem to be warming to the general idea of tolerance, but it is not possible, on the basis of these data alone, to tell whether these publics are tolerant about the same things. Nor is there any indication of whether this apparent surge in support for the *principle* of tolerance actually moves people to become more tolerant in the conduct of their day-to-day affairs.

Situational Tolerance

To delve into these significant practical aspects of tolerance requires more focussed evidence, and for that we can turn, once again, to the WVS data. The 1981 and 1990 surveys contained batteries of items that have been routinely used to probe public orientations to what some call "situational tolerance" (McCutcheon, 1985; Sniderman et al., 1989). Respondents were presented with identical lists of different groups of people and asked to indicate "Which groups of people you would *not* like to have as neighbours."[16] A factor analysis of responses to these questions reveals remarkably consistent cross-national patterns in how publics organize their responses. The results of the 1981 and 1990 pooled factor analysis, reported in Table 7-6, show that publics structure their responses along three quite specific dimensions. The first and most powerful dimension is the classic "political intolerance" dimension (McClosky & Zaller, 1984); it taps into antipathy for right-wing and left-wing extremists as neighbours. The second most important factor, labelled "social intolerance," explains about 18% of the variance, and in this case responses to

Table 7-6 Factor Analysis: The Dimensions of Situational Tolerance
(Principle Components Extraction Procedure with a Varimax Rotation)

Indicators	Political Intolerance	Social Intolerance	Racial Intolerance	Communality
Right-wing extremists	.91	.09	.07	.84
Left-wing extremists	.88	.18	.12	.82
Heavy drinkers	.17	.72	-.05	.55
People with a criminal record	.02	.71	.16	.53
Emotionally unstable people	.11	.67	.15	.48
People of a different race	.08	.11	.84	.72
Immigrants/foreign workers	.09	.10	.84	.72
Eigenvalue	2.34	1.23	1.08	
% of variance explained	33.4	17.6	15.4	

Question: "On this card are various groups of people. Could you please read out any that you would not like to have as neighbours? You can just read out the letters. (a) people with a criminal record, (b) people of a different race, (c) left-wing extremists, (d) heavy drinkers, (e) right-wing extremists, (f) people with large families, (g) emotionally unstable people, (h) Muslims, (i) immigrants and foreign workers, (j) people who have AIDS, (k) drug addicts, (l) homosexuals, (m) Jews, and (n) Hindus.
Source: 1981 and 1990 World Values Surveys.

three items systematically cluster together: "people with a criminal record," "heavy drinkers," and "people who are emotionally unstable." The third, a racial/immigrant dimension, accounts for just over 15% of the variance and captures responses clustered around two items: not wanting "people of a different race" and "immigrants/foreign workers" as neighbours.

Factor-analytic results drawn from pooled data, of course, can easily mask important cross-national and cross-time variations. But there is no indication of any significant cross-national differences in the structures of these attitudes. When the same factor analyses are repeated separately for each country at both time points, these basic dimensions seem to be both genuine and very robust. The 1981 pooled data produce the same factors, in the same order, and with almost identical loadings as those coming from the 1990 data.[17]

That the same three dimensions consistently organize beliefs about situational tolerance, or rather intolerance, in nearly every single country means that it is possible to make reliable cross-national comparisons about where publics stand on each of these dimensions, and to do so at both time points. The simplest strategy for undertaking such comparisons is to generate scales from the items that load into each factor and then to see where publics are located on those scales in 1981 and 1990. Notice that unlike the case of principled tolerance, these "situational tolerance" scales have a reversed polarity: the higher scores indicate a greater level of *intolerance*.

Table 7-7 reports the proportions of each national public scoring high on the three dimensions of situational intolerance. A number of arresting findings emerge from these summary data. The cross-national and cross-domain variations are striking: levels of political intolerance are far higher than levels of social or racial intolerance. About one in four respondents qualifies as politically intolerant compared to one in ten as socially intolerant and one in sixteen as racially intolerant. More intriguing, perhaps, is the direction of change. Since, we have established, there have been very sharp increases in support for the principle of tolerance, one would expect to find some reflection of that trend in the data concerning situational tolerance. But there is no trace of such a pattern. If anything, the shifts are counterintuitive. In the social and racial domains, nearly all changes are quite small and many are well within the margins of error. And the data suggest that people are becoming less tolerant rather than more.

What about the Canadian data? In this instance, the evidence is somewhat uneven. When it comes to political and racial intolerance, for example, Canadians do appear to be more tolerant, or rather less intolerant, than most Europeans or Americans. On the social intolerance dimension, however, Canadians are less tolerant than Europeans but more tolerant than Americans. On balance, the patterns of Canadian change are similar to those found elsewhere: most of the shifts are small enough that they could be attributable to measurement error, but the trajectories of change are the same—towards greater intolerance.

That situational intolerance is increasing is a perplexing finding, particularly when these results are placed in the context of the sharp and uniform increases in support for principled tolerance among these same publics (Table 7-5). What explains this apparent discrepancy? The statistical "explanation" is a very straightforward one: while orientations to the various dimensions of situational intolerance are connected to each other, support for principled tolerance turns out to be *unrelated* to support for *any* dimension of situational tolerance.[18] Consequently, the apparent increase in support for the principle of tolerance appears of little or no efficacy in predicting the tolerance of publics in specific situations. These findings, odd though they seem, are not isolated ones. Others have shown that support for abstract principles like tolerance can and does quickly evaporate when people are confronted with specific situations in which those principles may be expected to come into play (Prothro & Grigg, 1960; Sniderman et al., 1989; Sullivan, Pierson, & Marcus, 1979).

Another possible reason for these unusual findings is that the analytical

Table 7-7 Changes in Situational Tolerance (Percentages)

Country	Political Intolerance			Social Intolerance			Racial Intolerance		
	1981	1990	% change	1981	1990	% change	1981	1990	% change
France	7.0	19.1	+12.1	1.5	5.7	+4.2	1.8	6.6	+4.8
Britain	16.0	21.6	+5.6	11.6	13.4	+1.8	5.9	5.9	—
W. Germany	33.9	43.2	+9.3	11.0	11.5	+0.5	6.0	6.5	+0.5
Italy	29.9	24.9	-5.0	11.6	17.3	+5.7	2.2	8.3	+6.1
Netherlands	26.9	40.8	+13.9	5.3	9.1	+3.8	5.4	5.1	-0.3
Denmark	1.2	2.8	+1.6	2.8	4.5	+1.7	2.4	5.5	+3.1
Belgium	12.9	29.5	+16.6	4.7	8.7	+4.0	5.9	11.7	+5.8
Spain	18.8	22.3	+3.5	9.2	11.6	+2.4	0.8	6.2	+5.4
Ireland	12.7	17.6	+4.9	9.4	11.9	+2.5	1.9	2.6	+0.7
N. Ireland	19.9	27.0	+7.1	13.1	9.5	-3.6	5.8	3.6	-2.2
Europe average	17.9	24.9	+7.0	8.0	10.3	+2.3	3.8	6.1	+2.3
U.S.	18.5	23.7	+5.2	20.9	21.1	+0.2	2.5	4.5	+2.0
Canada	17.5	19.9	+2.4	11.1	13.9	+2.8	1.4	2.9	+1.5
English	19.7	22.8	+3.1	12.8	14.4	+1.6	1.4	2.8	+1.4
French	11.4	14.8	+3.4	6.3	9.1	+2.8	1.5	4.3	+2.8
New Canadians	—	17.4	—	—	17.4	—	1.6	—	—

Note: The political intolerance index includes those who do not want right-wing and/or left-wing extremists living next door. The index ranges from a low of 0 to a high of 2. The above table reports the percentages of each public scoring 2. The social intolerance index includes those who do not want heavy drinkers, criminals, and/or emotionally unstable people living next door. The index ranges from a low of 0 to a high of 3. The table reports the percentages of each public scoring 3. The racial intolerance index includes those who do not want people of a different race and/or immigrants/foreign workers living next door. The scale ranges from a low of 0 to a high of 2, and reports the percentages of each public scoring 2.
Source: 1981 and 1990 World Values Surveys.

strategy used is not sufficiently fine-grained and that there are other factors, perhaps country-specific conditions, that need to be incorporated into the analysis and given more weight. As noted earlier, most empirical explorations of tolerance have relied upon single-country data, and so the explanations for variations in tolerance are typically couched in country-specific terms. Of the twelve advanced industrial states considered here, there are wide national variations in factors that could well affect intercommunal relations: the balance and configuration of majorities and minorities, institutional contexts, cumulative historical experiences, socio-structural environments, and the communal distribution of economic resources and pressures. It is entirely plausible that these conditioning factors could combine in unique ways and help to account for some of the national differences that have been documented. The main advantage of the cross-national, cross-time WVS data, however, is that they allow us to tackle a more general question: Are there other factors, ones over and above these nationally unique conditions, that uniformly predict support for tolerance across these states?

Previous research, mostly of political and racial tolerance in the United States, indicates that support for tolerance varies consistently across a number of background variables. For example, it has been repeatedly shown that tolerance increases with rising education level (McClosky, 1964; Nunn, Crockett, & Williams, 1978; Prothro & Grigg, 1960; Stouffer, 1955), and the usual explanation is that formal education increases exposure to diversity of thought and values (Sullivan et al., 1985). It has also been demonstrated that support for tolerance varies with gender, age, and religious cleavages, even after the effects of education have been taken into account. Women are more tolerant than men, younger people more tolerant than older ones, and, in addition to variations across religious denominations, those who are subjectively more religious tend to be less tolerant than their more secular counterparts (Abramson, 1983; Davis, 1975; Hofstadter, 1964; Jackman, 1977; McClosky & Zaller, 1984; Nunn, Crockett, & Williams, 1987; Sullivan et al., 1985). Tolerance and support for civil liberties has also been linked to a variety of dispositions, including trust, self-esteem, and orientations towards conformity (Gibson, 1992; Segall, 1977; Sniderman, 1975; Sullivan, Piereson, & Marcus, 1981). It is conceivable, however, that these findings are unique to the American setting. Do they apply to Canadians? Indeed, are these findings generalizable to the other advanced industrial states? Specifically, to what extent, if any, do they apply to the situational and principled dimensions of tolerance?

To begin with, there is no particular reason to expect to find evidence of a clear or uniform pattern in which single predictors emerge as significant for each and every dimension; the absence of linkages between orientations to principled tolerance and the three aspects of situational tolerance could well mean that indicators predicting these different orientations will not be the same. On balance, the results of a more comprehensive multivariate analysis using pooled data reported in Table 7-8 supports that expectation. In no case

Table 7-8 Regression Analysis: The Predictors of Tolerance

Predictors	Principle of Tolerance	Political Intolerance	Social Intolerance	Racial Intolerance
Religious outlook:				
High church attendance	.01	-.03	.03	-.03
High importance of God	.01	.01	.03	-.02
Values:				
Postmaterialism	.08**	.001	-.05*	-.04*
Personal satisfaction:				
Life satisfaction	.01	-.01	-.004	-.05*
Job satisfaction	.01	-.03	-.03	-.0001
Financial satisfaction	-.02	-.01	.02	-.01
Socio-demographics:				
Age	.02	.14**	.06**	.08**
Male	-.07	.06**	-.02	.01
Employed	.03	.01	.02	.02
Caucasian	-.01	.001	-.10**	-.03
Education	.06**	.06**	.06**	-.03
Income	.01	.03	-.00001	-.04
Urban	.07**	.01	.11**	.09**
Nationality†:				
Canadian	.19**	.03	.07**	-.03
American	.11**	.04	.07**	-.04
Constant	.27*	.20	.97**	.17

*significant at $p < .05$; **significant at $p < .01$. †The reference group in this case is Europeans.
Source: 1981 and 1990 World Values Surveys.

does a single indicator significantly predict orientations to all tolerance dimensions. Post-materialist orientations come into play as significant predictors on three of the four dimensions, and all are in the expected direction: post-materialists are more likely than materialists to support the principle of tolerance and are less intolerant on the racial and social dimensions (Inglehart, 1990a). But the coefficients are small and, curiously, post-materialist orientations are unrelated to political intolerance.

Religious outlook has no impact whatsoever on any of the tolerance dimensions and levels of various aspects of subjective "life satisfaction" also have limited reach. The only significant finding here is that those with higher levels of general satisfaction are less likely to be racially intolerant. Socio-demographic indicators are more powerful predictors but, for the most part, their effects are also uneven. Age is a significant predictor of each of the three situational tolerance dimensions that are intercorrelated: in each case the old are less tolerant than the young. But as we have already seen (Figure 7-4), age is not a significant predictor of principled tolerance. More interesting are the cases of education and urban dwellers. The conventional wisdom is that tolerance rises with level of formal education. That wisdom has not gone unchallenged, and the WVS findings add grist to the argument, advanced by Sullivan and his colleagues (1979), that the connection between tolerance and education may be less straightforward than has been supposed.[19] Those who have high levels of formal education are more supportive of the principle of tolerance and are less likely to be racially intolerant. But they are *more inclined* than others to be politically and socially intolerant. Again, there is reason to expect the urban/rural divide to come into play, particularly in shaping respondent attitudes to the racial/immigrant dimension. Native-born citizens, after all, are more likely to come into contact with immigrants in the large urban settings that attract more immigrants. The urban/rural divide, however, is not a consistent predictor: urban dwellers exhibit *stronger* support for the principle of tolerance but are also *more* inclined than their rural counterparts to be racially and socially intolerant.

In short, even where there are good reasons to expect clear results, there is little evidence of a consistent pattern. Collectively, these findings are both awkward and puzzling. One implication is that the lessons coming from American research cannot simply be exported to other settings. It may be that national context, or nationally specific circumstances, are so powerful that they override the effects of the common background factors considered here. For example, the fact that levels of immigration have been five times higher in West Germany than in the other European states (OECD, 1992) may go a considerable distance towards explaining why levels of racial/immigrant intolerance are higher in that country. Another possibility is that as intolerance has become less socially acceptable it has also become more difficult to detect. The WVS indicators may not be sufficiently sensitive to flush out the more nuanced aspects of intolerance. Yet another possibility is that the failure to detect a uniform and cross-nationally stable pattern is attributable to the kinds of conceptual and measurement difficulties that have plagued other research on tolerance. The indicator of social intolerance, for example, could be challenged on the ground that it fails to capture the essence of tolerance or intolerance. It could be argued that "reasonable people" might object to "living next door" to "criminals" or "emotionally unstable" people for reasons that have little to do with tolerance or intolerance.

If aggregate levels of racial/immigrant tolerance/intolerance can be explained away by contextual factors and there are reasons to doubt the adequacy of our indicators of social tolerance/intolerance, what about political tolerance/intolerance? The political dimension deserves closer scrutiny for three reasons. First, not only are the proportions of these publics that qualify as intolerant on the social and racial dimensions much smaller (under 10%) than those who qualify as politically intolerant (around 25%), but the political dimension is also much more powerful in structuring public orientations. Second, there is now a substantial body of evidence indicating that most advanced industrial states have experienced considerable ideological flux in the last two decades (Dalton, 1988(b); Inglehart, 1990(b); Knutsen, 1993). Recall that the strategy used for exploring political intolerance followed conventional practice; it simply defined as politically intolerant those respondents reporting they did not want to live next door to right-wing or left-wing extremists. The assumption is that what people find objectionable, and what responses to that question measure, is a reaction to the idea of political extremism. But as others have pointed out (Sullivan, Piereson, & Marcus, 1982), such a strategy overlooks the possibility that respondents' own ideological preferences may have significant bearing on their responses: ideological bedfellows may be less likely than ideological opposites to find each other "intolerable." For example, those on the left may be more likely to be tolerant of others on the left even if the latter are characterized as "extremists." Aggregate results could also be misleading because they fail to take into account the varying distributions of "lefts" and rights" in different countries. A re-analysis of the WVS data, using an approximation of the "least-liked groups" approach, suggests that there is some substance to these concerns. It is not necessary to reproduce each twist and turn of this re-analysis; it suffices to summarize its three key findings.

One important finding is that a very substantial proportion of people—some 22% of respondents in 1981 and 16% in 1990—were *not* willing to place themselves anywhere on the left/right scale. Another 36% of respondents in 1981 (and 39% in 1990) occupy the middle ground of the left/right scale (Knutsen, 1993). In all, these "ideological indeterminates"—nonrespondents and those in the "middle ground"—account for more than half of all publics surveyed in both 1981 (58%) and 1990 (55%). In other words, somewhere between 42–45% of these publics are clearly identifiable as willing and unequivocal occupants of left/right ideological space.

For these particular groups there is evidence of significant shifts in mutual tolerance of ideological opposites (the lefts of the rights and the rights of the lefts) between 1981 and 1990. In general, clearly identifiable left-wingers became less tolerant of clearly identifiable right-wingers in the course of the decade. The cross-time shift amounts to some ten percentage points. The changes were particularly sharp in France, West Germany, the Netherlands, and Belgium, each of which experienced increases of twice the average rate, above twenty percentage points. It also shows that in 1980 right-wing antipathy to left-wingers was stronger than left-wing antipathy to the right by about a ten percentage point differential. By 1990, however, right-wing intolerance of left-wingers had clearly softened, and the discrepancy between right- and left-wingers' mutual antipathies had almost completely disappeared. There is some indication, then, that this apparent softening may be attributable to ideological "drift." The ideological centres of gravity of both the "lefts" and the "rights" shifted: those unambiguously on the left in 1981 drifted to the centre, as did those on the right. Together, these dynamics suggest that left and right self-locations may have become less meaningful than they once were to publics in advanced industrial states.

As left-right polarization has weakened, other kinds of shifts, such as post-materialist orientations, have taken on greater prominence.[20] The relative robustness of the post-materialism dimension and the evidence of a clear value shift raises rather different questions about the dynamics of political tolerance/intolerance. It is not possible, for obvious reasons, to determine whether materialists or post-materialists have become more or less mutually tolerant or intolerant.[21] But we can ask: Have materialist/post-materialist orientations, which some see as the most significant emerging axis of new value orientations, had any impact on the changing levels of tolerance towards the lefts and rights? The balance of the evidence indicates that they have. First, between 1981 and 1990 materialists became *less* tolerant of the rights; they also became *less* tolerant of the lefts. Although the ranks of those qualifying as materialists shrank during the decade, this group still accounts for a very substantial segment of all publics surveyed, and so the net effects of these shifts are far from negligible. Second, post-materialists, who are typically more tolerant in a number of other respects, are becoming increasingly less comfortable with the idea of living next door to right- or left-wing extremists. To be sure, post-materialists are "tougher" in their judgements about living next door to right-wing extremists and relatively "tender" in their judgements about left-wing extremists. The more significant point, however, is that post-materialists became significantly less tolerant of *both* types of extremist in the course of the decade. Moreover, the cross-time change was about the same, roughly seven percentage points in both cases.

Overall, these data suggest that part of the explanation for the increases in political intolerance is the growing salience of the intersecting materialist/post-materialist value divide. In both 1981 and 1990 a very significant proportion of materialists and post-materialists, between 40–46% of each group, qualified as "ideological indeterminates"; they were either unwilling to place themselves on the left-right scale or assigned themselves to the mid-point of that scale. At the same time, both materialists and post-materialists are becoming increasingly impatient with, and less tolerant of, extremists of both the traditional left and right.

Conclusions

Documenting each and every dimension of stability and change in social values would be an enormous task, and there is no sense in which the evidence considered so far can be regarded as comprehensive. By the same token, nor can the social values so far considered be dismissed as trivial. To this point, the indications are that some social values are in transition, and the shifts occurring on these dimensions follow a fairly consistent pattern. For example, regardless of which perspective is taken with respect to a variety of religious orientations, the general conclusion appears to be very much the same: publics in most of these countries are becoming more secular. Church attendance rates are falling, personal beliefs in God are on the decline, and the moral authority of churches is waning. The WVS data are not sufficient to determine whether the shifts towards secular outlooks are accelerating or decelerating, and it might be that the most radical shifts in religious orientations occurred before the 1980s (Halman & de Moor, 1993).

There are substantial cross-national variations in the levels of secularization and significant differences in the rates at which these changes are taking place. What interpretation we give of these shifts is very much a matter of perspective. Seymour Martin Lipset, for example, makes a compelling case that the "differences between religion in Canada and in the United States are large and clear" (1990: 80). According to both his evidence and our own, Lipset is absolutely right. As he suggests, these differences include variations in the organization of religion as well as in the religious outlooks of the two publics. Other data underscore these same cross-national conclusions. For example, the proportions of the American publics who qualify as "core members"— who attend church and are active volunteers in church activities—American is twice as high as in Canada (41% versus 21%). Between 1981 and 1990 there were very sharp increases in the proportions of Americans who qualified as "unchurched," nearly quadrupling from 6% to 23%. Even so, Americans still qualified as more religious than Canadians in 1990. By American standards, Canadians rate as a relatively secular people. But when all twelve countries are considered together, the striking finding is that Canadians are more religious than publics in most other advanced industrial states. In effect, the broader cross-national perspective highlights the extent to which the American public is the outlier.

Canadian and American religious values are moving along the same trajectory—towards greater secularization—but the *rate* of change is quicker in Canada, with the result that Canadian and American religious orientations appear to be diverging. These findings are interesting in their own right. More critical from the broader standpoint, however, is the supplementary evidence indicating that all of these trends are similarly related to the same background factors—to age, education, and value type. In a nutshell, those background factors that consistently shape orientations to basic political and economic dimensions of value change seem to have a similar impact on religious orientations.

The evidence concerning moral outlooks once again yields results that are consistent. As with religious orientations, the cross-national variations are quite striking. The shifts are generally in the same direction—towards greater permissiveness—but the aggregate shifts are not very dramatic in scope. Although the changes taking place in Canada are generally larger than those in most other countries, they are significantly larger than those in the United States. More impressive than the scope of these changes is the finding that they all are unmistakably related to the same background factors in similar ways. The clear implication is that these orientations are also part of the complex set of value shifts, and that they are related to generational change. The claim is *not* that every change examined has precisely the same root cause. Indeed, our own evidence (see Table 7-4) plainly demonstrates that the shifts in standards of moral permissiveness are better explained by religious outlooks than anything else. The point is that the shifts all appear to be connected. Orientations to moral permissiveness, for example, clearly are powerfully connected to orientations to civil permissiveness, and each is linked to the background indicators of generational change as well as religious orientations.

What about tolerance? Is there any substance to the claim that Canadians are more tolerant than other publics? To this question there is no simple answer. Straightforward cross-national comparisons of aggregate levels of tolerance are a starting point. In 1981 Canadians ranked seventh out of twelve countries in support for the principle of tolerance. By 1990 they had moved up to third out of twelve. Canadians also rate consistently low on political, social, and racial indicators of intolerance. By these measures, Canadians *are* relatively tolerant, but there is nothing to suggest that tolerance is a uniquely Canadian national trait. The conclusions to emerge from the preceding analysis present a more complex picture. The cross-time increases in racial intolerance are small and in most cases are within the margins of error. The same could be said for social intolerance, the dimension on which North Americans rate as significantly more intolerant than most of their European counterparts. Neither the rising support for the principle of tolerance nor the evidence of increased political intolerance can be dismissed as marginal. Most interesting, perhaps, is the finding that the emergent post-materialist divide does have a significant effect on citizen impatience with ideologues of the left and right. Citizens, it seems, pay lip service to the principle of tolerance, but this plainly does not mean they apply the principle to all spheres in equal measure.

In examining religious orientations, moral outlooks, and tolerance, we have focussed on stability and change in very general social values. The focus now shifts to consider stability and change in orientations to a very specific institution, the family, which is the primary locus of value acquisition and the intergenerational transfer of values.

NOTES

[1] In a more detailed analysis of these cross-national variations, Halman and de Moor contend that the variations are attributable to the fact that Ireland, Italy, Spain, and Portugal remain more "traditional" than the other countries. Consequently, they speculate that shifts in the religious orientations of these publics will likely quicken, and converge with those of other European countries, as the transition to late industrialism becomes more complete.

[2] The gamma coefficients are: Europe, age (.27), education (-.22), post-materialism (-.18); United States, age (.19), education (-.16), post-materialism (-.14); Canada, age (.24), post-materialism (-.16).

[3] In nearly every country belief in a "personal God" declined while belief "in some sort of spirit" increased very slightly. There were also decreases in the proportions of these publics indicating that they believe in "heaven," "hell," "reincarnation," and "life after death."

[4] The only exception is Dutch respondents, just under half (47.2%) of whom replied yes to the birth alternative. Typically, publics are most likely to think that there should be religious services for death. Marriage comes next.

[5] Is the church giving adequate responses to moral and family problems, by age education and value type (gamma coefficients)?

Country	Moral problems			Family problems		
	Age	Education	Value type	Age	Education	Value type
Europe	.32	-.25	-.31	.31	-.27	-.29
U.S.	.13	-.17	-.17	.11	-.11	-.13
Canada	.12	-.19	-.29	.13	-.17	-.25
English	.06	-.16	-.24	.09	-.20	-.20
French	.23	-.35	-.42	.23	-.26	-.38
New Cdn.	.20	-.06	-.24	.07	-.09	-.33

Question: "Generally speaking, do you think that your church is giving, in your country, adequate answers to:

A. the moral problems and needs of the individual

B. the problems of family life?

Source: 1981 and 1990 World Values Surveys.

[6] These moral permissiveness items are a discrete subset of responses coming from the same twenty-five-question battery that also provided us with the civil permissiveness dimension. As before, factor-analytic procedures were used to identify which particular items qualify as the components of the civil permissiveness dimension and which cluster into the "moral permissiveness" dimension.

[7] The eight items were: Married men/women having an affair, sex under the legal age of consent, homosexuality, prostitution, abortion, divorce, euthanasia (terminating the life of the incurably sick), and suicide.

[8] Some individual items have been analyzed elsewhere. For example, a comparative analysis of Canadian–American orientations towards abortion is explored in detail in Nevitte, Brandon, and Davis (1993).

[9] The index score is the percentage of those respondents in each country who score 8, 9 or 10 on *every* dimension.

[10] The gammas for age and moral permissiveness are Europe -.42, United States -.13, Canada -.23; for education and moral permissiveness Europe .46, United States .20, Canada .37; for value type and moral permissiveness, Europe .55, United States .32, Canada .35.

[11] In 1981 the gammas range from a low of .59 to a high of .82, and in 1990 the range is only slightly lower, from gamma = .45 to .70.

[12] Gibson properly cautions that the political relevance of tolerance/intolerance should

be understood not just in terms of the opinions of individuals, but also the extent to which a "culture of tolerance or intolerance" is more or less widespread (1992: 339). For Gibson, the crucial issue is the extent to which a climate of tolerance constrains others from being intolerant.

[13] The other values include good manners, hard work, feeling of responsibility, saving money and things, determination, religious faith, unselfishness, and obedience. Respondents were asked, "Please choose up to five [values]."

[14] For Europe, gamma = -.02; United States = .06; Canada = .06.

[15] For post-materialism and support for the principle of tolerance the gammas are: Europe = .28; United States = .20; Canada = .20. For education and support for the principle of tolerance, the gammas are: Europe = .14; United States = .14; Canada = .15.

[16] In the 1981 surveys the list included eleven groups: people with a criminal record, people of a different ethnicity, students, left-wing extremists, unmarried mothers, heavy drinkers, right-wing extremists, people with large families, emotionally unstable people, members of minority religious sects or cults, and immigrants or foreign workers. The 1990 surveys presented an expanded and modified version of the 1981 battery: people with a criminal record, people of a different race, left-wing extremists, heavy drinkers, right-wing extremists; people with large families, emotionally unstable people, Muslims, immigrants/foreign workers, people with AIDS, drug addicts, homosexuals, Jews, and Hindus. Considering both of these batteries as "equivalent" runs some risks. For instance, the simple fact that the 1990 batteries included more items than the 1981 survey would, *ceteris paribus*, decrease the chances of each 1990 item being mentioned. As we will see, the impact of this "noise" in the data may be less worrisome than might be supposed.

[17] West Germany, Belgium, and the Netherlands are the only exceptions to the general pattern, and they are exceptional only because the third and weakest factor, "social intolerance", failed to emerge as clearly as a discrete dimension. There are also differences in the order in which the factors emerge in the 1981 and 1990 Canadian results. In 1981 the social factor emerges second, while in 1990 the racial factor comes second.

[18] For example, the correlations between principled tolerance and the three indicators of situational intolerance average about gamma = .05, whereas the inter-item correlations between the three situational intolerance indicators are in the gamma = .2 range.

[19] There are significant variations in the impact education has on tolerance. Typically, where the Stouffer indicators of tolerance/intolerance are used, as in the General Social Surveys in the United States, researchers find a clear and positive link between education and tolerance. However, when the "least-liked" approach is used for measuring tolerance/intolerance, researchers report no evidence of a clear link between education and tolerance. See Sullivan, Piereson, & Marcus (1982), and Gibson (1992: 562–64).

[20] Notice that, in contrast to the left-right scale, more than 90% of all publics were able to respond to the items making up that scale.

[21] This is because post-materialist/materialist value typing is a conceptual construction, not a self-identification.

Appendix 7-A   Support for the General Principle of Tolerance by Age, Education, and Value
Type Within Canada
(Gamma Coefficients)

Groups within Canada	Age*	Education	Value type
English	.05	.06	.10
French	.05	.32	.31
New Canadians	.07	.21	.34

*The relationship between support for the general principle of tolerance and age appears to be
curvilinear.
Source: 1981 and 1990 World Values Surveys.

8: Family Values: Stability and Change

Since the 1960s, about the same time that researchers were beginning to identify broad value shifts among people in advanced industrial states, demographers noticed profound changes in the prevailing patterns of West European population replacement. The general contours of these demographic shifts, which some label the "second demographic transition," are now well documented. Birth rates began to fall below population replacement levels. Average family size declined while the number of single-parent families, as well as extra-marital births, increased. Climbing divorce rates led some to speculate that one-third of all contemporary West European marriages would end in divorce (Akker, Halman, & Ruud de Moor, 1993). At the same time, fewer people were deciding to marry; more were choosing to live alone, and those deciding to marry were doing so later in life. The scope and pace of these changes varied from one setting to the next. Northern European states, for example, seem to have led the trend, with their southern European counterparts, along with Ireland, lagging somewhat behind. The basic direction and consistency of the patterns were so similar from one country to the next that some suggested Western Europe might qualify as a single demographic unit (Roussel, 1992). Trends in North America correspond to those in Europe, and the net effect of these means that contemporary family life bears little resemblance to the stereotypes, rooted in the 1950s, that circulate about the traditional family.

What is the explanation for these profound shifts? Some contend that the changing shape of the family over the last three decades is a direct consequence of the broader structural shifts that are associated with the transition to late industrialism (Wrigley, 1977). As the evidence presented in Chapter 2 indicates, changing rates of marriage and divorce have been accompanied by sharp increases in the geographic and occupational mobility of populations, and these make it increasingly difficult for people to conduct their personal lives as did those in the single-earner household of yesteryear. In the last two decades in particular, there have been dramatic changes in the number of women in higher education and the paid workforce. Women still make up less than half of the paid workforce in Italy, Spain, and Ireland, but in each one of the countries considered here changes in the gender composition of the paid workforce have been in the same direction. One face of this shift is the rising number of wage earners in the average family. In 1961, for instance, Canadian single-income families outnumbered two-income families by a ratio of two to one. By 1981 the pattern had completely reversed; two-income families outnumbered single-income ones by two to one (Statistics Canada). These transformations undoubtedly place considerable strain on the traditional family unit.

An alternative perspective interprets the changes as having more to do with basic shifts in attitudes towards the family (Beaujot, 1991). Some characterize the shift pessimistically, as indicating the crumbling of one of society's pillars, while others celebrate changing "family values" as a form of liberation reflecting an "emancipation of alternatives" (Van den Akker, Halman, & de Moor, 1993). Either way, rising divorce rates, falling birth rates, the increases in single-parent families, increasing co-habitation, and other associated shifts are taken to mean that people now attach less importance to the family than they once did.

This chapter focusses on three aspects of "family values." The first part begins with general orientations towards marriage as an institution. Do people increasingly see marriage as an outdated institution? What qualities do people think are essential to a successful marriage? And how do these publics feel about women, work, and the family?

The second part examines orientations towards children and the two-parent family, concluding with an examination of what values people think are important for children to learn. In some respects, the WVS evidence produces surprising results. The survey data indicate that support for the traditional family unit remains quite strong; but they also show that there have been significant changes in what people expect from a marriage and in the kinds of values they think children should learn.

Orientations towards authority *within* the family is the issue taken up at the end of the chapter, and this part of the analysis parallels the investigation of changing political and economic orientations that formed the core of the concluding sections of Chapters 4 and 6. Two dimensions of family authority relations are singled out for detailed attention. The first has to do with spousal relations, on which there are clear, perceptible shifts towards more egalitarian spousal relations. The second dimension concerns parent–child relations; here there also seem to be significant shifts in orientations. These findings justify a broadening of the analysis: the final section takes up issues raised in our earlier analysis. It asks: Are changing orientations towards authority in the family also connected to comparable shifts in the workplace and the polity?

The Family and Marriage

Chapter 2 provided an initial glimpse of just how high "the family" ranks in the general priorities of people in all twelve countries. Respondents were

Table 8-1 Percentage Agreeing that Marriage is an Out-dated Institution

Country	1981	1990	% change
France	32.3	29.1	-3.2
Britain	14.5	18.4	+3.9
West Germany	17.3	15.0	-2.3
Italy	23.3	14.1	-9.2
Netherlands	15.8	21.1	+5.3
Denmark	19.4	18.0	-1.4
Belgium	18.5	23.2	+4.7
Spain	25.3	16.0	-9.3
Ireland	13.0	9.9	-3.1
Northern Ireland	14.4	14.4	—
European Average	19.4	19	-1.5
United States	9.2	8.0	-1.2
Canada	13.3	12.4	-0.9
English	11.9	11.0	-0.9
French	17.2	19.3	+2.1
New Canadians	—	8.6	—

Question: "Do you agree or disagree with the following statement? 'Marriage is an out-dated institution.'
Source: 1981 and 1990 World Values Surveys.

asked, "How important is—work, family, friends and acquaintances, leisure time, politics, religion—in your life?" The overwhelming majority (85%) of respondents in every country indicated that the family was "very important"— well ahead of the next closest response category, work, which about half (56%) said was "very important" (see Table 2-3). As an expression of general sentiments, these data are not at all difficult to accept. The extent to which they provide a reliable benchmark, however, is less clear. If historical experience is anything to go by, the lesson is that conceptions of the family have undergone many transitions, and the precise meanings people apply to "the family" may well have in recent decades become more ambiguous. For contemporary publics, the family may now encompass groupings that are more expansive than the traditional nuclear family.[1] And the absence of cross-time data on the priority people assign to the family means it is not possible to ascertain directly whether contemporary publics consider the family more important than did their predecessors. But the WVS provide other data that help to place these initial findings in context. In both 1981 and 1990 publics in the twelve countries were asked, "Do you agree or disagree with the following statement: `Marriage is an outdated institution'?" Marriage, of course, is not the same thing as family, but the basic findings, summarized in Table 8-1, indicate that a huge majority of respondents in every country do *not* think marriage is outdated. In 1981, for example, only 19% of Europeans thought marriage is outdated, and the figures were even lower for Americans (9%) and Canadians (13%). Nor is there any evidence that these orientations changed very much during the course of the 1980s. If anything, the marginal cross-time changes indicate that publics became less likely to say marriage is outdated. Regardless of soaring divorce rates, and despite the stress that sharp increases in geographic and social mobility place on marriages, the initial indications are that support for the institution of marriage is both high and quite stable. The social pressures to marry may be weaker than they once were (Thornton, 1989), but there is no indication whatsoever that the institution of marriage is under seige or that publics are progressively losing faith in the idea of marriage.

That support for the institution of marriage has remained relatively stable does not mean people's ideas about marriage have been entirely static (Festy, 1985; Hoffmann-Nowotny, 1987). Indeed, some argue that contemporary marriages are vulnerable precisely because partners have shifting expectations about the arrangement (Akker, Halman, & de Moor, 1993; Yankelovich, 1981). There is no reason to expect that people's ideas about marriage would have undergone any dramatic transformation in the 1981–1990 interlude. More instructive than the scope is the overall direction of the changes. The 1981 and 1990 surveys invited respondents to select from a comprehensive list those items thought to contribute to a successful marriage. Nine of these items cluster into three easily recognizable categories. First, there were those, such as "adequate *income*" and "good *housing*," that have to do with the material conditions of the household. The second cluster involves common background factors: "being of the same *social background*," "shared *religious beliefs*," "agreement on *politics*," and "*tastes and interests* in common." The third dimension clusters those factors that might be expected to shape the character of exchanges between spouses, including "*mutual respect and appreciation*," "*understanding and tolerance*," and "*sharing household chores*."

Two basic findings emerge from these cross-time data. The easiest place to start is with the direction of the overall shifts for the two domains on the left part of Table 8-2. Material conditions and common background factors are usually associated more with traditional considerations for successful marriages. In 1990 publics in ten of the twelve countries placed *less* emphasis on income and housing than in 1981; the exceptional cases are Belgium and Spain. The same pattern holds for attributes to common background factors; on balance, these considerations also became less important to people's evaluations of what makes for a successful marriage. Once again, there are some exceptions. With the American public, for example, shared social, religious, and political orientations became slightly more important. But where there are deviations from the larger pattern, they are small enough to be attributable to measurement error.

Now consider the third domain, in the right-hand panel of Table 8-2, dealing with egalitarian spousal relations. Here, the cross-time shifts are in the opposite direction. Between 1981 and 1990 publics became *increasingly* inclined to see egalitarianism in spousal relations as important to a successful marriage. There are other striking findings. Without exception, respondents in

Table 8-2 Important Attributes for a Successful Marriage (Percentages)

Country	Adequate Income and Housing				Common background								Equalitarian spousal relations					
	Income		Housing		Social		Religious		Political		Tastes and interests		Mutual respect and appreciation		Understanding and tolerance		Sharing household chores	
	1981	% Change by 1990	1981	% Change by 1990	1981	% Change by 1990	1981	% Change by 1990	1981	% Change by 1990	1981	% Change by 1990	1981	% Change by 1990	1981	% Change by 1990	1981	% Change by 1990
France	39.0	-1.0	41.9	-5.3	23.6	-2.7	16.9	-0.4	8.8	-1.3	39.1	-1.1	85.5	-1.2	72.9	+1.3	34.2	+1.0
Britain	43.9	-7.1	46.2	-6.2	22.0	-0.8	19.0	+0.8	7.0	+0.2	49.5	+0.1	86.4	-1.7	84.4	+1.7	40.8	+5.0
W. Germany	32.3	-6.6	30.1	-4.8	14.5	-3.1	17.6	-4.4	7.0	-0.5	53.4	-5.5	78.7	+0.3	78.8	-1.5	20.9	+0.6
Italy	39.8	-9.6	25.0	-1.7	16.8	-1.5	22.4	+0.8	9.5	-1.2	45.8	+3.7	89.7	+0.1	81.5	-2.0	31.1	-0.5
Netherlands	34.3	-8.2	46.7	-12.0	25.4	-3.1	22.5	-4.9	11.2	-3.3	32.2	-4.0	89.5	+3.0	88.9	-3.4	29.9	+4.0
Denmark	11.9	-1.4	35.5	-5.8	14.7	-3.2	17.1	-1.2	7.0	-3.2	22.6	-2.1	76.1	+7.2	77.9	+2.3	47.9	+0.1
Belgium	39.3	+5.8	35.2	+4.9	24.9	-2.6	27.0	-3.2	10.9	-0.6	42.5	-2.9	82.8	+2.4	74.3	+2.9	34.3	+3.7
Spain	37.3	+4.4	29.6	+6.6	26.7	-2.9	30.0	-3.6	18.0	-5.9	45.3	-1.9	73.0	+5.8	69.2	+4.6	25.9	+9.9
Ireland	55.2	-3.4	53.0	-6.8	29.6	-4.3	38.5	-5.6	5.9	-1.8	40.2	—	79.9	+3.4	78.0	+3.2	31.9	+6.3
N. Ireland	42.6	-2.5	37.8	-1.5	18.9	+2.5	40.7	-3.5	10.6	-0.7	49.8	-10.1	76.9	+6.0	84.3	-3.7	24.3	+20.6
U. S.	44.5	+0.9	42.0	-1.7	25.9	+2.7	42.9	+1.5	10.8	+1.0	52.8	-4.9	90.4	+1.6	85.2	-2.6	45.6	+1.4
Canada	40.6	-1.1	34.3	-1.4	21.4	-1.4	32.1	-4.2	7.7	-2.2	51.3	-1.5	92.6	-0.2	85.4	-1.7	46.5	+6.0
English	40.2	-0.6	32.9	-2.0	21.2	-3.5	33.9	-7.8	7.9	-2.6	54.5	-4.5	93.1	-1.9	89.0	-5.3	47.0	+3.8
French	41.7	+0.5	38.1	+0.9	22.1	+4.0	27.3	-0.3	7.2	-2.0	42.5	+3.5	91.0	+3.6	75.7	+6.2	45.0	+13.8
New Canadians	—	37.0	—	32.1	—	21.5	—	33.7	—	6.1	—	54.5	—	93.2	—	85.3	—	49.5

Question: "Here is a list of things which people think make for a successful marriage. Please tell me for each one, whether you think that it is very important, rather important or not very important for a successful marriage."
Source: 1981 and 1990 World Values Surveys.

every country indicated that "mutual respect and appreciation" and "tolerance and understanding" between spouses were the two most important factors contributing to the success of a marriage. In fact, the scores on these items were so high in 1981 that there is hardly any room for cross-time increases. Even so, the scores did increase marginally and, predictably, the increases were larger among those publics that scored lower in 1981. Of the three items in this domain it is sharing household chores that rates as least important to the success of marriages. Notice, too, that Canadians seem to attach more importance to these dimensions of egalitarianism than do publics in nearly every other country. Canadians, in other words, rate relatively high on all of these indicators of spousal egalitarianism.

Is there any evidence to indicate that these incremental shifts towards greater egalitarianism in marriage are related to the background factors that, together, are taken to signify generational change? To simplify the analysis, responses to the three component items within the spousal egalitarianism domain are added together to form a single composite score, an aggregate index score of spousal egalitarianism. Figure 8-1 reports the distributions on that index for all three background factors. Overall, the relationship between age and scores on the spousal egalitarianism index is a negative one: younger respondents are consistently more egalitarian than their older counterparts. The relationship between education and egalitarianism is consistently positive: those with higher education are more likely to be egalitarian, and post-materialists are significantly more likely than their materialist counterparts to say that egalitarianism is important to the success of a marriage. None of the relationships are particularly strong, but they are all consistent with the generational change interpretation.[2]

Figure 8-1 also illustrates the substantial gap between North Americans and Europeans. North Americans are consistently more egalitarian than Europeans when it comes to spousal relations, and Canadians are more egalitarian than Americans. There are a variety of reasons why one might expect to find significant gender differences lurking behind all of these results. If traditional families are characterized as being somewhat patriarchal, then one would anticipate the strongest impetus towards greater spousal egalitarianism to come from women.The WVS data provide some empirical support for that expectation. On balance, women are more supportive than men of greater egalitarianism between spouses. The differences, however, are surprisingly small; they amount to less than 2% on the spousal equalitarian index (European women, 28.8%, European men, 27%; American women, 39.1%, American men, 40.3%; Canadian women, 43.1%; Canadian men, 42.9%).

Women and Men, Family and Work

The influx of women into the paid workforce has been characterized as one of the most profound structural changes associated with emergent late industri-

Figure 8-1   Equalitarian Spousal Relations, by Age, Education, and Value Type

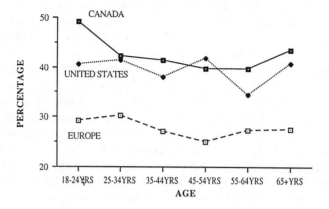

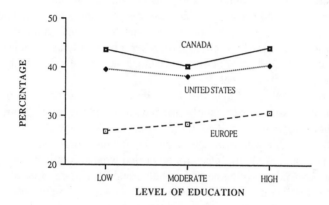

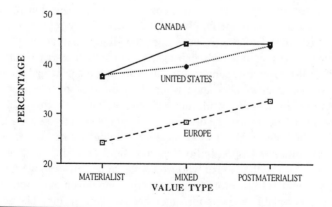

Source: 1981 and 1990 World Values Surveys.

alism, and it is that transformation, perhaps more than any single other, that analysts fix on as presenting the greatest challenge to the traditional family (Crouter & Manke, 1994; Ishi-Kuntz, 1994). Surely the heaviest burden of these changes has fallen on the shoulders of women trying to balance the demands of child-rearing with those of career and family. The difficulties flowing from these competing demands are legion and have been compellingly illustrated elsewhere (Schwartz, 1992). To bear children, women have to take time out from the full-time paid workforce. A variety of issues stem from this reality: Do employers take this factor into consideration when making decisions to hire women? Are the rules of employment rigid and tradition bound, or do they allow women to take time out from the paid workforce? To what extent do women pay career penalties because they bear children? What are the long-term economic consequences for the interrupted career path, for example, with respect to promotion and retirement benefits? These dilemmas are both contentious and difficult to resolve, but they speak only to the economic face of the changes that have taken place. As others have shown, the repercussions within the family of the growing numbers of women in the paid workforce are far more complex than just the economic costs and benefits (Schwartz, 1992). It is hardly conceivable that these transformations, with their profound ramifications, could have taken place without corresponding adjustments, on the part of both men and women, in women's roles in the family setting and the workplace.

Goldthorpe (1987) distinguishes three basic sets of attitudes about the employment of women, particularly married ones, and the implications each of these hold for family life. First, there is the "traditional view" that employment is incompatible with marriage. According to Goldthorpe, this view holds that "the normal and rightful place for a married woman is at home, supported by her husband, devoting herself to home-making and child care" (138). "Within the family, the husband/father is the breadwinner, responsible for the family's income, supporting wife and children. In recognition of that responsibility he is entitled to look for home comforts to the wife/mother. Men's and women's roles are segregated, and there is a clear-cut division of labour between the sexes both in the family and the wider society" (138).

Second is what Goldthorpe calls the "neo-traditional attitude" where "employment is compatible with marriage, but not with the care of infants and the aged" (138). From this perspective, "men are still the principal though no longer the sole breadwinners upon whom falls the responsibility for maintaining the family income, while the wife's contribution `helps.' If there is some blurring of the lines of the division of labour between the sexes, and men do some of the housework, this too is called `helping'—a key word, indicating that the ultimate responsibility for household tasks lies with women. Likewise it would be the mother who would absent herself from work to look after a sick child" (139). From this perspective, employers are prone to see women as less reliable workers than men because women may place family responsibilities ahead of their careers.

Third is the "radical egalitarian" attitude in which employment is seen as fully compatible with marriage and all other family responsibilities. This orientation "involves a radical rejection of the traditional division of labour between the sexes, and entails the sharing of all household tasks and responsibilities on a perfectly equal basis" (140). What balance is struck in the performance of household tasks, according to Goldthorpe, is not a matter of sex "but a process of negotiating individual agreements about who does what in the home on the basis of ability and preference" (140).[3]

These three sets of orientations might best be considered as constructs, ideal types that highlight the core differences in varying perspectives about women in the workplace and the family. The traditional orientation probably prevailed before 1945, while the neo-traditional attitude was probably dominant by the 1960s. In Goldthorpe's view, the "uncompromising egalitarian attitude ... is still probably the view of a small minority. Though some pay lip-service, few seem prepared to accept its full implications for their family lives" (140). Demographic data provide reasonable grounds for making these inferences about changing attitudes. In the early 1960s, for instance, 90% of mothers stopped working at the birth of their first child. Twenty years later, that figure dropped to 50% (Beaujot, 1991). There is also some scattered single-country data, mostly from the United States, that are consistent with these same conclusions. The biggest problem is that there is no systematic body of longitudinal cross-national attitudinal evidence that addresses all of these issues, and so it is not possible to determine where and when one prevailing ethos was replaced by another. In all likelihood, the transitions from one orientation to another have been gradual, incomplete, and subject to substantial variations rather than sudden, decisive, and uniform. Still, the categories developed by Goldthorpe and others are valuable because they provide guideposts that help to identify what kinds of attitudes lie at the core of these transitions, and which are more peripheral.

The WVS are not sufficiently comprehensive to fill this huge void because the questions most pertinent to this set of issues were not introduced until the 1990 survey. Nonetheless, the WVS can shed some light on selected aspects of the issue: the 1990 version of the surveys asked questions tapping attitudes that correspond reasonably well with some of the constructs identified by Goldthorpe. Six questions specifically probed attitudes towards "the changing roles of men and women today." Respondents were asked:

"How much do you agree or disagree with each of the following statements:
(a) A working mother can establish just as warm and secure a relationship with her children as a mother who does not work.
(b) A pre-school child is likely to suffer if his or her mother works.
(c) Having a job is the best way for a woman to be an independent person.
(d) A job is alright but what most women really want is a home and children.
(e) Both a husband and wife should contribute to household income.
(f) Being a housewife is just as fulfilling as working for pay."

Items (a), (c), and (e) probably come closer to the egalitarian perspective than any other. Items (b), (d), and (f), on the other hand, seem to capture orientations that are more consistent with the neo-traditional set of attitudes. Agreement with (b) and (d), in particular, certainly reflects Goldthorpe's characterization of the neo-traditional attitude, that "employment is compatible with marriage, but not with the care of infants" (1989: 138). Questions (a) and (b) reflect alternative views about the consequences for children of mothers in the paid workforce. Items (c) and (d) represent alternative perspectives on women's workplace-homelife motivations, and the (e) and (f) pair reflect different priorities concerning income.

What do the data show? First, Table 8-3 indicates that there are substantial cross-national variations in these orientations. To begin, consider just the responses to questions (a) and (b).[4] Overall, the percentages of these publics expressing strong agreement with statement (a) significantly outweigh the proportions strongly agreeing with (b). Among Danish respondents, those strongly agreeing with (a) outnumber those strongly agreeing with (b) by a ratio of about five to one, and in seven of the ten remaining countries the balance favouring (a) over (b) ratio is at least two to one. Ireland, Italy, and Holland are out of step with that pattern, but the most striking exception is West Germany, where those strongly supporting (b) outnumber those strongly agreeing with (a) by a ratio of three to one. There are also significant but less striking cross-national differences in the responses to statements (c) and (d). In five countries, there is at least a ten percentage point preference for (c), while in another five the differences are within the margins of error. French respondents, for instance, are three times more likely than Canadian, American, Irish, or British respondents to strongly agree that "having a job is the best way for a woman to be independent." There are also substantial national differences when it comes to whether both men and women "should contribute to the household income." Americans and Canadians are about evenly divided in their support for statements (e) and (f). Within Canada, francophone Canadians are significantly more likely than others to strongly agree that "a working mother can establish a warm and secure relationship with her children." They are also significantly more inclined to subscribe to the views that "being a housewife is just as fulfilling as working for pay" and that "both husband and wife should contribute to the household income."

The scope of these cross-national differences is striking. There are also significant differences between the responses of men and women, at least in the vast majority of cases. In all twelve countries, for example, women are significantly more likely than men to agree with statement (a). With one exception (Northern Ireland), they are also more likely than men to agree with the other items relating to greater egalitarianism between spouses, items (c) and (e). Still, these differences are substantially smaller than the cross-national variations; respondents' sex clearly matters, but not as much as their nationality.

Undoubtedly, there are multiple reasons for such striking aggregate differ-

Table 8-3   The Changing Roles of Women and Work

Country	(a) A working mother can establish a warm and secure relationship with her children	(b) A pre-school child is likely to suffer if his or her mother works	(c) Having a job is the best way for a woman to be an independent person	(d) A job is alright but what most women really want is a home and children	(e) Both husband and wife should contribute to the household income	(f) Being a housewife is just as fulfilling as working for pay
	Strongly agree	Strongly agree	Strongly agree	Strongly agree	Strongly agree	Strongly agree
France	40.0	22.1	36.7	23.0	37.5	21.1
	(43.5)	(22.4)	(41.6)	(25.2)	(39.1)	(24.1)
Britain	21.4	10.8	10.5	8.4	16.3	11.0
	(26.4)	(9.9)	(13.2)	(8.6)	(17.4)	(11.4)
West Germany	8.9	32.5	21.1	10.3	13.1	13.2
	(11.2)	(31.6)	(26.0)	(10.8)	(14.3)	14.2)
Italy	20.5	17.7	23.3	18.2	24.0	12.9
	(24.1)	(16.9)	(28.2)	(19.4)	(26.7)	(11.7)
Netherlands	29.9	21.3	15.0	10.0	8.5	17.9
	(33.3)	(19.0)	(17.6)	(11.8)	(10.1)	(19.7)
Denmark	52.1	9.3	35.3	7.0	29.8	18.7
	(57.2)	(8.3)	(37.6)	(8.2)	(32.5)	(23.0)
Belgium	40.6	19.3	27.2	20.4	27.4	26.2
	(44.6)	(18.5)	(30.0)	(21.6)	(29.1)	(25.4)
Spain	31.0	13.6	28.2	15.9	29.0	19.8
	(33.4)	(13.8)	(31.8)	(15.7)	(30.8)	(19.2)
Ireland	17.0	12.7	10.3	10.8	14.9	14.4
	(21.4)	(13.4)	(12.7)	(12.0)	(17.3)	(18.3)
N. Ireland	21.7	5.7'	11.0	8.2	21.5	10.7
	(20.8)	(4.6)	(8.9)	(4.6)	(19.2)	(9.9)
European Average	28.3	16.5	21.8	13.2	22.2	16.6
	(31.6)	(15.8)	(24.8)	(13.8)	(23.7)	(17.7)
United States	26.8	9.9	11.7	12.2	18.5	21.2
	(31.9)	(9.0)	(13.9)	(12.4)	(21.3)	(23.0)
Canada	27.0	9.8	12.5	9.0	18.8	19.7
	(30.8)	(9.7)	(13.8)	(9.9)	(19.4)	(23.1)
English	23.5	7.8	10.2	6.5	15.5	14.9
	(27.1)	(7.6)	(11.4)	(6.6)	(16.3)	(17.8)
French	38.5	13.6	17.8	14.7	26.8	33.9
	(42.4)	(13.7)	(18.3)	(16.9)	(25.5)	(38.0)
New Canadians	24.5	11.1	13.0	10.0	20.3	17.7
	(29.2)	(11.1)	(15.9)	(12.3)	(22.7)	(23.5)

Question: "People talk about the changing roles of men and women today. For each of the following statements I read, can you tell me how much you agree with each? Please use the responses on this card. (a) a working mother can establish just as warm and secure a relationship with her children as a mother who does not work, (b) a pre-school child is likely to suffer if his or her mother works, (c) a job is alright but what most women really want is a home and children, (d) being a housewife is just as fulfilling as working for pay, (e) having a job is the best way for a woman to be an independent person, and (f) both husband and wife should contribute to houshold income."

Note: Without brackets = percentages for entire sample; in brackets = percentages for women only

Source: 1990 World Values Survey.

ences. One is suggested by Goldthorpe's own line of investigation. It could be that national variations in the economic activity rates of women affect the timing of the transitions from neo-traditional to egalitarian attitudes. According to 1983 data from the European Community, for example, the levels of female paid workforce activity in Denmark were three times higher than for Irish females in the same age groups. Variations in attitudes to women in the workforce and family could also be dramatically affected by differences in the constitutions of national economies. Then there are significant national variations in the kinds of social supports available to women in the paid workforce. Other factors contributing to these cross-national variations are differences in the gender segregation of the workforce, differences in the size of the service sectors, and differences in pay. Variations in the character of economies and in the distribution of social supports affect both the opportunities and the costs facing women's entry into the paid workforce, as well as their incentives. If there are huge discrepancies between the wage rates of men and women, for example, if women get paid relatively little while men get a "family wage," there are then fewer incentives for women to become part of the paid workforce.

The joint effects of such contextual factors are probably powerful and possibly decisive. In all likelihood, a comprehensive explanation of women's participation rates in the paid workforce has to take into account how structural and attitudinal factors work together. Is there any indication that *individual*-level variations in attitudes to women, work, and the family are systematically associated with other features of late industrialism? Goldthorpe's (1987) analysis implies that attitudes to women, family, and work are gradually shifting from neo-traditional orientations towards more egalitarian ones. Schwartz expresses sentiments that echo those of Goldthorpe; she contends that women and men alike are in a "period of transition from the stability of defined roles … toward a time in which individuals will be able to determine the balance of work and family responsibilities they prefer independent of gender" (1992: 110). Are these emergent egalitarian orientations systematically associated with age, education level, and post-materialist orientations?

The effects of each of these three background variables on responses to the three statements that most closely correspond to the attitudes Goldthorpe associates with egalitarian views about women's employment (statements [a], [c], and [e] in Table 8-3) are mixed but intriguing. When the summary data presented in Figures 8-2, 8-3, and 8-4 are considered together, two patterns come into focus. First, according to Figure 8-2, there are clear traces of generation effects: agreement with the statement "a working mother can establish a warm and secure relationship with her children" is systematically linked to age, education, and post-materialist orientations. Regarding age, for example, the European and North American responses are similar: agreement is highest among the younger age groups and drops off significantly among those over 55 years. The impact of education is sharper among Europeans than North Americans, but in all cases the direction is consistent with the generational

Figure 8-2 Percentage Strongly Agreeing that "A Working Mother Can Establish a Warm and Secure Relationship with Her Children," by Age, Education, and Value Type

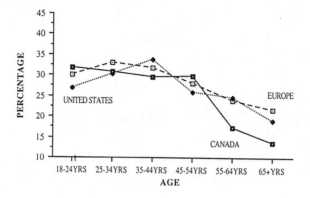

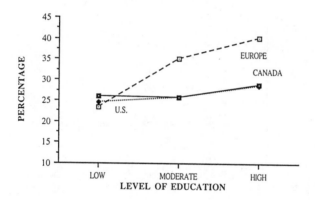

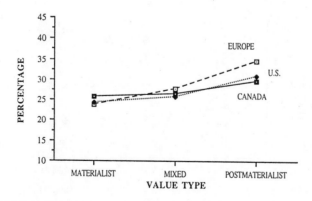

Source: 1990 World Values Survey.

Figure 8-3 Percentage Strongly Agreeing that "Having a Job Is the Best Way for a Woman to Be an Independent Person," by Age, Education, and Value Type

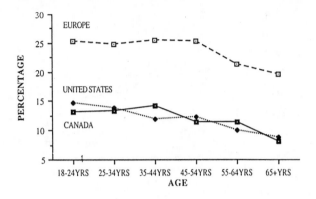

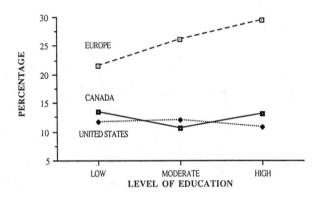

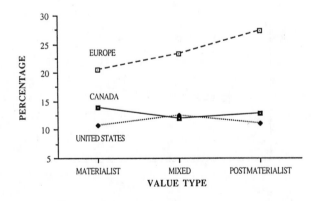

Source: 1990 World Values Surveys.

Figure 8-4 Percentage Strongly Agreeing that "Both Husband and Wife Should Contribute to the Household Income," by Age, Education, and Value Type

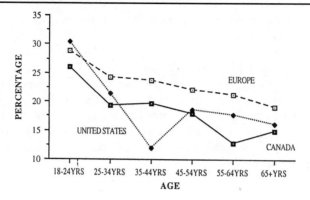

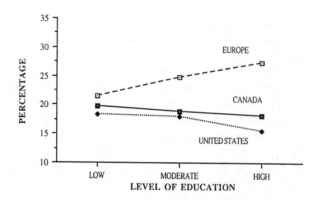

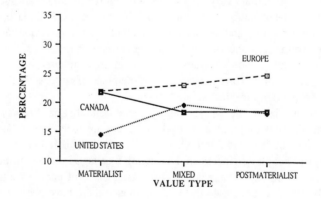

Source: 1990 World Values Survey.

change perspective: those with more education are more likely to agree with the statement. The effects of value type are essentially similar and also consistent.[5]

On the other two statements, "having a job is the best way for a woman to be an independent person" (Figure 8-3) and "both husband and wife should contribute to household income" (Figure 8-4), it is the differences between North Americans and Europeans that are most striking. In all cases, age effects are present—the young agree more with both statements—but after that, European and North American patterns diverge completely. On these dimensions, the European data on egalitarian attitudes to women's employment consistently point to the presence of generation effects. If generation effects are at play in the North American setting, there is no clear imprint of them from these data.

Parents and Children

That the social and economic functions of marriage and the family have undergone fundamental transformations is widely accepted. So, too, is the idea that norms about "the family" and about when people should marry have shifted. The WVS evidence complements the picture by showing that the expectations people have about marriage are in transition, as are the expectations about working mothers and the family (Rapoport, 1989). Some take these broad shifts to mean that individual preferences and expectations play an increasingly predominant role in marriages and external expectations and constraints have become less important (Akker, Halman, & de Moor, 1993). Others contend that contemporary marriage and family life are shaped less by traditional functional considerations, and the mutual obligations associated with those structures, and more by the emotional and expressive needs of individual partners (Roussel, 1989). Both interpretations focus on the theme of change. But the idea that everything to do with the family and marriage is in transition has to be balanced by another WVS finding: people still place a very high value on the family and on marriage. Much of the analysis undertaken so far has been primarily concerned with intra-generation interactions, with attitudes about the interaction of adults. What about cross-generational interactions within the family? Have attitudes about the place of children in the family setting changed, or are they stable?

The declining size of the average family is one trend that has been systematically tracked by demographers in each and every advanced industrial state: people are having fewer children (United Nations, 1992). If family size is decreasing and people are increasingly viewing marriage in terms of individual preferences, perhaps changes are also taking place in people's attitudes towards children? According to the WVS evidence there have been changes, but not all of them are in the expected direction.

Demographers typically attribute the shrinking size of the family to the

Table 8-4 Mean Scores: Ideal Number of Children in the Family

Country	1981	1990	% change
France	2.9	2.6	-0.3
Britain	2.7	2.5	-0.2
West Germany	3.3	2.2	-1.1
Italy	2.6	2.4	-0.2
Netherlands	3.3	2.6	-0.7
Denmark	3.5	2.6	-0.9
Belgium	3.3	2.5	-0.8
Spain	3.4	2.5	-0.9
Ireland	4.6	3.5	-1.1
Northern Ireland	3.6	3.1	-0.5
European Average	3.3	2.9	-0.6
United States	2.7	2.7	—
Canada	2.8	2.8	—
English	2.7	2.7	—
French	2.9	2.9	—
New Canadians	—	2.9	—

Question: "What do you think is the ideal size of family—how many children, if any?"
Source: 1981 and 1990 World Values Surveys.

joint effects of a constellation of factors, including the changing economic role of the family, the rapid increase in the number of women in the paid workforce, the availability of contraceptives, and geographic and occupational mobility. Compared to their predecessors, contemporary adults now face a much wider set of choices when making decisions about their own family. That people *are* self-consciously making different choices about family size is clear from the WVS evidence. In both 1981 and 1990 publics were asked, "What do you think is the ideal size of a family—how many children, if any?" According to the summary findings reported in Table 8-4, the ideal number of children in a family has fallen in every European country, and in some cases— West Germany and Ireland in particular—the declines have been quite sharp.[6] In 1981 Europeans reported that their ideal average family size was 3.3; in 1990 that average fell to 2.7. North American preferences, by contrast, have been much more stable: their ideal family size was 2.75 in 1981 and the same in 1990. Over the course of the decade, European preferences have converged with North American ones.

If marriage and family considerations really are driven less by traditional instrumental or functional considerations and more by personal expressive and emotional needs, then comparable changes may also have taken place in perspectives about children. In both 1981 and 1990, the WVS asked respondents in every country, "Do you think that a woman has to have children in order to be fulfilled?" The cross-national differences in responses to that question are substantial, and so are the continental variations: about half of all

Table 8-5 Percentage Agreeing that a Child Needs a Home with Both Parents in order to Grow Up Happily
(Percentages)

Country	1981	1990	% change
France	85.7	93.6	+7.9
Britain	65.5	73.8	+8.3
West Germany	90.6	94.1	+3.5
Italy	91.6	96.7	+5.1
Netherlands	76.9	78.6	+1.7
Denmark	57.8	72.8	+15.0
Belgium	87.5	92.0	+4.5
Spain	86.7	92.6	+5.9
Ireland	74.2	82.6	+8.4
Northern Ireland	77.9	80.7	+2.8
European Average	79.4	85.8	+6.4
United States	62.6	73.9	+11.3
Canada	66.1	78.3	+12.2
English	62.2	72.1	+9.9
French	76.8	93.2	+16.8
New Canadians	—	79.9	—

Question: "If someone says a child needs a home with both a father and a mother to grow up happily, would you tend to agree or disagree?"
Source: 1981 and 1990 World Values Surveys.

European respondents, compared to just one in four North Americans, said yes. There is also evidence of gender effects: men are consistently more likely than women to think that women have to have children in order to be fulfilled. In these respects, however, the cross-time changes are both tiny and inconsistent. As with general orientations towards the institution of marriage, the WVS data provide no indication of radical, or even significant, changes in this particular orientation.

Rising divorce rates mean that more children are growing up in a single-parent family setting. In 1986, for example, more than 10% of Canadian families were of the single-parent configuration (Beaujot, 1991), and the numbers continue to grow in Canada as elsewhere. It is reasonable to suppose that corresponding shifts will have taken place in public attitudes about children and the family. Single-parent families probably carry less stigma than they once did; they are far more common. Similarly, one might expect a greater willingness to embrace a wider array of alternatives in the structure of the "happy family." According to the WVS data, there have been changes. In 1981 and 1990 the WVS asked, "If someone says a child needs a home with both a father and a mother to grow up happily, would you tend to agree or disagree?" An overwhelming majority of publics in every country indicate that they agreed. Far more surprising is the direction of the cross-time changes. As Table 8-5 shows, levels of agreement with this traditional orientation *increased* significantly in every country between 1981 and 1990. The scope of these changes is not marginal, and so they cannot be explained in terms of measurement error. The changes are robust and consistent: a huge and increasing majority of people still cleave to the idea that a child needs a conventional family environment to "grow up happily."

There are other indications of stability. Conventional views about the obligations of parents to children remain essentially intact and stable. In both 1981 and 1990 the WVS asked respondents whether (a) "a parent's duty is to do their best for their children even at the expense of their own well-being," or (b) "parents have a life of their own and should not be asked to sacrifice their own well-being for the sake of their children." In both 1981 and 1990 an overwhelming majority of all publics supported the first option, and the aggregate changes were so small as to be inconsequential.[7]

These orientations have changed little over the decade, but others are in flux. One set of orientations that deserves particularly close attention concern the sets of values that parents want to pass on to their children. The transmission of values from parents to children is an important source of both value stability and change between generations. Not all parents are equally successful in explicitly teaching specific values to their progeny, but family environments can support some values and discourage others. And there have been systematic changes in the emphasis that adults place on key subsets of these child-rearing values.

In the 1981 and 1990 WVS respondents were told, "Here's a list of qualities that children can be encouraged to learn at home. Which, if any, do you consider to be especially important?" The interviewees were presented with a list of eleven values ranging from "good manners" and "hard work" to "imagination," and were asked to "choose up to five."[8] The responses to these questions have been analyzed in a variety of ways (Akker, Halman, & de Moor, 1993; Inglehart, Nevitte, & Basanez, 1996), and there is a consensus about what the key findings are and what they mean.

Table 8-6 itemizes the responses to seven individual items, and in a panel at the right-hand side of the table there is a third category labelled "egalitarian qualities." The first four items roughly correspond to the kind of traditional value orientations sometimes associated with the Protestant ethic. In this cluster, most publics indicate that responsibility is the most important value to teach children, and it is also the item that gained the most support during the 1981–1990 interlude. The increases were particularly sharp in Canada. Among those items that refer to social qualities, there were substantial cross-national shifts in support for good manners between 1981 and 1990. By comparison, the increases in the proportions of respondents identifying religious faith as especially important were relatively modest. The pattern of responses obtained provides yet another indication that this battery of questions elicits a projection of values from adults to children. With respect to general religious orientations, for example, the WVS data indicate that two countries stood out as being particularly religious: Ireland and the United States. These are also

Table 8-6 Parent-Child Interactions (Percentages)

| Country | Economic Qualities | | | | | | | | Social Qualities | | | | Religious faith | | Egalitarian Qualities | |
| | Hard work | | Determination/ perseverance | | Responsibility | | Thrift, saving money & things | | Good manners | | Unselfishness | | | | | |
	1981	% Change by 1990	1981	% Change by 1990	1981	% Change by 1990	1981	% Change by 1990	1981	% Change by 1990	1981	% Change by 1990	1981	% Change by 1990	1981	% Change by 1990
France	33.4	+19.3	18.3	+20.5	39.7	+31.8	30.7	+5.1	21.3	+31.7	21.7	+18.1	9.7	+3.0	10.8	+0.7
Britain	14.7	+13.5	18.2	+11.0	23.7	+22.3	8.2	+20.0	65.5	+24.5	40.7	+15.8	12.6	+7.3	15.3	+2.3
W. Germany	19.9	-5.6	27.7	+21.7	61.7	+23.2	28.8	+15.9	40.9	+25.2	4.4	+3.3	15.8	+3.5	27.3	+9.4
Italy	12.8	+10.8	18.0	+11.0	47.9	+35.5	18.2	+9.1	54.5	+23.5	2.2	+37.6	19.7	+15.6	10.4	+3.4
Netherlands	11.8	+1.8	16.1	+15.4	54.1	+31.2	16.7	+11.4	58.6	+20.1	9.0	+12.8	12.4	+1.8	20.9	+14.6
Denmark	2.1	+0.3	11.5	+18.9	62.3	+23.3	13.9	+4.7	48.6	+17.3	24.9	+25.5	6.9	+2.0	35.4	+17.2
Belgium	32.4	+1.8	20.6	+18.2	37.2	+33.5	35.5	+0.5	47.2	+25.2	14.3	+12.7	16.2	+1.0	7.3	+7.9
Spain	40.5	-3.3	12.7	+9.1	63.3	+14.8	10.6	+11.9	52.5	+28.5	4.4	+3.4	20.9	+3.6	18.8	+3.2
Ireland	23.5	+4.1	9.9	+15.7	22.2	+38.8	14.4	+7.5	64.7	+9.9	22.7	+29.9	41.1	+16.1	10.5	+4.8
N. Ireland	19.2	+10.1	9.9	+8.2	9.3	+28.9	7.7	+17.3	79.2	+15.5	29.5	+19.5	32.7	+11.7	6.1	+4.8
Europe Average	21.0	+5.3	16.3	+15.0	42.1	+28.3	18.5	+10.3	53.5	+22.1	17.4	+17.9	18.8	+6.6	16.3	+6.8
U.S.	26.3	+22.7	14.7	+20.7	42.7	+28.9	9.5	+19.4	62.5	+14.7	18.8	+18.0	38.2	+17.0	12.7	+8.4
Canada	20.2	+14.8	21.6	+16.1	40.4	+34.6	14.5	+6.7	53.7	+21.0	20.5	+21.8	23.4	+7.2	12.5	+12.1
English	21.1	+10.0	19.0	+14.6	37.7	+34.3	12.2	+5.8	57.4	+19.9	20.8	+23.4	24.6	+6.2	16.3	+12.5
French	17.7	+23.4	28.8	+21.7	47.7	+38.9	21.0	+9.6	43.2	+20.8	19.5	+23.0	20.1	+8.9	5.7	+17.8
New Canadians	—	40.1	—	35.0	—	71.3	—	19.6	—	78.9	—	35.6	—	30.9	—	25.6

Question: "Here is a list of qualities which children can be encouraged to learn at home. Which, if any, do you consider to be especially important? Please choose up to five. (a) good manners, (b) independence, (c) hard work, (d) feeling of responsibility, (e) imagination, (f) thrift, saving money and things, (g) determination, perseverance, (h) religious faith, (i) unselfishness, (j) obedience."

Note: The "egalitarian parent-child" relations index = "independence" important + "imagination" important + "obedience" not important + "one does not have the duty to respect and love parents who have not earned it by their behaviour and attitudes."

Source: 1981 and 1990 World Values Surveys.

the only two countries in which a majority say that religious faith is especially important for children.

It is possible to conduct a separate and detailed analysis of responses to each and every single one of these "children's values" items. But there are practical, as well as conceptual and empirical, reasons for adopting a less cumbersome approach. A background analysis of responses to all of these questions indicates systematic patterns in those responses. People tend to emphasize different clusters of responses. For example, respondents tend to emphasize *either* such values as independence and imagination, *or* values like obedience and good manners. The first set of orientations are those that encourage children to think for themselves, whereas the second set has more to do with conformity. A detailed investigation of these response patterns reveals a well-defined cluster of responses that clearly tap egalitarian orientations in parent-child interactions. The cluster, which forms a robust index of egalitarianism in those relations, is defined by a specific set of responses to four key items: respondents qualify as "egalitarian" if they identify both independence and imagination as important for children; if they do *not* select obedience as an important value; and if they indicate that "one does *not* have the duty to respect and love parents who have not earned it by their behaviour and attitudes."[9]

The column on the right-hand side of Table 8-6 indicates the proportion of each public qualifying as egalitarian on parent-child relations in 1981 and 1990. The basic finding is clear: all publics became more egalitarian during the course of the decade. In 1981 Danish, West German, and Dutch respondents scored high on this dimension, and Canadians (12.5%) and Americans (12.7%) were less egalitarian than Europeans (16.3%). The 1981–1990 increases were particularly substantial in Denmark, the Netherlands, and Canada. Consequently, by 1990 a significantly higher proportion of Canadians (25%) than Americans (21%) rated as egalitarian on this dimension. Within Canada, the increases were greatest among francophone Canadians.

That people are becoming more egalitarian in their child-rearing orientations and parents are less likely than before to demand conformity from their children are not isolated findings. Using longitudinal data for the thirty-year period between the 1950s and 1980s, Alwin (1986) demonstrates that there has been a gradual decline in the American public's emphasis on conformity in child-rearing, and a corresponding rise in autonomy orientations. Other investigators have also shown that there are consistent within-country variations in the distribution of these orientations. Kohn's pathbreaking research, for example, plainly indicates that occupation and class are vital. Families in which the head of the household has a manual occupation are the most likely to emphasize compliance with authority as an important value to teach children. Families in which the head of the household has a middle-class occupation are more likely to encourage children to turn to internal standards of conduct (1959: 341).

With the continued expansion of education, the shifting occupational structures associated with advanced industrialism, and the massive increases in the
size and character of the middle class, there are reasons to expect corresponding changes in child-rearing orientations. Such a shift might be regarded as a
functionally necessary adjustment to changing structural conditions. Adults
whose own work is driven more by information-processing, by the application
of knowledge, and who are rewarded for innovation are more likely than those
in more traditional occupations to see imagination and independence as
important. By the same token, the shifts could be attributed to transitions in
underlying values. According to the WVS data, there appears to be something
to both of these interpretations. Figure 8-5 illustrates a pattern suggesting that
the emergence of greater egalitarianism in parent-child relations is systematically connected to age, level of education, and post-materialist values.

In general, direction of the age effects is the same for Europeans and North
Americans: older respondents are much less egalitarian than the youngest age
groups in their views about important values for children. There are significant differences between Europeans and North Americans in the two youngest
age groups: Europeans are consistently more egalitarian than their Canadian
or American counterparts. For those over 35 years of age, however, the distributions are essentially the same. As one would expect, there is clear evidence
of education effects: those with high levels of education are twice as likely as
those with low levels to subscribe to egalitarian child-rearing values. The
impact of value type is similarly predictable: post-materialists are two to three
times more likely than materialists to express egalitarian child-rearing values.
Together, these findings consistently point to the interpretation that the shifts
in child-rearing values are related to generational change.

Each one of the findings about stability and change in the family, marriage,
orientations to the nexus between work-family-children, child-rearing, and
what are important values for children, deserves far more detailed investigation. In some respects, the findings raise more questions than they settle. It
would be fascinating, for example, to know more about the differences
between dual-career families that have children and those that do not. The
same could be said about the impact variations in people's own family structure might have. For example, do people who are in extended family environments have orientations towards primary relations that differ from those of
people in nuclear families? And what about people who head single-parent
families, and those who are single, or divorced? Have comparable changes
taken place within all of these groups? Answers to these kinds of questions are
essential to a deeper understanding of the important changes in the character
of primary relations. The possibilities for more detailed investigation are virtually endless.

Although the results examined so far just scratch the surface, there are two
aspects of shifting family values that are particularly central when viewed in
the context of our earlier findings. One has to do with emerging preferences
for more egalitarian spousal relations, the other with a similar shift towards

Figure 8-5 Egalitarian Parent-child Relations, by Age, Education, and Value Type

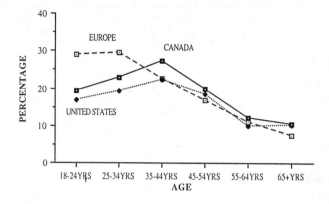

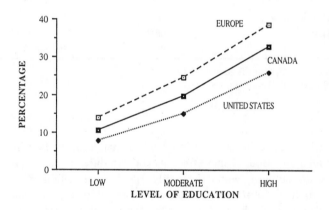

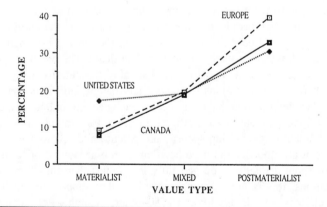

Source: 1990 World Values Survey.

Table 8-7   Regression Analysis: The Determinants of Egalitarian Spousal and Egalitarian
            Parent-Child Relations

Predictors	Egalitarian Spousal Relations	Egalitarian Parent-Child Relations
Change over time:		
1981–1990	.05**	.08**
Generational change:		
Postmaterialism	.06**	.18**
Education	.04**	.14**
Age	.02**	-.12**
Personal satisfaction:		
Household satisfaction	.09**	-.06**
Socio-demographics:		
Male	-.05**	.003
Income	.01	.02**
Non-manual occupation	-.002	.07**
Catholic	-.02**	-.17**
Nationality:		
Canadians	.08**	-.06**
Americans	.04**	-.04**

*significant at $p < .05$; **significant at $p < .01$.
Source: 1981 and 1990 World Values Surveys.

greater egalitarianism in what are inherently hierarchical relationships: parent-child relations. Both of these findings concern different aspects of orientations towards authority within the family. The findings in Table 8-7 summarize these findings from a slightly different vantage point; the multivariate
analysis identifies which variables are the significant predictors of orientations towards each of these two domains.

The first row in the table, for example, underscores an essential point: it
shows not only that people became more egalitarian in their outlook on
spousal and parent-child relations, but also that the 1981–1990 changes on
both of these dimensions were statistically significant. The results also confirm that age, education, and post-materialist value orientations are systematically connected to orientations to spousal and parent-child relations. More
than that, they demonstrate that the effects of each background factor are both
genuine and independent of each other. Education, for example, is a significant determinant of egalitarian spousal and parent-child relations even *after*
the effects of all other factors have been taken into account. Notice that the
results for spousal relations are generally less robust than those for parent-
child relations; this is not so surprising, given that support for egalitarian
spousal relations was already high in 1980—there is simply not much variation left to be explained.

Not every predictor works in precisely the same way for each dimension. The impact of the socio-demograph factors illustrates that point nicely. Notice that on the spousal relations dimension, the negative coefficient for "male" indicates that women are significantly more likely than men to favour more equality between spouses. Sex, however, has no effect whatsoever on parent-child relations, nor is there any particular reason to expect to find one. Neither income nor occupation has any significant impact on orientations to spousal relations, but both are significant predictors of orientation towards parent-child relations: those in lower-income groups and manual occupations are significantly less egalitarian in parent-child relations than are those in higher-income groups and with non-manual occupations. These results resemble findings reported by others (Kohn, 1959). Household satisfaction[10] is more difficult to fathom: people who are more satisfied with their home life are *more* likely to prefer egalitarian spousal relations, but they are *less* inclined to support more egalitarian parent-child relations. The impact of respondents' religious denomination, however, is consistent: Catholics are significantly less egalitarian than members of other denominations. And as the earlier analysis would lead one to believe, nationality is also significant and there are systematic continental variations. Canadians and Americans are significantly *more* egalitarian than Europeans when it comes to spousal relations, but significantly *less* egalitarian on the parent-child dimension. All in all, the multivariate analysis confirms that the shifts in orientations towards authority in the family are robust and significant ones. For reasons already outlined, the determinants of orientations towards parent-child relations are more robust than those for spousal relations, and the impact of these predictors, though not identical for each domain, broadly corresponds to other research findings. The finding that people have become more egalitarian, or less authoritarian, in their spousal relations and parent-child orientations is a result that also calls for more detailed investigation. The more immediate question here is: Do these findings help to shed any additional light on how to interpret the other shifts documented in preceding chapters?

Connecting Authority Orientations: The Family, Work, and the Polity

To place the analysis of shifting orientations in primary relations in the context of the cumulative findings, it is useful to revisit some of the broad themes that have emerged so far. In orientations towards the polity, one absolutely clear finding is that significant generationally driven changes have taken place in people's attitudes to political authority. There are two identifiable dimensions to these shifts: confidence in governmental institutions is declining while non-traditional, "elite-directing" forms of political participation are increasing. In political matters, people are becoming less deferential, less compliant, more inclined to speak out and to be more self-directing and more autonomous in reaching their own conclusions about the political world

(Figure 4-7). The evidence presented in Chapters 3 and 4 demonstrated unequivocally that these shifts are taking place simultaneously in all twelve advanced industrial states. The focus of the investigation then turned to what were broadly defined as economic orientations. Among other things, Chapters 5 and 6 document systematic shifts in the economic orientations of these publics. Once again, two dimensions of these changes turn out to be particularly striking: preferences about workplace participation are in transition, as are workplace motivations. People are increasingly interested in more meaningful participation in workplace decision-making, and their motivations for working are driven more by self-actualizing reasons and less by such traditional considerations as accumulation of wealth and status. As with the polity, these shifts in orientations towards authority in the economy are impressively consistent. They are taking place in all twelve countries, and there is evidence that the changes may be generationally driven.

Chapter 6 shifted the focus and entertained a more general set of possibilities by examining the empirical links between these two sets of findings: the central finding was that these transformations in the polity and the workplace are not just parallel changes that happen to be conceptually congenial to each other. The changes are systematically connected to each other (Figure 6-13); it appears that both of these broad transitions in orientations towards authority are part of a larger, complex pattern of change. On that general finding the empirical findings are absolutely clear: people who have traditional conceptions of political authority are also significantly more likely to have traditional notions about authority in the workplace. Conversely, people who hold to non-traditional orientations towards political authority, people who are less compliant, are also significantly more likely to hold non-traditional views about authority in the workplace. A more elaborate investigation of these multiple connections within and between different dimensions complicates the picture, but the findings from that more detailed analysis are reassuring for two reasons. First, they increase confidence in the conclusion that the results are not an artifact of measurement error; all of the results are genuine and robust. Second, it is obvious that these patterns are neither unique to one country nor limited to one continent. The same basic patterns emerge again and again in the twelve advanced industrial states. The same shifts are replicated more or less sharply from one setting to the next; they are even replicated within subsets of single populations. Moreover, the links between and within the domains hold up at both time points and in multiple countries. The patterns are coherent.

The findings introduced in this chapter provide a more complete picture as well as adding yet another dimension; they provide the building blocks for what looks to be a more comprehensive interpretation of the changes. With these basic empirical findings in mind, recall our preliminary discussion of authority relations, particularly the conceptual issues raised by the dialogue between Pateman (1970) and Eckstein (1966, 1969). Both of these pioneering investigators begin with slightly different questions in mind—Pateman is con-

Figure 8-6   Generalizing Authority Patterns

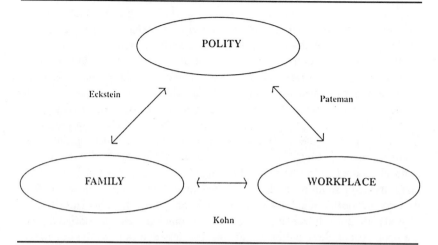

Note: The double-headed arrows do not represent causality, but merely a connection.

cerned about democratic participation and Eckstein more about democratic stability. Both analysts, however, arrive at similar perspectives: both see *all* authority relations as profoundly political, and each characterizes authority orientations as fundamental to understanding the character and dynamics of democratic life. And both subscribe to the important claim that patterns of authority are generalizable from one domain to the next. Their differences turn, among other things, on alternative evaluations of the importance of particular domains and competing assessments of the extent to which such domains as the workplace could become non-authoritarian. With respect to the workplace-polity dyad, Pateman uses selected case studies to make a convincing case that people generalize from their experiences with authority relations in the workplace to their perspectives on political authority. As we have seen, Chapter 6 provides substantial empirical support for Pateman's claim.

By placing greater emphasis on the implications of congruent, or discrepant, authority relations for democratic stability, Eckstein's investigations draw particular attention to the importance of the family-polity dyad.[11] If orientations towards authority really are generalizable, and if the Pateman and Eckstein perspectives are taken together, it takes no great leap of the intellectual imagination to recognize another possibility: What about a third dyad? Are orientations towards authority in the family connected to authority relations in the workplace? Posing these collateral questions pushes the inquiry forward by opening up a more comprehensive set of possibilities. Rather than just looking at authority relations between two discrete dyads (workplace-polity; parent-child relations-polity) where the polity is the focus, attention should be directed to a triangulated set of relations. Figure 8-6 schematically characterizes authority orientations in the polity, the workplace, and the family as potentially interdependent and as on equal conceptual footing.

There are two preliminary observations worth noting about such a reconfiguration. First, this elaboration does no violence whatsoever to the claims made by either Pateman or Eckstein. The reconfiguration simply takes their contributions and extends their insights in a slightly more deliberate way. Second, there is no reason to believe that this reconfiguration should be ruled out as implausible because it runs headlong into counter-evidence. The bulk of the available evidence about value orientations focusses primarily on within-domain concerns. Across-domain evidence is the exception, not the rule.[12] Matters of focus aside, the important point is that the limited data that are available yield findings that are quite consistent with the family-workplace connection implied in Figure 8-6. In explaining the democratic stability of the class-divided Britain of the 1960s, for example, Eckstein sees close parallels between authority relations in family life and those in associational life. "Family life in the lower strata," he notes, "is much more authoritarian than in the upper strata; there is less reasonableness, less consultation, less courtesy, less formality, more punishment, and more arbitrariness" (1966, 246). The finding is not an isolated one. Other systematic evidence that more explicitly connects work and family authority orientations is provided by Kohn (1959), Kohn and Schooler (1969), and others who demonstrate that where parents sit in corporate hierarchies is consistently related to the kinds of behaviours they attempt to instill in their children. They find that middle-class people, those who occupy positions that allow for greater self-direction, are more likely to encourage their children to appreciate the virtues of autonomy, whereas people whose occupations allow less room for self-direction are more likely to teach their children the values of conformity and obedience.

Such scattered findings are suggestive and encouraging, but they fall far short of clinching the case that authority orientations are generalizable across the three domains.[13] Before we tackle the larger question head on, there is a necessary preliminary step. Chapter 6 demonstrated that there is empirical support for Pateman's contention that workplace authority orientations are related to authority orientations in the polity. The next question is: Does the WVS evidence provide any support for Eckstein's parallel claim that authority orientations in the family are related to those in the polity?

As in Chapter 6 the easiest place to begin is with the broad picture. The first part of this chapter identified seven individual WVS questions that qualify as indicators of orientations towards authority in the family. Combining those seven indicators into a simple additive scale produces an aggregate measure of each respondent's orientations towards authority in the family.[14] Table 8-8 provides an overview of the extent to which orientations towards authority in the family are related to three other dimensions, each of which has been examined before.

First, consider the left-most panel in Table 8-8. This summarizes for each country the relationship between orientations towards authority in the family

Table 8-8   The Links between Orientations Towards General, Political, Workplace, and Family
Authority, by Country

Country	General Orientations and Family Orientations	Political Orientations and Family Orientations	Workplace Orientations and Family Orientations
France	-.21	.29	.20
Britain	-.19	.17	.18
West Germany	-.17	.36	.34
Italy	-.20	.38	.28
Netherlands	-.24	.43	.36
Denmark	-.13	.33	.37
Belgium	-.11	.24	.30
Spain	-.25	.32	.30
Ireland	-.19	.25	.30
Northern Ireland	-.06	.05	.21
European Average	-.18	.28	.28
United States	-.22	.19	.24
Canada	-.26	.32	.24
English	-.23	.33	.24
French	-.40	.31	.25
New Canadians	-.17	.29	.17

Note: The above figures are gamma coefficients for the merged 1981 and 1990 data.
Source: 1981 and 1990 World Values Surveys.

and a single indicator of general orientations toward authority. Recall that the latter come from a single question response: those saying that "greater respect for authority in the future would be a 'good thing.'" The expectation is that those supporting greater egalitarianism in the family should disagree with that question, and the negative sign on the gamma coefficient reported in the first column indicates that there is a consistent pattern bearing out that expectation. The links are quite strong (in excess of gamma +/- .2) for Dutch, Italian, Spanish, and American respondents. They are stronger still in Canada, and are remarkably robust among Canadian francophones. More important, the relationships are in the same predicted direction for every single public.[15]

The data in the middle panel of Table 8-8 deserve particularly close attention because they provide a proximate test of Eckstein's claim (1966, 1969; Eckstein & Gurr, 1972). These findings are more robust. In every single country, orientations towards authority in the family do seem to be related to orientations towards political authority.[16] The data from Northern Ireland are somewhat limp. But in every other country the relationships are at least moderately strong, and they are particularly powerful in the Netherlands, Italy, West Germany, Denmark, and Canada.[17]

Now to the right-most panel in Table 8-8: these findings amount to a plausibility probe of our own extension of the Pateman-Eckstein line of reasoning; it is the more novel third side of the triangle that was introduced in Figure 8-

6. The argument is simple: if the general rule applies and orientations towards authority really are generalizable from one domain to the next, then there should be evidence of such a connection when it comes to the less explored relationship between orientations towards authority in the family and the workplace. The findings do support that claim, and the evidence is both systematic and quite robust. The strengths of these relationships oscillate within a relatively narrow range: they are never weaker than in Britain (.18) or stronger than in Denmark (.37). On balance, the association between family and workplace authority orientations is about as strong as the family-polity dyad and a good deal stronger than the family-general dyad. So far, there are fairly persuasive reasons for believing that authority orientations are generalizable and that the line of speculation proposed earlier has some merit—that the family-workplace dyad does form a significant but neglected part of a more comprehensive pattern.

These initial findings need to be unpacked; they need to be examined in greater detail and pushed further. Are these results stable? And do the basic findings hold up when scrutinized from different vantage points? One indication of whether findings are truly robust is whether results from one setting have parallels in others. Another is the cross-time dimension, which is why so much emphasis has been placed on the cross-time consistency of the data: each and every public has become less deferential on each and every one of the aspects of authority considered. A third indication of robustness has to do with "connectedness." Here, the presumption is that if the relationships between these three domains are genuinely tied to each other, then those connections should hold up regardless of whether publics are more or less deferential and regardless of whether the measurements are taken in 1981 or 1990. Robustness, in other words, is not just about *levels* of deference; it also has to do with the *connectedness* of these orientations within and between the three domains under different circumstances. If the claim that orientations toward authority are generalizable is plausible and is one that should be taken seriously, then it has to be shown that people generalize from one domain to the next regardless of the levels of deference, the national setting, or the particular moment when the comparable measures are taken.

Figure 8-7 unpacks the aggregate data for both time points, and these data help to satisfy some of these concerns. Portions of these findings have been presented before (Figure 6-13); the left-most and centre parts of the figure present no new data. It is the addition of the right-most column that places the earlier findings in the expanded perspective proposed above (Figure 8-6).

There are two aspects of Figure 8-7 to focus on: first compare the 1981 and 1990 findings. The cross-time variations in the sizes of the coefficients are generally quite small: with the exception of the workplace-general authority dyad, they are in the range of +/- .03 (gamma coefficient). So while people became less deferential between 1981 and 1990, the connectedness of these orientations remained essentially the same; they are stable. What about the strength of the connectedness? On this score there is some variation. Consider

Figure 8-7 The Links between Orientations towards General, Political, Workplace, and Family Authority in 12 Advanced Industrial States

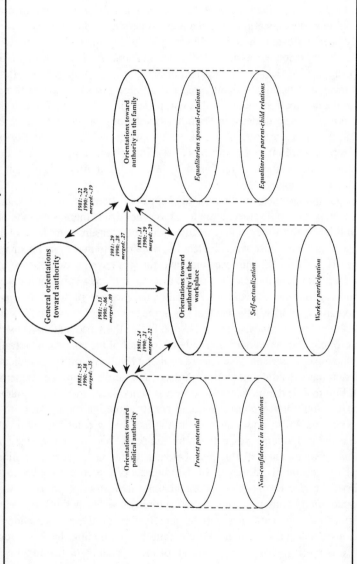

Source: 1981 and 1990 World Values Surveys.
Note: The above figures are gamma coefficients.

the links between general authority orientations and each of the three domains. The strongest ties, indicated by the larger coefficients, are between political and general orientations. Next comes the family, and the weakest associations are with the workplace. That is, when people think about "authority" or, more precisely, "greater respect for authority," they are more likely to be thinking about political and familial matters than about the workplace. But what about the connections between the other three dimensions? As has already been indicated, there is stable support for Pateman's claim that workplace authority orientations are linked to views about political authority. There is also support for Eckstein's view that orientations to authority in the family are connected to political orientations. The strongest links, however, turn out to be in the connections between the workplace and the family. The key finding is not that a new dimension of authority relations has been "discovered"; it is that the basic structure of the more comprehensive set of authority relations proposed in Figure 8-6 survives a basic but crucial empirical test. From this vantage point, there is reason to believe that authority orientations are indeed generalizable.

This preliminary step in the analysis supplies a summary overview, but it tells less than the whole story; it remains too general, and there is room to push the findings still further. There is the issue of measurement to take into account. Rare is the case when indicators, responses to questions on surveys, are exactly right for the purposes that investigators have in mind. Some indicators might be described as "too thin": they are on target but do not uncover very much about the key concept. Arguably, the measure of "general orientations towards authority," the one that sits at the top of Figure 8-7, suffers from that problem.[18] Other measures can be "too fat" in the sense that they cover so much ground it becomes hard to decide which part of the conceptual terrain is really the most important. That charge could be levelled against the indicators of orientations towards political, workplace, and family authority. Remember that in Figure 8-7, the indicators of political, workplace, and family authority come from multiple responses to some twenty-three questions. More to the point, Figure 8-7 also draws attention to the fact that orientations within each of these three domains are really more nuanced. Within each of the three domains, people make distinctions between different aspects of political, workplace, and family authority. In the interests of presenting the broad picture first, the general measures, the *combined* indicators of political, workplace, and family authority orientations, ignored those distinctions. But a great deal more can be learned about the architecture of these orientations by unpacking the data and bringing those within-domain findings back into focus.

There is no simple way to present all of the relevant evidence in an easily digestible format. Considering at the same time the connections between just the three domains is easy enough. Viewing the connections between six dimensions is harder but still manageable. Navigating all possible combinations of the domains and dimensions is complicated no matter how you look at it. Nonetheless, it is important to be able to see the entire picture. Figure 8-8

Figure 8-8 The Linkages between Dimensions of Orientations towards Political and Workplace Authority

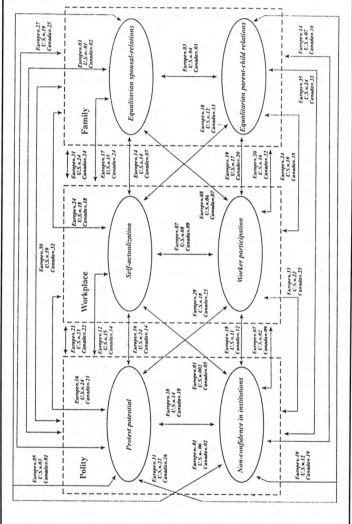

Source: 1981 and 1990 World Values Surveys.

Note: The above figures are gamma coefficients for the merged 1981 and 1990 data.

presents all of the connections within a single schematic. Fathoming this schematic becomes less daunting when approached with some basic rules for interpretation in mind.

There are two initial observations that help to clear the way. First, there is no longer any pressing need to be concerned about the general orientations towards authority dimension. That capstone concept becomes less useful now: more meaningful than a thin indicator of an expansive concept are the underlying dimensions, the supporting structure, that fleshes out notions of authority in more precise ways. Second, neither is it any longer necessary to present all of the cross-time findings. That there *have* been significant cross-time shifts in both public orientations towards each domain and on each dimension within those domains is now well established. With these considerations set aside, what should be the focus of attention?

There are three immediate priorities. First and foremost are the relationships between the six different dimensions of authority orientations. Think of Figure 8-8 as an architectural plan; it is the connections between the various elements in that plan that hold the structure together. The six dimensions at the core of the schema can be thought of as pillars. There is no reason to suppose that all of those pillars, each part of the structure, will be equally important to the stability of the entire edifice. Some will be critical "supporting beams"; they are load bearing and hold the edifice together. Other elements may make far more modest contributions. From this standpoint, the key question to begin with is: Where are the supporting beams? On the other side of the same issue is a second question that is far from trivial: Which connections are not load bearing? And following the same logic as before, the third question is: Do the dynamic properties of these structures work similarly or differently from one place to the next?

Each pair of vertically stacked ellipses is surrounded by cross-hatched rectangles that represent the three domains, or compartments, of the overall structure. The polity is in the left part of the schematic, workplace is in the middle, and family is at the right. Notice that the strength of connections between the three domains is very much like that reported in Figure 8-7. They are all fairly robust, but they provide one additional piece of corroborating evidence: they report cross-national findings. The connections are somewhat stronger for European and Canadian publics than for their American counterparts, and from this perspective the connections between the family-polity dyad are the strongest (gamma coefficients: Europe = .30, Canada = .32, United States = .19) and the polity-workplace dyad the weakest (Europe = .23, Canada = .22, United States = .21). In other words, not only is the basic structure stable across time (Figure 8-7), it is also stable across different national settings.

To fathom what holds the structure up, one needs to look at the connections between the pillars. Notice that the *direction* of the coefficients is uniformly positive, which indicates that, to a greater or lesser extent, all of the dimensions are helping to support the overall structure. The variations in size of the coefficients indicate that there are primary, load-bearing parts of the structure; these have connections in the range of gamma = .2. Then there are secondary contributors, the supporting beams, with connections that are somewhat weaker (gammas of about .14). Finally, there are what by usual criteria would be considered essentially irrelevant connections, those less than gamma = .1; these are the sheetrock and wall paper. By these benchmarks there are five basic connections that seem to be doing most of the work (have gamma coefficients around .2). Three of these involve the "protest potential" dimension and another three implicate the "parent-child" dimension. Worker participation has two such connections, while non-confidence in institutions and self-actualization have one each. First and foremost is the direct connection between protest potential (polity) and parent-child relations (family); these are all relatively strong (Europe = .31, Canada = .26, United States = .21). The connections between protest potential (polity) and worker participation (workplace) are not quite as strong (Europe = .29, Canada = .23, United States = .18). Non-confidence in institutions (polity) and self-actualization (workplace) then come into play as important contributors to the primary structure.

In effect, of the six pillars identified in the preceding analysis, five feature more or less directly as load-bearing parts of the basic structure; only "spousal relations" is not of primary importance. Even so, the spousal relations dimension cannot be written off or dismissed as inconsequential. This dimension is essentially irrelevant to both of the polity dimensions, but it is a part of the secondary supporting structure. Spousal relations is connected to the workplace "compartment" and particularly to "self-actualization." The other parts of the secondary supporting structure include the parent-child relations (family)–self-actualization (workplace) dyad, the worker participation (workplace)–non-confidence in institutions (polity) dyad, and the protest potential (polity)–non-confidence in institutions (polity) dyad.[19]

Much more could be said about each one of these detailed findings, but the crucial question is: What do these results collectively mean? And what broader conclusions can be drawn from the more complete but rather complex network of relationships? First and foremost, Figure 8-8 provides compelling support for the fundamental idea that people do indeed generalize about orientations towards authority. Put most boldly, the data seem to indicate that people generalize from one dimension to the next and from one domain to the next. As Pateman neatly puts it, people "appreciate the connection between the public and private spheres" (1970: 110).[20] This finding is itself a significant contribution. In proposing that congruence of authority patterns is conducive to democratic stability (Eckstein) and that workplace authority patterns are related to political efficacy and thence to political participation (Pateman), the two theorists relied exclusively on selected case studies for their supporting evidence. In Eckstein's case the main focus was on Britain and Germany, in Pateman's case Britain and Yugoslavia. Both Eckstein and Pateman saw their efforts as "theory building" and in need of far more systematic evidence. Using a rather different strategy, the WVS data both supply that evidence and provide greater confidence in that general theory by demonstrating that, in their basic form, the very same patterns hold up across time and in multiple national settings.

A second general conclusion elaborates the first: orientations toward authority are plainly not undifferentiated. People discriminate between various aspects of authority orientations. The point, brought into sharp focus by Figure 8-8, is a simple one, but here also the WVS data make a contribution of a different sort: they identify additional relevant sites in the "grid" of authority orientations. Both Eckstein and Pateman were aware that patterns of authority can infuse all relationships between people, but the WVS give firmer empirical shape to that general proposition. Eckstein was primarily interested in the connections between family and political relations. Within the family, he was primarily concerned with parent-child relations. The WVS evidence provides some justification for that preoccupation, but the WVS findings also reveal that "spousal relations" are a second dimension of "family" authority patterns that deserve attention. Within the polity, Eckstein's primary interest is in "associational life," which corresponds most closely, perhaps, to the institutional dimension of the political domain. The WVS findings point to "protest potential" as a second relevant dimension of the political domain. Similarly, the WVS highlight a second aspect of "workplace" authority patterns as another site for analysis. Because Pateman is primarily concerned with participation, her focus is primarily upon the connection between workplace participation and political participation. The WVS justify that concern, but they also draw attention to "self-actualization" as a second relevant dimension. All in all, the WVS findings explicitly identify and further elaborate a more extended field of play.

Third, knowing that public orientations towards authority are more nuanced—that people distinguish not only between authority in the polity, the workplace, and the family, but also between different aspects of authority *within* each of these domains—raises a variety of other issues about both the *levels* and the *connectedness* of deference. Making generalizations about levels of deference is no longer so simple. The conventional wisdom is that Canadians are more deferential than Americans, but now a more subtle question has to be asked: *In what respects* are Canadians more or less deferential than Americans? When it comes to the connectedness of authority orientations, the complications are of a different order. People do generalize authority orientations across and between domains and dimensions, but they do not do so with equal efficiency: some dimensions are more closely interconnected than others, some parts of the structure more tightly integrated with the rest of the edifice than others. One implication is that shifts in authority orientations will reverberate more or less powerfully depending on the point of origin. Shifts in spousal authority orientations, for example, may have a negligible effect on the entire pattern, a mere ripple, because spousal relations are relatively peripheral to the entire structure. By contrast, a change of similar magnitude in any of four more centrally connected dimensions—protest potential, worker participation, parent-child relations, or non-confidence in institutions—would reverberate far more powerfully.

This observation raises yet another set of questions. What of the point of origin? Or more particularly, can anything be said of the *directions* of change? Theoretically at least, there are three sets of possibilities each of which takes a different domain as the point of origin. Shifts in authority relations may begin with the family and filter through to the workplace and polity; or they may begin with the workplace and be generalized to the family and the polity; or they might originate within the polity and be generalized to the family and workplace. If we take account of the order in which the process of generalization filters through to the second and third domains, the number of possible combinations multiply. They expand again if the focus becomes dimensions rather than just domains. There is no simple way to empirically demonstrate a point of origin or to definitively isolate the precise pathways by which authority orientations are generalized. But at least two sources, points of origin, seem plausible. Socialization theorists argue that basic orientations towards the world begin to crystallize during an individual's formative years. This is the reason that Eckstein and Gurr (1975) pay so much attention to parent-child relations:

> The young child first becomes aware of the simple fact that his world is inhabited by powerful beings—parents or their surrogates—who issue directives and use rewards and deprivations to back them ... It is likely that shortly after children discover supers [superordinates], they become aware that some of their own actions are regularly subject to directives ... while others are not." (1975: 363).

The presumption is that families are salient, and on this point the evidence seems clear: families rate highest in people's priorities.

Socialization theory also acknowledges that life-cycle effects matter, and on this count the workplace is again a plausible point of origin. Basic orientations toward authority might originate in the family setting, but such early dispositions can be significantly modified by experience. Adults spend many of their waking hours in the workplace, and it is here that people daily confront the more complex realities of superordination and subordination in an institutional setting. The workplace provides concrete experiences, the stuff of office politics, that modify the orientations learned in family settings. It may well be through the workplace that higher-order distinctions about authority orientations are learned, refined, and tested. Next to the family, work is also salient; people attach a high priority to work (Figure 2-6), and there are incentives to be attentive to workplace authority relations. If such factors as primacy, immediacy, salience, and attentiveness are relevant to points of origin, to where people learn about authority, then the least likely scenario, surely, is that people begin with the polity and generalize from it to the family and the workplace. People pay relatively little attention to politics; politics rates low on their priorities (Figure 2-6), and to the extent that it does command attention, the demand is typically short and episodic (Zaller, 1992). All this is about where authority orientations may originate. How they are expressed, and where they are generalized to, is a different issue, about which more will be said in the next chapter.

Conclusions

This chapter began by highlighting some of the spectacular demographic shifts that have taken place in the character of the family over the last two decades. On the strength of that evidence alone, it is tempting to conclude that the changing nature of the family must have been accompanied by equally dramatic shifts in "family values," in people's preferences about the family. The WVS data do not cover every aspect of family values, but they do touch on some of the more important ones. Clearly, there have been important changes, particularly for women, in the relationships between work, family, and child-rearing. Not surprisingly, these shifts complement what is arguably the most dramatic trend of the last two decades: the rapid influx of women into the full-time paid workforce. Even so, there are surprising levels of stability in the cross-time benchmark data. The family remains one of the most important priorities in people's lives, and huge majorities of publics still consider marriage to be important. There is also some evidence of stability in what might be considered fairly traditional attitudes to the family and marriage. That said, there are also indications of systematic change, and there are two dimensions that, in light of the findings presented in earlier chapters, are particularly noteworthy. One is that there are clear shifts in preferences about spousal relations: both women and men want spousal relations to be more egalitarian. The other is that parent-child relations are in transition: they are becoming less hierarchical. The scope of these shifts is not particularly dramatic; if anything, they are incremental. Not only are the shifts consistent across the twelve advanced industrialized states, but they are also systematically related to other background factors.

The substantively important aspect of these findings is how they contribute to the larger picture that began to emerge from analysis of political and economic value changes. Orientations toward authority is one coherent and recurring theme that unites some of the core changes that have taken place in the polity, the economy, and the family. And an explicit investigation of the relationships between these domains clearly indicates that these connections are systematic. If deference to authority is a core value, then one key dimension of change between 1981 and 1990 is that all publics in these twelve states became less deferential in their outlooks towards politics, the workplace, and family life. The connectedness of these orientations and the shifts in levels jointly indicate the coherence of the pattern of change. Not all of the connections are uniformly powerful, and in some respects it is the variations that are intriguing. The task now is to look at our main findings, to consider them in their totality, and to return to the questions that were raised at the very start of this inquiry.

NOTES

[1] For an overview of the evolving character of the family in western societies, see Goldthorpe (1987).

[2] Most are less than gamma = .12. Note, too, that the age-spousal egalitarianism relationship is somewhat curvilinear, particularly among the Canadian and European publics. This may indicate the presence of some interaction with life-cycle factors. It is also possible to get sharper results by considering selected subgroups of each public. Those in the very youngest and oldest groups, for example, are least likely to have children in the household and less likely to have their decisions about the domestic divisions of labour "complicated" by child-related duties. The oldest respondents are also the most likely to be retired and so least likely to have "career effects" impinging on their orientations.

[3] For a slightly different but congenial interpretation of the rates of European change, see Jallinoja (1989).

[4] Note that the reported percentages are for those indicating they "strongly agree" with each statement.

[5] The associations are not particularly powerful, but they are all in a consistent direction. For age: Europe, gamma = -.15, United States = -.16, Canada = -.21; for education: Europe, gamma = .26, United States = .08, Canada = .11; for value type: Europe, gamma = .16, United States = .09, Canada = .09.

[6] The proportions of each sample indicating that the ideal family size was "no children" was minuscule, and there were no perceptible changes in this response between 1981 and 1990.

[7] In 1981 and 1990 the proportions agreeing with option (a) were as follows: United States, 72% and 75%; Canada, 66% and 67%; European countries, 68% and 70%, respectively.

[8] The list included good manners; independence; hard work; feeling of responsibility; imagination; tolerance and respect for other people; thrift, saving money and things; determination and perseverance; religious faith; unselfishness; and obedience. Note that responses to one item—"tolerance and respect for others"—were separately analyzed in the preceding discussion of tolerance (see Chapter 7).

[9] This index is similar to the conformity scale used by others (Akker, Halman, & de Moor, 1993; Inglehart, Nevitte, & Basanez, 1996). More precisely, it amounts to an expanded version of the non-conformity polarity of that scale.

[10] This is a WVS indicator that asks: "Overall, how satisfied or dissatisfied are you with your home life?" Respondents use a ten-point scale (1 = dissatisfied, 10 = satisfied) to indicate their level of satisfaction/dissatisfaction.

[11] It is important to note that Eckstein is not just interested in the family-polity dyad;

his investigations are more far-reaching and extend to superordinate-subordinate relations in all manner of "associational life"—schools, unions, professional associations, and so on. The point is that Eckstein places greater emphasis than Pateman on the family.

[12] For completely understandable reasons, researchers typically concentrate their efforts on within-domain issues: economists focus on economic questions, political scientists are preoccupied with the polity, and sociologists worry more about primary relations.

[13] Eckstein's case studies of Germany and Britain are intended to be "theory informing" and the other available data are limited because they are country specific and gathered at a single time point.

[14] Indicators of public attitudes toward authority in the family:
1. Mutual respect and appreciation makes for a successful marriage: (very important or rather important = 1; not very important = 0).
2. Understanding and tolerance makes for a successful marriage: (very important or rather important = 1; not very important = 0).
3. Sharing household chores makes for a successful marriage: (very important or rather important = 1; not very important = 0).
4. One does not have the duty to respect and love parents who have not earned it by their behaviour and attitudes: (agree = 1; disagree = 0).
5. Children should be encouraged to learn independence at home (important = 1; not important = 0).
6. Children should be encouraged to learn imagination at home (important = 1; not important = 0).
7. Children should be encouraged to learn obedience at home (important = 1; not important = 0).

[15] These data are the merged 1981 and 1990 findings. The very same finding emerges in every country at both time points.

[16] As with the general indicator of authority orientations in the family, the measure of political authority orientations relies on a composite additive index of the nine items identified in Chapter 3 as the components of political authority.
Indicators of public attitudes toward authority in the polity:
1. Signing a petition: (have done or might do = 1; would never do = 0).
2. Joining in boycotts: (have done or might do = 1; would never do = 0).
3. Attending unlawful demonstrations: (have done or might do = 1; would never do = 0).
4. Joining unofficial strikes: (have done or might do = 1; would never do = 0).
5. Occupying buildings or factories: (have done or might do = 1; would never do = 0).
6. Non-confidence in the armed forces: (not very much or not at all = 1; a great deal or quite a lot = 0).
7. Non-confidence in the police: (not very much or not at all = 1; a great deal or quite a lot = 0).
8. Non-confidence in parliament: (not very much or not at all = 1; a great deal or quite a lot = 0).

9. Non-confidence in the civil service: (not very much or not at all = 1; a great deal or quite a lot = 0).

[17] In selecting the cases of Britain and Germany to illustrate these connections, the WVS data indicate that Eckstein chose one "strong case" (Germany) and "weak" one (Britain).

[18] To say that "greater respect for authority" is a "good thing" provides a partial picture. The unanswered questions might be: What kind of authority? How much more "authority" do people have in mind? Why is it a "good thing"?

[19] The connections that are least relevant are in the following dyads: self-actualization–non-confidence in institutions, self-actualization–worker participation, spousal relations–non-confidence in institutions, spousal relations–parent-child relations, and spousal relations–worker participation.

[20] Notice here that many of the connections across domains are stronger than those within domains. This might provide more strong evidence that people readily generalize across domains. Recall, though, that the dimensions were determined by factor-analytic techniques that limit within-domain correlations.

9: Patterns of Change

The WVS are a massive and extraordinarily rich body of evidence. Huge volumes of detailed information are an enormously valuable resource, but they present awkward problems of another sort—how to make sense of it all. Do you start with a theory, some sort of conceptual roadmap that guides all of the analysis that follows? Or do you begin with "thick description," immersing yourself in all of the evidence in the hope that some light will go on, that there will be a flash of insight that brings order to the mass of detail? There are pitfalls either way. The risk with the first approach is that the roadmap, or theory, determines the scope and focus of the search. Quite aside from the possibility that the theory may not pan out, the danger is that preoccupation with the roadmap introduces subtle blinkers, a tunnel vision that screens out important pieces of evidence, perhaps even the big story, which may have little or nothing to do with the theory one started with. The immersion approach is a good way to get a feel for the evidence, but how do you know which details are "important"? And what happens if there is no flash of inspired insight? Absent any guidelines whatsoever, the danger is that one ends up flailing about in an ever-thickening fog of incomprehensible detail.

The strategy adopted here has been an exploratory one that steers a middle course between these options. The starting point was a very basic observation: since the 1980s, Canadians seem to have experienced an extraordinary degree of turmoil, and much of that turbulence surfaced as clashes over values, fundamental differences in basic orientations to the political, social, and economic world. That observation was followed by what can best be described as hunches about what the sources of the turmoil might be. Hunches fall well short of a theory, but they do flag a range of possible explanations. The task then became one of combing the available evidence to see which hunches survived a more detailed probing and which ones fell by the wayside. The approach is short on elegance, but the pay-off is that a wider range of possibilities remain open longer.

One central claim has been that there is detectable order in the value shifts that have occurred, that the trajectories of value change conform to a coherent pattern. It is simply not possible to present all of the evidence at once, but seeing different chunks of evidence a piece at a time makes it difficult to get a clear fix on just how extensive or coherent the patterns really are. What does the pattern look like when the key findings are brought together and considered from a broader vantage point? Table 9 -1 summarizes nearly all of the

Table 9-1 Directions of Value Change in 12 Advanced Industrial Countries, 1981–1990

Dimensions	Direction of Change		Correlated with:		Value Type
			Age	Education	
Political Orientations					
Interest in politics	rising	12/12	yes (+)	yes (⌒)	yes (-)
Confidence in government institutions	falling	10/12	yes (-)	yes (-)	yes (+)
Confidence in Non-government institutions	falling	10/12	yes (+)	yes (-)	yes (+)
Protest potential	rising	11/12	yes (⌒)	yes (+)	yes (+)
Civil permissiveness	rising	9/12	yes (+)	yes (+)	yes (-)
General deference	falling	10/12	yes (-)	yes (-)	yes (-)
National pride	rising	7/12	yes (-)	yes (-)	yes (-)
Cosmopolitanism	rising	8/12	yes (+)	yes (+)	yes (+)
Economic Orientations					
Importance of work	falling	9/11	yes (-)	yes (+)	yes (-)
Support for meritocracy	rising	12/12	yes (+)	yes (+)	yes (+)
Pride in work	rising	12/12	yes (v)	yes (+)	yes (-)
Worker expressiveness	falling	7/12	yes (+)	yes (-)	yes (+)
Workplace obedience	falling	6/12	yes (-)	yes (+)	yes (-)
Worker participation	rising	6/12	yes (+)	yes (-)	yes (+)
Job satisfaction	falling	8/12	yes (+)	yes (+)	yes (-)
Financial satisfaction	falling	7/12	yes (+)	yes (+)	yes (-)

Social Orientations

Importance of God	falling	10/12	yes (+)	yes (-)	yes (-)
Church attendance	falling	10/12	yes (+)	yes (-)	yes (-)
Moral permissiveness	rising	10/12	yes (-)	yes (+)	yes (+)
Principle of tolerance	rising	12/12	weak	yes (+)	yes (+)
Social intolerance	rising	11/12	yes (+)	yes (-)	yes (-)
Racial intolerance	rising	9/12	yes (+)	yes (-)	yes (-)
Political intolerance	rising	11/12	yes (-)	yes (-)	yes (-)
Egalitarian spousal relations	rising	12/12	yes (-)	yes (+)	yes (+)
Egalitarian parent-child relations	rising	12/12	yes (-)	yes (+)	yes (+)

Note: The dimensions in boldface are the six indicators of authority orientations.
Source: 1981 and 1990 World Values Surveys.

various dimensions of change that have been the focus of more detailed investigation in the previous chapters. Most of the indicators included in the table are not just single responses to individual WVS questions: nearly all are compound indicators that aggregate multiple items from the WVS. The robustness of these indicators has been repeatedly documented elsewhere. The regularity of these findings is truly impressive. Begin with the left-most column and consider first the directions of change. In every advanced industrial state considered, citizens became more interested in politics. Over the same period, citizen confidence in a whole array of governmental institutions (parliaments and civilian bureaucracies of one sort or another) dwindled, as did confidence in a variety of non-governmental institutions such as the education system, the media, and churches. At the same time, people became more inclined to approve of protest types of political behaviour, and support for a variety of social movements increased. Politics became more boisterous and citizens more cranky.

The pattern is striking in two respects. First, there is the extent to which the directions of the shifts are replicated from one setting to the next. The interpretive issue hinges on plausibility: Are these shifts just random? Could they be just a matter of happenstance? Suppose, for the sake of illustration, that the shifts in one country have nothing to do with what happens in others. In this extreme hypothetical case, the value dynamics of one public are assumed to be unrelated to the dynamics of others; they are independent[1]. For that interpretation to hold water, there should be evidence of "randomness" in the aggregate findings. One indication of random dynamics would be that, on any single value dimension, publics in six of the twelve states are moving in one direction while publics in the other six states are moving in the opposite direction. By these standards, *some* value shifts, such as national pride, may indeed be more or less random: national pride increased in seven countries and declined in the other five. In the economic domain, aggregate support for greater employee participation inched up, but there were clear increases only in six of the twelve countries considered. These particular findings, however, are isolated ones; they are exceptions not the rule. According to Table 9-1, there is decisive evidence that the value shifts have been moving in the same direction in an overwhelming number of cases. Expressed numerically, publics in at least two-thirds of the twelve countries moved in the same direction on twenty-one of the twenty-five value dimensions considered. Equally striking is the *breadth* of the changes. These dynamics are plainly *not* limited to the political domain; significant shifts are taking place across a whole range of economic and social values as well and, indeed, the shifts in social values are the most consistent of all.

As regards the directions of change, then, the most plausible interpretation is that there *have* been significant value shifts and the transformations are *not* random. That conclusion has a variety of implications, and prompts yet another question: What are the root causes of these shifts?

We began by considering the issue of Canadian value change, and from that vantage point Chapter 1 canvassed three possibilities, or hunches, about why Canadians experienced value shifts between 1981 and 1990. The first viewed Canada as an advanced industrial state and suggested that the turmoil Canadians experienced might be traceable to the rhythms of late industrialism that are common to such states. The second hunch raised the possibility that Canadian value change had something to do with the country's position on the North American continent. From this perspective, Canadians are characterized as unusually well-exposed receptors of value dynamics that flow *from* the United States *to* Canada. The third hunch focussed on patterns of population replacement. Canada is a society with an atypically high volume of immigrants; perhaps the influx of large numbers of people not socialized in the country is a significant source of net value change. The three perspectives work at different levels of analysis and emphasize alternative sources of value change, and there is no reason to believe they are mutually exclusive. It may be, for instance, that advanced industrialism is responsible for some value shifts and proximity to the United States accounts for others, with yet other shifts attributable to the influx of new people. Keeping in mind that there are a variety of possible combinations, however, there is still the question: do the cumulative findings favour one perspective over others?

Canada as an Advanced Industrial State: Perspective 1

The cross-national consistency of the directions of value change (the left-most column of Table 9-1) is impressive; it provides strong circumstantial evidence in favour of the first perspective. If the value changes across multiple value dimensions are consistent across all of these advanced industrial states, then the shifts might well be attributable to the common features shared by these states. Other evidence in Table 9-1 reinforces that same conclusion. For example, the same background variables, age and education, are related to each of the various dimensions in strikingly similar ways in different countries. In all twelve countries, older people and those with more education tend to be more interested in politics. In nearly all countries, older people and those with less formal education have more confidence in governmental institutions. The patterns emerge with impressive regularity across a wide range of political, social, and economic values. The young and the better educated, for example, tend to be more cosmopolitan; they give a higher priority to worker expressiveness and are more likely to want greater participation in workplace decision-making. The young and the better educated are also more secular, express higher levels of "moral permissiveness" and "civil permissiveness," and are consistently more egalitarian than their older counterparts in their attitudes to spousal and parent-child relations. Where education, or age, is related to particular values in one country, it is nearly always related in the same way to the same values in other countries. The very same patterns are replicated again and again in different countries.

Few doubt that the "rhythms of late industrialism" *are* associated with a variety of such shifts. More contentious are two other issues: Where do these shifts come from? And where are they going to? Some observers site the origins of these changes in the weakening of the traditional class divide, whereas others variously connect the shifts to the collapse of the welfare state, the evolution of new ideological axes, the rising "cognitive capacity" of publics, the emergence of new values, or some combination of these factors (Dalton, 1990; Halman and de Moor, 1993; Huntington, 1974; Inglehart, 1990(a); Kitschelt, 1989; Offe). It is not possible to provide a definitive direct test of every conceivable explanation, but there is very strong evidence that the changes documented are consistent with Inglehart's (1990(a)) post-materialist value change explanation. As the right-most column of Table 9-1 demonstrates, value type is systematically associated with every single value domain considered, and once again the links between value type and each value dimension are replicated in country after country. The conclusion to draw from that finding is not that emerging post-material orientations are the *only* cause of every value change documented, for the post-materialist explanation is consistent with other accounts. But the result does mean that the emergence of post-materialism remains a candidate explanation for the political, economic, and social value shifts in the twelve publics.

When all of the data in Table 9-1 are considered together, another important theme emerges: many of these shifts may be generationally driven, they are most deeply embedded within a particular generation and are carried by that increasingly influential generation throughout its life-course. With cross-sectional evidence of the sort coming from the WVS, it is not possible to prove that every one of these changes is generational in nature. A huge volume of panel data collected in every country for two or three decades would surely help to increase the certainty of such an interpretation. Lacking those data, the issue, in the final analysis, turns on a matter of plausibility. Inglehart and others have gone to great lengths to determine whether post-materialist value orientations are generational or not, and the weight of the evidence is that they are (see Abramson & Inglehart, [1995, 1992]; Clarke & Dutt, [1991]; Inglehart, [1988, 1990]). Other disinterested investigators using a variety of different strategies have examined the same kind of evidence and arrived at a similar conclusion: values, like ideologies, are generationally transmitted (Jennings, 1987). For reasons already outlined, a simple correlation between age and values is not sufficient to make the case for generational change; only when a number of different indicators all point in the same direction does the case for generational change become compelling. Throughout this investigation, the argument has been that a stronger case for generational interpretation can be made if at least three conditions are satisfied: the value dimension must be related to an indicator of population turnover—age; it must *also* be related to an indicator of structural change—education; *and* it must be related to an indicator of value orientations—Inglehart's post-materialism index. A significant number of the value dimensions in Table 9-1 do meet all three of these conditions. Consider the case of confidence in governmental institutions. Levels of citizen confidence in these institutions are falling, and this orientation is systematically associated with the young, *and* those with high levels of education, and post-materialists. In the political domain, the same holds for deference, civil permissiveness, and national pride and cosmopolitanism. Using the same three criteria, the evidence suggests that shifting economic orientations may also be generationally driven. Generational effects may underpin shifts in how much importance people attach to work, worker expressiveness, workplace deference, and employee participation. As for social orientations, generational patterns seem most clearly to apply to moral permissiveness, religious orientations, tolerance, and aspects of family relations.

These findings do not mean that all of the value changes documented in Canada and elsewhere can only be caused by the rise of post-materialist values. All of this evidence favouring the advanced-industrial state-perspective has to be considered in a broader context. Is there also empirical support for rival explanations?

Canada as a North American State: Perspective 2

What about the perspective of Canada as a North American state? The WVS data are particularly pertinent to this perspective, not least of all because they are the only data available for undertaking direct comparisons of the economic, social, and political values of both North American publics. That they do so across time makes them even more valuable. That Canadian value change is a consequence of proximity and exposure to the United States is a well-worn theme, that draws on convincing accounts of how cultural orientations travel from one setting to the next. Furthermore, this perspective contains very clear expectations about both the directions and consequences of value change. As Irving Louis Horowitz (197) has cogently argued, the value differences between Canada and the United States may reflect longstanding structural differences between the two countries. But if the value differences between the two countries are attributable to structural differences, then as those structural conditions change, so should values. There is ample evidence indicating that American and Canadian structural conditions have become more alike (Chapter 1); following Horowitz's line of argument, then, we might expect Canada's "cultural lag" behind the United States to have become less pronounced. But there is another implication to be drawn from this argument: regardless of whether the value differences between the two countries really are attributable to structural differences, the clear expectation is that Canadian values would follow behind those in the United States. It is in this respect that the United States shows Canada the picture of its own future. Do the WVS data support this line of interpretation?

Table 9-2 considers the same value dimensions reported in Table 9-1, but

Table 9-2 Value Change in the United States and Canada, 1981–1990

Dimensions	Direction of Change	U.S.–Canada Movement from 1981–1990	Leader of Trend in 1990 (U.S.–Canada)	Overall Leader of Trend in 1990 highest/lowest
Political Orientations				
Interest in Politics	rising	parallel	Canada	W. Germany
Confidence in government institutions	falling	converging	Canada	Italy
Confidence in non-government institutions	falling	converging	Canada	Netherlands
Protest potential	rising	diverging	Canada	Italy
Civil permissiveness	rising	parallel	Canada	Belgium
General deference	falling	parallel	Canada	W. Germany
National pride	falling	parallel	Canada	Germany
Cosmopolitanism	rising	diverging	U.S.	Italy
Economic Orientations				
Importance of work	falling	parallel	Canada	Belgium
Support for meritocracy	rising	converging	U.S.	U.S.
Pride in work	rising	parallel	U.S.	U.S.
Worker expressiveness	falling	parallel	Canada	France
Workplace obedience	falling	converging	Canada	Italy
Worker participation	rising	parallel	Canada	Spain
Job satisfaction	U.S. (rising) Canada (falling)	converging	—	Denmark (highest) France (lowest)
Financial satisfaction	U.S. (rising) Canada (falling)	converging	—	Netherlands (highest) France (lowest)

Social Orientations

Importance of God	falling	parallel	Canada	Denmark
Church attendance	U.S. (rising) Canada (falling)	diverging	—	Ireland (highest) Denmark (lowest)
Moral permissiveness	rising	diverging	Canada	Netherlands
Principle of tolerance	rising	diverging	Canada	Netherlands
Social intolerance	rising	parallel	U.S.	U.S.
Racial intolerance	rising	parallel	U.S.	Belgium
Political intolerance	rising	parallel	U.S.	W. Germany
Egalitarian spousal relations	rising	parallel	Canada	Canada
Egalitarian parent-child relations	rising	diverging	Canada	Denmark

Note: The dimensions in boldface are the six indicators of authority orientations.
Source: 1981 and 1990 World Values Surveys.

this time the focus narrows to just Canada and the United States. As before, begin with the *directions* of change. In nearly every case, Canadian and American values seem to be shifting more or less in tandem. Between 1981 and 1990 the directions of change were the same on twenty-two of the twenty-five dimensions presented. Of the only three exceptions, two involve economic indicators—job satisfaction and financial satisfaction—and in both of these instances Americans reported rising levels, whereas Canadian levels fell. The other exception is church attendance: between 1981 and 1990 church attendance rates in Canada fell, as they did in Europe, but they climbed marginally in the United States.

What were the *consequences* of these shifts? Were the value orientations of Canadians and Americans more alike in 1990 than in 1981? On this point, a neat and decisive answer is more difficult to supply, but key to this particular interpretation are the data in the second column of Table 9-2. Theoretically at least, there are three possible trajectories of 1981–1990 value shifts: (1) Canadian and American values may have converged—become more alike; (2) they may have diverged—become less alike; or (3) the prevailing value shifts may have simply moved along a parallel trajectory, which is to say that they may have both risen or fallen and been no closer in 1990, give or take the margin of error, than they were in 1981. A straightforward arithmetic count indicates that the prevailing pattern is one of parallel value change, and that finding is not surprising, because the 1981–1990 period is a relatively short time frame for shifts in basic orientations to take place. Of the twenty-five dimensions, there is parallel change on thirteen dimensions, convergence on six dimensions, and divergence on six others. In other words, Canadians and Americans became more alike in some respects but more different in others. The problem with a simple arithmetic count, however, is that it is a very rough metric; it pays no heed to what, arguably, are the substantively more intriguing features of these results: the patterns of value change are *not* evenly distributed. When it comes to the cluster of *political* values, there is no easily identifiable distributional pattern: Canadian and American orientations converge on two dimensions, diverge on two others, and for the remainder the trajectory is one of parallel change. When it comes to the other two domains, however, there are detectable variations in the patterns: between 1981 and 1990, the period during which free trade was an issue of vital interest to Canadians, Canadian and American publics became more alike in their economic orientations: they *converged*. With social values, however, the trend is in the opposite direction and the evidence, on balance, indicates *divergence*.

What about the cultural lag part of the explanation? Is there any support for Horowitz's (1973) idea that Canadian values follow along behind American ones? Once again, the answer is not so simple. Where the trajectories of value change are the same in the two countries, that is, where both are rising or both are falling (column 1, Table 9-2), the critical question becomes: Which public leads the trend?[2] Key to this interpretation are the data in the right-most half of Table 9-2. Column 3 reports the Canada–United States comparisons, and column 4 indicates which of the twelve countries leads the prevailing trend. Of the twenty-five dimensions considered, twenty-two qualify for these kinds of lead-lag evaluations[3], and of these it is the values of Canadians, not Americans, that lead. There is no ambiguity on this score: Canadian value shifts led on sixteen of the dimensions considered, and Americans on six. In other words, Canadian value shifts led American ones by a ratio of better than two to one. Nor do the clusterings of the data indicate any particular sphere of values—the political, economic, or social—in which Canadians lag their American counterparts. It could be, of course, that American values led Canadian value shifts in the past, but the argument that Canadian values lag American ones or, more radically, that Canadian values are changing because they are becoming "Americanized," finds little support in these data—at least for these particular value dimensions and the particular period covered by the WVS. In the broader context, American values seem to lead those taking place throughout the advanced industrial states on three dimensions, two of which, pride in work and support for meritocracy, amount to what others have identified as core American economic values (McClosky & Zaller, 1984). But are Americans so exceptional in even these respects? West Germans and Danes are each leaders on four dimensions, and the Dutch lead on three. Canadians lead on one dimension: egalitarian spousal relations.

Canada as an Immigrant Society: Perspective 3

With the third perspective, focus narrows once again: attention now shifts to within-Canada value differences and variations. At the core of this perspective is the expectation that new Canadians, those not born in the country, may bring to Canada values that are significantly different from those of the cultural mainstream—anglophone and francophone Canadians. As before, context is everything, and judgements about whether new Canadians qualify as outliers depends on where this particular group stands in relation to the others.[4] Among non-immigrants, for example, is there evidence of value convergence or divergence? As before, Table 9-3 brings together cumulative evidence from preceding chapters, beginning with the directions of value change.

In the vast majority of cases, on nineteen of the twenty-five dimensions considered, anglophone and francophone trajectories of value change are the same. Once again, however, of greater interest than the actual count are the locations of the discrepant shifts. Some are entirely predictable. For instance, in the political domain "national pride" declined among francophones between 1981 and 1990 and increased among anglophone Canadians over the same period. Notice, though, that there are *no* discrepancies between the two groups in the directions of social value change, and the values of the two groups actually shifted in opposite directions on fully *half* of the economic values. The divergence-convergence consequences of these shifts vary depending on the domain being considered. On balance, anglophone and

Table 9-3 Value Changes Within Canada, 1981–1990

Dimensions	Direction of Change		English-French Movements 1981–1990	Are New Canadians Outliers?
	English	French		
Political Orientations				
Interest in politics	rising	rising	parallel	yes (+)
Confidence in government institutions	falling	rising	parallel	no
Confidence in non-government institutions	falling	falling	parallel	no
Protest potential	rising	rising	diverging	no
General deference	falling	falling	parallel	no
National pride	rising	falling	diverging	no
Cosmopolitanism	rising	rising	diverging	yes (+)
Economic Orientations				
Importance of work	falling	falling	converging	no
Support for meritocracy	rising	rising	converging	no
Pride in work	rising	falling	diverging	no
Worker expressiveness	falling	falling	diverging	no
Workplace deference	rising	rising	converging	yes (−)
Worker participation	rising	falling	converging	yes (+)
Job satisfaction	stable	stable	parallel	no
Financial satisfaction	falling	rising	diverging	no

Social Orientations

Importance of God	falling	falling	diverging	no
Church attendance	falling	falling	converging	*
Moral permissiveness	rising	rising	diverging	no
Principle of tolerance	rising	rising	converging	*
Social intolerance	rising	rising	parallel	*
Racial intolerance	rising	rising	parallel	*
Political intolerance	rising	rising	parallel	no
Egalitarian spousal relations	rising	rising	parallel	*
Egalitarian parent-child relations	rising	rising	diverging	no

Note: * indicates that the value lies within the margin of error (± 3%), (+) indicates that the 1990 value for new Canadians was highest, (-) indicates that the 1990 value for new Canadians was lowest. The dimensions in boldface are the six indicators of authority orientations.
Source: 1981 and 1990 World Values Surveys.

francophone respondents seem to have *diverged* in their political orientations and *converged* on economic ones.

To determine precisely where new Canadians fit into this larger matrix of Canadian values, and to identify exactly the scope and origins of the variations and similarities, would require huge amounts of extremely detailed data. For example, chances are slim that new Canadians of non-European origin would have social, economic and political values identical to descendants of Canadians of European origin who settled generations ago. To provide a comprehensive account of precisely what contribution each immigrant group makes to the larger Canadian value matrix would require far more detailed documentation of the value profiles of each immigrant group. Lacking those data, another strategy is to ask: When all new Canadians are considered together, are there aggregate differences between this segment of the population and the two other groups—francophone and anglophone Canadians who were born in the country? The results reported in the right-most column of Table 9-3 are based on a rough calculation: they simply take the aggregate scores for anglophones and francophones on each value dimension as the upper and lower limits—the range of Canadian-born respondents. Then the question becomes: Do the aggregate scores for new Canadians' values fall within, or outside, that range? If the scores for new Canadians consistently lie *outside*, then the claim that the influx of new Canadians is a significant source of value change is a credible one. But if they are consistently *within* this range, it becomes more difficult to argue that the influx of new Canadians is responsible for steering "Canadian values" off in novel directions. These results have to be interpreted with a great deal of caution, but they are instructive.[5] Surprisingly, new Canadians qualify as outliers on only four of the twenty-five dimensions analysed. New Canadians turn out to be more interested in politics than others, a finding that can be attributed to the relatively high level of education of this group. Not surprisingly, new Canadians are also more cosmopolitan, more likely to think of themselves as "world citizens." When it comes to the workplace, new Canadians are more inclined than others to want more participation in workplace decision-making, and they are least inclined to exhibit unswerving obedience in following workplace instructions. The most remarkable finding, perhaps, is that there appear to be *no* significant differences between new Canadians and others on *any* of the social values.

Which of the three perspectives is the most compelling? Judgements about the merits of alternative explanations are necessarily comparative ones. What counts is not just how much empirical support there is for a perspective, but whether that perspective does better than its rivals. On balance, the findings favour the first perspective: the direction, content, and style of Canadian value change has a great deal in common with the transformations taking place in other advanced industrial states. First, there are the striking similarities between the patterns of value change in Canada and in other advanced industrial states. Second is the consistent impact of such structural factors as age and education. Also impressive is the extent to which the indicators of one variant of the advanced industrial state perspective, post-materialism, consistently line up behind nearly all of the value changes in ways that the theory predicts. Furthermore, the empirical support for each of the other two perspectives is relatively weak, in some respects surprisingly so. Why, for instance, is there is so little support for the second perspective, the popular and intuitively appealing hunch that attributes Canadian value change to the influence of the United States? One possibility that has to be taken seriously is that the time frame captured by the data is the "wrong one." Arguably, the findings might have been different had the WVS data covered another and ideally longer period. Then again, it might be that survey data are just not adequate to the task or that the WVS simply do not ask the right questions. There is yet another possibility: the lack of support for the "Americanization of Canada" perspective could also have something to do with post-materialism. Recall that of the twenty-five value dimensions considered, nearly all are systematically related to post-materialist orientations; so it is conceivable that Canadians may lead their American counterparts on many of these value dimensions because they are "further ahead," or have been more deeply affected by the values associated with late industrialism. As has already been demonstrated, post-materialist value orientations emerged earlier and are more widespread in Canada than in the United States (figure 2-15).

There is both comfort and risk in settling on a single explanation. In some respects, the advanced industrial state explanation is an attractive one; there is a sense in which this particular account makes the turmoil Canadians have faced since the early 1980s easier to understand and even to accept. One implication is that the conflicts Canadians experienced during the decade should not be taken to mean that Canadian institutions are peculiarly inadequate, or the country's leadership is unusually inept. Instead, the perspective suggests that the roots of the turbulence are byproducts of transformations that, to a lesser extent, are of our own making. There is a risk, though, of attributing too much to one explanation. It is one thing to claim that the deeper causes of Canada's turbulence have something in common with the causes of similar phenomena in other states. But to argue that all of the difficulties of the decade are wholly attributable to, and merely derivative of, the "rhythms of late industrialism" is not at all convincing. For one thing, such a claim is excessively deterministic; it runs into trouble because it leaves no room for other, demonstrably important, factors. For example, what about the role of institutions? Institutions are vital, and institutional environments interact with and mediate values in complex ways (North, 1990; Putnam 1993). Citizens of the twelve countries do not live in identical institutional settings, and those settings undoubtedly shape interests and public values in quite different ways. In some environments, institutional frameworks may constrain or mute the expression of particular behaviours and values, while in other settings, the national matrix of institutions may provide outlets, opportunities, that amplify them. Then again, what about structural conditions? To say that the twelve countries are structurally similar does not mean they are identical. Nowhere in these pages is it argued that values are "disembodied," that values fly free of structural or institutional conditions, that they are immune to profound structural transformations, or even that they respond to such structural shifts in identical ways. The extent to which value changes induce structural transformation or are merely reflections of structural change remains a profoundly controversial and largely unresolved issue. But there are very powerful reasons for supposing that structural shifts and value changes are intimately connected. To claim that all of the changes experienced by Canadians are wholly attributable to the value shifts associated with late industrialism and that value shifts stand aloof from institutional arrangements or structural conditions of a national setting is hardly credible. The point, rather, is that of the three hunches that have been explored throughout the book, one version of the advanced industrial state explanation—the post-materialist variant—does much better than the others.

There are other risks too. One is that in accepting a single explanation too wholeheartedly, we take a chance that the search for alternative accounts will become less enthusiastic. The antidote to that hazard is skepticism. For analytical purposes, try a mental experiment. Suppose that, for whatever reason, one has reservations about the advanced industrial state perspective, or more particularly, that one finds the post-materialist version of that perspective troubling or unconvincing. Post-materialism might "explain" too much or too little. Perhaps there are doubts about the way the theory combines notions of security with socialization effects. Or concern could be rooted in more technical considerations: Are the indicators adequate? Do they really measure what they are supposed to measure? Is the post-materialism/materialism value divide genuinely a unidimensional one, or does the instrumentation behind the index force undimensionality on the data? All of these issues have been vigourously thrashed out elsewhere (Bean & Papadakis, 1994; Boltken & Jagodzinski, 1985; Flanagan, 1987; Lafferty and Knutsen, 1985; Marsh, 1975, 1977; Van Deth, 1983), and the balance of the case still seems to favour Inglehart's theory (Abramson & Inglehart, 1995; Bakvis & Nevitte, 1987; Bean & Papadakis, 1994(a), 1994(b); de Graaf, 1988; Hellevik, 1994; Inglehart, 1994). If after all this dust has cleared, one still remains unconvinced, then another serious question arises: Is there anything left from all of the preceding analysis if the post-materialist component is set aside?

The question is a challenging one, and there are at least two preliminary observations to make before attempting a reply. First, quibbling with one particular explanation, or one variant of a perspective, does not alter any of the other basic findings that have been documented throughout. That is, after the post-materialist interpretation is set aside and if all those aspects of the findings are thrown out the window, there still remains the problem of providing an explanation for the remarkably consistent patterns of economic, political, and social value change that have been documented. The conceptual problem does not go away just because one particular explanation is found to be unattractive. Instead, the ground shifts to another question: Is there a better alternative explanation for all of the regularities in the patterns of value change?

Second, as the investigation has unfolded other strands of interpretation have emerged. One set of findings, findings that cut across political, economic, and social domains alike, concern coherent and systematic shifts in orientations towards authority. These findings are substantively important, and they stand on their own merits regardless of what one makes of the post-materialist perspective. Disqualifying, ruling out, or "setting aside" the post-materialist interpretation shifts the analytical spotlight and gives far more prominence to these particular results. Looking for "what is left" necessarily means adopting an alternative focus and searching in other directions. The challenge then becomes one of knowing what to make of this second unifying theme. For these reasons, it is useful to continue the mental experiment, to revisit the issue of orientations towards authority from a slightly different vantage point, and to press this line of investigation a little further.

Revisiting Authority Orientations

The longstanding justification for examining authority relations is that it is "a neglected concern." No such justification is necessary in the Canadian case, because if there is one well-entrenched self-image it is the idea that Canadians are "deferential," that they are relatively passive, that they are attracted to "order" and unusually acquiescent to elite direction (Bell, 1992). That image, like other conventional wisdoms, may well have been true in the past, and one has to look no further than Porter's (1965) pioneering study of Canadian society to find a persuasive and influential body of evidence substantiating it: deference is an orientation that is entirely consistent with, even necessary to, a society in which elites are closely interconnected and whose place in Canadian society, until relatively recently, was relatively unchallenged. Quite aside from the opportunity to explore the contemporary relevance of conventional wisdoms about Canadian culture, there are far more compelling reasons to be interested in authority traits. Orientations towards authority are fundamental to how democracies work. Eckstein and Gurr eloquently capture the central issue: "the traits of authority that members of social units think of as most important are those that determine how and whether members comply, cooperate, resist, or work for transformation" (1975: 361). From this standpoint, authority orientations are not just like any other set of orientations. They are profoundly political and intimately connected to the democratic culture of a society; they are fundamental to legitimacy, and to the stability and effectiveness of collective life (Eckstein & Gurr, 1975).

The world of Canadian politics seems to provide some of the most dramatic illustrations of just how divisive and contentious Canadian public life has been since the 1980s and it may be no coincidence that the most coherent and striking findings to emerge from the analysis are the pervasive shifts in orientations towards political authority. Shifting the analytical spotlight away from post-materialism and fixing instead on orientations towards authority brings at least two other questions immediately into view: What are the explanations for shifting orientations towards authority? Are those shifts in any way related to the recent turbulence of Canadian politics?

There are at least two kinds of explanations for why such shifts in orientations towards political authority might have taken place. One takes us back to advanced industrial society explanations, and the other draws on congruency theory. Of the late industrialism genre there are at least three testable variants. First, the familiar post-materialist argument cannot be ignored because Inglehart (1990(a)) explicitly shows that the spread of post-material orientations encourages new styles of political action, including elite-challenging behaviours. The presumption, then, is that the rise of post-materialist *values* will be associated with the decline of deference. At first blush, configuring the problem this way round seems a not so subtle way of bringing this perspective in through the back-door in order to keep it "in play." But as will become immediately apparent, the post-materialist perspective now faces a more crowded theoretical field; it becomes just one among many possibilities.

The second variant to come from the advanced industrial states genre places the emphasis on *structural changes*, particularly the link between rising levels of education and growing interest in politics—citizens are more "cognitively mobile" than before, and "cognitive mobilization means that citizens possess the level of political skills and resources necessary to become more self-sufficient in politics" (Dalton, 1988: 18). Consequently, when it comes to making important political decisions these more knowledgeable, skilled, and attentive publics are not only more likely to know and care about these issues, but are also less reliant on cues from traditional sources of political authority (Dalton, 1988). More than that, the narrowing of the skill gap between elites and publics is emancipating in the sense that it makes citizens and leaders more equal.

The third variation concerns a newly emerging set of *ideological beliefs*. According to Herbert Kitshelt (1989, 1990, 1994), a keen observer of west European social democratic movements, a "new left libertarian" ideology is transforming the traditional ideological landscape of advanced industrial states in vital ways. Kitschelt contends that "new left libertarians" differ from the traditional left in that they are highly mobilized citizens who "accept important issues on the socialist agenda, but reject traditional socialism's paternalistic-bureaucratic solutions [centralized state planning] as well as the primacy of economic growth over 'intangible' social gratifications" (1990(a): 180). New left libertarians advocate increased levels of participatory democracy and believe that groups and individuals should have the autonomy to define their economic, political and cultural institutions without interference from the marketplace or bureaucracies. The clear implication is that the decline of deference may be linked to the emergence of new left libertarian beliefs.

At one level, these three "explanations" are close allies: they are all concerned with different aspects of a common underlying dynamic, the transition from smokestack industrialism to late industrialism. But on closer inspection it is also clear that each explanation is analytically quite distinct. Values, knowledge skills, and ideology are not the same things; they tap individual characteristics that are conceptually different. Furthermore, each explanation implicates different variables as the chief culprit behind changing public orientations towards authority; for that reason it should be possible to mount distinct empirical tests that evaluate the merits of each explanation quite separately.

To these three explanations two more can be added, each of which comes from different specifications of congruency theory (the idea that orientations towards one aspect of authority are linked to others). If, as has already been demonstrated in Chapters 4, 6, and 8, orientations towards authority are generalizable from one domain to the next, then it is entirely possible that shifts in orientations towards *political* authority may, as Eckstein (1966, 1969) argues, be related to shifts in orientations towards authority in the *family*. Alternatively, as Pateman (1970: 50–53) suggests, orientations to political authority may be rooted in shifts in authority in the *workplace*.

There are a variety of ways to evaluate the relative merits of these five plausible explanations, but at this stage two considerations are paramount. What is required is a strategy that discriminates between each of the theoretically plausible accounts and pits each explanation against the others. In evaluating these competing perspectives it is also useful to try to screen out "noise," sources of variation that could be attributable to other factors. A slightly more complicated multivariate approach, regression analysis, addresses these concerns; it can be configured to consider in a single estimation *all* of the theoretically important indicators that are plausible predictors of orientations towards political authority. In practical terms, this means entering as predictors indicators of post-materialist value orientations (Inglehart's post-materialism index); indicators of cognitive mobilization (Dalton's combined index that includes level of formal education, frequency of political discussion, and levels of political interest); and an indicator tapping Kitschelt's new left libertarianism. Also included are the two measures of orientations towards workplace (Pateman) and family (Eckstein) authority. Then, to make the test a conservative one and to screen out sources of noise, "cynics" are included—those people whose irritations with the political order are traceable to unhappiness with life in general (life satisfaction) or personal financial situation (financial satisfaction).[6] Following conventional practice, a variety of standard socio-demographic markers are included in these estimations. Now to the substantive findings.

Table 9-4 reports the results of four separate regression analyses, each of which explores how well the various standardized "predictor variables" (those in the left-most column) determine orientations towards political authority. The left-most column of coefficients provides the benchmark data—the aggregate findings for all twelve countries. The remaining columns report the

Table 9-4 Regression Analysis: Predictors of Political Authority Orientations
(Standardized Beta Coefficients)

Predictors		12 Advanced Industrial Countries	Western Europe	United States	Canada
Personal	Life satisfaction	-.06**	-.07**	-.05	-.08**
satisfaction	Financial satisfaction	-.07**	-.06**	-.12**	-.08**
Broad-gauged shifts	Postmaterial orientations	.15**	.17**	.10**	.09**
	Cognitive mobilization	.15**	.13**	.19**	.19**
	Left libertarianism	.07	.09**	.005	.02
Authority	Worker-expressiveness	.01	-.01	.08**	.06**
orientations	Worker-participation	.10**	.12**	.05	.10**
	Spousal relations	.01	.01	-.04	.01
	Parent-child relations	.11**	.12**	.10**	.09**
Religiosity		-.10**	-.13**	-.08**	-.12**
Socio-	Age	-.20**	-.18**	-.17**	-.19**
demographics	Male	.05**	.06**	.04	.08**
	Income	-.001	.004	.05	.09**
	Catholic	.01	.03**	-.02	.05*
	Constant	.47**	.44**	.59**	.50**
	R-squared	.25	.29	.19	.24

*significant at $p < .05$; **significant at $p < .01$.
Source: 1981 and 1990 World Values Surveys (weighted results).

results for the same tests applied separately to three subgroups: the ten West European countries, then the United States and, separately, Canada.

As has been shown elsewhere, levels of personal and financial satisfaction do have a bearing on people's political orientations, and with the single exception of the United States (life satisfaction), all findings are significant and in the predicted direction. People with lower levels of life/financial satisfaction also tend to be less deferential to political authority.[7] After these "screening" considerations are set aside, the substantively more intriguing question is: Which of the five plausible remaining accounts best predicts orientations towards political authority? The important consideration here is that the regression strategy means each of the explanations, in effect, competes against the others. Consequently, the coefficients listed in Table 9-4 indicate how much of the variation in orientations towards political authority is attributable to each predictor *after* the effects of the other predictors have been taken into account.

First, consider the three variants of the late industrial state perspective—what are labelled the broad-gauged shifts. Of these, the first two—Inglehart's post-materialist values and Dalton's cognitive mobilization account—are significant predictors in all cases, but there is variance in how well they work. Post-materialism is as good as, or better than, cognitive mobilization in predicting the aggregate and Western European data. Cognitive mobilization, however, is clearly a far stronger predictor for the two North American countries. The new left libertarian explanation only features as a significant predictor in Western Europe, a finding that might well be attributable to the absence, in North America, of a West European style of social democratic tradition.

What about the two other possible explanations, those that come directly from congruency theory? In this case, each dimension of workplace and family authority orientations is considered in its decomposed form. On balance, and supporting Eckstein's prediction, parent-child authority orientations seem to be a slightly stronger predictor of orientations towards political authority. It is a significant predictor of orientations to political authority in every setting with about the same effect; the coefficients are stable. Worker participation is also significant, but there are also variations; the estimates are less uniform. As Pateman's theory predicts, people who want more participation in workplace decision-making are *less* deferential. That finding applies to both Western Europe and Canada. Notice, though, that it does *not* apply to the United States. There are also continental variations. In both the United States and Canada, worker expressiveness significantly predicts orientations towards political authority, but that finding is not replicated among the west European publics. If we are forced to choose between the five explanations, then, the conclusions turn out to be slightly different for different settings. In Western Europe post-materialist values seem to count the most, whereas in North America it is cognitive mobilization that has the strongest empirical support.

Socio-demographic indicators are also important. Indeed, in the Canadian case, every single socio-demographic indicator turns out to be a significant predictor of orientations towards political authority. Of all indicators considered, age is consistently the most powerful single predictor: the young are consistently less deferential than their older counterparts. That age *and* post-materialist value orientations *and* cognitive mobilization are all significant predictors and that the impact of each predictor is still significant *after the effects of the others are taken into account* are substantively important findings. They point to the conclusion that the shifting orientations towards political authority involve more than just life-cycle effects; they are not just a matter of people becoming more "authoritarian" as they get older, so that the young will mellow and grow out of their rebelliousness with the passage of time. A more likely explanation is that these coherent shifts are generationally driven. Orientations to political authority seem to be the product of a combination of values and structural factors. If the shifts are indeed bound up in the dynamics of generational change, then the decline of deference cannot be dismissed as a short-term "blip"; it is more likely to be a relatively robust and long-term feature of political life.

What about within the Canadian polity? Do the same interpretations apply to francophones, anglophones and new Canadians? Here there are significant between-group variations, with the most striking differences between new Canadians and those in the other two groups. The detailed findings are reported in Appendix 9-A. The sharpest contrasts are between anglophones and new Canadians. For anglophone Canadians, eleven out of the fourteen indicators are statistically significant predictors of orientations towards political authority. But for new Canadians, only three of the fourteen predictors are statistically significant. Moreover, for this group there is support for only one of the five explanations proposed at the outset—parent-child relations. Along with parent-child relations, religiosity and gender count the most: those who are the least religious and males are significantly less deferential than their religious and female counterparts. The surprising finding is that for new Canadians age does not count at all. The anglophone-francophone variations are less dramatic, but they are nonetheless interesting. Post-materialist orientations, worker expressiveness, parent-child relations, are all significant predictors of political authority orientations for anglophones but not francophones; for the latter, cognitive mobilization turns out to be by far the most important predictor.[8]

The results coming from the multivariate analysis are helpful in a number of respects. Certainly, the picture that emerges is more nuanced, but it is one that illustrates quite plainly an important general point. First, the results very clearly demonstrate that more than one aspect of the "rhythms of late industrialism" accounts for shifts in orientations towards political authority. Both structural (cognitive mobilization) and value (post-material) aspects of late industrialism jointly, and separately, contribute to the decline of political deference. Second, the results also indicate some support for the predictions of congruency theory: different aspects of family and workplace authority orientations are also relevant, and these are separately and independently significant predictors. Overall, the post-materialist value change interpretation remains a plausible source of a core set of changes, even after other explanations are brought into play. Significantly, however, other structural aspects of late industrialism also contribute to the changes described. The predictive power of indicators of family and workplace authority orientations could have overwhelmed the other predictors.[9] The point to underscore is that they did not.

Authority Orientations and the Status Quo

These additional findings can be taken in several directions. One interpretation that brings all of the results together is that changing orientations towards political authority is one defining face of the political life of late industrial states. Certainly, that interpretation complements the observations of analysts working from very different perspectives. For instance, Rosenau, who is mainly interested in transnational dynamics, characterizes the "puzzle of the 1980s" in terms of a reallocation of authority (1992: 256). Flanagan argues that a central feature of domestic socio-political change is a shift from "a devotion to authority to cynicism and self-assertiveness" (1982: 403–43), and Ester and colleagues (1993), analyzing similar evidence, attach the label "individualization" to the process. There is productive overlap, perhaps, in the perspectives coming from both congruency theorists (Eckstein & Gurr, 1975; Pateman, 1970) and analysts of late industrialism (Huntington, 1974): the turmoil of the last decade or so, the challenges to the political status quo, may be part of the rhythms of late industrialism, but they also appear to be more specifically grounded in changing orientations towards authority.

Definitively demonstrating that the *dynamics* of authority orientations are connected to challenges to the political status quo is more difficult. The WVS contain no single indicator that cleanly captures citizen orientations towards the political status quo. Nonetheless, for the purposes of conducting a "plausibility probe," we can turn to an indirect indicator of "support for changing the political status quo" that is configured from a combination of responses to two questions used in the 1990 version of the WVS. Respondents were presented with two separate statements and asked to indicate where they stood on each (disagree completely; disagree somewhat; neither agree nor disagree; agree somewhat; agree completely): (a) "our government should be made much more open to the public," and (b) "political reform in this country is moving too rapidly."

The basic findings, presented in Table 9-5, are straightforward: a huge majority of citizens in every country believes that government should be more open, and Canadians are among the most enthusiastic supporters of that idea. On whether political reform is too rapid there is less consensus. For the purposes of a plausibility test, the indirect indicator of attitudes towards the political status quo can be configured from those respondents who agree (somewhat or completely) with statement (a) and who also disagree (somewhat or completely) with statement (b) Column 3 of Table 9-5 combines both of these responses into a single additive index that taps *support* for changing the political status quo.[10]

This index is a rough gauge but it may be sufficient to detect any hint of a connection between orientations towards various aspects of authority and support for changing the political status quo. If authority orientations are congruent and if publics have become progressively less deferential, then it seems improbable that citizens would be as content as before with the political status quo. The approach is broad and inclusive: it considers both the indicator of general orientations towards authority with which we began and the two indicators of the two dimensions of political, economic and family authority orientations. Figure 9-1 reports the connections (gamma coefficients) for the merged results from all twelve countries and then those for the West European publics. Figure 9-2 reports exactly the same links for the United States and Canada.

Table 9-5 Support for Changing the "Political Status Quo" 1990

Country	Government should be made more open	Political reform is moving "too slow"	Support for changing the current political status quo
France	95.1	44.6	41.7
Britain	85.8	45.5	45.4
West Germany	88.6	37.6	39.7
Italy	86.1	55.0	55.3
Netherlands	77.8	63.5	50.7
Denmark	85.5	38.8	39.3
Belgium	85.7	35.8	38.0
Spain	85.7	39.7	45.9
Ireland	88.1	61.0	62.9
Northern Ireland	84.0	51.4	49.6
United States	82.9	46.6	46.6
Canada	90.8	44.1	49.9
English	91.1	44.3	53.1
French	92.0	39.1	38.4
New Canadians	88.3	48.8	52.6

Questions: "I am going to read out some statements about the government and the economy. For each one, could you tell me how much you agree or disagree? Please use the responses on this card.

    A. Our government should be made much more open to the public
        1. Disagree completely
        2. Disagree somewhat
        3. Neither agree nor disagree
        4. Agree somewhat
        5. Agree completely
    B. Political reform in this country is moving too rapidly
        1. Agree completely
        2. Agree somewhat
        3. Neither agree nor disagree
        4. Disagree somewhat
        5. Disagree completely"
Column 1 above includes those that "agree somewhat," and "agree completely" with question A, while column 2 includes those that "disagree somewhat" and "disagree completely" with question B. Column 3 is an additive index composed of columns 1 and 2.
Source: 1990 World Values Survey.

The general findings correspond to what one would expect: people who are *least* deferential are also *most* inclined to want changes to the political status quo. Not surprisingly, the general authority orientations indicator is reasonably strong.[11] Nor does it come as any surprise to discover that the "protest activity" indicator is strongly related to support for changing the political status quo; indeed, it would be remarkable if it were not. On spousal relations, the links are stable but also relatively weak, and this too is entirely consistent with the previous findings. In all of these respects, the results ring true.

Far more interesting are the variations in the strength of the other connections. Compare the Canadian and American results (Figure 9-2) with the West

Figure 9-1 Links between Authority Orientations and Public Support for the "Political Status Quo"

12 Advanced Industrial Countries

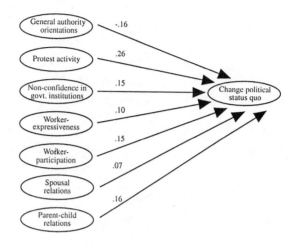

Western Europe

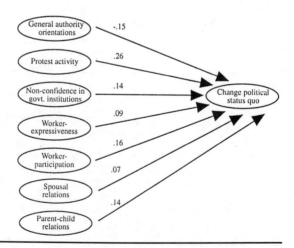

Source: 1990 World Values Survey.

European results (Figure 9-1). For one thing, the connections between non-confidence in governmental institutions and support for *changing* the political status quo are significantly stronger for North Americans than for Europeans. More interesting still are the Canadian results for worker participation and parent-child relations: in both cases the links to support for changing the status quo are powerful, much stronger than for any other public. Indeed, the Canadian parent-child relations coefficients are about twice as strong as those

Figure 9-2   Links between Authority Orientations annd Public Support for the "Political Status Quo"

United States

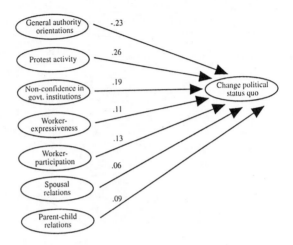

Canada

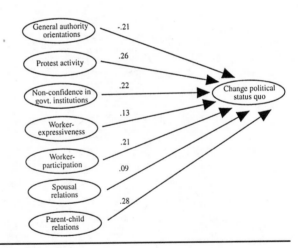

Source: 1990 World Values Survey.

found in Europe, and are stronger even than the coefficient for protest activity. A more detailed investigation indicates that these findings are replicated among anglophone and francophone Canadians (Appendix 9-B). In sum, it is in the Canadian setting that congruency theory seems to work best.

This re-assessment of authority orientations was prompted by a challenge: is there anything left from the preceding investigation if post-materialist value change considerations are set aside? The answer, surely, is yes. Shelving

Inglehart's broad-gauged account of value change in late industrial states is a revealing experiment for two reasons. First, the strategy shifts the analytical spotlight onto other substantive findings, findings that may have been given too little attention. Second, the alternative perspective injects balance and underscores an important earlier point: post-material value orientations is but one of several candidate interpretations of late industrialism. Bringing authority orientations to the centre of the analysis reinforces the conclusion that post-materialist values do indeed count: under more stringent and controlled conditions post-materialist orientation still has significant explanatory power when it confronts rival explanations even after key structural characteristics are taken into account. At the same time, it also becomes clear that post-materialism does not account for everything; it does not, for example, decisively outperform other explanations. As has just been demonstrated (Table 9-4), Dalton's cognitive mobilization account, a structural explanation, does just as well as Inglehart's post-material-value-based account in explaining orientations towards political authority. If the decline of deference is one of the defining characteristics of late industrialism, then according to the analysis above, it is rooted in more than value shifts; it is attributable to *both* structural and value dynamics.

Searching for patterns, weighing alternative perspectives, and conducting mental experiments are retrospective strategies that help increase confidence in the interpretations of the findings. What emerges? Some findings are crystal clear. Significant value changes have taken place in Canada, and the scope and direction of those changes look very much like those experienced by publics in other advanced industrial states. Some conventional wisdoms about Canadian values do not appear to hold water, and many of the findings also challenge long-standing interpretations of Canadian-American value differences and similarities. Our purpose, though, is not to take aim at these specific interpretations; it is to see what can be learned about Canadian values and value change by taking the broad view, a viewpoint that both places Canadian values in the context of other advanced industrial states and explores the connections between the economic, political, and social value domains.

As pure description, the investigation of direct and comparable value evidence yields an intriguing portrait. There is more to it, though, than description; there is progress on the theoretical front. In addition to demonstrating that Canadian value change is consistent with explanations provided by analysts of late industrialism, the results put empirical flesh on the bones of congruency theory. This in several respects: there is a clear demonstration that authority traits are multidimensional. Indeed, one core finding is that there are more dimensions to authority orientations than others have supposed. Also clearly illustrated is the coherent structure of these orientations. Significantly, the very same structure is replicated in multiple countries at different time points. Furthermore, in empirically probing the architecture of authority orientations—the connectedness of these orientations—we find indications that authority orientations are generalizable. People do not generalize from one authority domain to another with equal efficiency; the crucial point that has both theoretical and practical implications is that some authority orientations are both generalizable and in transition.

The process of empirically poking around authority orientations has been revealing in other respects: the findings shed light on some key limitations of earlier versions of congruency theory. As others have observed, congruency theory pays no attention to the *dynamics* of shifting authority orientations (Barry, 1978). The theory is underspecified in other respects as well: Precisely when do patterns of authority qualify as "congruent"? At what point do differences in authority orientations become significant disjunctures or important discrepancies? Are there critical thresholds that, when breached, induce democratic instability or plummeting support for the status quo? All of these unanswered questions are as intriguing and important now as when they were first proposed. They become far more complex when dynamic considerations are introduced. The twelve countries analyzed in this volume are probably not the ideal ones for pursuing these questions further: in the broad scheme of things, all qualify as stable democracies. More information about the relations between patterns of authority and democratic stability could be gleaned from a broad range of countries some of which qualify as unstable, with a mixture of rapid and slow shifts in authority orientations. With such a range of cases, it would also be useful to investigate the implications of discrepancies in authority traits for democratic stability. These large issues remain to be investigated.

Quite aside from these descriptive and theoretical aspects of findings, there are practical questions. Do the patterns of change and the spread of post-materialist value orientations mean that Canadians, and citizens in other late industrial states, are doomed to a future marked by increasing levels of turmoil and confrontation? And are the trajectories of change stable or transitory? Post-materialist value orientations are contingent upon economic conditions, and those conditions do not always follow a smooth path. For that reason, Inglehart does not claim that post-materialist value orientations will grow at all times or at a steady pace. Think back to the initial demonstration of the generational bases of post-materialist value orientations. The evidence is that the ranks of the post-materialist legions are swelling, or at least they have been since the late 1960s. Even so, there are clear indications that post-materialist value orientations are sensitive to shifts in the economic environment, and particularly to people's sense of economic security (Figure 2-4). Levels of post-materialism actually declined during the oil price crisis of the late 1970s and the economic slowdown of the early 1980s. The impacts of those particular downturns were relatively short lived, and equally impressive is the extent to which levels of post-materialist orientations recovered, returning to something like the "normal" pattern for the post-war period. It is possible, of course, that with prolonged hard times, the growth of post-materialist orientations could stall or even reverse. If the rhythms of late industrialism were only a matter of values, then it would be much easier to make the case that these transformations are unstable or transitory. As much of the preceding analysis makes clear, however, structural factors are also implicated, and it is less probable that structural conditions are as variable.

The rise of educated publics may well be rooted in profound structural changes in the characteristics of advanced industrial states and be driven by technological demand, by the needs of an increasingly sophisticated workplace, the need to be competitive in a world where information is increasingly vital to economic prosperity. It is unlikely that the shift from the old economy to the new will simply reverse. If the "object-processing occupations" continue to decline and "client-interactive occupations" continue to emerge (Kitschelt, 1994), demand for an educated workforce (perhaps even better educated) will also continue. The further expansion of educational opportunities and rapid dissemination of information have a variety of consequences: people are better informed, are better able to independently process information and make sense of the information available to them. The expansion of educational opportunities also means people will become more interested in and attentive to public life; and a growing body of evidence indicates that informed and interested people make decisions differently from those who are uninformed and less interested (Johnston et al., 1996; Sniderman, Brady, & Tetlock, 1991). In short, the rise of an increasingly competent and sophisticated public also means the emergence of a less compliant public.

These structural changes place a premium on key elements of creative thinking—analytical capacity, curiosity, willingness to challenge old assumptions—all of which are the prerequisites of innovation, the engine of competitive new economies. In increasingly "information-sensitive" economies, it is sound economic practice to encourage publics to sharpen these skills, to create environments in which they will flourish, and to structure incentives around the acquisition of these capacities. But how realistic is it to suppose that citizens so equipped will then place limits on how and where these information-acquiring and -processing skills are applied? The essential point comes from our own evidence: people do generalize from one environment to the next. Having flatter hierarchies in the workplace, for example, has implications that go well beyond the confines of the economy. It is unlikely that accumulation of these skills, which are inspired by structural shifts in the economy, is a trend that will go into reverse. Precisely how people choose to use these skills, however, may have much more to do with values.

In the abstract, of course, there is reason to welcome the emergence of a public that is increasingly interested, attentive, knowledgeable, and articulate. These are just the kind of citizens that all democracies should want. By the same token, such publics present significant challenges for governance. Perhaps the most vivid illustration of the growing independence of citizens in recent Canadian experience is the Charlottetown Accord. Nearly all of the country's "respectable" elites urged Canadians to vote yes in that referendum. But citizens voted no. The difficulties of governing, perhaps, would be most keenly felt by organizations that still cling to hierarchical structures. For them the challenge is how to adjust their institutional frameworks to accommodate the new reality. One implication of the findings presented is that the new citizens are less likely than their predecessors to be satisfied with any form of authoritarianism, be it of the political right or the political left. Nor are they as satisfied with authoritarianism in the workplace or the family. Citizens cut from the newer cloth, certainly, are more attracted to formations that are "bottom-up," but they are also better equipped to separate the reality from the rhetoric and to act on the basis of the judgements they reach.

The decline of deference, whatever its source, presents a monumental challenge. How to restore faith in government? How to renew confidence in leaders and institutions, and to restore the depleted reservoirs of trust? And how to reverse a deeper slide into cynicism? The chances of successfully meeting these challenges begins with an understanding of the shifting *priorities* of publics. That understanding also has to take into account the impressive expansion in the *capacities* of citizens. But these alone are not enough; they must be accompanied by an appreciation of the reality that citizen evaluations of their political world are intimately tied to their social and economic worlds.

NOTES

[1] The opposite extreme is that all of the identifiable changes are interdependent, in which case all of the changes for each and every public would be the same.

[2] For example, if between 1981 and 1990 Canadian values approached American 1981 levels, then this is taken to indicate support for the "cultural lag" explanation: American values lead their Canadian counterparts. But if American 1981–1990 value changes approach Canadian 1981 levels, then Canadian values lead those of their American counterparts.

[3] As has already been indicated, three do not qualify because Canadians and American values are not moving in the same direction: job satisfaction, financial satisfaction, and church attendance.

[4] Recall that the categories are defined broadly: anglophone Canadians are defined simply as those outside of Quebec who were interviewed in English and were born in Canada. Francophones are those who were interviewed in French in Quebec and were born in Canada. New Canadians are all respondents who indicated they were not born in Canada.

[5] These data have to be interpreted extremely cautiously because mean scores do *not* indicate the variance. It is theoretically possible that each individual group of immigrants scores in the "outlier" range but when the data for all groups are aggregated the resulting mean falls within the range. Recall, too, that the data for new Canadians come from a single time point only (1990). Thus, the data in column 3 of Table 9-3, compare new Canadians with those in the other groups at that time point only.

[6] There are a number of variations of the connection between levels of personal satisfaction/disatsifaction and support for the status quo; see Tomassen (1990). In the Canadian setting, analysis shows that this segment of the public is relatively small but

nonetheless significant (Kanji & Nevitte, 1995). For present purposes, the goal is to screen out other sources so that we can, as far as possible, isolate the independent effects of each of the primary theories under consideration.

[7] Notice that there are striking differences between financial satisfaction of American and West European respondents: for Americans the financial satisfaction coefficient is twice as powerful.

[8] Notice, too, that the socio-demographic variables are also much more powerful predictors for francophones.

[9] Family and workplace authority orientations, after all, are conceptually closer to political authority orientations than are the other indicators.

[10] The indicator clearly taps a political dimension, but the results based on the index have to be interpreted cautiously. The index assumes that "more open government" is the key direction of change and that the rate of change is critical.

[11] The negative sign on the coefficient is a conceptually consistent finding, not a perverse one, because the item taps those *agreeing* with the statement "a greater respect for authority in the future would be a *good thing*."

Appendix 9-A   Regression Analysis: Predictors of Political Authority Orientations within Canada
(Standardized Beta Coefficients)

Predictors		English Canadians	French Canadians	New Canadians
Personal satisfaction	Life satisfaction	-.09**	-.09**	-.06
	Financial satisfaction	-.09**	-.07	-.02
Broad-gauged shifts	Postmaterial orientations	.10**	.07	-.01
	Cognitive mobilization	.18**	.25**	.01
	Left libertarianism	.02	.02	.06
Authority orientations	Worker-expressiveness	.07**	.01	.12
	Worker-participation	.11**	.11**	.06
	Spousal relations	-.02	.03	.10
	Parent-child relations	.08**	.08	.19*
Religiosity		-.12**	-.05	-.18**
Socio-demographics	Age	-.22**	-.22**	-.01
	Male	.06*	.13**	.14*
	Income	.07*	.11*	.15
	Catholic	.02	.12**	-.07
	Constant	.55**	.44**	.36**
	R-squared	.24	.30	.22

*significant at $p < .05$; **significant at $p < .01$.
Source: 1981 and 1990 World Values Surveys (weighted results).

Figure 9-B   Links between Authority Orientations and Public Support for the "Political Status Quo"

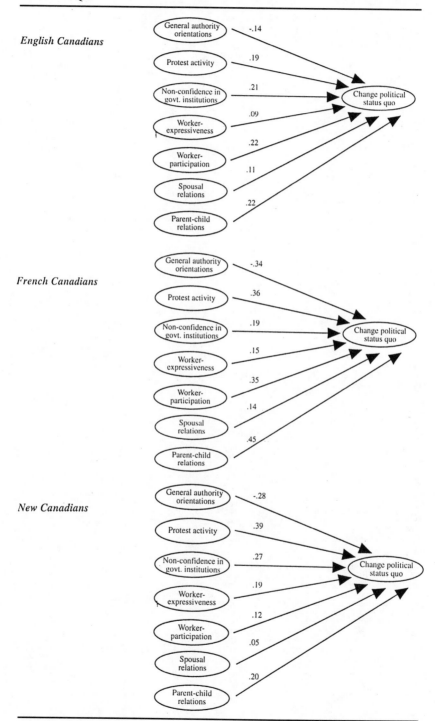

Appendix: World Values Survey

SHOW CARD A
116 Please say, for each of the following, how important it is in your life.

	Very important	Quite important	Not important	Not at all important	DK
A Work	1	2	3	4	9
B Family	1	2	3	4	9
C Friends and acquaintances	1	2	3	4	9
D Leisure time	1	2	3	4	9
E Politics	1	2	3	4	9
F Religion	1	2	3	4	9

122 When you get together with your friends, would you say you discuss political matters frequently, occasionally or never?

Frequently	1
Occasionally	2
Never	3
Don't know	9

123 When you, yourself, hold a strong opinion, do you ever find yourself persuading your friends, relatives or fellow workers to share your views? If so, does it happen often, from time to time, or rarely?

Often	1
From time to time	2
Rarely	3
Never	4
Don't know	9

SHOW CARD B
124 I am now going to read out some statements about the environment. For each one I read out, can you tell me whether you agree strongly,

agree, disagree or strongly disagree? (Read out each statement and code an answer for each)

	Strongly agree	Agree	Disagree	Strongly disagree	DK
A I would give part of my income if I were certain that the money would be used to prevent environmental pollution	1	2	3	4	9
B I would agree to an increase in taxes if the extra money is used to prevent environmental pollution	1	2	3	4	9
C The Government has to reduce environmental pollution but it should not cost me any money	1	2	3	4	9
D All the talk about pollution make people too anxious	1	2	3	4	9
E If we want to combat unemployment in this country, we shall just have to accept environmental pollution	1	2	3	4	9
F Protecting the environment and fighting pollution is less urgent than often suggested	1	2	3	4	9

130 Taking all things together, would you say you are ... (Read out, reversing order for alternate contacts)

Very happy	1
Quite happy	2
Not very happy	3
Not at all happy	4
Don't know	9

SHOW CARD C

131 Please look carefully at the following list of voluntary organizations and activities and say ...
   a) which, if any, do you belong to? (Code all 'yes' answers under (a))
   b) which, if any, are you currently doing unpaid voluntary work for? (Code all 'yes' answers under (b))

	a	b	
A Social welfare services for elderly, handicapped or deprived people	1	1	
B Religious or church organizations	1	1	
C Education, arts, music or cultural activities	1	1	
D Trade unions	1	1	
E Political parties or groups	1	1	
F Local community action on issues like poverty employment, housing, racial equality	1	1	
G Third world development or human rights	1	1	
H Conservatives, the environment, ecology	1	1	
I Professional associations	1	1	
J Youth work (e.g. scouts, guides, youth clubs etc.)	1	1	
K Sports or recreation	1	1	
L Women's groups	1	1	
M Peace movement	1	1	
N Animal rights	1	1	
O Voluntary organizations concerned with health	1	1	
P Other groups	1	1	
None	1	-	
Don't know	9	-	
None	-	1	Skip to
Don't know	-	9	Q. 216

SHOW CARD D

167 Thinking about your reasons for doing voluntary work, please use the following five point scale—where "1" means "unimportant" and 5 means "very important"—to indicate how important each of the reasons below have been *in your own case*.

	Unimportant			Important	DK
A A sense of solidarity with the poor and disadvantaged	1	2 3 4		5	9
B Compassion for those in need	1	2 3 4		5	9
C An opportunity to repay something, give something back	1	2 3 4		5	9
D A sense of duty, moral obligation	1	2 3 4		5	9
E Identifying with people who were suffering	1	2 3 4		5	9
F Time on my hands, wanted something worthwhile to do	1	2 3 4		5	9
G Purely for personal satisfaction	1	2 3 4		5	9

H Religious beliefs	1	2 3 4	5	9
I To help give disadvantaged people hope and dignity	1	2 3 4	5	9
J To make a contribution to mylocal community	1	2 3 4	5	9
K To bring about social or political change	1	2 3 4	5	9
L For social reasons, to meet people	1	2 3 4	5	9
M To gain new skills and useful experience	1	2 3 4	5	9
N I did not want to, but could not refuse	1	2 3 4	5	9

SHOW CARD E

216   On this card are various groups of people. Could you please read out any that you would not like to have as neighbours? (Code an answer for each)

	Mentioned	Not Mentioned
A People with a criminal record	1	2
B People of a different race	1	2
C Left wing extremists	1	2
D Heavy drinkers	1	2
E Right wing extremists	1	2
F People with large families	1	2
G Emotionally unstable people	1	2
H Muslims	1	2
I Immigrants/foreign workers	1	2
J People who have kids	1	2
K Drug addicts	1	2
L Homosexuals	1	2
M Jews	1	2
N Hindus	1	2

230   All in all, how would you describe your state of health these days? Would you say it is (Read out reversing order for alternate contacts)

Very good	1
Good	2
Fair	3
Poor	4
Very poor	5
Don't know	9

231 We are interested in the way people are feeling these days. During the past few weeks, did you ever feel ... (Read out and mark one code for each statement)

	Yes	No
A Particularly excited or interested in something	1	2
B So restless you couldn't sit long in a chair	1	2
C Proud because someone had complimented you on something you had done	1	2
D Very lonely or remote from other people	1	2
E Pleased about having accomplished something-	1	2
F Bored	1	2
G On top of the world/feeling that life is wonderful	1	2
H Depressed or very unhappy	1	2
I That things were going your way	1	2
J Upset because somebody criticized you	1	2

241 Generally speaking, would you say that most people can be trusted or that you can't be too careful in dealing with people?

Most people can be trusted   1
Can't be too careful   2
Don't know   9

SHOW CARD F
242 Some people feel they have completely free choice and control over their lives, and other people feel that what they do has no real effect on what happens to them. Please use this scale to indicate how much freedom of choice and control you feel you have over the way your life turns out?

None at all								A great deal		Dk
1	2	3	4	5	6	7	8	9	10	99

SHOW CARD G
244 All things considered, how satisfied are you with your life as a whole these days? Please use this card to help with your answer.

Dissatisfied								Satisfied		Dk
1	2	3	4	5	6	7	8	9	10	99

SHOW CARD H
246a Why are there people in this country who live in need? Here are four possible reasons. Which one reason do you consider to be most important? (Code one under (a) below)

247b And which reason do you consider to be the second most important?
(Code one under (b) below)

	Most important	Second most important
Because they are unlucky	1	1
Because of laziness and lack of willpower	2	2
Because there is injustice in our society	3	3
It's an inevitable part of modern progress	4	4
None of these	5	5
Don't know	9	9

SHOW CARD I

248 Here are some aspects of a job that people say are important. Please look at them and tell me which ones you personally think are important in a job? (Code all mentioned)

A Good pay   1
B Pleasant people to work with   1
C Not too much pressure   1
D Good job security   1
E Good chances for promotion   1
F A job respected by people in general   1
G Good hours   1
H An opportunity to use initiative   1
I A useful job for society   1
J Generous holidays   1
K Meeting people   1
L A job in which you feel you can achieve something   1
M A responsible job   1
N A job that is interesting   1
O A job that meets one's abilities   1
   None of these   1

ASK ALL WORKING (Others skip to question 270)

265 How much pride, if any, do you take in the work that you do? (Read out)

A great deal	1
Some	2
Little	3
None	4
Don't know	9

SHOW CARD J

266 Overall, how satisfied or dissatisfied are you with your job?

Dissatisfied								Satisfied		Dk
1	2	3	4	5	6	7	8	9	10	99

SHOW CARD K

268 How free are you to make decisions in your job? Please use this card
to indicate how much decision-making freedom you feel you have.

None at all								A great deal		Dk
1	2	3	4	5	6	7	8	9	10	99

ASK ALL

SHOW CARD L

270 Here are some statements about why people work. Irrespective of
whether you have a job or not, which of them comes closest to what
you think?

Work is like a business transaction. The more I get paid, the more I do; the less I get paid, the less I do	1
I will always do the best I can, regardless of pay	2
Working for a living is a necessity, I wouldn't work if I didn't have to	3
I enjoy working but I don't let it interfere with the rest of my life	4
I enjoy my work; it's the most important thing in my life	5
I never had a paid job	6
Don't know	9

277 Imagine two secretaries, of the same age, doing practically the same
job. One finds out that the other earns $50 a week more than she does.
The better paid secretary, however, is quicker, more efficient and more
reliable at her job. In your opinion is it fair or not fair that one secretary is paid more than the other?

Fair	1
Unfair	2
Don't know	9

SHOW CARD M

278 There is a lot of discussion about how business and industry should be
managed. Which of these four statements comes closest to your opinion? (Code one only)

The owners should run their business or appoint the managers   1
The owners and the employees should participate in the selection
   of managers   2
The government should be the owner and appoint the managers   3
The employees should own the business and should elect the
   managers   4
Don't know   9

SHOW CARD N

279 People have different ideas about following instructions at work.
Some say that one should follow instructions of one's superiors even
when one does not fully agree with them. Others say that one should
follow one's superior's instructions only when one is convinced that
they are right. With which of these two opinions do you agree?

Should follow instructions   1
Must be convinced first   2
Depends   3
Don't know   9

316 Do you agree or disagree with the following statements?

	Agree	Disagree	Neither	DK
A When jobs are scarce, men have more right to a job than women	1	2	3	9
B When jobs are scarce, people should be forced to retire early	1	2	3	9
C When jobs are scarce, employers should give priority to Canadian people over immigrants	1	2	3	9
D It is unfair to give work to handicapped people when able bodied people can't find jobs	1	2	3	9

SHOW CARD O

320 How satisfied are you with the financial situation of your household?

Dissatisfied								Satisfied		DK
1	2	3	4	5	6	7	8	9	10	99

322 How often, if at all, do you think about the meaning and purpose of
life? (Read out in reverse order for alternate contacts)

Often	1
Sometimes	2
Rarely	3
Never	4
Don't know	9

323 Do you ever think about death? Would you say ...

Often	1
Sometimes	2
Rarely	3
Never	4
Don't know	9

324 I am going to read out a list of statements about the meaning of life. Please indicate whether you agree or disagree with each of them. (Read out in reverse order for alternate contacts)

	Agree	Disagree	Neither	Dk
A Life is meaningful only because God exists	1	2	3	9
B The meaning of life is that you try to get the best out of it	1	2	3	9
C Death is inevitable, it is point-less to worry about it	1	2	3	9
D Death has a meaning only if you believe in God	1	2	3	9
E If you have lived your life, death is a natural resting point	1	2	3	9
F In my opinion, sorrow and suf-fering only have meaning if you believe in God	1	2	3	9
G Life has no meaning	1	2	3	9

SHOW CARD P

331 Here are two statements which people sometimes make when dis-cussing good and evil. which one comes closest to your own point of view?

A There are absolutely clear guidelines about what is good and evil. These always apply to everyone, whatever the circumstances.

B There can never be absolutely clear guidelines about what is good and evil.

What is good and evil depends entirely upon the circumstances at the time.

Agree with statement A   1
Agree with statement B   2
Disagree with both   3
Don't know   9

332a   Do you belong to a religious denomination?

Yes	1	Go to Q. 333b
No	2	Go to Q. 334c

333b   (If yes) Which one? (Code under (b) below)

334c   (If no) Were you ever a member of a religious denomination? Which one? (Code under (c) below)

	b	c
Roman Catholic	1	1
Church of England (Protestant)	2	2
Free Church/Non-Conformist/Evangelical	3	3
Jew	4	4
Muslim	5	5
Hindu	6	6
Buddhist	7	7
Other (Specify) _____	8	8
Never	-	0
Did not state	9	9

ASK ALL
335   Were you brought up religiously at home?

Yes	1
No	2

SHOW CARD Q
336   Apart from weddings, funerals and christenings, about how often do you attend religious services these days?

More than once a week	1
Once a week	2
Once a month	3
Christmas/Easter day	4
Other specific holy days	5
Once a year	6
Less often	7
Never/Practically never	8

337 Do you personally think it is important to hold a religious service for any of the following events?

	Yes	No	Dk
Birth	1	2	9
Marriage	1	2	9
Death	1	2	9

340 Independently of whether you go to church or not, would you say you are ... (Read out reversing order)

A religious person	1
Not a religious person	2
A convinced atheist	3
Don't know	9

341 Generally speaking, do you think that your church is giving, in your country, adequate answers to ... (Read out and code one answer for each)

	Yes	No	Dk
A The moral problems and needs of the individuals	1	2	9
B The problems of family life	1	2	9
C People's spiritual needs	1	2	9
D The social problems facing our country today	1	2	9

345 Do you think it is proper for churches to speak out on ...

	Yes	No	Dk
A Disarmament	1	2	9
B Abortion	1	2	9
C Third World problems	1	2	9
D Extramarital affairs	1	2	9
E Unemployment	1	2	9
F Racial discrimination	1	2	9
G Euthanasia	1	2	9
H Homosexuality	1	2	9
I Ecology & environmental issues	1	29	
J Government policy	1	2	9

355 Which, if any, of the following do you believe in? (Read out and code one answer for each)

	Yes	No	Dk
A God	1	2	9

B	Life after death	1	2	9
C	A soul	1	2	9
D	The devil	1	2	9
E	Hell	1	2	9
F	Heaven	1	2	9
G	Sin	1	2	9
H	Resurrection of the dead	1	2	9
I	Reincarnation	1	2	9

SHOW CARD R

364 Which of these statements comes closest to your beliefs? (Code one answer only)

There is a personal God	1
There is some sort of spirit or life force	2
I don't really know what to think	3
I don't really think there is any sort of spirit, God or life force	4
Did not state	9

SHOW CARD S

365 And how important is God in your life? Please use this card to indicate—where 10 means very important and 1 means not at all important.

Not at all									Very	DK
1	2	3	4	5	6	7	8	9	10	99

367 Do you find that you get comfort and strength from religion?

Yes	1
No	2
Don't know	9

368 Do you take some moments of prayer, meditation or contemplation or something like that?

Yes	1
No	2
Don't know	9

369 How often do you pray to God outside of religious service? Would you say ...

Often	1
Sometimes	2
Hardly ever	3

Only in times of crisis	4
Never	5
Don't know	9

SHOW CARD T
370 Overall, how satisfied or dissatisfied are you with your home life?

Dissatisfied								Satisfied		DK
1	2	3	4	5	6	7	8	9	10	99

372 Are you currently ... (Read out and code one only)

Married	1
Living as married	2
Divorced	3
Separated	4
Widowed	5
Single	6

373 Have you been married before?

Yes, more than once	1
Yes, only once	2
No, never	3

ASK ALL EXCEPT SINGLES
374 Do (did) you and your partner share any of the following? (Read out and code all mentioned)

Attitudes towards religion	1
Moral standards	1
Social attitudes	1
Political attitudes	1
Sexual attitudes	1
None of these	1
Don't know	1

ASK ALL
416 And how about your parents? Do (did) you and your parents share any of the following? (Read out and code all mentioned)

Attitudes towards religion	1
Moral standards	1
Social attitudes	1
Political attitudes	1

Sexual attitudes	1
None of these	1
Don't know	1

423 If someone said that individuals should have the chance to enjoy complete sexual freedom without being restricted, would you tend to agree or disagree?

Tend to agree	1
Tend to disagree	2
Neither/it depends	3
Don't know	9

SHOW CARD U

424 Here is a list of things which some people think make for a successful marriage. Please tell me, for each one, whether you think it is very important, rather important or not very important for a successful marriage?

	Very important	Rather important	Not very important	DK
A Faithfulness	1	2	3	9
B An adequate income	1	2	3	9
C Being of the same social background	1	2	3	9
D Mutual respect and appreciation	1	2	3	9
E Shared religious beliefs	1	2	3	9
F Good housing	1	2	3	9
G Agreement on politics	1	2	3	9
H Understanding and tolerance	1	2	3	9
I living apart from your in-laws	1	2	3	9
J Happy sexual relationship	1	2	3	9
K Sharing household chores	1	2	3	9
L Children	1	2	3	9
M Tastes and interests in common	1	2	3	9

437 Have you had any children? If yes, how many?

No children	0	Skip to Q. 439
1 children	1	
2 children	2	
3 children	3	
4 children	4	
5 children	5	

6 children or more	6
Did not state	9

438 How many of them are still living at home?

None	0
1 children	1
2 children	2
3 children	3
4 children	4
5 children	5
6 children or more	6
Did not state	9

ASK ALL

439 What do you think is the ideal size of a family–how many children, if any?

No children	0
1 children	1
2 children	2
3 children	3
4 children	4
5 children	5
6 children	6
7 children	7
8 children	8
9 children	9
10 children or more	10
Don't know	99

441 If someone says a child needs a home with both a father and a mother to grow up happily, would you tend to agree or disagree?

Tend to agree	1
Tend to disagree	2
Don't know	9

442 Do you think that a woman has to have children in order to be fulfilled or is this not necessary?

Needs children	1
Not necessary	2
Don't know	9

443 Do you agree or disagree with the following statement? (Read out)

	Yes	No	Dk
Marriage is an outdated institution?	1	2	9

444 If a woman wants to have a child as a single parent but she doesn't want to have a stable relationship with a man, do you approve or disapprove?

Approve	1
Disapprove	2
Depends	3
Don't know	9

SHOW CARD V

445 People talk about the changing roles of men and women today. For each of the following statements I read out, can you tell me how much you agree with each. Please use the responses on this card.

	Strongly Agree	Agree	Disagree	Strongly Disagree	Dk
A A working mother can establish just as warm and secure a relationship with her children as a mother who does work	1	2	3	4	9
B A pre-school child is likely to suffer if his or her mother works	1	2	3	4	9
C A job is alright but what most women really want is a home and children	1	2	3	4	9
D Being a housewife is just as fulfilling as working for pay	1	2	3	4	9
E Having a job is the best way for a woman to be an independent person	1	2	3	4	9
F Both the husband and wife should contribute to household income	1	2	3	4	9

SHOW CARD W

451 Which of these two statements do you tend to agree with? (Code one answer only)

A Regardless of what the qualities and faults of one's parents
   are, one must always love and respect them   1

B One does not have the duty to respect and love parents who
   have not earned it by their behaviour and attitudes   2

   Don't know   9

SHOW CARD X

452 Which of the following statements best describes your views about
parents' responsibilities to their children? (Code one only)

Parents' duty is to do their best for their children even at the
   expense of their own well-being   1

Parents have a life of their own and should not be asked to
   sacrifice their own well-being for the sake of their childrens   2

Neither   3

Don't know   9

SHOW CARD Y

453 Here is a list of qualities which children can be encouraged to learn at
home. Which, if any, do you consider to be especially important?
Please choose up to five. (Code five only)

	Important
Good manners	1
Independence	1
Hard work	1
Feeling of responsibility	1
Imagination	1
Tolerance and respect for other people	1
Thrift, saving money and things	1
Determination, perseverance	1
Religious faith	1
Unselfishness	1
Obedience	1

SHOW CARD Z

465 Do you approve or disapprove of abortion under the following circumstances?

	Approve	Disapprove	DK
A Where the mother's health is at risk by the pregnancy	1	2	9
B Where it is likely that the child would be born physically handicapped	1	2	9

C Where the woman is not married	1	2	9
D Where a married couple does not want to have any children	1	2	9

471 How interested would you say you are in politics?

Very interested	1
Somewhat interested	2
Not very interested	3
Not at all interested	4
Don't know	9

SHOW CARD AA

472 Now I'd like you to look at this card. I'm going to read out some different forms of political action that people can take, and I'd like you to tell me, for each one, whether you have actually done any of these things, whether you might do it or would never, under any circumstances, do it?

	Have done	Might do	Would Never do	Dk
A Signing a petition	1	2	3	9
B Joining in boycotts	1	2	3	9
C Attending lawful demonstrations	1	2	3	9
D Joining unofficial strikes	1	2	3	9
E Occupying buildings or factories	1	2	3	9

SHOW CARD BB

477 Which of these two statements comes closest to your own opinion?

A I find that both freedom and equality are important. But if I were to choose one or the other, I would consider personal freedom more important, that is, everyone can live in freedom and develop without hindrance   1

B Certainly both freedom and equality are important. But if I were to choose one or the other, I would consider equality more important, that is, that nobody is underprivileged and that social class differences are not so strong   2

Neither   3

Don't know   9

SHOW CARD CC

478 In political matters, people talk of the left and the right. How would you place your views on this scale, generally speaking?

Left   Right   Dk
1   2   3   4   5   6   7   8   9   10   99

SHOW CARD DD

480 On this card are three basic kinds of attitudes about the society we live in. Please choose the one which best describes your own opinion. (Code one only)

The entire way our society is organized must be radically
changed by revolutionary action   1
Our society must be gradually improved by reforms   2
Our present society must be valiantly defended against all sub-
versive forces   3
Don't know   9

SHOW CARD EE

516 Now I'd like you to tell me your views on various issues. How would you place your views on this scale? Each card I show you has two contrasting statements on it. Using the scale listed, could you tell me where you would place your own view? 1 means you agree complete-ly with the statement on the left, 10 means you agree completely with the statement on the right, or you can choose any number in between.

A Incomes should be made   There should be greater incen-
   more equal   tives for individual effort   Dk
   1   2   3   4   5   6   7   8   9   10   99

B Private ownership of   Government ownership of
   business and industry   business and industry should
   should be increased   be increased   DK
   1   2   3   4   5   6   7   8   9   10   99

C Individuals should take   The government should take
   more responsibility for   more responsibility to ensure
   providing for themselves   that everyone is provided for   DK
   1   2   3   4   5   6   7   8   9   10   99

D People who are unemploy-
   ed should have to take any   People who are unemployed
   job available or lose their   should have the right to refuse
   unemployment benefits   a job they do not want   DK
   1   2   3   4   5   6   7   8   9   10   99

E Competition is good. It
   stimulates people to work   Competition is harmful. It

hard and develop new ideas brings out the worst in people DK
1   2   3   4   5   6   7   8   9   10   99

F In the long run, hard work
usually brings a better life

Hard word doesn't generally
bring success–it's more a matter
of luck and connections DK
1   2   3   4   5   6   7   8   9   10   99

G People can only accumu-
late wealth at the expense
of others

Wealth can grow so there's
enough for everyone DK
1   2   3   4   5   6   7   8   9   10   99

SHOW CARD FF

530 There is a lot of talk these days about what the aims of this country should be for the next ten years. On this card are listed some of the goals which different people would give top priority. Would you please say which one of these you, yourself, consider the most important? (Code one answer only)

531 And which would be the next most important? (Code one answer only)

	First choice	Second choice
Maintaining a high level of economic growth	1	1
Making sure this country has strong defence forces	2	2
Seeing that people have more say about how things are done at their jobs and in their communities	3	3
Trying to make our cities and countryside more beautiful	4	4
Don't know	9	9

SHOW CARD GG

532a If you had to choose, which one of the things on this card would you say is most important? (Code one answer only)

533b And which would be the next most important? (Code one answer only)

	First choice	Second choice
Maintaining order in the nation	1	1

Giving people more say in important government decisions	2	2
Fighting rising prices	3	3
Protecting freedom of speech	4	4
Don't know	9	9

SHOW CARD HH

534a Here is another list. In your opinion, which one of these is most important? (Code one answer only)

535b And what would be the next most important? (Code one answer only)

	First choice	Second choice
A stable economy	1	1
Progress toward a less impersonal and more humane society	2	2
Progress toward a society in which ideas count more than money	3	3
The fight against crime	4	4
Don't know	9	9

536 Of course we all hope that there will not be another war, but if it were to come to that, would you be willing to fight for your country?

Yes	1
No	2
Don't know	9

537 Here is a list of various changes in your way of life that might take place in the near future. Please tell me for each one, it it were to happen whether you think it would be a good thing, a bad thing, or don't you mind?

	Good	Bad	Don't mind
A Less emphasis on money and material possessions	1	2	3
B Decrease in the importance of work in our lives	1	2	3
C More emphasis on the development of technology	1	2	3
D Greater emphasis on the development of the individual	1	2	3
E Greater respect for authority	1	2	3

F More emphasis on family life	1	2	3
G A simple and more natural lifestyle	1	2	3

544 In the long run, do you think the scientific advances we are making will help or harm mankind?

Will help	1
Will harm	2
Some of each	3
Don't know	9

SHOW CARD II

545 Please look at this card and tell me, for each item listed, how much confidence you have in them, is it a great deal, quite a lot, not very much or none at all? (Code one answer for each item–read out reversing order for alternate contacts)

	A great deal	Quite a lot	Not very much	None at all
A The church	1	2	3	4
B The armed forces	1	2	3	4
C The education system	1	2	3	4
D The legal system	1	2	3	4
E The press	1	2	3	4
F Trade unions	1	2	3	4
G The police	1	2	3	4
H Parliament	1	2	3	4
I Civil service	1	2	3	4
J Major companies	1	2	3	4
K The social security system	1	2	3	4
L The European Community	1	2	3	4
M NATO	1	2	3	4

SHOW CARD JJ

559 On this card are listed some things people have said make them proud of Canada. Do any of these things make you proud of this country? (Circle one only under first mention below)

560 Is there anything else? And is there anything else? (Circle up to two mentions and record mention below)

	First mention	Second mention
Canadian scientific achievements	1	1
Canadian political system	2	2
Canadian sporting achievements	3	3

Canadian culture and arts	4	4
Canadian economic achievements	5	5
Canadian health & welfare system	6	6
None of these things make me proud	7	7
Don't know	9	9

561 Generally speaking, would you say that this country is run by a few big interests looking out for themselves, or that it is run for the benefit of all the people?

Run by a few big interests	1
Run by all the people	2
Don't know	9

562 How much do you trust the government in Ottawa to do what is right? Do you trust it almost always, most of the time, only some of the time, or almost never?

Almost always	1
Most of the time	2
Only some of the time	3
Almost never	4
Don't know	9

SHOW CARD KK

563 There are a number of groups and movements looking for public support. For each of the following movements which I read out, can you tell me whether you approve or disapprove of this movement? Please use the responses on this card. (Read out and code one answer for each)

	Approve strongly	Agree somewhat	Disapprove somewhat	Disapprove strongly	Dk
A Ecology movement or nature protection	1	2	3	4	9
B Anti-nuclear energy movement	1	2	3	4	9
C Disarmament movement	1	2	3	4	9
D Human rights movements (at home or abroad)	1	2	3	4	9

E Women's movement	1	2	3	4	9
F Anti-apartheid movement	1	2	3	4	9

SHOW CARD LL

569 Please tell me for each of the following statements whether you think it can always be justified, never be justified, or something in between, using this card. (Read out statements reversing order for alternate contacts. Code one answer for each statement)

Never									Always	Dk
1	2	3	4	5	6	7	8	9	10	99

A Claiming government benefits which you are not entitled to
B Avoiding a fare on public transport
C Cheating on tax if you have the change
D Buying something you knew was stolen
E Taking and driving away a car belonging to someone else (joyriding)
F Taking the drug marijuana or hashish
G Keeping money that you have found
H Lying in your own interest
I Married men/women having an affair
J Sex under the legal age of consent
K Someone accepting a bribe in the course of their duties
L Homosexuality
M Prostitution
N Abortion
O Divorce
P Fighting with the police
Q Euthanasia (terminating the life of the incurably sick)
R Suicide
S Failing to report damage you've done accidently to a parked vehicle
T Threatening workers who refuse to join a strike
U Killing in self-defence
V Political assassinations
W Throwing away litter in a public place
X Driving under the influence of alcohol

SHOW CARD MM

648a Which of these geographical groups would you say you belong to first of all?

649b And the next?

	first	next
Locality or town where you live	1	1
Region of country where you live	2	2
Your country as a whole	3	3
North America	4	4
The world as a whole	5	5
Don't know	9	9

650 How proud are you to be Canadian?

Very proud	1
Quite proud	2
Not very proud	3
Not at all proud	4
Don't know	9

SHOW CARD NN

651 Now I want to ask you some questions about your outlook on life.
Each card I show you has two contrasting statements on it. Using the
scale listed, could you tell me where, you would place your own
view? 1 means you agree completely with the statement, 10 means
you disagree completely with the statement on the right, or you can
choose any number in between.

A One should be cautious
  about making major
  changes in life

You will never achieve
much unless you act
boldly   DK

| 1 | 2 | 3 | 4 | 5 | 6 | 7 | 8 | 9 | 10 | 99 |

B Ideas that have stood
  the test of time are
  generally the best

New ideas are generally
better than old ones   DK

| 1 | 2 | 3 | 4 | 5 | 6 | 7 | 8 | 9 | 10 | 99 |

C When changes occur in my
  life, I worry about the
  difficulties they may
  cause

When changes occur in my
life, I welcome the pos-
sibility that something new
is beginning   DK

| 1 | 2 | 3 | 4 | 5 | 6 | 7 | 8 | 9 | 10 | 99 |

SHOW CARD OO

657 A variety of characteristics are listed here. Could you take a look at them and select those which apply to you?

A I usually count on being successful in everything I do	1
B I enjoy convincing others of my opinion	1
C I often notice that I serve as a model for others	1
D I am good at getting what I want	1
E I own many things others envy me for	1
F I like to assume responsibility	1
G I am rarely unsure about how I should behave	1
H I often give others advice	1
None of the above	1

SHOW CARD PP

666 I am going to read out some statements about the government and the economy. For each one could you tell me how much you agree or disagree? Please use the responses on this card.

	Agree completely	Agree somewhat	Neither agree nor disagree	Disagree somewhat	Disagree completely	Dk
A This country's economic system needs fundamental changes	1	2	3	4	5	9
B Our government should be made much more open to the public	1	2	3	4	5	9
C We are more likely to have a healthy economy if the government allows more freedom for individuals to do as they wish	1	2	3	4	5	9
D If an unjust law were passed by the government I could do nothing at all about it	1	2	3	4	5	9

E Political reform
in this country
is moving too
rapidly   1   2   3   4   5   9

SHOW CARD QQ

671   I now want to ask you how much you trust the following groups of people. Using the responses on this card, could you tell me how much you trust ... (Read out each and code one answer for each)

	Trust them completely	Trust them a little	Neither trust nor distrust them	Do not trust them very much	Do not trust them at all	Dk
A Your family	1	2	3	4	5	9
B Canadian people in general	1	2	3	4	5	9
C French Canadians	1	2	3	4	5	9
D Recent immigrants	1	2	3	4	5	9
E Americans	1	2	3	4	5	9
F Mexicans	1	2	3	4	5	9
G Russians	1	2	3	4	5	9
H Chinese	1	2	3	4	5	9

679   Were you born in Canada?

Yes   1   Skip to Q. 711
No   Continue
If 'NO', ask:
Where were you born?

Latin America   2
United States   3
Asia   4
Europe   5
Africa   6
Other   7

680   In what year did you come to Canada?

Within past 2 years   1
Within past 3-5 years   2
6-10 years ago   3

| 11-15 years ago | 4 |
| More than 15 years ago- | 5 |

SHOW CARD RR
711 To which of the following groups do you belong, above all? Just call out one of the letters on this card.

A Above all, I am a French Canadian	1
B Above all, I am an English Canadian	2
C Above all, I am an ethnic Canadian	3
D Above all, I am a Canadian first and a member of some ethnic group second	4
E Above all, I am a Canadian First and only	5

Thinking now about economic issues.

SHOW CARD SS
748 In your opinion, should Canada have closer, or more distant, economic ties with ...

	Yes, much closer	Somewhat closer	A bit more distant	No, much more distant	Dk
Western Europe	1	2	3	4	
Japan	1	2	3	4	9
Mexico	1	2	3	4	9
United States	1	2	3	4	9
Eastern Europe	1	2	3	4	9

753 Most countries like our own depend on trade. Here is a list of various ways of dealing with trade issues. Please tell me how much you agree or disagree with eachof the following statements:

	Strongly agree	Agree	Disagree	Strongly disagree	Dk
There should be no restrictions on the free flow of goods and services across international borders	1	2	3	4	9
We should allow goods and services to flow more freely across our borders as long as Canadians don't lose jobs	1	2	3	4	9

We should give countries
free access to our markets
only if they give us free
access to theirs   1   2   3   4   9

756   More than a year ago, Canada signed a Free Trade Agreement with the United States. Thinking about that agreement today, which phrase best describes your opinion? (Read list and code one answer only)

I'm a strong supporter of the Free Trade Agreement	1
On balance, I support the Free Trade Agreement	2
On balance, I oppose the Free Trade Agreement	3
I absolutely oppose the Free Trade Agreement	4
Don't know	9

757   What do you think would be the main advantages of Canada and the United States forming one country? PROBE: Any other advantages?

763   And what do you think would be the main disadvantages? PROBE: Any other disadvantages?

769   Would favor or oppose Canada and the United States forming one country ...

	Yes	No	Dk
If it meant that you would enjoy a higher standard of living	1	2	9
If it meant losing Canada's cultural identity	1	2	9
If it meant that we could deal more effectively with environmental issues like acid rain and air pollution	1	2	9
If it meant that Canada would form 12 new states in the United States	1	2	9
If it meant slightly lower taxes but fewer government services	1	2	9
If it meant a better quality of life	1	2	9
If it meant a privately funded rather than a government funded health care system	1	2	9

776   All things considered do you think that we should do away with the border between Canada and the United States?

Favor	1
Oppose	2
Don't know	9

777 Over the past few months, there has been much debate over the proposed Meech Lake Constitution Accord. Which of the following statements comes the closest to your own opinion on the Accord? (Code only one answer)

I strongly support the Meech Lake Accord	1
The Accord may have flaws, but it is the best that we can do	2
I would support the Accord, but only if it is amended	3
The Accord should be rejected	4
I don't know enough about the Accord to have an opinion	5
Refused or no answer	9

778a If there were a federal election tomorrow, for which party would you vote? IF DON'T KNOW, ASK: Which party appeals to you most?

778b And which party would be your second choice?

	778a first choice	778b second choice
Liberal	1	1
Progressive Conservative	2	2
N.D.P.	3	3
Reform Party	4	4
Other Party (Write in)		
_____	5	
_____		5
Refused	6	6
Not eligible	7	7
Don't know/None	9	9

DEMOGRAPHICS

779 Record sex of respondent:

Male	1
Female	2

780a Can you tell me the date of your birth please?

780b This means you are years old.

781 At what age did you (or will you) complete your full-time education, either at school or at an institution of higher education? Please exclude apprenticeships.

Write in age:

782   Do you live with your parents?

    Yes   1
    No   2

783a Are you, yourself, employed now or not?

    If Yes:
    About how many hours per week do you work?
    30 hours a week or more   1
    Less than 30 hours per week   2
    Self-employed   3

    If No:
    Retired/pensioned   4
    Housewife not otherwise employed 5
    Student   6
    Unemployed   7
    Other (specify) _____ 8

783b In what profession/industry do you or did you work? (If more than
    one job, ask for main job)

783c What is/was your job there?

784   Are you the chief wage earner?

    Yes   1   Skip to Q. 786
    No   2   Continue

785a Is the chief wage earner employed now or not?

    Yes   1
    No   2

785b In which profession/industry does/did he (she) work?

785c What is/was his/her job?

ASK EVERYONE:
786   Here is a scale of incomes and we would like to know in what group
    your household is, counting all wages, salaries, pensions and other
    incomes that come in. Just give the letter of the group your household
    falls into, before taxes and other deductions.

C	Under $10,000	1
D	$10,000-$14,999	2
E	$15,000-$19,999	3
F	$20,000-$24,999	4
G	$25,000-$29,999	5
H	$30,000-$39,999	6
I	$40,000-$49,999	7
J	$50,000-$59,999	8
K	$60,000-$69,999	9
L	$70,000 & over	10
	Refused	99

787 Interviewer record only, do not ask:

AB	(upper, upper-middle class)	1
C1	(middle, non-manual workers)	2
C2	(manual workers–skilled, semi-skilled)	3
DE	(manual workers–unskilled, unemployed)	4

788 Time at the end of the interview:

789 Total length of interview:

_____ Hours _____ Minutes

790 During the interview the respondent was ...

Very interested	1
Somewhat interested	2
Not very interested	3

791 Interviewer record ethnic group, do not ask:

Caucasian (White)	1
Negro (Black)	2
South Asian (Indian, Pakistani, etc.)	3
East Asian (Chinese, Japanese, etc.)	4
Arabic	5
Other	6

792 Are you a ...

Canadian citizen	1
Landed Immigrant	2
or	

| A visitor | 3 |
| Refused | 9 |

RECORD IF:

Farm	1
Rural, non-farm	2
Urban	3
Language _____	

Bibliography

Abramson, Nancy, Linda Briskin, and Margaret McPhail. 1988. *Feminist Organizing for Change: The Contemporary Women's Movement in Canada.* Toronto: Oxford University Press.

Abramson, Paul R. 1982. *Political Attitudes in America: Formation and Change.* San Francisco: W.H. Freeman & Company.

———. 1983. *Generational Change in American Politics.* Lexington, MA: Lexington Books.

———. 1992. "Of Time and Partisan Stability in Britain." *British Journal of Political Science,* 22: 381-95.

Abramson, Paul R., and Ronald Inglehart. 1987. "The Future of Postmaterialist Values: Population Replacement Effects 1975-1985 and 1985-2000." *Journal of Politics,* 49 (February): 231-41.

———. 1995. *Value Change in Global Perspective.* Ann Arbor, MI: University of Michigan Press.

Akker, P. van den, Loek Halman, and Ruud de Moor. 1993. "Primary Relations in Western Societies." In Peter Ester, Loek Halman, and Ruud de Moor (eds.), *The Individualizing Society: Value Change in Europe and North America* (pp. 97-127). Tilburg, Netherlands: Tilburg University Press.

Almond, Gabriel, and Sidney Verba. 1963. *The Civic Culture.* Princeton: Princeton University Press.

Alwin, Duane. 1986. "Religion and Parental Child-Rearing Orientations: Evidence of a Catholic-Protestant Convergence." *American Journal of Sociology,* 92: 412-40.

Andrian, Charles F. 1980. *Politics and Economic Policy in Western Democracies.* Massachusetts: Duxbury Press.

Arendt, Hannah. 1959. *The Human Condition.* Garden City, NY: Doubleday.

Bakvis, Herman, and Neil Nevitte. 1987. "In Pursuit of Postbourgeois Man: Postmaterialism and Intergenerational Change in Canada." *Comparative Political Studies,* 70: 357-89.

———. 1990. "The Greening of the Canadian Electorate: Environmentalism, Ideology and Partisanship." Paper presented at the annual meeting of the Canadian Political Science Association, Victoria.

———. 1992. "The Greening of the Canadian Electorate: Environmentalism, Ideology and Partisanship." In Robert Broadmand (ed.), *Canadian Environmental Policy: Ecosystems, Politics and Process* (pp. 144-63). Toronto: Oxford University Press.

Banfield, Edward C. 1958. *The Moral Basis of a Backward Society.* Chicago: Free Press.

Barber, Benjamin. 1984. *Strong Democracy.* Berkeley: University of California Press.

Barnes, Samuel, Max Kaase, Klaus Allerback, Barbara Farah, Felix Heunks, Ronald

Inglehart, Kent Jennings, Hans Klingemann, Alan Marsh, and Leopold Rosenmay. *Political Participation: Mass Participation in Five Western Democracies.* Beverly Hills: Sage.

Baron, R.A., and D. Byrne. *Social Psychology: Understanding Human Interaction.* Boston: Allyn and Bacon.

Bashevkin, Sylvia B. 1991. *True Patriot Love: The Politics of Canadian Nationalism.* Toronto: Oxford University Press.

Bean, Clive, and Elim Papadakis. 1994a. "Polarized Priorities or Flexible Alternatives? Dimensionality in Inglehart's Materialism-Postmaterialism Scale." *International Journal of Public Opinion Research,* 6, 3: 264-88.

————. 1994b. "Polarized Priorities and Flexible Alternatives: Response to Inglehart and Hellevik." *International Journal of Public Opinion Research,* 6,3: 295-97.

Beaujot, Roderic. 1991. *Population Change in Canada: The Challenges of Policy Adaptation.* Toronto: McClelland & Stewart.

Beaujot, Roderic, and Peter J. Rappak. 1988. *Immigration from Canada: Its Importance and Interpretation.* Population Working Paper No. 4. Policy Department. Ottawa: Employment & Immigration Canada.

Beck, Nathaniel, and John C. Pierce. 1977. "Political Involvement and Party Allegiances in Canada and the United States." *International Journal of Comparative Sociology,* 18: 23-43.

Bell, Daniel. 1973. *The Coming of Post-Industrial Society.* New York: Basic Books.

————. 1976. *The Cultural Contradictions of Capitalism.* New York: Basic Books.

Bell, David. 1992. *The Roots of Disunity: A Study of Canadian Political Culture,* 2nd ed. Toronto: Oxford University Press.

Black, Jerome H. 1991. "Reforming the Context of the Voting Process in Canada: Lessons from Other Democracies." In Herman Bakvis (ed.), *Voter Turnout in Canada.* Vol. 15. Research Studies for the Royal Commission on Electoral Reform and Party Financing. Toronto/Oxford: Dundurn Press.

Böltken, F., and W. Jagodzinski. 1985. "Postmaterialism in the European Community, 1970-1980: Insecure Value Orientations in an Environment of Insecurity." *Comparative Political Studies.* 17: 453-84.

Brand, K.W. "Cyclical Aspects of New Social Movements: Waves of Cultural Criticism and Mobilization Cycles of New Middle Class Radicalism." In R. Dalton, and M. Kuechler (eds.), *Challenging the Political Order: New Social and Political Movements in Western Democracies* (pp. 23-42). New York: Oxford University Press.

Brzezinski, Zbigniew. 1970. *Between Two Ages: America's Role in the Technetronic Era.* New York: Viking.

Buchannan, William, and Hadley Cantril. 1953. *How Nations See Each Other: A Study in Public Opinion.* Urbana: University of Illinois Press.

Budge, Ian, Ivor Crewe, and David Farlie (eds.). 1976. *Party Identification and Beyond.* New York: Wiley.

Bürklin, Wilhelm P. 1985. "The Greens: Ecology and the New Left." In George Romoser and Peter Wallach (eds.), *West German Politics in the Mid-Eighties* (pp. 187-218). New York: Praeger.

Burt, Sandra. 1988. "Legislators, Women and Public Policy." In Sandra Burt, Lorraine Code, and Lindsay Dorney (eds.), *Changing Patterns: Women in Canada* (pp. 129-56). Toronto: McClelland & Stewart.

Cairns, Alan. 1990. "Citizens (Outsiders) and Governments (Insiders) in Constitution

Making: The Case of Meech Lake." In Douglas Williams (ed.), *Disruption: Constitutional Struggles, from the Charter to Meech Lake.* Toronto: McClelland & Stewart.

———. 1993. "A Defence of the Citizen's Constitution Theory: A Response to Ian Brodie and Neil Nevitte." *Canadian Journal of Political Science*, 26, 2: 261-67.

Cherrington, D. 1980. *The Work Ethic: Working Values and Values that Work.* New York: Amacon.

Clark, Samuel D. 1962. *The Developing Canadian Community.* Toronto: University of Toronto Press.

Clarke, Harold. D., and Nitish Dutt. 1991. "Measuring Value Change in Western Industrialized Society: The Impact of Unemployment." *American Political Science Review*, 85: 905-20.

Clarke, Harold D., Lawrence LeDuc, Jane Jenson, and Jon H. Pammett. 1991. *Absent Mandate: Interpreting Change in Canadian Elections.* Toronto: Gage.

Clarke, Harold D., and Allan Kornberg. 1993. "Evaluations and Evolution: Public Attitudes toward Canada's Federal Political Parties, 1965-1991." *Canadian Journal of Political Science*, 26: 287-311.

Cohen, Marshall, Thomas Nagel, and Thomas Scanlon (eds.). 1977. *Equality and Preferential Treatment.* Princeton, NJ: Princeton University Press.

Crawford, Craig, and James Curtis. 1979. "English Canadian—American Differences in Value Orientations: Survey Comparisons Bearing on Lipset's Thesis." *Studies in Comparative International Development*, 14: 23-44.

Crewe, Ivor. 1981. "Electoral Participation." In David Butler, Howard R. Penniman, and Austin Ranney (eds.), *Democracy at the Polls* (pp. 216-63). Washington: American Enterprise Institute.

Crick, Bernard. 1973. *Political Theory and Practice.* New York: Basic Books.

Crouter, Ann C., and Beth Manke. 1994. "The Changing American Workplace." *Family Relations*, 43, 11: 117-24.

Dalton, Russell J. 1984a. "Cognitive Mobilization and Partisan Dealignment in Advanced Industrial Democracies." *Journal of Politics*, 46: 264-84.

———. 1984b. *Electoral Change in Advanced Industrial democracies: Realignment or Dealignment?* Princeton, NJ: Princeton University Press.

———. 1988a. *Citizen Politics in Western Democracies: Public Opinion and Political Parties in the United States, Great Britain, West Germany and France.* Chatham, NJ: Chatham House.

———. 1988b. "The Environmental Movement and West European Party Systems." Paper presented at the annual meeting of the Midwest Political Science Association. Chicago.

———. 1992. *Politics in Germany.* New York: Harper Collins.

Dalton, Russell, J. Scott Flanagan, and Paul Beck (eds.). 1984. *Electoral Change in Advanced Industrial Democracies.* Princeton, NJ: Princeton University Press.

Dalton, Russell J., and Manfred Kuechler (eds.). 1990. *Challenging the Political Order: New Social and Political Movements in Western Democracies.* New York: Oxford University Press.

Dalton, Russell J., Manfred Kuechler, and Wilhelm Burklin. 1990. "The Challenge of New Movements." In Dalton and Kuechler (eds.), *Challenging the Political Order: New Social and Political Movements in Western Democracies* (pp. 3-20). New York: Oxford University Press.

Dalton, Russell J., and Martin P. Wattenberg. 1993. "The Not So Simple Act of

Voting." In Ada W. Finifter (ed.), *The State of the Discipline II* (pp. 193-218). Washington: American Political Science Association.

deGraaf, Nan Dirk. 1988. *Postmaterialism and the Stratification Process: An International Comparison.* Utrecht: University of Utrecht.

Deutsch, Karl W. 1952. *Nationalism and Social Communication.* Cambridge: MIT Press.

————. 1957. *Political Community and the North Atlantic Area.* Princeton: Princeton University Press.

————. 1963. "Social Mobilization and Political Development." *American Political Science Review,* 55: 493-517.

————.1966. *Nationalism and Social Communication: An Inquiry into the Foundation of Nationality.* Cambridge: MIT Press.

————. 1968. *Political Community and the North Atlantic Area.* Garden City, NY: Doubleday.

Diebold, William Jr. (ed.). 1988. *Bilateralism, Multilateralism and Canada in U.S. Trade Policy.* New York: Ballinger.

Durkheim, E. 1961. *The Elementary Forms of Religious Life.* New York: Collier.

Dye, Thomas, and Harmon Zeigler. 1970. *The Irony of Democracy.* Belmont: Duxbury.

Eckstein, Harry. 1966. *Division and Cohesion in Democracy.* Princeton: Princeton University Press.

————. 1969. "Authority Relations and Governmental Performance." *Comparative Political Studies,* 2: 269-325.

————.1992. *Regarding Politics: Essays on Political Theory, Stability and Change.* Berkeley: University of California Press.

Eckstein, Harry, and T.R. Gurr. 1975. *Patterns of Authority: A Structural Basis for Political Inquiry.* New York: Wiley & Sons.

The Economist. 1994 October 22:20.

Ester, Peter, Loek Halman, and Ruud de Moor (eds.). 1993. *The Individualizing Society: Value Change in Europe and North America.* Tilburg, Netherlands: Tilburg University Press.

Festy, P. 1985. "Evolution contemporain du mode de formation des familles en Europe occidentale." *European Journal of Population,* 1: 179-205.

Fiorina, Morris P. 1992. *Divided Government.* New York: Macmillan.

Flanagan, Scott C. 1982. "Changing Values in Advanced Industrial Societies: Inglehart's Silent Revolution from the Perspective of Japanese Findings." *Comparative Political Studies,* 14: 403-44.

————. 1987. "Value Change in Industrial Society." *American Political Science Review.* 81: 1303-19.

Fox, Bonnie J. 1989. "The Feminist Challenge: A Reconsideration of Social Inequality and Economic Development." In Robert J. Byrm with Bonnie Fox, *From Culture to Power: The Sociology of English Canada* (pp. 120-67). Toronto: Oxford University Press.

Frohlich, Norman, and Irvin Boschman. 1986. "Partisan Preference and Income Redistribution: Cross-national and Cross-sexual Results." *Canadian Journal of Political Science,* 19: 53-69.

Fry, Earl H. 1980. *Financial Invasion of the U.S.A.: A Threat to American Society?* New York: McGraw-Hill.

Fuchs, Dieter, and Hans-Dieter Klingemann. 1990. "The Left-Right Schema." In M. Kent Jennings, Jan W. Van Deth, Samuel H. Barnes, Dieter Fuchs, Felix J. Heunks,

Ronald Inglehart, Max Kaase, Hans-Dieter Klingemann, and Jacques J.A. Thomassen. *Continuities in Political Action: a Longitudinal Study of Political Orientations in Three Western Democracies.* Berlin: Walter de Gruyter.

Furnham, Adrian. 1990. *The Protestant Work Ethic: The Psychology of Work-Related Beliefs and Behaviours.* London: Routledge.

Gelb, Joyce. 1990. "Feminism and Political Action." In Russell Dalton and Manfred Kuechler (eds.), *Challenging the Political Order: New Social and Political Movements in Western Democracies* (pp. 137-55). New York: Oxford University Press.

Gevers, J.K.M. 1992. "Legislation on Euthanasia: Recent Developments in the Netherlands," *Journal of Medical Ethics*, 18: 138-41.

Gibbins, Roger, and Neil Nevitte. 1985. "Canadian Political Ideology: A Comparative Analysis." *Canadian Journal of Political Science*, 18, 3: 577-98.

Gibson, James L. 1992. "Alternative Measures of Political Tolerance: Must Tolerance Be 'Least Liked'?" *American Journal of Political Science*, 36: 560-77.

Glazer, Nathan. 1988. *The Limits of Social Policy.* Cambridge: Harvard University Press.

Glenn, Noval D. 1977. *Cohort Analysis.* Beverly Hills: Sage.

Golthorpe, J.E. 1987. *Family Life in Western Societies.* Cambridge: Cambridge University Press.

Gourevitch, Peter. 1986. *Politics in Hard Times: Comparative Responses to International Economic Crises.* Ithaca, NY: Cornell University Press.

Gundelach, Peter. 1991. "Research on Social Movements in Denmark." In Dieter Rucht (ed.), *Research on Social Movements: The State of the Art in Western Europe and the U.S.A.* (pp. 264-94). Frankfurt/Boulder, CO: Campus Verlag/Westview Press.

Guppy, L. Neil. 1984. "Dissensus or Consensus: A Cross-national Comparison of Occupational Prestige Scales." *Canadian Journal of Sociology*, 9: 69-84.

Haas, Ernst B. 1958. *The Uniting of Europe.* Stanford: Stanford University Press.

Halman, Loek, and Ruud de Moor. 1993. "Comparative Research on Values." In Peter Ester, Loek Halman and Ruud D. Moor (eds.), *The Individualizing Society: Value Change in Europe and North America* (21-36). Tilburg, Netherlands: Tilburg University Press.

Harding, S. 1986. "Contrasting Values in Western Europe: Some Methodological Issues Arising from the EVSSG European Values Project." Paper presented at the Third Cross-National Research Seminar Language and Culture in Cross-National Research, at Aston University. Birmingham, U.K.

Hartz, Louis. 1964. *The Founding of New Societies.* New York: Harcourt, Brace & World.

Hay, P.R., and M.G. Haward. 1988. "Comparative Green Politics: Beyond the European Context?" *Political Studies*, 36: 433-48.

Heidenheimer, Arnold, and Peter Flora. 1981. *The Development of the Welfare State.* New Brunswick, NJ: Transaction Books.

Heidenheimer, Arnold, Hugh Heclo, and Carolyn Adams. 1983. *Comparative Public Policy*, 2nd. ed. New York: St Martin's.

Hellevik, Otto. 1994. "Measuring Cultural Orientation: Rating versus Ranking." *International Journal of Public Opinion Research*, 6,3: 292-94.

Hildebrandt, Kai, and Russell Dalton. 1978. "The New Politics." In Max Kaase and K. von Beyme (eds.), *German Political studies: Elections and Parties*, vol. 3. Beverly Hills: Sage.

Hoberg, George, and Kathryn Harrison. 1991. "Setting the Environment Agenda in Canada and the United States: The Cases of Dioxin and Radon." *Canadian Journal of Political Science*, 24 1: 3-28.

Hochschild, Jennifer. 1981. *What's Fair? American Beliefs about Distributive Justice*. Cambridge: Harvard University Press.

Hoffmann-Nowotny, H. 1987. "The Future of the Family." Plenaries European Population Conference, Helsinki, IUSSP/EAPS/FINNCO, Central Statistical Office, 113-200.

Hofstadter, Richard. 1964. *The Paranoid Style in American Politics, and Other Essays*. New York: Knopf.

Horowitz, Gad. 1966. "Conservatism, Liberalism and Socialism in Canada: An Interpretation." *Canadian Journal of Economics and Political Science*, 32, 143-70.

Horowitz, Irving Louis. 1973. "The Hemispheric Connection." *Queen's Quarterly*. 80, 3: 327-59.

Huntington, Samuel P. 1974. "Post-Industrial Politics: How Benign Will It Be?" *Comparative Politics*, 6: 147-77.

———. 1981. *American Politics: The Promise of Disharmony*. Cambridge, MA: Harvard University Press.

Inglehart, Ronald. 1971. "The Silent Revolution in Europe: Intergenerational Change in Post-Industrial Societies." *American Political Science Review*, 65: 991-1017.

———. 1977 *The Silent Revolution*. Princeton, NJ: Princeton University Press.

———. 1981. "Postmaterialism in an Environment of Insecurity." *American Political Science Review*, 75: 880-900.

———. 1988. "Cultural Change in Advanced Industrial Societies: Postmaterialist Values and Their Consequences." *International Review of Sociology*, 3: 77-100.

———. 1990. *Culture Shift in Advanced Industrial Society*. Princeton: Princeton University Press.

———. 1990. "Values, Ideology, and Cognitive Mobilization in New Social Movements." In Russell Dalton and Manfred Kuechler (eds.), *Challenging the Political Order: New Social and Political Movements in Western Democracies* (pp. 43-66). New York: Oxford University Press.

———. 1993. "Public Support for Environmental Protection: Objective Problems and Subjective Values." Paper presented at Conference on Social Values, Tilburg University, Netherlands, September 16-18.

———. 1994. "Polarized Priorities or Flexible Alternatives? Dimensionality in Inglehart's Materialism-Postmaterialist Scale: A Comment." *International Journal of Public Opinion Research*. 6, 3: 289-92.

Inglehart, Ronald and Paul Abramson. 1994. "Economic Security and Value Change." *American Journal of Political Science*, 88, 2: 336-54.

Inglehart, Ronald and David Appel. 1989. "The Rise of Postmaterialist Values and Changing Religious Orientations, Gender Roles and Sexual Norms." *International Journal of Public Opinion Research*, 1, 1: 45-75.

Inglehart, Ronald, Neil Nevitte and Miguel Basanez. 1994. *Convergencia en Norteamerica*. Mexico: Siglo xxi editores.

———. 1996. *The North American Trajectory: Social Institutions and Social Change*. New York/Berlin: Aldine de Gruyter.

Innis, Harold. 1956. *Essays in Canadian Economic History*. Toronto: University of Toronto Press.

Ishi-Kuntz, Masako. 1994. "Work and Family Life: Findings from International Research and Suggestions for Future Study." *Journal of Family Studies*, 15, 3: 490-506.

Jackman, Mary R. 1978. "General and Applied Tolerance: Does Education Increase Commitment to Racial Integration?" *American Journal of Political Science*, 22: 302-24.

Jackman, Robert N. 1972. "Political Elites, Mass Publics, and Support for Democratic Principles." *Journal of Politics*, 34: 753-73.

Jackson, Robert and Doreen Jackson. 1994. *Politics in Canada*, 3rd. ed. Scarborough: Prentice Hall.

Jallinoja, Riitta. 1989. "Women Between the Family and Employment." In Katja Boh, Maren Bak, Cristine Clason, Maja Pankratova, Jens Qvortrup, Giovanni B. Sgritta, and Kari Waerness (eds.), *Changing Patterns of European Family Life: A Comparative Analysis of Fourteen European Countries* (pp. 95-122). London: Routledge.

Jennings, M. Kent. 1984. "The Intergenerational Transfer of Political Ideologies in Eight Western Nations." *European Journal of Political Research*. 12: 261-76.

————. 1987. "Residues of a Movement: The Aging of the American Protest Movement." *American Political Science Review*. 82. 367-82.

Johnson, Harry G. 1965. "An Economic Theory of Protectionism, Tariff Bargaining and the Formation of Customs Unions." *Journal of Political Economy*, 73, 256-83.

Johnston, Richard, André Blais, Henry Brady, and Jean Crête. 1992. *Letting the People Decide*. Montreal/Kingston: McGill-Queen's University Press.

Johnston, Richard, André Blais, Elisabeth Gidengil and Neil Nevitte. 1996. *The Challenge of Direct Democracy: The 1992 Canadian Referendum*. Montreal/Kingston: McGill-Queen's University Press.

Kaase, Max. 1990. "Mass Participation." In M. Kent Jennings and Jan W. Van Deth (eds.), *Continuities in Political Action* (pp. 23-66). Berlin: de Gruyter.

Kaase, Max, and Alan Marsh. 1979. "Political Action Repertory: Changes over Time and a New Typology." In Samuel Barnes, Max Kaase, *et al* (eds.), *Political Action*. Beverly Hills: Sage.

Kanji, Mebs and Neil Nevitte. 1995. "North American Reactions to Environmentalism." *Border Demographics and Regional Interdependency—A Trinational Symposium—Canada/U.S./Mexico*. Bellingham, Washington.

Keohane, Robert. O. 1977. "Reciprocity in International Relations." *International Organization*, 1, 40: 1-28.

Keohane, Robert. O., and Joseph S. Nye. 1976. *Power and Interdependence: World Politics in Transition*. Boston: Little, Brown.

King, Desmond. 1987. *The New Right: Politics, Markets and Citizenship*. Chicago: Dorsey.

Kitschelt, Herbert. 1984. *Der okologische Diskurs*. Frankfurt: Campus Verlag.

————. 1988. "Organization and Strategy in Belgian and West German Ecology Parties." *Comparative Politics*, 20: 127-54.

————. 1989. *The Logics of Party Formation: Structure and Strategy of Belgian and West German Ecology Parties*. Ithaca, NY: Cornell University Press.

————. 1990. "La gauche libertaire et les écologistes français." *Revue Française de Science Politique*, 40, 3: 339-65.

————. 1994. *The Transformation of European Social Democracy*. New York: Cambridge University Press.

Kitschelt, Herbert, and Staff Hellemans. 1990. "The Left-Right Semantics and the New Politics Cleavage." *Comparative Political Studies*, 23, 2: 210-38.

Klandermans, Bert. 1988. "The Formation and Mobilization of Consensus." In Bert Klandermans, Hans Peter Kriesi, and Sidney Tarrow (eds.), *From Structure to Action: Comparing Movement Participation across Cultures*. Greenwich, CT: JAI Press.

————. 1991. "New Social Movements and Resource Mobilization: The European and American Approach Revisited." In Dieter Rucht (ed.), *Research on Social Movements: The State of the Art in Western Europe and the U.S.A.*, Frankfurt/Boulder, CO: Campus Verlag/Westview Press.

Knutsen, Oddbjorn. 1993. "Value Orientations and Party Choice: A Comparative Study of the Impact of Old Parties and New Politics Value Orientations on Voting Intention." Paper presented at the conference on European Value Change, Tilburg University, Netherlands, November.

Kohn, Melvin K. 1959. "Social Class and Parental Values." *American Journal of Sociology*, 64, 4: 337-51.

Kohn, Melvin K., and Carmi Schooler. 1969. "Class, Occupation, and Orientation." *American Sociological Review*, 34: 659-78.

Koop, C.E. "Decisions at the end of life," *Issues in Law and Medicine*, 5: 101-15.

Krieger, Joel. 1986. *Reagan, Thatcher and the Politics of Decline*. Cambridge: Polity Press.

Kuechler, Manfred, and Russell J. Dalton. 1990. "New Social Movements and the Political Order: Inducing Change for Long-Term Stability?" In Russell Dalton and Manfred Kuechler (eds), *Challenging the Political Order: New Social and Political Movements in Western Democracies* (pp. 277-300). New York: Oxford University Press.

Lafferty, William, and Oddbjorn Knutsen. 1985. "Postmaterialism in a Social Democratic State: An Analysis of the Distinctness and Congruity of the Inglehart Value Syndrome in Norway." *Comparative Political Studies*, 17: 411-31.

Landes, Ronald G. 1977. "Political Socialization Among Youth: A Comparative Study of English-Canadian and American School Children." *International Journal of Comparative Sociology*, 18: 63-80.

Laponce, Jean. 1972. "In Search of the Stable Elements of the Left-Right Landscape." *Comparative Politics*, 41: 455-75.

Lasch, Christopher. 1971. *Haven in a Heartless World*. New York: Basic Books.

Leduc, Lawrence. 1984. "Canada: The Politics of Stable Dealignment." In Russell Dalton, Scott C. Flanagan, and Paul Allen Beck (eds.), *Electoral Change in Advanced Industrial Democracies: Realignment of Dealignment?* (pp. 402-24). Princeton, NJ: Princeton University Press.

Lerner, Daniel. 1958. *The Passing of Traditional Society*. New York: Free Press.

Letwin, William (ed.). 1983. *Against Equality: Readings on Economic and Social Policy*. London: Macmillan.

Lindberg, Leon, and Stuart Scheingold. 1970. *Europe's Would-Be Polity: Patterns of Change in the European Community*. Englewood Cliffe, NJ: Prentice-Hall.

Lipset, Seymour Martin. 1950. *Agrarian Socialism: The Cooperative Commonwealth Federations in Saskatchewan*. Berkeley: University of California Press.

————. 1960. *Political Man*. New York: Doubleday.

————. 1963. *The First New Nation: The United States in Historical Comparative Perspective*. New York: Basic Books.

————. 1963. *Political Man*. Garden City, NY: Doubleday.

————. 1979. "The New Class and the Professoriate." In Bruce-Giggs (ed.), *The New Class?* New Brunswick: Transaction Books.

————. 1990. *Continental Divide: The Values and Institutions of the United States and Canada.* Ottawa: C.D. Howe Institute.

Lipsey, Richard. G. 1985. "Canada and the United states: The Economic Dimension." In John F. Sigler and Charles H. Doran (eds.), *Canada and the United States: Enduring Friendship, Persistent Stress.* Englewood Cliffs, NJ: Prentice-Hall.

Lortie, Pierre. 1991. *Report of Royal Commission on Electoral Reform and Party Financing* (ed.), Herman Bakvis, vol 14, Ottawa: Supply & Services.

Lower, A.R.M. 1964. *Colony to Nation.* Toronto: Longman's.

Luhmann, Niklas. 1979. *Power and Trust.* New York: Wiley.

Luskin, Robert. 1987. "Measuring Political Sophistication." *American Journal of Political Science,* 31: 856-99.

Lustig, Michael. 1994. "The Limits of Rent Seeking: Why Protectionists Become Free Traders." Tallahassee: Florida State University.

Marsh, Alan. 1975. "The Silent Revolution, Value Priorities, and the Quality of Life in Britain." *American Political Science Review,* 69: 1-30

————. 1977. *Protest and Political Consciousnmess.* Beverly Hills: Sage.

Maslow, Abraham. 1954. *Motivation and Personality.* New York: Harper.

McAllister, Ian. 1992. *Political Behavior: Citizens, Parties and Elites in Australia.* Sydney: Longman Cheshire.

McCloskey, Herbert. 1964. "Consensus and Ideology in American Politics." *American Political Science Review,* 18: 361-82.

McCloskey, Herbert, and Alida Brill. 1983. *Dimensions of Tolerance: What Americans Believe about Civil Liberties.* New York: Russel Sage Foundation.

McCloskey, Herbert, and John Zaller. 1984. *The American Ethos.* Cambridge, MA: Harvard University Press.

McCutcheon, A.L. "A Latent Class Analysis of Tolerance for Nonconformity in the American Public." *Public Opinion Quarterly,* 49: 474-88.

McDaniel, Susan D. 1988. "The Changing Family: Women's Roles and the Impact of Feminism." In Sandra Burt, Lorraine Code and Lindsay Dorney (eds.). *Changing Patterns: Women in Canada* (pp. 103-28. Toronto: McClelland & Stewart.

McRae, Kenneth D. 1964. "The Structure of Canadian History." In Louis Hartz (ed.), *The Founding of New Societies.* New York: Harcourt, Brace & World.

Merrit, Richard L., and Donald J. Puchala. 1968. *Western European Perspectives on International Affairs.* New York: Praeger.

Milbrath, Lester W. 1965. *Political Participation: How and Why People Get Involved in Politics.* Chicago: Rand McNally.

Miller, Warren E., and Teresa Levitin. 1976. *Leadership and Change.* Boston: Winthrop.

Milner, Helen V. 1988. *Resisting Protectionism: Global Industries and the Politics of International Trade.* Princeton, NJ: Princeton University Press.

Milner, Helen V., and David B. Yoffie. 1989. "Between Free Trade and Protectionism: Strategic Trade Policy and a Theory of Corporate Trade Demands." *International Organization,* 43,2: 239-72.

Mishler, William. 1979. *Political Participation in Canada.* Toronto: Macmillan.

Morton, W.L. 1961. *The Canadian Identity.* Madison: University of Wisconsin Press.

Müller-Rommel, Ferdinand. 1985. "Social Movements and the Greens: New Internal Politics in Germany." *European Journal of Political Research,* 13: 53-67.

————. 1990. "New Political Movements and 'New Politics' Parties in Western

Europe." In Russell Dalton, and Manfred Kuechler (eds.). *Challenging the Political Order: New Social and Political Movements in Western Democracies* (pp. 209-31). New York: Oxford University Press.

Naegele, Kaspar D. 1971. "Canadian Society: Some Reflections." In Bernard Blishen, Frank E. Jones, Kaspar D. Naegele, and John Porter (eds.), *Canadian Society: Sociological Perspectives*, 3rd. ed. Toronto: MacMillan.

Naisbitt, John. 1982. *Megatrends*. New York: Warner Books.

Nevitte, Neil. 1991. "New Politics, the Charter and Political Participation." In Herman Bakvis (ed.). *Representation, Integration and Political Parties in Canada*, 14: 355-417. Research studies for the Royal Commission on Electoral Reform and Party financing. Toronto/Oxford: Dundurn Press.

———. 1994. "New Trading Partners: What Survey Research Reveals about Canadians and Mexicans." Paper presented at Third Tinker Conference on Mexican Policy Studies, Tulane University, New Orleans, September 16.

———. 1995. "Bringing Values `Back In': Value Change and North American Integration." In Donald Barry (ed.), *Toward a North American Community? Canada, the United States and Mexico* (pp. 185-209). Boulder, CO: Westview.

Nevitte, Neil, W. Brandon, and Lori Davis. 1993. "The American Abortion Controversy: Lessons from Cross-National Evidence." *Politics and the Life Sciences*, 12,1: 245-60.

Nevitte, Neil, and Ian Brodie. 1993. "Evaluating the Citizens' Constitution Theory." *Canadian Journal of Political Science*, 26: 235-59.

———. 1993. "Clarifying Differences: A Rejoinder to Alan Cairns's Defence of the Citizens' Constitution Theory." *Canadian Journal of Political Science*, 26: 269-72.

Nevitte, Neil, and Roger Gibbins. 1990. *New Elites in Old States: Ideologies in the Anglo-American Democracies*. Toronto: Oxford University Press.

———. 1991. "New Politics, the Charter and Political Participation." In Herman Bakvis (ed.), *Representation, Integration and Political Parties in Canada* (pp. 355-417). Toronto: Dundurn Press. (Vol. 14 *Report of the Royal Commission on Electoral Reform and Party Financing*).

Nevitte, Neil, and Ron Inglehart. 1995. "North American Value Change and Integration: Lessons from Western Europe." In Ruud de Moor (ed.), *Values in Western Societies*. Tilburg, Netherlands: Tilburg University Press.

Nevitte, Neil, and Mebs S. Kanji. 1995. "Explaining Environmental Concern and Action in Canada." *Applied Behavioural Science Review*. 3, 1: 85-102.

Nevitte, Neil, and Allan Kornberg (eds.). 1985. *Minorities and the Canadian State*. Oakville, ON: Mosaic Press.

North, Douglas. 1990. *Institutions, Institutional Change and Economic Performance*. New York: Cambridge University Press.

Nincic, Miroslav, and Bruce Russett. 1979. "The Effect of Similarity and Interest on Attitudes toward Foreign Cultures." *Public Opinion Quarterly*, 1, 43: 68-78.

Nunn, Clyde Z., Harry J. Crockett, Jr., and J. Allen Williams, Jr. 1978. *Tolerance for Nonconformity*. San Francisco: Jossey-Bass.

Nye, Joseph S. 1968. "Comparative Regional Integration: Concept and Measurement." *International Organization*, 14,22: 855-80.

———. 1977. "Transnational Relations and Interstate Conflicts: An Empirical Analysis." In Annette Baker Fox, Alfred O. Hero, Jr., and Joseph Nye (eds.), *Canada and the United States: Transnational and Transgovernmental Relations* (pp. 367-402). New York: Columbia University Press.

———. 1988. "Neorealism and Neoliberalism." *World Politics*, 40: 238-39.

OECD, Statistics Directorate. 1992. Paris: OECD

Offe, Claus. 1984. *Contradictions of the Welfare State*. Cambridge, MA: MIT Press.

———. 1985. "New Social Movements: Changing Boundaries of the Political." *Social Research*, 52: 817-68.

———. 1987. "Challenging the Boundaries of Institutional Politics.: In Charles S. Maier (ed.), *Changing the Boundaries of the Political: Essays on the Evolving Balance Between the State and Society, Public and Private in Europe* (pp. 63-105). New York: Cambridge University Press.

Ostheimer. N.C., and J.M. Ostheimer. 1976. *Life or Death-Who Controls?* New York: Springer.

Paehlke, Robert. 1989. *Environmentalism and the Future of Progressive Politics*. New Haven, CT: Yale University Press.

Pammett, Jon H. 1991. "Voting Turnout in Canada." In Herman Bakvis (ed.), *Voter Turnout in Canada*, vol 15. Research Studies for the Royal Commission of Electoral Reform and Party Financing. Toronto/Oxford: Dundurn Press.

Pateman, Carole. 1970. *Participation and Democratic Theory*. London: Cambridge University Press.

Pelinka, A. 1991. "The Study of Social Movements in Austria." In Rucht, D. (ed), *Research on Social Movements: The State of the Art in Western Europe and the U.S.A.* (pp. 230-46). Boulder, CO: Westview Press.

Phillips, Kevin. 1991. *The Politics of Rich and Poor*. New York: Harper Perennial.

Pinard, Maurice. 1973. "Third Parties in Canada Revisited." *Canadian Journal of Political Science*, 6: 439-60.

Popkin, Samuel. 1991. *The Reasoning Voter*. Chicago: University of Chicago Press.

Porter, John. 1965. *The Vertical Mosaic: An Analysis of Social Class and Power in Canada*. Toronto: University of Toronto Press.

Powell, G. Bingham. 1982. *Contemporary Democracies*. Cambridge, MA: Harvard University Press.

Presthus, Robert. 1977. "Aspects of Political Culture and Legislative Behaviour: United States and Canada." *International Journal of Comparative Sociology*, 18: 7-22.

Price, Vincent. 1992. *Public Opinion*. Newbury Park, CA: Sage.

Protho, James W., and Charles Grigg, "Fundamental Principles of Democracy: Basis of Agreement and Disagreement." *Journal of Politics*, 22: 276-94.

Pruitt, Dean G. 1965. "Definition of the Situation as a Determinant of International Action." In Herbert C. Kalman (ed.). *International Behavior: A Social-Psychological Analysis* (pp. 391-432). New York: Holt, Rinehart and Winston.

Puchala, Donald J. 1968. "The Pattern of Contemporary Regional Integration." *International Studies Quarterly*, 12: 38-64.

Putman, Robert D. 1988. Diplomacy and Domestic Politics: The Logic of Two-Level Games." *International Organization*, 42,3: 436-40.

———. 1993. *Making Democracy Work: Civic Traditions in Modern Italy*. Princeton, NJ: Princeton University Press.

Rapoport, R. 1989. "Ideologies About Family Forms." In Katja Boh, *et al.* (eds.). *Changing Patterns of European Family Life: A Comparative Analysis of Fourteen Countries* (pp. 53-70). London: Routledge.

Redekop, J.H. 1978. *Approaches to Canadian Politics*. Scarborough, ON: Prentice-Hall.

Reitz, Jeffrey. 1988. "Less Racial Discrimination in Canada, or Simply Less Racial

Conflict? Implications of Comparisons with Britain." *Canadian Public Policy*, 14,4: 424-41.

Rochon, T.R. 1988. *Mobilizing for Peace: The Antinuclear Movements in Western Europe*. Princeton, NY: Princeton University Press.

———. 1990. "The West European Peace Movement and the Theory of New Social Movements." In Russell Dalton and Manfred Kuechler (eds.). *Challenging the Political Order: New Social and Political Movements in Western Democracies* (pp. 106-121). New York: Oxford University Press.

Rogowski, Ronald. 1989. *Commerce and Coalitions: How Trade Affects Domestic Political Alignments*. Princeton, NJ: Princeton University Press.

Rokeach, Milton. 1968. *Beliefs, Attitudes and Values*. San Francisco: Jossey-Bass.

———. 1973. *The Nature of Human Values*. New York: Free Press.

Rosenau, James N. 1992. "The Relocation of Authority in a Shrinking World." *Comparative Politics*, 24,3: 253-71.

Roussel, Louis. 1989. "Les changements demographiques des vingt derniers annes: Quelques hypotheses sociologiques." In J. Legare, T.R. Balakrishnan, and R. Beaujot (eds.), *The Family in Crisis: A Population Crisis?* Ottawa: Royal Society of Canada.

———. 1992. "La famille en Europe occidental: Divergences et convergences." *Population*, 47: 133-52.

Rucht, Dieter (ed.). 1990. "Campaigns, Skirmishes and Battles: Anti-Nuclear Movements in the U.S.A., France and West Germany." *Industrial Crisis Quarterly*, 4,3: 193-22.

———. 1991. *Research on Social Movements: The State of the Art in Western Europe and the U.S.A.* Frankfurt/Boulder, CO: Campus Verlag/Westview Press.

Schmitter, Philippe C. 1971. "A Revised Theory of Regional Integration." In Leon Lindberg and Stuart Scheingold (eds.), *Regional Integration: Theory and Research* (pp. 253-300). Cambridge, MA: Harvard University Press.

Schott, Jeffrey J., and Murray G. Smith (eds.). 1988. *The Canada-United States Free Trade Agreement: The Global Impact*. Washington: Institute for International Economics.

Schwartz, Felice N. 1992. *Breaking with Tradition: Women and Work- The New Facts of Life*. New York: Warner Books.

Simeon, Richard (ed.). 1977. *Must Canada Fail?* Montreal/Kingston: McGill-Queen's University Press.

Smith, Murray G. 1988. "The Free Trade Agreement in Context: A Canadian Perspective." In Jeffrey J. Schott and Murray G. Smith (eds.). *The Canada-U.S. Free Trade Agreement: The Global Impact* (pp. 37-64). Washington, DC/Ottawa: Institute for International Economics/Institute for Research on Public Policy.

Sniderman, Paul M. 1975. *Personality and Democratic Politics*. Berkeley, CA: University of California Press.

Sniderman, Paul M., Richard Brody, and Philip Tetlock. 1991. *Reasoning and Choice: Explorations in Political Psychology*. Cambridge: Cambridge University Press.

Sniderman, Paul M., Philip Tetlock, James Glaser, Donald Philip Green, and Michael Hout. 1989. "Principled Tolerance and the American Mass Public." *British Journal of Political Science*, 19: 25-45.

Stairs, Denis. 1994. "Change in the Management of Canada-United States Relations in the Post-War Era." In Donald Barry (ed.), *Toward a North American Community?* (pp. 53-74). Boulder, CO: Westview Press.

Statistics Canada. 1965-1972. *Canada Census Data*. Ottawa: Statistics Canada.

————. 1991. *Canada 1991: An International Business Comparison*. Ottawa: Supply and Services.

————. 1993. *National Forum on Family Security: Keynote Paper*. Ottawa: The Canadian Council on Social Development.

Stouffer, Samuel. 1955. *Communism, Conformity and Civil Liberties*. Garden City, NY: Doubleday.

Sullivan, John L., James E. Piereson, and George E. Marcus. 1979. "An Alternative Conceptualization of Political Tolerance: Illusory Increases 1950s-1970s." *American Political Science Review*, 73: 781-94.

————. 1980. "Political Tolerance: An overview and Some New Findings." In John C. Pierce and John L. Sullivan (eds.). *The Electorate Reconsidered* (pp. 157-78). Beverly Hills, CA: Sage.

————. 1982. *Political Tolerance and American Democracy*. Chicago: University of Chicago Press.

Sullivan, John L., Michal Shamir, Patric Walsh, and Nigel S. Roberts. 1985. *Political Tolerance in Context: Support for Unpopular Minorities in Israel, New Zealand, and the United States*. Boulder, CO: Westview Press.

Thompson, Michael, Richard Ellis, and Aaron Wildavsky. 1990. *Cultural Theory: Foundations of Socio-Cultural Variability*. Boulder, CO: Westview Press.

Thornton, Arland. 1989. "Changing Attitudes to Family Issues in the United States." *Journal of Marriage and the Family*. 51: 873-93.

Tilly, Charles. 1988. "Social Movements, Old and New." *Research in Social Movements: Conflicts and Change*. 10: 1-18.

Tiryakian, Edward A., and Ronald Rogowski. 1985. *New Nationalism of the Developed West: Toward Explanation*. Boston: Allen & Unwin.

Toffler, Alvin. 1980. *The Third Wave*. New York: Morrow.

Tomassen, Jacques, J.A. 1990. "Economic Crisis, Dissatisfaction, and Protest." In M. Jennings, Jan Van Deth, *et al.* (eds.), *Continuities in Political Action*. Berlin: Walter de Gruyter.

Touraine, Alan. 1981. *The Voice and the Eye: An Analysis of Social Movements*. Cambridge: Cambridge University Press.

Truman, Tom. 1971. "A Critique of Seymour Martin Lipset's Article `Value Differences Absolute or Relative: The English Speaking Democracies.'" *Canadian Journal of Political Science*, 4: 497-525.

Turner, B.S. 1991. *Religion and Social Theory*. London: Sage.

Underhill, Frank. 1960. *In Search of Canadian Liberalism*. Toronto: Macmillan.

United Nations. 1976. *UN Demographic Yearbook*. Department of International Economic and Social Affairs, Statistical Office. New York: United Nations.

————. 1982. *UN Demographic Yearbook*. Department of International Economic and Social Affairs, Statistical Office. New York: United Nations.

————. 1990. *UN Demographic Yearbook*. Department of International Economic and Social Affairs, Statistical Office. New York: United Nations.

————. 1992. *UN Demographic Yearbook*. Department of International Economic and Social Affairs, Statistical Office. New York: United Nations.

UNESCO. 1976. *UNESCO Statistical Yearbooks*. Paris: UNESCO.

————. 1992. *UNESCO Statistical Yearbooks*. Paris: UNESCO.

Van den Broek, Andries, and Felix Heunks. 1993. "Political Culture: Patterns of Political Orientations and Behaviour." In Peter Ester, Loek Halman, and Ruud de

Moor (eds.), *The Individualizing Society: Value Change in Europe and North America*. Tilburg, Netherlands: Tilburg University Press.

Van Deth, Jan W. 1983. "The Persistence of Materialist and Postmaterialist Value Orientations." *European Journal of Political Research*. 11: 83-109.

Verba, Sidney. 1971. "Cross-National Survey Research: The Problem of Credibility." In Ivan Vallier (ed.), *Comparative Methods in Sociology* (pp. 305-56.). Berkeley: University of California Press.

Verba, Sidney, Norman Nie, and Jae-on Kim. 1971. *The Modes of Democratic Participation*. Beverly Hills, CA: Sage.

———. 1978. *Participation and Political Equality*. New York: Cambridge University Press.

Wattenberg, Martin P. 1982. "Party Identification and Party Images: A Comparison of Britain, Canada, Australia and the U.S." *Comparative Politics*, 15,1: 23-40.

———. 1990. *The Decline of American Parties: 1952-1988*. Cambridge: Harvard University Press.

Weaver, R. Kent (ed.). 1992. *The Collapse of Canada?* Washington, DC.: The Brookings Institution.

Weber, Max. 1958. *The Protestant Ethic and the Spirit of Capitalism*, trans. Talcott Parsons. New York: Scribner's.

Wildavsky, Aaron. 1987. "Choosing Preferences by Constructing Institutions." *American Political Science Review*, 81: 3-21.

Wilson, B. 1992. *Religion in Sociological Perspective*. Oxford: Oxford University Press.

World Bank. 1992. *The World Development Report*. New York: Oxford University Press.

World Values Surveys. 1981 and 1990. Are available from the I.S.R. University of Michigan. Ann Arbor, MI.

Wrigley, E. Anthony. 1977. "Reflections on the History of the Family." *Daedelus*, 71-85.

Wylie, Laurence. 1957. *Village in the Vaucluse*. Cambridge: Harvard University Press.

Yankelovich, D. 1981. *New Rules*. New York: Random House.

Yankelovich, D., H. Zetterberg, B. Strümpel, and M. Shanks. 1985. *The World at Work: An International Report on Jobs, Productivity and Human Values*. New York: Octagon Books.

Younger, S.J. 1986. *Human Values in Critical Care Medicine*. New York: Praeger.

Zaller, John R. 1992. *The Nature and Origins of Mass Opinion*. New York: Cambridge University Press.

Zanders, H. 1993. "Changing Work Values." In Peter Ester, Loek Halman, and Ruud de Moor (eds.). *The Individualizing Society: Value Change in Europe and North America* (pp. 129-53). Tilburg, Netherlands: Tilburg University Press.

Index